ARUNDEL CASTLE

MAILSHIPS OF THE UNION-CASTLE LINE

Above: A Union liner, probably the Mexican, *leaving the Alfred Basin, Cape Town, circa 1885.*
Title page: The ship's bell on the Windsor Castle *(1960).*

C J HARRIS & BRIAN D INGPEN

MAILSHIPS

OF THE UNION-CASTLE LINE

PAINTINGS: PETER BILAS

PSL
Patrick Stephens Limited

Mailship passengers enjoy an evening of dance, circa 1900.

FIRST PUBLISHED 1994

THIS EDITION IS PUBLISHED IN BRITAIN IN 1994 BY PATRICK STEPHENS LTD, AN IMPRINT OF HAYNES PUBLISHING, SPARKFORD, NR YEOVIL, SOMERSET BA22 7JJ

ORIGINAL EDITION PUBLISHED IN SOUTH AFRICA IN 1994 BY FERNWOOD PRESS

ISBN: 1 85260 485 9

A CATALOGUE RECORD OF THIS BOOK IS AVAILABLE FROM THE BRITISH LIBRARY

PRINTED AND BOUND IN SINGAPORE

A morning muster on board a Cape mailship, circa 1900.

CONTENTS

From the Year Book and Guide to East Africa *(1950 edition)*.

ACKNOWLEDGEMENTS

The authors wish to express their deepest gratitude to the following individuals and institutions for the invaluable assistance received while researching and compiling this book:

The Rt. Hon. Lord Cayzer; David Holgate for the loan of his grandfather's diary; former Union-Castle employees, particularly Captains Reg Kelso and Ricky Flint, and Messrs Desmond Lawrence, Jim Inkson, Bill McEwan, Jasper Gleave, Jack Newlan and Brian Simpson for their patience in answering what may have appeared foolish questions; Peter Humphries for the loan of newspaper cuttings; the Ship Society of South Africa for the use of their library and other resources; the South African Marine Corporation Ltd, for making research in Britain and Northern Ireland possible; the Mayhew family for allowing access to the photographic collection of the late Commodore George Mayhew; the staff of the National Maritime Museum, Greenwich, particularly David Hodge for his tireless efforts to locate specific photographs and to document the contents of photographs; the librarian of the *Southern Evening Echo*, Southampton; Michael McCaughan and the librarians at the Ulster Folk and Transport Museum, Belfast; the staff of the South African Library and State Archives, Cape Town, as well as those at the Local History Museum in Durban.

Finally, we wish to thank Pieter Struik (publisher), Peter Borchert (editorial advisor), Valerie Streak (editor) and Willem Jordaan (designer) for their collective and individual efforts which have made this book both possible and exceptional.

AUTHORS' NOTE

In compiling this work, a wide range of records was consulted, including many newspaper articles, several of which came into our hands as newspaper clippings from private collections. They were undated and unsourced, but they were original. It was therefore decided to use them but in quoting from them it has not been possible to provide full references.

It is also drawn to the reader's attention that, at times, there may appear to be certain inconsistencies in the text in respect of tonnage, length of ship and passenger capacity. While official records have been used wherever possible, some discrepancies may have arisen from the use of a variety of sources, some of which have provided different figures. Further, it is pointed out that, in accordance with maritime tradition, distances at sea have been given in nautical miles.

When the decimalization of the South African currency came into effect on 14 February 1961, the new currency unit (the rand) was equivalent to ten of the old South African shillings. In other words, R2 was equal to SA£1 (just under £1 sterling). Initially, the rand remained steady against sterling but with a firmer gold price in the seventies and an increasingly complex political situation developing in South Africa, the rand unit began to fluctuate. For the benefit of those readers who may wish to convert to sterling the rand references in the text the following table gives the approximate value of the rand against the pound for the period concerned.

1970	1,7164	1972	1,9331	1974	1,5897	1976	1,5721
1971	1,7427	1973	1,7083	1975	1,6349	1977	1,5175

Permission to reproduce extracts from various published and unpublished material has kindly been given by: Chick Breetze (assorted correspondence); *The Argus* and *Cape Times* of Cape Town, the Durban *Daily News* and the Port Elizabeth *Eastern Province Herald* (news reports); Lloyds (*Lloyds List* and *Lloyds Weekly Shipping Index*); John Murray Publishers (*John Smith Moffat*); Longmans (*Union-Castle Chronicle*); Dan Overett (letter from Lucy Nottage); Oxford University Press (*Ships and South Africa* and *War in the Southern Oceans*); Sir Laurens van der Post and Chatto & Windus (*Yet Being Someone Other*) and George Young (*Ships that Pass*).

PUBLISHERS' NOTE

It is with regret that we record the death of Captain C. J. Harris during the final stages of preparing this book for publication. It is a great sadness that, as the initial motivator of this work, he was unable to see the fruits of his endeavours.

The Edinburgh Castle *off the Needles, Isle of Wight.*

FOREWORD

For more than a century mailships plied the route between the ports of South Africa and Southampton, the majestic vessels with their distinctive lavender hulls winning a place in the hearts of all who saw and travelled in them. When in 1977 this regular mail service drew to an end, it was a matter of great sadness for so many people.

For me, the sense of personal loss was particularly intense, as I had been a member of the committee appointed by the South African Government to examine the future of shipping. As such, I had been party to the decision to containerize the Europe-South Africa trade, a decision that effectively sealed the fate of those beautiful mailships, which had been such an integral part of the South African way of life for so long. The decision to phase out the mailships also affected the lives of thousands of Union-Castle personnel, many of whom had known no other employer.

This book traces the colourful history of the mail service from its infancy to the poignant final departure of the *Southampton Castle*, the last mailship to leave South Africa. I commend it as a demonstration of exhaustive enquiry and balanced judgement as well as for the deep nostalgia it evokes for a time that has passed.

DESMOND B LAWRENCE
LAST MANAGING DIRECTOR OF UNION-CASTLE STEAMSHIP COMPANY (SOUTH AFRICA) LIMITED

The Windsor Castle *loading for Southampton at A Berth and the* Transvaal Castle *inward from Britain at F Berth, Cape Town.*

INTRODUCTION

Those who remember the lavender-hulled Union-Castle mailships with their black-topped, brilliant vermilion funnels cannot but reflect with deep nostalgia upon a way of life that will never return. Theirs is the memory of a time when travel was leisurely and enjoyable, and a holiday in itself; when elaborate meals were freshly prepared and brought to the table in a flurry of silver and white napery; when service was polite and efficient, and days were spent lazing under warm sunny skies, making new friends and having fun.

Testimony to the pleasure those recollections evoke is the quantity of memorabilia and souvenirs that is still treasured in many homes in South Africa and Britain, each item calling to mind such cameos of life on board as the traditional Crossing the Line ceremony, the captain's cocktail party, fancy-dress competitions, deck sports and the bumper farewell dinner. And then there were the diving boys at Madeira and the buffeting in the notorious Bay of Biscay when, tongue in cheek, the captain would declare it to be the worst he had experienced in a lifetime at sea!

Passengers about to board the boat train at Waterloo Station.

Sailing day from Southampton provided its own special atmosphere, heralded by the arrival from London's Waterloo station of the 'boat train'. At Berth 104, anxious and excited – often bewildered – passengers would hasten to keep pace with porters who expertly wove their way through crowds in the shed and on to the quay, brushing past bustling deliverymen at every turn and florists' runners bearing farewell bouquets for departing friends.

Once on board passengers were greeted by well-drilled reception staff who checked passage tickets and escorted the bearers to cabins that would be their home-from-home for the next two weeks. Prior to sailing, those travelling cabin (tourist) class queued in their dining saloon for place allocations for first or second sitting. Naturally, those in first class had their seating arrangements planned for them, while a few special passengers were invited by the captain – with an occasional prompt from head office – to share his table.

At 16:00 precisely, with hatches battened down and everything secured, moorings were slipped and, to much waving and calling, the liner would draw slowly away from the quay to move sedately down Southampton Water. The pilot customarily disembarked off the Needles or, if the weather was bad, near the Nab Tower under the lee of the Isle of Wight. Then, with the engine room telegraph at 'full ahead', a slight tremble would run through the ship as the giant engines gradually picked up speed to the 21 knots required for the voyage of 5 978 nautical miles to Cape Town.

On the other side of the equator, early risers in Cape Town might see on a Thursday the weekly mailship picking up her pilot from the coal-fired tender off the Table Bay breakwater. To the traditional log-book entry of 'Proceeded to master's orders and pilot's advice', the great liner would make its dignified way into the inner harbour, and commuters on their way to work would silently greet her.

For many of the 700 or so passengers on board it would be their first visit to South Africa: some confident in the anticipation of an exciting holiday, some apprehensive about their future in a strange land. Others, native to the country, might be returning from holidays or business trips, and in each ship there was sure to be a contingent headed for the Rhodesias, Bechuanaland or Basutoland to begin a new life or take up postings in the British colonial service. Whatever their reasons for making the voyage, few would ever forget it, and in the thrill of arrival many would even forgo the camaraderie of the final breakfast in order to experience the breathtaking spectacle of Table Mountain in one of its many moods and the city spread out below.

On mailship day the passenger terminal and wharfside thronged with people anxious and eager for the first glimpse of a friend, relative or business associate. As faces

The purser's bureau – source of all information for passengers.

Visitors and passengers crowd the promenade deck on sailing day.

were recognized, frantic exchanges would span the narrowing gap between ship and quay, but before the welcomes or reunions a period of impatient waiting had to be endured while immigration and customs officials verified all documentation.

High above the crowds on the quayside and the passengers on deck, the captain would observe yet another dawn arrival from the vantage point of the bridge. Once again, his commission to deliver the 'English' mail had been fulfilled.

By far the majority of South Africans who sailed in Union-Castle ships booked for the coastal voyage. In 1962 the ten-day return voyage from Cape Town to Durban cost R57, and even six years later the fare had been increased by only R6. Such moderate rates brought the thrill of a sea voyage within the reach of most white people, and it became an extremely popular form of family holiday, with ships booked to capacity during the school vacations.

The cruise included calls at Port Elizabeth, East London and Durban, and at each port maximum leisure time was provided for passengers to tour nearby places of interest, perhaps visit friends or family, shop, play or simply soak up the sun and enjoy the warm waters of the Indian Ocean. Altogether it was the perfect holiday. At the same time, the liner performed its function as carrier of urgently required imports and such priority exports as wool, fruit, wine and gold.

Back in Cape Town on a Tuesday morning, even as the coastal voyagers were disembarking, frenetic preparations got under way for the northbound sailing.

It was a well-advertised fact that one could set one's watch by the Friday departure of the mailship. It waited for no-one. And that certainty precipitated a hectic scramble to complete all loading and storing, and the embarkation of the approximately 700 passengers in good time for the four o'clock sailing.

Invariably, the final rush included a telegraph boy bounding up the gangway with a last-minute telegram, or the late arrival of a delivery van with parting gifts of fruit and flowers as the third warning bell sounded for all visitors to hasten ashore. The last cars already secured on the boatdeck, two harbour tugs would connect towing hawsers to their massive charge, and from the bridge the captain and pilot would watch the crew single up moorings fore and aft. Finally, at 16:00 precisely, the last mooring line would be slipped, the Blue Peter lowered from the yardarm on the foremast and the tugs would take the strain on their steel hawsers. With three deep vibrating blasts of the sailors' farewell bellowing from her foghorn, the twin screws of the liner would begin to churn the water. And as she moved almost imperceptibly away from the quay, hundreds of paper streamers linking passengers and well-wishers would stretch and snap. For many the experience of a lifetime had begun.

A special feeling of excitement accompanied the start of a voyage.

The basis of the service that Union-Castle and its forebears had provided so effectively for 120 years was, of course, the carriage of mail, and it was the ships' strict adherence to a specified schedule – embedded in each Ocean Mail Contract – that made the line a virtual symbol of reliability. On no other trade – including the Cunard services across the North Atlantic and those of P&O to the East – did liners operate with such punctiliousness. Delays of arrival and departure were only countenanced in instances of the severest weather conditions, and so rarely did they occur that reports of such delays were guaranteed prominence in the South African newspapers. Indeed, such was the importance attached to punctuality in the mail service that the utmost priority for berthing and cargo-handling was accorded the mailships wherever they called.

At no time has this deference to the carrying of the mail been better illustrated than on the occasion when a

With the pilot on board, the Carnarvon Castle *heads for the Victoria Basin.*

Loading liquor, fruit and wool – the main cargo of northbound mailships.

Union-Castle mailship, outward bound for South Africa, was leaving the calm waters of the Solent at the time of Royal Naval manoeuvres in the English Channel. The mailship's captain was interrupted on the bridge by a signal received from the flag officer of the Royal Naval squadron. It informed him that his ship was impeding the exercising of His Majesty's fleet. Without a moment's hesitation, the captain dictated this reply: 'And you, sir, are impeding the passage of His Majesty's mails.' At this, ships of the awesome Royal Navy opened up their columns to make way for the mailship.

Because of the vital transport role that Union-Castle played in the history of South Africa, and because so many people had sailed in the great liners, the company, as well as the names of its ships, became household words in South Africa and, to a lesser extent, in Southampton. The launching of a ship, and particularly a maiden voyage arrival, became a talking-point at dinners, tea parties and at The Club. Any change of command in the mailships, or a new promotion to mailship master, again received prominent press coverage.

A typical Cape Town departure.

The masters of mailships were all highly accomplished seamen, hand-picked by Union-Castle's board of directors from experienced men with fine records of command of units of the cargo fleet and the intermediates. The ultimate honour for a Union-Castle captain was to be appointed commodore of the fleet – a prestigious position akin, in the minds of South Africans, to the Royal Naval commander-in-chief of the South Atlantic station.

Alas, the harsh reality of economics brought an end to it all. In the closing years of this once fine service, thousands of people who had been loyal to the company over decades – some being third or fourth generation mailship men – were retrenched, and on the mud flats of Kaohsiung and Hong Kong acetylene torches cut those splendid ships to pieces.

The poignancy of their demise is summed up in a signal passed from the *Pendennis Castle* to the *Edinburgh Castle* when the ships passed during the last voyage of the latter in 1976:

REVELATIONS 18, VERSE 11

And the merchants of the earth shall weep and mourn over her, for no man buyeth their merchandise any more.

1

1
The Ocean Mail Contract
1851-1883

2

Almost 200 years of haphazard communications between the Cape Colony and Europe were to pass before the first Ocean Mail Contract was signed in 1851; its purpose – to establish a regular mail service between Britain and the Cape. It was short-lived. Steam was in its infancy and the General Screw Steam Shipping Company with whom the British Admiralty had entered into the contract suffered one misfortune after the other. Breakdowns at sea and penalties exacted for failure to meet its contractual obligations brought financial disaster to the shipping company and the contract to an end. But in those three short years the foundation had been laid for a mail service that would not only endure for 120 years but whose implementation would also entirely revolutionize maritime transport to South Africa.

From 1652, when the Dutch East India Company had established a victualling station at the Cape of Good Hope for its merchant ships trading with the East, until the second British occupation of the colony in 1806, communications between the Cape and Europe had been few and sporadic. Instructions to officials and personal letters from home formed the bulk of what little mail was brought on those tediously long southbound voyages. And on their return from the Indies, running before the south-east trade winds, the small and vulnerable sailing vessels would bear the Cape governor's reports to the Heeren XVII in Amsterdam – and later to the British Colonial Office – together with a small bag of correspondence from the tiny, but expanding, community of settlers at that remote outpost.

The irregularity of this 'mail service' and the protracted voyages meant that lengthy periods elapsed before reports or replies to letters were received. Also, owing to the frequency of ships foundering, there was every prospect that important communications would never reach their destinations. But a mail service was neither the chief, nor the only, benefit to be derived from ships anchoring at the Cape en route for the East. They also brought essential military, agricultural, construction and domestic equipment from

3

Europe, as well as new settlers, and on the return journey they filled their holds with such cargoes as indigenous timber, dried fish and seal skins. Fundamental to the maintenance and development of the young colony, these early maritime links with Europe pioneered what was to evolve in later years into one of the world's most extensive and sophisticated shipping services.

After the second British occupation of the Cape in 1806, the Cape Colony assumed a greater sense of permanence and structure as attempts were made to consolidate the numerous settlements, mission stations and farms that were scattered over an area stretching from Namaqualand in the north-west to the Great Fish River in the east. In the latter region, military posts had been established by 1812 as a bulwark against the threat posed by the Xhosa, whose land was under pressure from European settlers. Associated with this drive towards consolidation and an improved infrastructure, was the need for increased means of conveying more immigrants for settlement in the frontier regions and, as a consequence, more cargo and more mail. This, in turn, led to progressively more regular and structured shipping services, particularly between Britain and the Cape – a trend that was to increase still further as the vast natural resources of southern Africa were discovered and exploited.

The first mineral to be mined in any great quantity was copper. For centuries the indigenous people of Namaqualand had known of the sites of several deposits, and as early as 1685, under the direction of Governor Simon van der Stel, European prospecting had taken place in the area. Then, in the 1840s, renewed prospecting in Namaqualand revealed further deposits of copper and kindled in the minds of some several interesting, if unfeasible, schemes. One such scheme was proposed when applications were invited for shares in the South African Mining Company which was to open mines in the Kamiesberg area. It was suggested that the ore be transported to the Orange River, thence on lighters and rafts to the sea, where it would be transferred to waiting vessels for direct export to England! Despite many other impractical export schemes, a flourishing copper trade did emerge and ore mined in the Okiep and Nababiep area was carried by wagon – and later by narrow-gauge railway – to Hondeklip Bay and Port Nolloth from where it was exported.

Coal deposits were discovered in Natal in 1840, and fifteen years later samples were tested successfully in the furnaces of the British sloop HMS *Hydra*. Although no large-scale mining had begun, it was evident that as a source of fuel for the increasing number of steamers, Natal would be invaluable.

In 1843, the British annexation of Port Natal, where traders had been active for more than a decade, had an immediate impact upon shipping services and, as the hinterland of Port Natal was being opened up, the economic potential of the region became increasingly evident. A report in the *Cape of Good Hope & Port Natal Shipping and Mercantile Gazette* of 1844 commented that 'Natal is likely to become of some commercial importance at no distant period', while a letter to the *Gazette* of 9 February 1844 claimed that Natal 'is one of the most fertile parts of Africa . . . fifty miles from the sea, the growth of vegetation is indescribable . . .' It added that because of the subtropical climate and

1 *The first Union mailship,* Dane, *seen here off the Needles. Her inaugural voyage on the mail service took forty-four days.*

2 *Arthur Anderson, founder of the Union Line.*

3 *An English East Indiaman victualling in Table Bay, circa 1658. The fort here depicted was built by Van Riebeeck's men in 1652 but it was soon to be replaced by the Castle of Good Hope, which was begun in 1666 and completed in 1678. Two mailships, the* Capetown Castle *(1938) and the* Good Hope Castle *(1965), bore names inspired by the later fortification.*

ARTHUR ANDERSON
FOUNDING CHAIRMAN OF THE UNION STEAMSHIP COMPANY

Born at Gremista in the Shetlands on 19 February 1792, Arthur Anderson received no formal education as a child, and indeed grew up in poverty in his native islands. Hoping for better things in life, the energetic and imaginative young Shetlander decided to try life in the Royal Navy. Initially as a midshipman and then as a captain's clerk, he served in the Baltic and along the French and Spanish coasts, after which, in 1814, he was paid off, though he returned for the Hundred Days' War in 1815.

Virtually penniless after his discharge, he made his way to London. There he found employment with a shipbroker, Brodie McGhie Willcox, whose small company ran a sailing ship to Portugal. In the early 1830s it ran guns for the royal houses of Portugal and Spain during their civil wars, and in 1835, at the instigation of the Spanish, the company began a steamship service from London to the Iberian Peninsula. Hard work on the part of Willcox and his astute protégé, Anderson, made possible the formation of a new company. Initially known as the Peninsular Steam Navigation Company, its services began in earnest in 1837 with the signing of a contract to carry mails between Britain and the Iberian Peninsula. In time, the company grew, operating further afield into the Mediterranean Sea. As trade with the Far East expanded, they cast their eyes beyond the isthmus of Suez and, in 1842, sent one of their vessels, the Hindustan, *via the Cape of Good Hope to India to operate between Bombay and Suez. In this way they complemented an existing service from Britain to Alexandria, whence an overland route to Port Suez took cargo and passengers bound for the East. So began the prestigious Peninsular & Oriental Steam Navigation Company (P&O), the word 'Oriental' being added once the company had forged its eastern links.*

Anderson became one of three managing directors of P&O, and in 1862 he assumed its chairmanship. (It is less commonly known that he was also a major role player in the founding of the Union Steamship Company.)

At the age of 30 Anderson had married Mary Hill, but there were no children from the marriage. Without the usual family commitments, he assumed a growing interest in public life. This led him to found a short-lived newspaper, The Shetland Journal, *in 1836 and to establish a scheme to encourage Shetland emigration to Brazil. It also led to his election as a Liberal member of parliament for Orkney and Shetland from 1847 to 1852. In later years, he demonstrated his concern for education and the plight of widows and the aged, particularly in the Shetlands. His death in February 1868 brought to a close the life of one of Britain's major shipping entrepreneurs and a man known for his generosity.*

the undulating terrain of the Natal coastal belt, wheat, maize, barley, oats, cotton and tobacco grew well. But it was soon realized that of all crops, sugar would be the most profitable to cultivate.

As early as 1815, in an attempt to fulfil the need for more regular contact with the Cape Colony, the British Government had sponsored a monthly mail service to Mauritius and India via the Cape, but because the sailing ships employed had taken 114 days for the voyage the project was short-lived. Nonetheless, the extent and pace of development in southern Africa demanded both increased speed and a greater degree of sophistication in maritime links with Britain, and ultimately these requirements led to the signing of the first Ocean Mail Contract between the British Admiralty commissioners and the General Screw Steam Shipping Company. Inaugurating sailings in terms of that contract, the first official mail steamer, *Bosphorus*, arrived in Table Bay on 27 January 1851 after a passage of forty days from Plymouth, five days longer than provided for by the contract. Soon other vessels were brought on to the service.

Launched in October 1851, the *Queen of the South*, a ship of 1 777 tons, was the first of the bigger vessels built for the General Screw Steam Shipping Company. She had a conventional propeller rather than paddle wheels and was described in one contemporary press report as

> a noble specimen of naval architecture, well calculated to excite the utmost confidence . . . The provision for passengers is especially excellent . . . As to the engines . . . they combine to an unprecedented degree economy of space with efficiency of action; the most perfect form of marine action, which in simplicity most nearly approaches direct action, has been developed by the screw propeller, and the fact is at once a valuable acquisition to mechanical science and a silent testimony to the importance of that new field of enterprise upon which the General Steam Company have entered.

She began her maiden voyage on 20 June 1852 when, carrying mail, she sailed from Plymouth for India via the Cape. Thirty-seven days later she dropped anchor in Table Bay. The ship did not have a successful career, however, owing to repeated problems with her propeller. Other units of the General Screw Steam Shipping Company also experienced mechanical breakdowns. The *Hydaspes*, for example, developed engine trouble on her maiden voyage and had to return to England under sail. Coal consumption by the early vessels proved greater than expected too. On one occasion, the *Propontis* ran out of coal and had to be towed to Table Bay by her consort *Sir Robert Peel.*

Eventually, because of the difficulties experienced in maintaining the rigorous schedule, the enterprise became a financial failure and within four years the service of the General Screw Steam Shipping Company had ceased.

Merchants at the Cape who were lobbying continually for a regular mail service must have been heartened to read the following article in the *South African Commercial Advertiser* in March 1856:

> *STEAM COMMUNICATION WITH ENGLAND*
>
> We are glad to find that there are now fair grounds for believing that we shall soon again have the monthly steam communication with England. Several tenders have been sent in to the Home Government, and it was rumoured that the Government had accepted that of the General Screw Steam Navigation Company. This rumour, however, has been denied, and it is stated that no tender has yet been accepted. But that tenders have been lodged for the performance of the mail service monthly between England and the Cape by screw steamers is certain. We may, therefore, expect to see the first of the liners in two or three months.

The speculation of the press proved partly correct, for a second contract, this time with a government subsidy of £28 000 per annum and requiring a thirty-six-day passage, was awarded to a shipping company owned by the British member of parliament, W. S. Lindsay. The inaugural voyage was made by the *England* in August 1856 but because the voyages regularly took more than fifty days the service was abandoned the following year. With the economic development of southern Africa proceeding steadily and immigration to the region increasing by the month, the scene was nonetheless set for a reliable mail service between southern Africa and Britain.

For their steamers trading to the Mediterranean, the embryonic Peninsular and Oriental Steam Navigation Company (P&O) needed an assured supply of coal at the port of Southampton, which had become the British terminus of their mail service to Portugal

THE DANE

COMMISSIONED: *1855*
BUILT BY: *Messrs Lungley & Co., Deptford*
LENGTH: *53,9 metres*
BREADTH: *7,5 metres*
TONNAGE: *526 tons*
SPEED: *7,5 knots under steam only*
(The Dane *was also fitted with sails, which gave her another 4 knots and, of course, conserved the coal bunkers.)*

In 1857, the Dane *made the inaugural voyage of the mail service. She was moved to the Mauritius service in 1864, and from 1865 was to have been used by the Admiralty as a transport in the naval operation to suppress slave-trading along the East African coast, particularly around Zanzibar. En route from Simon's Town to East Africa, however, and under the command of a certain Captain Waldeck, she was wrecked on Thunderbolt Reef near Port Elizabeth on 1 December 1865 without loss of life. An extract from the* Eastern Province Herald *of 2 December 1865 describes the wreck:*

TOTAL LOSS OF THE UNION COMPANY S.S. DANE
PASSENGERS AND CREW SAVED

Yesterday afternoon about 5 o'clock, our port was thrown into a state of considerable excitement by the report that the screw steamer Dane *was on shore off Cape Receife, and we are sorry to add that the report was true. She had struck on the point known as White Sands Reef, about a mile this side of the lighthouse.*

About half-past 4 o'clock, the Dane *was seen by officers of the* Saxon *rounding Cape Receife, and presently it was observed that she was drifting ashore and was seen to strike.*

Signals were made to shore and Captain Ricketts of the Saxon, *who half an hour before had himself seen the* Dane *to be westward of Receife, at once signalled to his chief officer to get up steam which was immediately done. About 6 o'clock the* Saxon, *with steam up, weighed anchor, having on board Captain Edington of the* Albany, *Captain Way of the* Golden Fleece *and Mr Skead, Mr Ebden, Mr MacDonald and a few other friends.*

In the meantime, the Sailors Friend *and one of the Union Boating Company's boats had proceeded to the scene of the disaster and one of the* Dane's *boats, with three passengers and the little luggage they could save, arrived at and were received on board the* Saxon . . .

At daylight this morning, Captain Ricketts was on deck, steam was up, and everything ready to render every assistance [to tow the Dane *from the reef] but to everyone's amazement, there was not a vestige of the wreck to be seen.*

All of the ship's company were rescued.

THE THIRD OCEAN MAIL CONTRACT

The terms of the third (1857) Ocean Mail Contract for the carriage of mail by steamship to the Cape – the first to be signed by the Union Steamship Company – provided for:

* *A monthly service in both directions.*
* *Steamships with a capacity of not less than 530 tons.*
* *A voyage of not more than forty-two days.*
* *The British departure port to be Plymouth (to allow for the latest possible delivery of mail from London by train). The Cape terminus to be either Table Bay or Simon's Bay, depending on the weather. (The swell and onshore prevailing wind during winter made the open roadstead in Table Bay extremely dangerous.)*
* *An annual subsidy of £33 000 to be paid to the contractor by the British Government.*
* *Ships to call at St Helena and Ascension islands on the homeward voyage.*

and Spain. Also operating out of Southampton were several other steamship companies with similar fuel requirements, and in the face of high railway rates, as well as irregular sailing ship services from the coal ports of southern Wales, there was clearly a demand for steam colliers to move coal from Cardiff and Swansea to Southampton.

In response to this demand for coal, Arthur Anderson, then managing director of P&O, initiated the formation of the Union Company, of which the shipping arm was initially registered in 1853 as the Southampton Steam Shipping Company. In view of its primary function, however, the company changed its name to the Union Steam Collier Company. Orders for five ships were placed with two Thames shipyards: the *Union*, *Briton* and *Saxon* were to be built by the Samuda Brothers, while the larger *Norman* and *Dane* were to come from Lungleys. All were designed to carry more than 500 tons of coal.

By March 1854, when Britain found herself embroiled in the Crimean War, none of Union's ships had been completed, but many of the vessels belonging to other shipping companies trading out of Southampton, including those of P&O, were requisitioned by the Government as transports. This resulted in the scheduled services being badly dislocated by the war and an inevitable downturn in the usual commercial activity at the Hampshire port.

Although the *Union*, commissioned in May 1854, had discharged her first cargo of coal at the end of June 1854, it was not long before she and the other Union ships were diverted by Anderson for use on several of the services that P&O had been obliged to discontinue. Nonetheless, it became obvious that it would only be a matter of time before the Union ships too would be pressed into government war service. The first so used was the *Norman* which, in December 1854, took a hundred prefabricated huts to the Crimea for use by the troops during the winter.

Surprisingly, government service proved so financially beneficial to the Union Steam Collier Company that a sixth ship, the *Celt*, was ordered. But when the end of the war came and the government transports were released to their owners, not only had coal been stockpiled in Southampton but also there were surplus ships available, meaning that alternative employment had to be found for the Union vessels. Services to South America and to Hamburg were both unsuccessful. Indeed, the former, being regarded as an intrusion into the preserve of the Royal Mail Line, had led to Captain Charles Mangles, a director of Royal Mail, resigning from the board of Union, on which he had served since its inception.

Fortuitously, the British Admiralty, frustrated by the failure of the Cape mail service that had been operated by both the General Screw Steam Shipping Company and W. H. Lindsay, decided to invite tenders for the third contract to carry mail to and from the Cape. The Union Steamship Company – it had shed 'Collier' from its name – tendered for and won the contract, which was duly signed in London on 12 September 1857 and was to be in force for five years.

Commanded by Captain William Strutt, the first Union mailship, *Dane*, left Southampton on 15 September 1857. Forty-four days later, after battling against strong south-east trades for much of her passage south of the equator, the small ship – a mere 526 tons – anchored among sixty sailing ships in Table Bay on 29 October 1857.

Taking the opportunity to conduct a major public relations programme while the *Dane* was in these waters, the Union Steamship Company (later referred to as the Union Line) invited fifty prominent citizens of Cape Town to join the ship for a cruise from Table Bay to Hout Bay. This generated enthusiastic response from commerce, and support was immediately forthcoming for the ship's northbound voyage. To allow time for answers to urgent letters from Britain, the *Dane* was required to wait in Table Bay until three days after the arrival of the next Union liner, the *Celt*, whereupon the pioneering Union liner sailed for Southampton via St Helena and Plymouth. In her hold was the largest consignment of mail yet shipped from the Cape.

One of many renowned men to travel in ships of the Union Line was the missionary, the Reverend John Smith Moffat, CBE, son of the Reverend Robert Moffat of Kuruman. Following his ordination for missionary work, John Moffat, together with his wife, left Southampton in April 1858 to continue his father's work in southern Africa. This is how he described the voyage:

RMS Briton, *circa 1865.*

There was only one mail despatched a month and the contract time for the passage was forty-two days. Our boat, the Norman, was five hundred tons burden . . . There was not much to be done in the way of carrying cargo. All the stowage room was required for the necessary coal to be consumed on the passage, so that when we arrived in Table Bay, our vessel was floating like an empty barrel . . . whereas at our start we were so deeply loaded that, when our vessel rolled, the water would wash across at midships, where the main deck was lowest.

We had an exceedingly rough beginning to our voyage, so much so that on the first night at sea, the whole of our livestock on deck, consisting of poultry intended for the table, was swept overboard. A few sheep which happened to be in a more sheltered corner, were served to us to eke out our supplies. There was no 'cold storage' in those days, and it was an unceasing wonder how we were all fed, and that very well too. Fortunately, there were only about sixteen passengers in the saloon. With the exception of the one usual grumbler, we were all happy and contented. My wife was a poor sailor, and it was a long time before she could take a proper meal . . . There was an army surgeon on board, a Dr Scott, who was going to join his regiment at the Cape. There were only nine berths available for the more favoured passengers in a sort of deckhouse. The other seven passengers had to make the best of berths down below, where there must often have been suggestions of the Black Hole of Calcutta.

There was a French Chevalier on board with his wife and daughter . . . bound to St Helena, but as we did not call there, they had not only the tedious voyage to the Cape, but also the return voyage to their destination . . . When we had accomplished about two-thirds of our voyage, our engines broke down, and for eight days we were under sail, whilst our plucky and indomitable engineer, a Scotsman, wrestled with his difficulties, and managed to make the necessary repairs. In spite of this drawback, we managed to scrape in just to contract time.

Constant pressure was being exerted by the colonists for an accelerated mail service, for which the contract at that stage demanded a voyage duration of not more than forty-two days. In response, the Cape Legislative Assembly voted in 1859 to pay the Union Line a bonus of £250 for each day pared from the expected average voyage of thirty-five days. After five such voyages had earned substantial bonuses for the company, the postmaster-general's report of 1860 stated: 'The packets which made these voyages most frequently in less than the contract or appointed time were those, between Devonport and the Cape of Good Hope, belonging to the Union S.S. Company, the next most successful packets being those of the Cunard Line.' When one considers the impeccable reputation of Cunard, even in those distant days, the postmaster-general's remarks must have induced great satisfaction among Union's board of directors.

Despite the economic doldrums in which southern Africa found itself at this time, two important projects were initiated in the sixties which, in a few short years, were to be crucial to the development of the region. The first was the construction of a sheltered harbour for Cape Town. The north-westerly gales that struck the Cape each winter had taken a heavy toll of shipping over the previous two centuries, and although various moles and jetties had been built, they were totally inadequate to offer protection to ships at anchor in Table Bay. In 1860, work began on an inner and an outer basin, as well as a 546-metre-long stone breakwater. The scheme, inaugurated by Queen Victoria's son, Prince Alfred, took nine years to complete. In the interim, ships in the bay continued to be subject to the ravages of winter gales and heavy swell and to be at the mercy of the savage south-easters that blew in summer.

The Reverend John Moffat, whose children were to be taken to boarding school in England in 1867, describes their embarkation in Table Bay before completion of the Alfred Basin project:

> We arranged for them [the children] to sail in the Norseman, which was timed to leave on the 19th of November. When the day came, there was a gale of unusual violence blowing. There were no docks, and vessels had to ride at anchor far out from the shore. It looked as if embarkation would be impossible, but a clerk in one of the principal shipping offices . . . said they were sending off a boat. There were three gentlemen who had agreed to pay three pounds each, and there were two or three cases of ostrich feathers, for the embarkation of which one pound each would be paid . . . Our boat was a cutter of ten tons with a covering deck before the mast. The passage to the steamer was comparatively easy, as the wind was with us, but when we got alongside, and had to round up with our head to the sea, the real tug-of-war began. The boat plunged violently against the check of the hawser which held us to the ship. It would have been impossible to have used the ladder. The basket would have been useless. The only way was to wait for the moment when the boat sprang up and was level with the deck of the steamer, where a sailor stood in readiness and caught the children as they were thrown over into his arms. Their little lady guardian had to be dealt with in the same fashion. I managed to jump across and to take the last farewell on deck, and then we started back for the shore, which we reached after a thorough drenching, as we had to beat up against the wind.

While the speed and comfort of sea travel were continually improving, two centuries of colonization at the Cape had seen little progress in overland travel. It had been the early trekboers, missionaries and traders who had first pioneered routes from the Cape and Port Natal into the interior, and with few exceptions, little attempt had been made in the intervening years to upgrade what were nothing more than tracks. Nor had the mode of travel seen much change. Long journeys were still undertaken by the tediously slow ox-wagon. Then in 1860, applications for shares were invited for the formation of the Natal Railway Company – the first of its kind in South Africa – the purpose of which was to link the Point area on Durban Bay with the town – a distance of 3,2 kilometres. This was followed in 1862 by the completion of the first stage of the Cape Town to Wellington line. It was an important advance in the colony's communications system and one, in fact, to which the Union Steamship Company could claim some slim connection, for among the six passengers brought to the Cape by the *Dane* on her first voyage was William Brounger who, as resident engineer of the Cape Town Dock and Railway Company, had led much of the planning for the Wellington line.

Without economic growth in the interior of the country, however, there was little incentive to extend the lines further afield. Like the economy of the region as a whole, railway development required some substantial stimulus before rapid expansion could take place.

That stimulus came at last with the discovery of southern Africa's mineral wealth. Although isolated finds of alluvial diamonds along the middle courses of both the Orange and Vaal rivers had been made in 1867, they did not have the impact of the Star of South Africa – a magnificent 82,5 carat diamond, found in 1869 in Griqualand West. It was initially sold for £11 000 but shortly thereafter changed hands again for the astounding sum of £25 000. The true diamond rush was on.

The opening of dry diggings at Kimberley drew thousands of fortune seekers into the interior, which, until then, had been sparsely settled by indigenous people, stock farmers, traders and missionaries. In response to the sudden demand for mining equipment, food, clothing and shelter, as well as transport for the droves of people who were making their way to Kimberley, plans were drawn up for the immediate extension of the Cape Town-Wellington line to the diamond fields. By 1885, Cape Town, Port Elizabeth and East London were all linked by rail to Kimberley.

For shipping companies sailing regularly to South Africa, the diamond rush and the associated boom meant good business. With full complements of passengers, many living under considerable hardship in the austere steerage class, or even in open berths on deck, the ships came not only from Britain and Europe, but also from Australia and America. To cater for the unprecedented demand for consumer goods and mining equipment, additional operators came on to the South African trade. Yet despite these interlopers, cargo space was at a premium. There was also considerably more mail for conveyance between Britain and South Africa. The time was clearly ripe for further major developments on the maritime scene.

Of all the shipping personalities associated with the South African trade, Donald Currie is probably the best known and, in the opinion of some, the most controversial. His was a simple, almost obscure, background. One of ten children, he was born in Greenock on the Clyde in 1825 and moved with his family to Belfast the following year. Yet although he grew up with little formal education, he rose to exert greater influence on South African maritime matters than many before or since.

His first encounter with the world of commerce was at the age of fourteen when he entered the office of the sugar merchants, MacFie, as a lowly clerk. For the young Currie that experience was vital, since his next step, three years later, was to join the firm of Charles McIver – one of the founders of the great Cunard Steamship Company – where he found the opportunity to display both insight and initiative in commerce, and particularly in shipping. In 1849 he was sent to Le Havre as the Cunard agent, a position he occupied with such great zeal that he was soon able to extend the Cunard influence to other areas in north-western Europe.

That Donald Currie was an individualist – and an ambitious one at that – is evidenced by his determination to operate his own ships rather than those of another. In 1862, he left Cunard and formed Donald Currie & Company, chartering sailing ships for trade with India via the Cape of Good Hope. It was not long before he owned his own fleet of sailing ships – all with the suffix 'Castle' – many bearing names that, perpetuated by later ships, were to become ingrained in the maritime history of southern Africa: *Pembroke Castle*, *Roslin Castle*, *Kenilworth Castle*, *Tantallon Castle*, *Carisbrooke Castle*, *Stirling Castle*, *Carnarvon Castle*, *Arundel Castle* and *Warwick Castle*.

Currie's first venture into steamships was in 1869, mainly as a baulk against the opening of the Suez Canal which, he reasoned, would probably sound the end of the sailing ship trade to India. In the meantime, while still continuing with his sailing ships to India, he established the Liverpool & Hamburg Steamship Company to operate a feeder service from Britain to Europe, and within a few years he had begun the construction of steamers for his Indian trade.

It was at about this time that Currie's interest in the South African trade was aroused. George Payne of the Cape & Natal Line (formed in 1871 as the Steam Navigation Company) approached Currie for assistance. Cape & Natal was then engaged in fierce competition with the Union Line and Payne required two ships to charter. Currie could not release any of his own but he arranged with the Leith, Hull & Hamburg Line, of which his brother James was the manager, to charter the *Iceland* and the *Gothland* to Payne. On the day that the *Iceland* sailed from Dartmouth for the Cape (23 February 1872), Currie's first 'Castle' steamship, the *Dover Castle*, was launched on the Clyde, though she was fated never to sail on the Cape run as a fire caused her to founder off the Chilean coast while on a chartered voyage to South America.

Within days of the first voyage of the *Iceland*, the Cape & Natal Line was declared bankrupt. Encouraged by the promised support of Cape merchants for a new shipping line, and in preference to using his steamers on the Indian trade (which he was soon to abandon altogether), Currie decided to continue where Cape & Natal had left off. A major factor influencing his change to the Cape run was the positive trend in the economy of the region following the diamond rush. At the same time, his entry into the

Cape Town harbour's Alfred Basin, circa 1880.

1

South African sphere fulfilled part of the intensifying demand for ships to carry the hordes of people seeking passage to the diamond fields, not to mention the increasing volume of cargo awaiting shipment.

A number of chartered vessels paved the way for Currie's venture into the South African trade, but it fell to the *Westmoreland* – of the Liverpool & Hamburg Line – to be the first of his own ships on a regular service to South Africa.

Carrying what were called 'private mails' and arriving before the appointed Union vessel, Currie's ships began to challenge seriously the monopoly held by the Union Line on the mail contract, and one of his chartered ships, the *Penguin*, even set a new record for a passage to the Cape when, in May 1872, she covered the distance from Dartmouth in a mere twenty-four days and eighteen hours.

In October 1872 the arrival of the *Walmer Castle*, the first steamer bearing a 'Castle' name to call at a South African port, brought a new dimension to the competition between the Union and Castle lines, for besides her British cargo, she brought cargo from Bordeaux in France, where she had called in the hope of generating trade between France and southern Africa, as well as the Indian Ocean islands. More significantly, she brought telegraphic news and other communications that had been cabled to her in Bordeaux; thus the news she carried was more recent – if only marginally – than that brought by the following Union liner. And yet another record passage was made in 1873, this time by the *Windsor Castle*, which arrived in Table Bay from Dartmouth after only twenty-three days at sea.

No matter how trivial such aspects might seem in retrospect, they were not lost on the community at the Cape and, more particularly, they were not lost on the Cape Colonial Government.

Prior to 1876, the British Imperial Government had been responsible for the Ocean Mail Contract, and the Cape Colony contributed its share of the cost by paying the British Government eighty-three per cent of the revenue collected in the colony for overseas postage. In terms of that contract, the Union Line had to provide two sailings a month between Britain and the Cape, while another contract required the Union Line to have an additional sailing each month to convey mail between the Cape and Zanzibar. To supplement the Zanzibar service and to encourage competition on the England-Cape run, the Cape Government paid the Castle Line a £12 000 'gratuity', as it was called by the postmaster-general in his report for the year, for the Castle ships to operate a monthly mail service. Currie was also offered a bonus of £150 for every day shaved off the mail contract time of thirty days. Certain other concessions were granted to the Castle Line too, and although no formal contract had been drawn up, to all intents and purposes the line's operations were recognized by the Cape as part of the mailship service.

FROM THE LOG OF THE ICELAND

(The steamer Iceland *was on a chartered voyage from London to Algoa Bay.)*

SEPTEMBER 8 1872 — *Lat. 2 degrees 37 minutes S*
Long. 9 degrees 2 minutes E
Stopped the allowance of flour to the crew, and gave them preserved potatoes as a substitute.

OCTOBER 8 1872 — *Port Elizabeth*
Charles —, AB, got the noise for drinking. Used abusive language to the 1st Mate, also struck at him. Was put in irons and subsequently released on his promising to behave himself. He afterwards went in the forecastle and commenced to fight with some of the hands.

OCTOBER 10 1872 — *Port Elizabeth*
Chas. —, AB, was this day sentenced to imprisonment with hard labour for assaulting the 1st Mate.

OCTOBER 14 1872 — *Port Elizabeth*
The above-named seaman, Chas. — was this day taken from prison and signed his release and was discharged before the Shipping Master 'Indebted to Ship 6s 6d'.

EXTRACT FROM THE CAPE ARGUS 5 OCTOBER 1872

ARRIVAL OF THE MAIL.

The Royal Mail Steamer *Saxon*, Capt. F. Diver, anchored in Table Bay shortly after 3 o'clock on Monday morning, after a passage of thirty-five days. She left Southampton on the 26th August and Madeira on the 2nd ultimo. Nothing of any importance occurred during the voyage. She brought out for this port and Algoa Bay a large cargo of general merchandise and fifty passenger,s of whom the following is a list :—For Madeira,—Mr. Perreira. For Cape Town,—Mr. Lazarus, Miss Lyars. Mr. H. Barkly, Mr. Ridley, Mr. W. A. Lippert, Mr. Thornley, Mr. Edie, Mr. and Mrs Peabody, Mrs. Tweed, Mr. W. Boas, Mr. Sidney, Mr. Westuton, Mr. Pfuhl, Mr. Price, Mr. Raby, Mr. Roberts, Mr. Mann, Mr. Tomlinson, Mr H. F. Teitz. For Algoa Bay,—Mr. and Mrs. Henman, Mr. Mills, Mr. D. Manhall, Mr. Brandt, Mr. Michaelis, Mr. R. Soames, Mr. Hay, Mr. and Master Saenger, Miss McCalle. For Natal,—Mr. Tricket, Mr. A. Bateman, Mr. Wright, Mr. Wright, Mr. Humphrey. Mr. Fawcett, Mr. Broner, Mrs. Dunning, two children, Mr. Rosevere, Mr. Mackenzie and man servant, two Messrs. Wichausen, Mr. Bray, Mr. Basset, Mr. Dinning, Mr. Abel, Mr. Bennett, Mr. Kemp, Mr. J. Winter, Miss Smith, Mr. F. Bell.[2]

On the expiry of the contract in 1876, the Cape Government assumed responsibility for its renewal, and on account of the encouragement it had given to Donald Currie, it was inevitable that the new contract should consider his claims as a genuine competitor. This became reality when the contract, signed on 5 October 1876, was shared equally between the two companies. In his report for the year 1876, the postmaster-general wrote:

> Contracts have been entered into with the Union Company and Donald Currie & Co. for the conveyance of a weekly mail service to and from England, which came into force on the 1st October 1876 and are to terminate on the 30th September 1882. It is stipulated in them that the voyages are to be performed in 26 days, and in 27 days when the packet is appointed to touch either at St Helena or Ascension. Premiums for speed at the rate of £4/3/4 are allowed for every complete hour in which the passage is made under the period of 26 or 27 days and at the rate of £6/5/- per hour for each such passage under the period of 23 or 24 days respectively. The contractors are further entitled to receive the postage collected on the mails they convey. (Letters 6d half oz. Newspapers 1d each. Book packets and samples 3d for 4oz.)

Included in the contracts was a prohibition on an amalgamation between the Union and Castle lines, and on any working agreements between them without the approval of the Cape Government. This set the stage for ferocious competition, something the Cape Government wished to encourage so that an improved service could be provided.

It was at this time that Currie changed the operating name of his company: first to The Castle Packets Company and then, in 1881, to The Castle Mail Packets Company, retaining Donald Currie & Co. as the managing company.

Since speed was one of the focuses of competition between the rival companies, each sought to outdo the other when ordering new ships. Within five years of the joint mail contract being signed, and to cope with the booming South African economy, the Union Line had taken delivery of seven new mailships, and the Castle Line eight. Both companies had every reason to boast of their achievements as they expanded their fleets with bigger, better and faster ships. But they had had their disasters too. Between 1875 and 1881 there had been five accidents involving ships of the Union and Castle lines.

The first news that the general public received of the wreck of the *Celt*, was a short report that appeared in the *Cape Argus* of 9 February 1875. The *Celt* had left Table Bay for the east coast run on Saturday, 6 February.

WRECK OF THE CELT

> A telegram was posted early yesterday morning at the Commercial Exchange announcing the wreck at 4 a.m. on Sunday of the RMS *Celt* at the boundary of Rattel River and Hagel Kraal. The passengers, crew and mails were saved and landed . . .

According to a later report in the newspaper, the vessel carried 'an unusually heavy mail, a considerable number of passengers and a large cargo, a good deal of which . . . was uninsured'. Another bulletin, still in telegraphic language, from a correspondent in the town of Caledon reported that no survivors had arrived there:

> Three large carts sent up from Cape Town by Wm. Anderson and Co. sent to the scene of the wreck this afternoon. Civil Commissioner sent off mail-wagons for the mails last Monday evening. Can hardly be expected back before tomorrow night owing to heavy and sandy state of the road. Celt total wreck, cargo all more or less damaged.

The full story emerged only when the passengers and crew arrived in Cape Town aboard the *Zulu*, which had been diverted from Port Elizabeth to rescue the shipwreck victims. Again, the *Cape Argus* of 13 February carried the report of the stranding:

> About four o'clock [on the morning of Sunday, 7 February], it was discovered that the vessel was close in shore; the officer sang out 'land ahead' several times, but before there was time to adopt any precautionary measures, the ship struck and bumped the rocks with a loud grating sound, the force of the concussion throwing some of the passengers out of their bunks . . .

---

1 *This fine oil is of the* Carnarvon Castle, *one of Sir Donald Currie's early vessels, most of which were employed predominantly on the Indian trade.*

2 *The arrival of the mail was news indeed. Even early this century, notices similar to this appeared in the press to announce the arrival of a mailship.*

ACCIDENT AT SEA

Returning to Britain for furlough and missionary deputation work, the Reverend John Moffat recorded the following tragic event:

> *We embarked at Port Elizabeth on the 27th of February 1872 in the* Danube, *a comfortable enough ship, but small [compared] to the great liners which now make the passage with unvarying regularity . . . One untoward incident broke the comparative monotony of the voyage. We called at Madeira. As we were leaving again, the boatswain, while busy completing the stowage of the anchor, fell overboard. We were by this time going at full speed. The alarm was given but by the time the vessel could be brought to a standstill, the unfortunate man, who could not swim, was far astern. Meanwhile, a boat was being lowered in hot haste. A number of passengers, well-meaning but blundering, rushed to assist. In the confusion, they lowered one end of the boat too quickly, with the result that three more men were thrown into the water, of whom two sank at once before our eyes. The third, who could swim, calmly availed himself of one of the lifebuoys that had been thrown over, and waited patiently till he could be picked up. When at last a boat was properly lowered and went back to the spot where the boatswain had fallen over, there was nothing to be seen but his cap floating on the water . . . We reached Southampton on the 1st of April. To eyes accustomed to the arid wastes of Bechwanaland, it was a sensation never to be forgotten to gaze upon the wonderful green of the meadows and hedgerows of Old England.*

EXTRACT FROM THE CAPE TIMES OF 30 MAY 1877

LAUNCH OF A NEW CAPE MAIL-STEAMER.

On Tuesday, the 1st inst., Messrs. Robert Napier launched from their yard at Govan, Glasgow, a new steamer of 3,000 tons register for the mail service between England and the South African Colonies. This vessel, one of six now building on the Clyde for Messrs. Donald Currie & Co. and intended for the same trade, was named the *Dublin Castle* by Miss Bessie Currie as proxy for the Duchess of Manchester—the steamer being named in honour of the Duke of Manchester, the last elected Knight of St. Patrick, who is President of the Royal Colonial Institute.

The *Dublin Castle* will take up her station on the line between England and the Cape in July next.

The plating of the *Warwick Castle* is nearly completed, and the *Conway Castle* is in frame. Both steamers are intended for the same owners and, service and will be ready during the summer. They are each of 2,900 tons.

The trial trip of the steamer *Melrose*, which has been built by Messrs. Robert Steele & Co., of Greenock, for Messrs. Donald Currie & Co.,
1 took place yesterday.

> The spot where the passengers were destined to lead a Robinson Crusoe kind of existence was anything but inviting, for all around there was nothing discernible but a sandy waste dotted over with low scrubby bush . . .
>
> Many of the passengers were quite jolly over the event, and thought shipwreck under favourable circumstances not such a bad thing after all . . .

Then came a bitter blow to the stranded people. The Castle liner, *Edinburgh Castle*, which had sighted the wrecked ship, turned inshore and signalled. Excitedly, the chief officer of the *Celt* rallied seamen to launch a boat to row out to the *Edinburgh Castle* and arrange for the evacuation of the people on the beach, but when they had progressed a mile, the liner began to turn seawards and resumed her voyage to Cape Town. This incident drew an angry response from the passengers, some of whom later alleged that the master of the *Edinburgh Castle* had not displayed the traditional spirit of brotherhood of the sea by leaving the unfortunates on the beach. Captain Penfold of the *Edinburgh Castle* presented a different point of view. It was reported in the *Cape Argus* of 11 February, also in telegraphic format:

> At 5.15 p.m. sighted a vessel on shore about one mile from Quoin Point when we immediately altered our course towards her and found it a brig-rigged steamer with black funnel, having a blue ensign flying half-mast at the main Union down. Supposed to be the *Celt*. Upon nearing the shore, guns were fired to attract attention and the signal 'Do you need assistance?' hoisted, but after waiting some time, the flag was hauled down from the vessel on shore, and no other notice being taken of our signal, we proceeded on our course at 6.23 p.m., concluding that no assistance was required. The boats were all gone from the davits and a number of tents were erected on the beach, and people could be distinguished walking about. The vessel was lying broadside to the sea which was breaking heavily outside her. Vessel heading ESE compass. A large clump of rocks apparently on the port bow, she was lying over very much, and a brisk south east wind blowing at the time the *Edinburgh Castle* sighted her.

The newspaper agreed that Captain Penfold had acted with the best intentions, and reported: '. . . those on board the *Edinburgh Castle* deny having seen any boat, and we feel assured that . . . Captain Penfold is too renowned a seaman to have been guilty of such neglect and want of consideration. As it was, he placed his vessel in no small jeopardy.'

At the inquiry, Captain George Bird was found guilty of negligence as he had set a course too close to land, had neither checked the compass error, nor the bearings taken earlier. The court also found that second officer John Miller had not kept a proper watch. Both had their certificates suspended for a year.

'Transportation would have been better than that!' fumed Captain Bird at the court's sentence, to which the magistrate retorted, 'I cannot help that!'

Eighteen months later, the Castle Line suffered a major loss. In the early hours of 19 October 1876, the *Windsor Castle*, inward to Table Bay from Dartmouth, grounded on the rocky Dassen Island some sixty miles from Cape Town. Captain John Hewat had been alerted to there being a light ahead and had rushed up on deck. He saw the island but assumed it to be more distant, and continued to scan the horizon for the light which had been reported to him. No sooner had he ordered the helm a point more to starboard, than he felt the ship grind on to the rocks. He called for full astern, but the chief engineer reported that the vessel was taking water in the engine room. Hewat ordered the boats to be swung out and he sent the chief officer away in a gig to search for a safe landing place. At daybreak, the ship was abandoned, the boats making for a small beach on the island that the chief officer had located. The fourth officer and two volunteers, Lieutenant Mellville and a Mr Searle, went to the mainland in search of help. They walked for many kilometres over rough terrain before arriving at the hamlet of Darling, where they hired, at the exorbitant rate of £20, a horse and cart with which they hastened to Cape Town. The loss of a mailship was a most serious event and received extensive coverage in the press. The *Cape Argus* of 24 October carried the following report:

WRECK OF THE WINDSOR CASTLE

> The most startling piece of intelligence that goes home to England by the present mail is the loss of Donald Currie and Company's fine steamer *Windsor Castle* which occurred at Dassen Island early on the morning of the 19th inst. Although the gravity of the disaster is somewhat relieved by the fact that the passengers, crew and mail bags were all saved, that so splendid a mail boat whose speed was almost as proverbial,

2

> should have been wrecked within a few miles of port on a fine night is a matter for universal and unfeigned regret . . .
>
> The *Windsor Castle* was several days overdue and her arrival from England was being anxiously awaited when news of the wreck reached here by two of the passengers . . .
>
> The news soon spread through Cape Town and the office of the agents Messrs Anderson and Murison was besieged by persons having friends on board . . . The excitement was somewhat alleviated by the fact that the passengers and mails were reported to be saved, but no time was lost in dispatching the *Florence* to the scene . . .

All the passengers were returned safely to Cape Town. As in the case of the *Celt*, the master and second officer were found guilty of negligence but, as the account of the court's proceedings read, '. . . taking into consideration that after the ship struck, the master performed his duty for the preservation of life and property in a manner most creditable to an officer and a seaman, and his fifteen years' service as a master without an accident . . .' the court suspended his certificate for nine months and that of the second officer for three months.

The 2 271-ton *European* had been bought as a three-year-old vessel by the Union Line in 1872. On a regular mail voyage from the Cape to Southampton in December 1877, she left Madeira in good weather and three days later passed Cape Finisterre some 25 miles to starboard. On 5 December, her master, Captain Robert Ker, ordered that she heave to so that soundings could be taken, as he was unsure of her exact position due to there being an indraught into the Bay of Biscay. No bottom was found and they resumed their passage, this time steering north-northeast for three hours before further soundings were taken. Again, no bottom was found and, since Captain Ker thought the vessel to be too far westward, he altered course to steer north-northeast. Soundings were taken later that evening and the bottom was found at 48 fathoms, and a slight alteration to the course was made.

At eight bells that evening, Captain Ker and the chief officer went below and were relieved by the second and third officers. On a visit to the bridge later that night, Ker found that the course being steered was not to his satisfaction and ordered a further change. Shortly thereafter, the Ushant light was sighted off the port bow when it should have been to starboard. When breakers were sighted off the starboard bow, and thinking his way was clear to port, the captain ordered the engines full ahead. Within minutes the ship had struck the rocks, which ripped her open to the sea, flooding the forward holds and engine room. In miraculously moderate conditions, the lifeboats were lowered and all reached St Malo safely.

Censured by the court of inquiry for keeping his ship on a course too close to the coast, for 'not sufficiently attending the soundings which he had obtained and comparing them to the chart', as well as for having ordered the engines full ahead when he was unsure of the ship's exact position, Captain Ker had his master's certificate suspended for six months.

With sixty-eight passengers and seventy-six crew members on board, the 2 484-ton Union liner *American* left Southampton for Table Bay on 8 April 1880. In view of the premium on cargo space on the South African trade at the time, she was well loaded with general cargo, much of which was destined for the diamond fields. It was the morning of 23 April. The ship was about 200 miles south-west of Cape Palmas, a promontory on the Liberian coast; the watchkeepers had changed and within an hour the first passengers would awake to take in the balmy tropical air.

Down in the engine room where stokers and engineers had sweated all night to keep the furnaces fired, the fourth engineer suddenly heard a crash and the engines began to race. Instantly, he turned off the steam but discovered to his horror that water was pouring in through the propeller-shaft tunnel. (The cause of the crisis was a fracture in the propeller shaft which had pierced the ship's side.) He managed to close the tunnel door, preventing the immediate flooding of the engine room. However, the after bulkhead had also been damaged, and because that bulkhead did not carry up to the spar deck, water had easy access to the after hold and, within an hour, to the engine room.

On deck, Captain Wait ordered the boats to be provisioned, then he calmly sent

---

1 *Since the carriage of the mail was of such importance to South Africa, news of launchings and maiden voyages received considerable press coverage.*

2 *An etching depicting the* Windsor Castle *ashore on Dassen Island, 1876.*

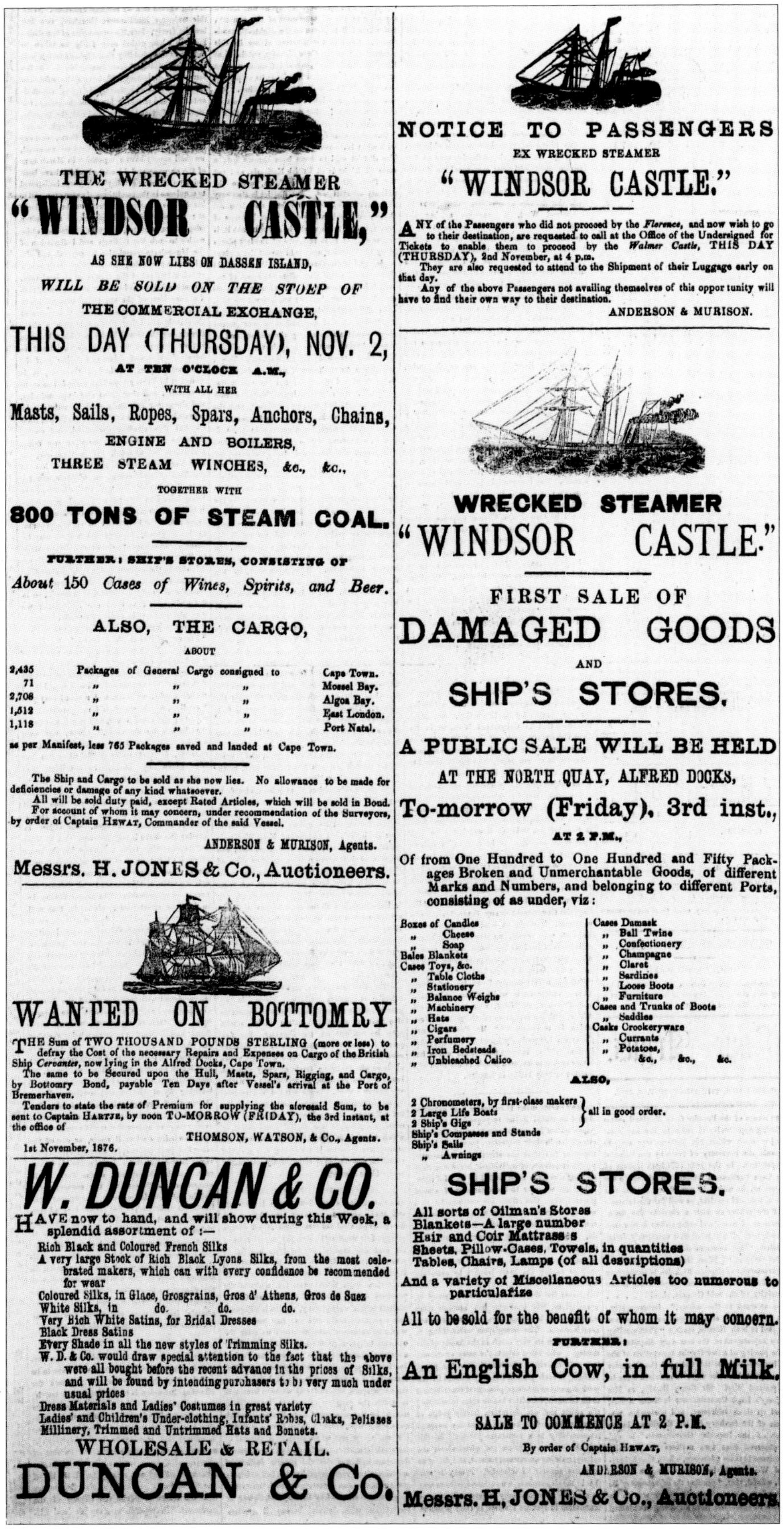

THE WRECKED STEAMER

"WINDSOR CASTLE,"

AS SHE NOW LIES ON DASSEN ISLAND,

WILL BE SOLD ON THE STOEP OF

THE COMMERCIAL EXCHANGE,

THIS DAY (THURSDAY), NOV. 2,

AT TEN O'CLOCK A.M.,

WITH ALL HER

Masts, Sails, Ropes, Spars, Anchors, Chains,

ENGINE AND BOILERS,

THREE STEAM WINCHES, &c., &c.,

TOGETHER WITH

800 TONS OF STEAM COAL.

FURTHER: SHIP'S STORES, CONSISTING OF

About 150 Cases of Wines, Spirits, and Beer.

ALSO, THE CARGO,

ABOUT

2,435	Packages of General Cargo	consigned	to	Cape Town.
71	"	"	"	Mossel Bay.
2,708	"	"	"	Algoa Bay.
1,512	"	"	"	East London.
1,118	"	"	"	Port Natal.

as per Manifest, less 765 Packages saved and landed at Cape Town.

The Ship and Cargo to be sold as she now lies. No allowance to be made for deficiencies or damage of any kind whatsoever.

All will be sold duty paid, except Rated Articles, which will be sold in Bond.

For account of whom it may concern, under recommendation of the Surveyors, by order of Captain HEWAT, Commander of the said Vessel.

ANDERSON & MURISON, Agents.

Messrs. H. JONES & Co., Auctioneers.

WANTED ON BOTTOMRY

THE Sum of TWO THOUSAND POUNDS STERLING (more or less) to defray the Cost of the necessary Repairs and Expenses on Cargo of the British Ship *Cervanter*, now lying in the Alfred Docks, Cape Town.

The same to be Secured upon the Hull, Masts, Spars, Rigging, and Cargo, by Bottomry Bond, payable Ten Days after Vessel's arrival at the Port of Bremerhaven.

Tenders to state the rate of Premium for supplying the aforesaid Sum, to be sent to Captain HARTJE, by noon TO-MORROW (FRIDAY), the 3rd instant, at the office of

THOMSON, WATSON, & Co., Agents.

1st November, 1876.

W. DUNCAN & CO.

HAVE now to hand, and will show during this Week, a splendid assortment of :—

Rich Black and Coloured French Silks

A very large Stock of Rich Black Lyons Silks, from the most celebrated makers, which can with every confidence be recommended for wear

Coloured Silks, in Glace, Grosgrains, Gros d' Athens, Gros de Suez

White Silks, in do. do. do.

Very Rich White Satins, for Bridal Dresses

Black Dress Satins

Every Shade in all the new styles of Trimming Silks.

W. D. & Co. would draw special attention to the fact that the above were all bought before the recent advance in the prices of Silks, and will be found by intending purchasers to be very much under usual prices

Dress Materials and Ladies' Costumes in great variety

Ladies' and Children's Under-clothing, Infants' Robes, Cloaks, Pelisses Millinery, Trimmed and Untrimmed Hats and Bonnets.

WHOLESALE & RETAIL.

DUNCAN & Co.

NOTICE TO PASSENGERS

EX WRECKED STEAMER

"WINDSOR CASTLE."

ANY of the Passengers who did not proceed by the *Florence*, and now wish to go to their destination, are requested to call at the Office of the Undersigned for Tickets to enable them to proceed by the *Walmer Castle*, THIS DAY (THURSDAY), 2nd November, at 4 p.m.

They are also requested to attend to the Shipment of their Luggage early on that day.

Any of the above Passengers not availing themselves of this opportunity will have to find their own way to their destination.

ANDERSON & MURISON.

WRECKED STEAMER

"WINDSOR CASTLE."

FIRST SALE OF

DAMAGED GOODS

AND

SHIP'S STORES.

A PUBLIC SALE WILL BE HELD

AT THE NORTH QUAY, ALFRED DOCKS,

To-morrow (Friday), 3rd inst.,

AT 2 P.M.,

Of from One Hundred to One Hundred and Fifty Packages Broken and Unmerchantable Goods, of different Marks and Numbers, and belonging to different Ports, consisting of as under, viz :

Boxes of Candles	Cases Damask
" Cheese	" Ball Twine
" Soap	" Confectionery
Bales Blankets	" Champagne
Cases Toys, &c.	" Claret
" Table Cloths	" Sardines
" Stationery	" Loose Boots
" Balance Weighs	" Furniture
" Machinery	Cases and Trunks of Boots
" Hats	" Saddles
" Cigars	Casks Crockeryware
" Perfumery	" Currants
" Iron Bedsteads	" Potatoes,
" Unbleached Calico	&c., &c., &c.

ALSO,

2 Chronometers, by first-class makers }
2 Large Life Boats } all in good order.
2 Ship's Gigs }
Ship's Compasses and Stands
Ship's Sails
" Awnings

SHIP'S STORES.

All sorts of Oilman's Stores
Blankets—A large number
Hair and Coir Mattrasses
Sheets, Pillow-Cases, Towels, in quantities
Tables, Chairs, Lamps (of all descriptions)

And a variety of Miscellaneous Articles too numerous to particularize

All to be sold for the benefit of whom it may concern.

FURTHER:

An English Cow, in full Milk.

SALE TO COMMENCE AT 2 P.M.

By order of Captain HEWAT,

ANDERSON & MURISON, Agents.

Messrs. H. JONES & Co., Auctioneers.

1

everyone to enjoy a hearty breakfast. This action succeeded in neutralizing panic and facilitated the later orderly abandoning of the vessel. At 07:30, when the vessel began to settle rapidly, the women and children were put into the boats. By 11:00 the stern was under water and Wait gave the order to abandon ship, he himself being the last to leave the vessel, which sank an hour later. The eight lifeboats were headed for Cape Palmas but became separated. After several days in the small boats, and enduring the blistering heat of a tropical sun, the survivors were becoming desperate. Then, on Sunday 25 April, two boats were sighted by the steamer *Congo*, the occupants rescued and landed at Madeira. Survivors in another three boats were picked up by the American barque, *Emma F. Herriman*. To accommodate these extra people aboard a relatively small vessel would have been a problem; it is therefore not surprising that the master transferred them some days later to the liner *Coanza*, which landed them at Grand Bassa in Liberia. Others were not so fortunate. Rescued by the British Africa liner *Senegal* while that vessel was homeward bound to Britain, one boat-load had just begun to relax after their ordeal when the *Senegal* itself ran aground near Las Palmas. All were rescued from their second shipwreck within a fortnight, apart from the Cape member of parliament, John Paterson, who was precipitated into the sea when a lifeboat launch went awry and was struck by the ship's propeller.

The Union liner *Teuton* had sighted the *Senegal* ashore and returned posthaste to Las Palmas with the news of the wreck. Within a few days, carrying the survivors landed at Las Palmas, she headed for Madeira to pick up those landed by the *Congo*, before resuming her voyage to the Cape. The *Senegal* was refloated some weeks later.

There were still two of the *American*'s lifeboats unaccounted for. One was sighted six weeks after the sinking by the German schooner *Moltke*, which rescued the survivors, transferring them later to the German ship *Kamerun* for landing at Madeira. News of the plight of the last boat reached Britain months later, when it was reported from Luanda that the Portuguese brig *Tarujo* had landed the boat's occupants there on 21 July.

Sitting in July 1880, the court of inquiry found the sinking of the *American* to be totally accidental and praised the officers and men of the ship for their exemplary conduct. Captain Wait became the recipient of congratulations from many quarters for the calm manner in which he had handled the abandoning of the ship. Ordering that last breakfast aboard the stricken liner had indeed been an inspired move.

The fifth disaster was the sinking, in August 1881, of one of the vessels that had assisted in the rescue of survivors of the *American* – the intermediate liner *Teuton*. Another victim of the treacherous reefs off Quoin Point on the southern Cape coast, she was sliced open by the rocks and although her master turned her to head for Simon's Town, she sank suddenly near Cape Hangklip with great loss of life.

The considerable jockeying for favour between Union and Castle continued away from the sea lanes, each company seeking any and every means to exhibit its prowess or to gain the ear of influential people. Following the loss of the *Windsor Castle*, a public display of the animosity between the two companies erupted when Currie accused the Union Line's Captain Baynton, master of the *Nubian*, of ignoring the plight of the passengers and crew of the *Windsor Castle*, wrecked on Dassen Island in October of the previous year. He alleged that Baynton had neither rendered assistance nor had he reported the mishap to the Lloyds agents on arrival in Britain. Currie's accusations were contained in correspondence which he claimed had been ignored by the Union Line's management and which he then sent to the press. He was at pains to point out that the Castle Line officers were under instructions to offer aid wherever necessary and quoted the case of the *Edinburgh Castle* standing by the wrecked *Celt* near Danger Point in 1875. He further alleged deceit on the part of the Union Line because it had appointed extra hands in the stokehold of the *Nyanza* in an attempt to increase her speed, contrary, he maintained, to the spirit of the mail contract.

In a letter to the *Cape Argus* of 14 June 1877, Thomas Fuller, the Union Line's general manager for South Africa, repudiated these allegations with sarcasm and disdain. It was the first time that there had been public hostility between the two companies.

There is no denying Currie's considerable skills as a strategist. In the hope of lucrative benefits to his company, he did not hesitate to go the extra mile – and further – to humour dignitaries. His association with influential South African and British personalities brought many favours in return. When the dour President Thomas Burgers of the Transvaal Republic was in Britain in 1875, it was Currie who used his influence to assist him in obtaining the finance for a rail link between the Transvaal and Delagoa Bay. In return the Castle Line was given a provisional undertaking that it would be given the

THE INTERMEDIATE FLEET

Before the joint contract was drawn up between the Castle Mail Packets Co. Ltd and the Union Steamship Company, the Union Line had to provide thirty-six sailings each year. In terms of the new contract, both companies had to provide one vessel each alternate week. This left the Union Line with surplus ships. As, however, the Eastern Province had persistently lobbied for a more regular service to Algoa Bay, it was logical that the Union Line should employ its extra ships to provide a monthly service to Algoa Bay direct from England, a service which was extended and became known as the 'intermediate service'; hence the ships were referred to as 'intermediates' (or occasionally as 'extras') to distinguish them from those vessels employed in terms of the mail contract.

After the amalgamation of the Union and Castle lines, the intermediate ships were employed on routes other than that stipulated by the mail contract, and gradually the service was extended, initially up the East African coast and then to a 'round Africa service'. During periods of heavy demand for passenger berths or for cargo space, some vessels came directly from Britain and turned at Cape Town.

There were, of course, other itineraries, such as that of the Bloemfontein Castle *which, from her entry to the service in 1950 until her sale to Greek owners in 1959, plied the London-Cape Town-Beira trade with calls at all the major southern African ports, including Walvis Bay and Lourenço Marques (now Maputo).*

There was always a unique atmosphere surrounding the intermediate service, for it reflected to a greater degree than the mail service those more leisurely times when the British Empire was at its peak. High Commissioners, military attachés, civil servants and a host of other expatriates from the East and Central African colonies travelled in these ships which called at picturesque, exotic ports such as palm-fringed Dar-es-Salaam or Mombasa, the crowded anchorage at Aden and, of course, the bustling maritime convergence points of Suez and Port Said. Frequently the voyage included calls at Naples, Genoa or Marseille, adding a Continental bonus for the passengers and attracting those travelling between Britain and South Africa who might otherwise have chosen the mailship.

2

3

4

5

1 *Press advertisements announce the sale of salvaged goods from the wreck of the* Windsor Castle. *Among the more interesting items offered for sale is 'An English Cow, in full Milk'. She would have been carried aboard the liner to provide fresh milk for those passengers travelling first class. How the animal was removed from the wrecked ship and taken to the island and thence to the mainland is not recorded.*

2 *The* Llangibby Castle, *an intermediate liner employed on Union-Castle's round-Africa service from 1929 to 1954.*

3 *The* Braemar Castle, *one of the early intermediate liners.*

4 *The intermediate liner* Durham Castle, *which made a few voyages on the mail service after World War I.*

5 *The* Durban Castle, *one of the intermediates that undertook several sailings on the mail service until the delivery of the* Pretoria Castle *in 1948.*

1

2

EXTRACT FROM A LETTER TO DONALD CURRIE

From the Cape Town office of The Castle Mail Packets Co. Ltd.

The letterhead bears the embossed words 'South African Royal Mail Service' and is dated 23 January 1883. The contents, relating to subsidized immigration schemes promulgated by the Cape Colonial Government, illustrate the fluctuations in the relationship which Currie – and indeed the Union Line too – enjoyed with the Cape Government which was intent on ensuring that it obtained its pound of flesh.

I have seen Mr Merriman [the influential Cape statesman, politician and future prime minister] with reference to the immigration contract and pointed out to him how unfair the Mail Companies have been treated in this matter, and repeated what you wrote to me and to Captain Murison as to the manner in which the agent general had gone about offering the Contract to the Union Company if they would break with the Castle Company, and vice versa, and inducing outside steamers to tender, which style of doing business was, to say the least of it, beneath the dignity of the representative of the Colony.

Mr Merriman would not go into the question further, than to express his regret that the mail companies had not accepted the 1881 rates offered by the Government which he considered notwithstanding your remarks to the contrary, fair and reasonable. I pointed out to him how much more convenient it would be to the Government to have the Immigrants landed here fortnightly in small batches by the Mail Steamers than by the International Line in larger numbers at irregular intervals, and how the Colony might be brought into disrepute through the action of the Government in refusing the reasonable terms offered by the Mail Companies, and accepting the tender of a much inferior class of vessel at an unremunerative rate, which would possibly result in the bad treatment of the Immigrants, all of which he admitted to a certain extent might be the case, but he still justified the position which the Government had taken up with regard to this matter.

He told me that he would have been prepared to make special arrangements for the conveyance of the Italian immigrants had the scheme been carried out, but he would not say what scheme he would have proposed.

It is quite clear to me that so long at least as Mr Merriman is in office, we need not expect that any special consideration will be shown to the mail Companies, notwithstanding their obligations to carry out the Mail Contract under difficulties and severe competition from outside steamers which are not obliged to load home.

contract to carry Transvaal mails to Britain at the conclusion of the agreement with the Union Line. Similarly, when President Brand of the Orange Free State visited Britain, Currie acted as an intermediary during the diamond fields dispute, a role which earned him the CMG from Queen Victoria. Prime Minister Gladstone was among his personal friends and was frequently invited on special voyages on his ships. In 1881, in recognition of his services and achievements, Currie was knighted, and at a banquet on board the *Garth Castle* to mark the opening of a new dock at Leith, he was toasted on his knighthood by none other than the Duke of Edinburgh.

With such diplomatic gains to his credit, Currie was clearly the leading contender in the struggle for dominance in the mail service.

3

2

A duel for supremacy

1883-1900

4

The linking of the Cape to Britain by undersea telegraph cable in 1880 meant more than the mere facilitating of urgent communications between the colony and Britain. Indirectly, the very speed at which messages could be transmitted both ways further stimulated development in the region. As a result, spurred on by the spiralling demand for both passages and cargo space, the mail companies further increased the size of their fleets as well as the size of individual ships.

Union led the way with the *Mexican* in 1883. This was the first mailship over 4 000 tons and it was followed closely by the *Tartar*, another 4 000-tonner. Not to be outdone, the Castle Line quickly responded by introducing a brand new trio to the run: the *Hawarden Castle*, the *Norham Castle* and the *Roslin Castle*. These ships were also capable of greater speeds, for the new mail contract of 1883 stipulated that the outward voyage from Dartmouth to Table Bay should not exceed twenty-one days and twelve hours, and penalties were to be enforced for any voyage taking longer than twenty-three days. In wording similar to that of previous contracts, the new contract also called for 'a sufficient number of good substantial and efficient steam vessels of adequate power and supplied with first rate appropriate steam engines and in all respects suited to the performance of the services hereby agreed to be performed with the respective terms herein stipulated'.

By this time a number of other companies had entered the South African

1 *Durban, circa 1890.*
2 The Saxon, *the first Union liner to dock in the Alfred Basin in November 1870.*
3 The Scot *in Cape Town.*
4 *Sir Donald Currie, founder of the Castle Line and first chairman of the Union-Castle Mail Steamship Company.*

1

GOVERNMENT PASSENGERS : THE OCEAN MAIL CONTRACT OF 1883

The contract entered into between the Cape Colonial Government on the one hand and the Castle Mail Packet Company and Union Steamship Company on the other, specified requirements for the treatment of government passengers on board the companies' ships:

> *The said first class and second class passengers shall be accommodated in cabins properly fitted up and the said third class passengers shall be accommodated in hammocks or bunks placed between decks.*
>
> *The messing of the said first class passengers, their wives and children shall be the same as is usually allowed to chief cabin passengers, their wives and children. The messing of the said second class passengers, their wives and children shall be the same allowed to second class passengers, their wives and children, including a reputed pint of good sound bottled or draught ale or beer per diem, but the said messing shall never be less or inferior in quantity or quality to that required by the Regulations of Her Majesty's Transport Service and the victualling of the said third class passengers, their wives and children shall be in accordance with the scale of victualling contained in the said regulations.*

trade, which was then regarded as one of the most profitable. Bullard King and Rennie's Aberdeen Direct Line, two companies that had been operating sailing vessels between Britain and Natal since 1858, had both opted for steamers in 1880, introducing considerable competition for the mail companies. During the following year, the arrival in Table Bay of the *Clan Lamont* signalled the entry of The Clan Line Steamers to the trade, a new venture for this shipping company, for it had previously been interested in services to India. Within a year it had eight ships calling at southern African ports and was gradually extending its operations to include East Africa and Mauritius. Another two new entrants using irregular sailings by chartered ships – the International Line and the South African Line – presented still more competition. The International Line had secured a significant portion of the mail companies' potential passengers when it won the immigration contract from the Cape Government.

A brief, but potentially damaging, freight rates war ensued – to the detriment of all the participating lines. To counteract this, and in an attempt to give each of the various parties a proportional share in the trade, Donald Currie convened a series of discussions, culminating in September 1883 with the formation of the first South African Shipping Conference – a body which was to act as a watchdog to control, *inter alia*, excessive competition, freight rates and passenger traffic.

With their longer experience of the Cape route, their larger, faster ships, their substantial influence and nurtured contacts, and above all, the Ocean Mail Contract, the two mail companies completely dominated the discussions and, indeed, all subsequent proceedings of the Conference – as it was called – for the next few decades. Certainly, the figure of Sir Donald Currie featured prominently at all the meetings. None could match

2

THE CAREY MURDER

In 1882, the British secretary for state for Northern Ireland had been cold-bloodedly murdered by members of the Fenian Society. At the trial of the murderers, one of the accomplices, James Carey, turned Queen's evidence and, based largely on his testimony, the others were convicted, condemned and later executed. The Fenians swore revenge. Carey and his family were therefore spirited out of the country aboard the Kinfauns Castle (I) *to start a new life in Port Elizabeth, but leaked information led the Fenians to place an agent by the name of O'Donnell on the liner when she left for South Africa. His instructions were to liquidate the traitor.*

On reaching Cape Town, the Carey family and O'Donnell were transferred to the Castle coaster Melrose, *which ran a shuttle service up the South African east coast. Unbeknown to Carey, his cabin companion on that voyage was his intended assassin. On 29 July 1883, a day after the tiny coaster had left Table Bay, three shots rang out. Carey was found dead in the saloon. O'Donnell, who appears to have made no attempt to disguise his culpability, was immediately arrested by the second officer of the* Melrose *and landed at Port Elizabeth. He was sent back to England, where he was tried, found guilty of murder and sentenced to death. This was the first recorded murder to take place on a Castle liner.*

his incisiveness or his flamboyant style, not to mention his general flair for managing maritime trade.

No sooner had the Conference been formed, however, than the interior of southern Africa was struck by a severe drought and, exacerbated by a fall in the diamond price, an extended period of recession descended on the region, stemming the flow of immigrants seeking passage to the Cape and causing a decline in the demand for cargo space. Nor did the recession affect only those companies that had more recently entered the Cape trade; the mail companies too were obliged to lay up ships for a while.

The depressed state of the economy did not last long. In 1886 another fortune scramble with even greater implications for southern Africa was precipitated by the discovery of the main gold reef on the farm Witwatersrand in the Transvaal. Looking ahead to an improved economy based on the latest gold discoveries, Currie – always the innovator – decided in 1887 that a visit to South Africa would be a wise investment in the future. It was a move no Union Line chairman had ever made and it initiated a practice that was to be continued by all subsequent chairmen after the amalgamation of the two companies.

To ensure maximum publicity, Currie chose to travel in the *Norham Castle*, one of

---

1 *The* Grantully Castle *leaving the south Devonshire port of Dartmouth, circa 1889, where the mailships would call to pick up mail and additional passengers before proceeding to South Africa.*

2 *The* Athenian, *a Union Line mailship from 1882 to 1897, twice broke the record for the passage from Cape Town to England.*

1

2

the largest Castle liners at the time, and for company on the outward voyage he invited the Transvaal consul-general in Britain to join him. Currie's tour covered most of the important centres in southern Africa, including towns in the two Boer Republics where, in view of his assistance to Presidents Brand and Burgers during their visits to Britain, he was warmly received – by Brand in the Orange Free State and, in the Transvaal Republic, by President Paul Kruger, whom Currie had also previously met in London.

The tour was a great personal triumph for Currie, who assumed virtual ambassadorial status. At every opportunity he delivered addresses on current subjects to financiers, government officials and mining tycoons, and wherever he went he built up valuable contacts with key people.

The timing of the visit had been perfect. The rush to the Witwatersrand soon transformed bare veld into a series of mushrooming settlements that rapidly grew into towns. The largest of these was Johannesburg which, by 1895, was linked by rail to all three major Cape ports (Cape Town, Port Elizabeth and East London) as well as those at Durban and Lourenço Marques (Maputo). The effect on the development of the interior, not to mention shipping, was startling.

The bottom line in much, if not all, that Currie did was to make his company more profitable. To this end he frequently endowed people in influential positions, particularly politicians, with gifts – a practice he employed to nurture his newly won South African allies. This is made clear by the contents of a letter dated 8 October 1891, sent from his Fenchurch Street office.

3

Messrs.
The Castle Mail Packets Co. Limited
Cape Town Agency

Dear Sirs,

By the "Scot", Sir Donald Currie sent in charge of Captn Travers, a haunch of venison for Sir Henry Lock, and we have now to give you the following instructions with regard to other 4 haunches in separate boxes, which go out in the "Hawarden Castle" and will be delivered to you by Captn Duncan.

While leaving you to judge of their fittest disposal, Sir Donald Currie suggests that you might give a haunch to Mr Rhodes if he is in town, and further, he thinks that you should send a haunch to the President of the Transvaal, and another to the President of the Orange Free State with his best regards, providing you consider the venison would be properly forwarded, and that it would arrive in good, or fair, condition.

Besides the venison, Sir Donald Currie has also sent by "Hawarden Castle" 5 boxes of pheasants, namely :- a box for your Agency, 1 for Mossel Bay, 1 for Algoa Bay, 1 for East London, and 1 for Natal, and Captn Duncan has instructions with regard to the best care possible being taken of the birds on the voyage, and with regard to their delivery at the different ports.

The box for your agency contains 15 brace, and our principal is desirous that in the distribution which you make, you should bear in mind the Ministry, the Post Master General, the Dock Master, the General Commanding, the Editors of the "Cape Times", the "Cape Argus", and the "Volksstem", not forgetting Mr John Noble, and Mr Silverwright.

Yours faithfully,

[Signature indistinct but it is possibly that of Sir Donald Currie himself.]

P.S. Enclosed are four labels which you can use for the venison.

1 *During an extensive refit, the* Moor, *a sister ship to the* Athenian, *was lengthened by nearly 16 metres, and was given two tall funnels in place of her original single funnel. She was the first mailship on the South African trade to be converted to an armed merchant cruiser when, in 1885, war between Britain and Russia seemed imminent. She was the last Union Line vessel to sail from Southampton before the official amalgamated service began in March 1900.*

2 *Deck space was limited on the early liners, as can be seen in this photograph taken on the* Roslin Castle. *Passengers also had to contend with the fall-out of soot from the funnel, a discomfort that increased on windless days when soot was deposited on the deck in even greater quantities.*

3 *The* Roslin Castle *(seen here in the Alfred Basin, Cape Town) was built in 1883. Re-engined and modified in 1888, she became one of the fastest vessels on the mail service at the time.*

1

Another letter in similar vein, dated 19 December 1891, was addressed to:

L. MacLean, Esq. and/or D.C. Andrew, Esq.
Cape Town

Dear Sirs,

Sir Donald Currie has sent by the "Hawarden Castle", addressed to yourselves, a case containing a haunch of venison, and has desired us to advise you that, if Mr Rhodes is in town, the haunch is given to him with Sir Donald Currie's compliments. Failing Mr Rhodes, you are to give the venison either to Mr Hofmeyr, or to Sir G. Gordon Sprigg, whichever of these gentlemen did not get a haunch before, or if both have already had venison, you can give the present haunch to Sir Henry Loch.

We are, Dear Sirs,
Yours faithfully,
Donald Currie.

A letter in copperplate handwriting and dated 14 November 1891 related to a promising student, a 'Mr Smuts', later to become a Boer general, a field marshal and prime minister of South Africa.

Messrs.
The Castle Mail Packets Co. Ltd
Cape Town Agency

Dear Sirs,

Referring to your letter of 23rd Sept. enclosing another from Dr Cameron with reference to the passage money of Mr Smuts and the other Cape Students, we beg to inform you that Sir Donald Currie has himself sent £5 to young Mr Smuts to help him in his studies at Cambridge and we have proposed to the Union Company to put students of the Cape University on the same footing as Missionaries. We shall advise you the result of our proposal.

Yours faithfully,
for DONALD CURRIE & CO.

An addition in the margin of this letter indicated that a ten per cent reduction would be granted to 'students from the Cape University'.

The new wave of mass immigration and the extraordinary amount of cargo for shipment again made shipping a most profitable enterprise. Between 1886 and 1890, the Union Line added two intermediate vessels, two cargoships and two coasters, but Currie

EXTRACT FROM THE NATAL GOVERNMENT CONTRACT FOR THE CONVEYANCE OF IMMIGRANT PASSENGERS

The Government of Natal entered into its own contracts with shipping companies for the carriage of both mail and immigrants. The following is an extract from the Natal Government's contract for the conveyance of immigrants by the Union Steamship Company and the Castle Mail Packets Company, signed on 23 February 1894:

For each adult emigrant, the contractor shall provide a weekly scale of victualling not less than or inferior to the following that is to say –

1½ lbs Beef	*½ lb Molasses*	*3 lbs Preserved Meat*
6 oz Suet	*1 lb Pork*	*3 lbs 10oz Biscuits*
4½ lbs Flour	*6 oz Butter*	*½ pint Peas*
½ lb Potatoes	*1½ lb Rice or Oatmeal*	*½ lb Onions*
½ lb Raisins	*½ lb Carrots*	*2 oz Coffee*
1 lb Sugar	*1½ oz Tea*	*½ lb Mixed Pickles*
½ oz Mustard	*6½ oz Lime juice*	*2 oz Salt*
½ oz Pepper	*6 oz Cheese*	

About 0,5 cubic metres of baggage space was allowed. The fares for emigrants from England to Natal were:

On intermediate or 'extra' steamers	*£10 2s 0d for open berths (men only)*
	£12 12s 0d for closed berths
On mail steamers	*£15 2s 0d per person.*

There was a further clause concerning 'Scotch' or Irish immigrants: 'Should the embarkation of emigrants from any Scotch or Irish ports be desired to suit the convenience of the Agents . . . the contractor shall have the option of conveying such emigrants from Scotch or Irish ports.'

2

decided to take what he considered to be a substantial leap ahead. Carefully, but swiftly, he drew up plans for what was to be a sensational rival for the Union Line. She would have two funnels and three masts – the first Castle liner so fitted – accommodation for 360 passengers and, more importantly, she would have the capacity to smash the existing record for a passage between England and South Africa. Thus, when the completed *Dunottar Castle* drew away from the quay at the Fairfield Yard in September 1890, there was every anticipation that this ship would greatly boost Currie's already substantial influence in the maritime world. And perform she did. Over the measured mile in the Firth of Clyde, and with black smoke belching from her funnels, she surpassed expectations with a speed of 17,5 knots.

A very satisfied Sir Donald embarked with guests for a cruise around the Scottish coast, an excursion that covered two functions: it was a shake-down cruise for the ship's company, during which time they would test every aspect of the machinery and other equipment, and it was also a splendid opportunity for Currie to advertise his new mail-ship, particularly as she would inaugurate the new Castle Line mail service from Southampton to Table Bay. (Formerly, the Castle liners left for the Cape from London via Dartmouth.)

More media coverage came his way when the first British rugby team to visit South Africa was found to be among the passengers booked for the Cape. At a banquet on board the liner shortly before she left, Currie presented the team with a large gold cup, which he requested that they hand to their South African hosts to use as a trophy for an internal rugby competition. Thus the Currie Cup was introduced to South African rugby. A similar cup was later presented to the cricket authorities in South Africa.

The arrival of the *Dunottar Castle* in Table Bay was sensational, for, with a passage of seventeen days and twenty hours, she had trimmed by nearly a day the record set by the *Drummond Castle* nine years previously.

Then came the *Scot*, the Union Line's trump card, with which it stole the limelight from Currie for several years. Built at the Dumbarton yards of William Denny & Brothers Shipbuilding Company in 1891, she had deliberately been designed to create a sensation as both a record-breaker and a vessel of the most graceful lines yet seen in a mailship. Not only was she the answer to Currie's *Dunottar Castle*, but she was also a superior vessel in aspects such as speed (on trials, she had done 19,176 knots for six hours when fully laden), length and tonnage. She was quite unlike any of her predecessors in the Union fleet as well, being half as long again as the *Mexican* and having twin screws.

Her arrival in Table Bay on 10 August 1891 on her maiden voyage could not have been more remarkable, for she had completed the passage from Southampton in 15 days, 9 hours and 25 minutes, paring more than a day off the record set by Currie's *Dunottar Castle*. Then, after a round of receptions and much publicity at the Cape, she further enhanced her reputation by racing homeward to break the northbound record as well. Her ultimate triumph, by which she gained a place in history, occurred in March 1893. It is recalled by Marischal Murray in the *Union-Castle Chronicle*:

> Tuesday was then the normal day for the arrival of the mail from England. Men still talk of the excitement caused in Cape Town on that Sunday morning when suddenly and unexpectedly, the mail flag was hoisted from the look-out station up on Signal Hill. It was just before luncheon; crowds began to line the Sea Point waterfront to see what it might mean. Soon a vessel, unmistakably the Scot, showed up from under the horizon, and shortly after half-past one, with Captain de la Cour Travers on the bridge, the mail steamer came round the breakwater. The Scot had come out from England in 14 days 18 hours 57 minutes, a record passage that was not equalled for nearly half a century.

There is no doubt that she was an exceptional vessel. Indeed, many commentators believe that apart from some of the North Atlantic liners of the immediate pre-1939 era, she was the most elegant of all vessels. She represented a radical change in mailship design, such as would influence the design of all new ships until the advent of the four-funnelled *Arundel Castle* in 1921.

Towards the end of the century, agricultural developments in South Africa pointed to

1 *Currie's record-breaking* Dunottar Castle *in Cape Town harbour.*
2 *On board the* Scot, *circa 1892.*

1

RMS SCOT

When the Union Line was planning this remarkable vessel, its intention was to build a record-breaker. The contract that was signed with William Denny & Brothers Shipbuilding Company on 28 November 1889 therefore specified that she should be able to maintain a service speed of 18,5 knots when loaded to a draught of 7 metres. To achieve this speed, she had two sets of triple expansion steam engines powered by six boilers, and twin screws, which would certainly contribute to her capacity for speed, as well as improving the manoeuvrability of the ship. With the losses of the American *and the* Teuton *still fresh in the memory, safety was also a high priority – hence the* Scot *had a double bottom and fourteen thwartship bulkheads, of which ten were watertight.*

It was also specified that she should meet the Admiralty requirements for chartering for trooping duties and for operation as an armed merchant cruiser, a role in which her speed would have been an attribute had she ever been called upon to fulfil either of these functions.

Her 208 first class passengers were accommodated mainly in one- or two-berth cabins. The outside bulkheads of the cabin alleys were panelled in polished American ash, with the pilasters stained a darker colour than the panels. The inside bulkheads of the cabins had feathered and grooved pine panels. The dining saloon in the deckhouse on the spar deck had a ceiling of yellow pine, with ornate paintings and gildings, while the saloon tables were of mahogany, completing one of the most exquisitely decorated public rooms yet seen on the Cape run. There was the children's nursery, a music room whose carpet was patterned with the Union house flag, a ladies' 'boudoir' adjoining the music room, and three ladies' waiting rooms on the main deck. (The custom was for the men to move to the smoking room after dinner, while the ladies would retire to the 'waiting rooms'.) Such was the luxurious nature of the fittings on the ship that the male card-players in the smoking room dealt on marble-topped tables. One hundred berths were provided for second class passengers who were accommodated in the poop – an unusual feature in the early mailships as that was the conventional first class area. The 100 third class passengers slept in nine-berth cabins on the main deck aft. Their saloon, which also served as a recreation area, had long tables with benches, rather different to the elegance of the more affluent first class.

But it was the external appearance of the ship that attracted most attention, for her graceful lines, curved stem, counter stern, as well as her raked funnels and masts, contrasted sharply with the dumpy profile of the Dunottar Castle. *The yacht-like appearance of the* Scot *was enhanced with a carving of the Royal Coat of Arms of Britain on each quarter, the Lion of Scotland in the centre of the stern and a striking figurehead (an effigy of Sir William Wallace) flanked by beautifully gilded scrollwork. These peripherals indicated that no expense had been spared in the fitting out of the ship.*

2

The Scot*, though, proved expensive to operate. She consumed 170 tons of coal per day, compared to the* Arundel Castle *– three times the size – which used only a little more in her coal-burning days. Something had to be done to make her more economical to operate. When she broke down with severe mechanical trouble during an outward voyage in 1895 and had to put into Vigo, Spain, Union Line took the opportunity to modify her, for which purpose she went to Belfast. There Harland & Wolff cut her in two, added 18 metres ahead of the bridge – thereby enlarging her cargo capacity as well as her passenger accommodation – and made adjustments to her engines. Many of the interior fittings installed by Harland & Wolff were the inspiration of Sir William Pirrie, chairman of the shipyard, and based on his studies of the décor in leading American and European hotels.*

Although the Scot *did use less coal when she returned to the mail service in July 1896, she remained a financial burden for her owners, and in 1904, with the larger* Armadale Castle *about to enter service, she was withdrawn from the mail schedule. Once the pride of the Union Line's fleet, the* Scot *lay at anchor off Netley on Southampton Water for nearly two years before her sale to Hamburg-Amerika Linien. After three subsequent owners and name changes, she was finally broken up in Italian scrapyards in 1927.*

It was from the deck of the Scot*, in 1897, that mining magnate Barney Barnato jumped into the sea, presumably to commit suicide. Seeing him go overboard, Fourth Officer Clifford leapt after him in a vain rescue attempt, nearly drowning in the process. His courageous action brought high praise from many quarters.*

1 *The* Scot *at the Denny yards in Dumbarton. With the* Scot*, the livery of the Union Line changed from black to yellow funnels and a light buff superstructure. Shortly before her refit in 1895, her hull and superstructure were repainted white, a colour used for all subsequent Union Line mailships. (It is interesting to note the timber supports for the ship under construction in the background. These were replaced by steel girders in later shipbuilding techniques.)*

2 *Sailing day for the* Scot*. Having brought passengers and their friends to the jetty, the horse-drawn cabs shown here would wait to transport some of the well-wishers back to the town centre after the vessel had sailed.*

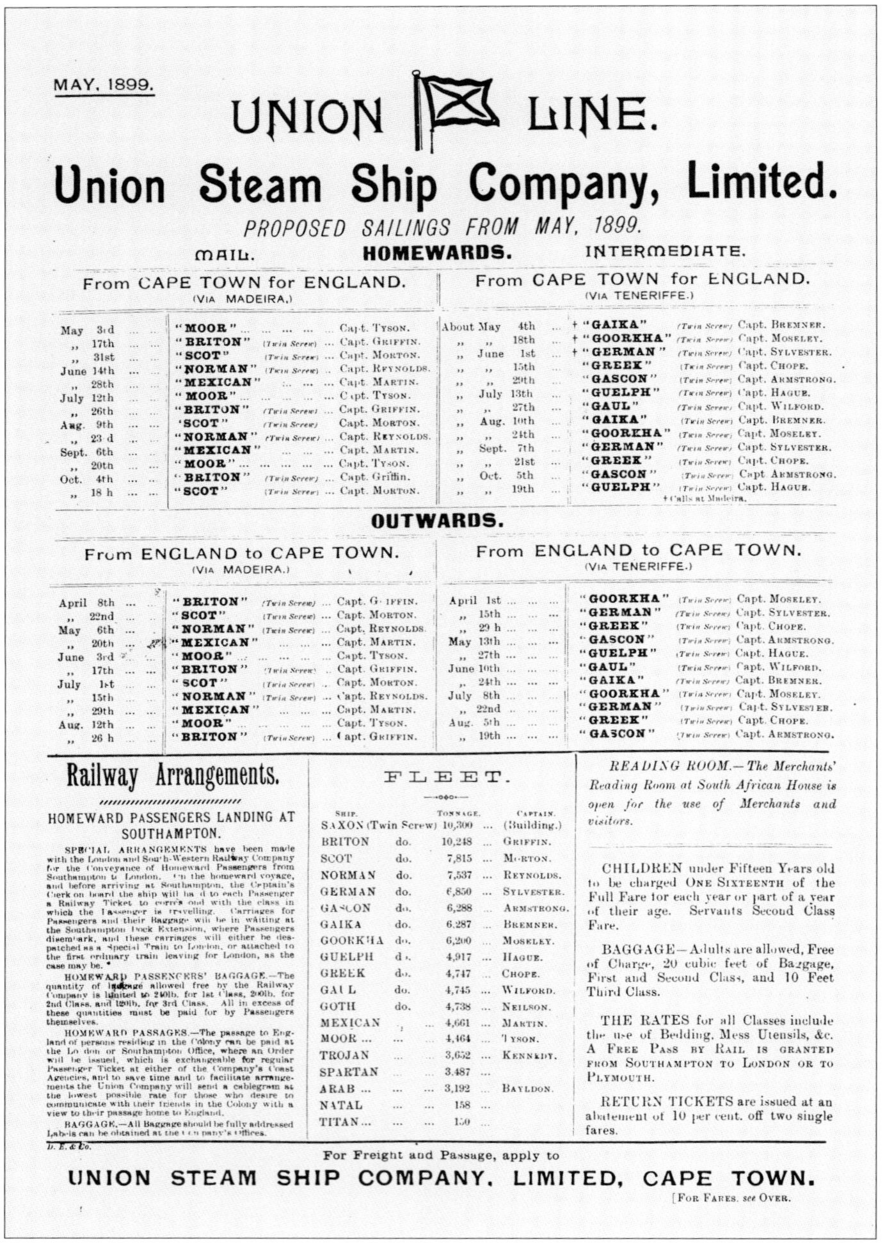

MAY, 1899.

UNION LINE.

Union Steam Ship Company, Limited.

PROPOSED SAILINGS FROM MAY, 1899.

HOMEWARDS.

MAIL. — From CAPE TOWN for ENGLAND. (VIA MADEIRA.)

May 3rd	"MOOR"	Capt. Tyson.
" 17th	"BRITON" (Twin Screw)	Capt. Griffin.
" 31st	"SCOT" (Twin Screw)	Capt. Morton.
June 14th	"NORMAN" (Twin Screw)	Capt. Reynolds.
" 28th	"MEXICAN"	Capt. Martin.
July 12th	"MOOR"	Capt. Tyson.
" 26th	"BRITON" (Twin Screw)	Capt. Griffin.
Aug. 9th	"SCOT" (Twin Screw)	Capt. Morton.
" 23rd	"NORMAN" (Twin Screw)	Capt. Reynolds.
Sept. 6th	"MEXICAN"	Capt. Martin.
" 20th	"MOOR"	Capt. Tyson.
Oct. 4th	"BRITON" (Twin Screw)	Capt. Griffin.
" 18th	"SCOT" (Twin Screw)	Capt. Morton.

INTERMEDIATE. — From CAPE TOWN for ENGLAND. (VIA TENERIFFE.)

About May 4th	+ "GAIKA" (Twin Screw)	Capt. Bremner.
" " 18th	+ "GOORKHA" (Twin Screw)	Capt. Moseley.
" June 1st	+ "GERMAN" (Twin Screw)	Capt. Sylvester.
" " 15th	"GREEK" (Twin Screw)	Capt. Chope.
" " 29th	"GASCON" (Twin Screw)	Capt. Armstrong.
" July 13th	"GUELPH" (Twin Screw)	Capt. Hague.
" " 27th	"GAUL" (Twin Screw)	Capt. Wilford.
" Aug. 10th	"GAIKA" (Twin Screw)	Capt. Bremner.
" " 24th	"GOORKHA" (Twin Screw)	Capt. Moseley.
" Sept. 7th	"GERMAN" (Twin Screw)	Capt. Sylvester.
" " 21st	"GREEK" (Twin Screw)	Capt. Chope.
" Oct. 5th	"GASCON" (Twin Screw)	Capt. Armstrong.
" " 19th	"GUELPH" (Twin Screw)	Capt. Hague.

+ Calls at Madeira.

OUTWARDS.

From ENGLAND to CAPE TOWN. (VIA MADEIRA.)

April 8th	"BRITON" (Twin Screw)	Capt. Griffin.
" 22nd	"SCOT" (Twin Screw)	Capt. Morton.
May 6th	"NORMAN" (Twin Screw)	Capt. Reynolds.
" 20th	"MEXICAN"	Capt. Martin.
June 3rd	"MOOR"	Capt. Tyson.
" 17th	"BRITON" (Twin Screw)	Capt. Griffin.
July 1st	"SCOT" (Twin Screw)	Capt. Morton.
" 15th	"NORMAN" (Twin Screw)	Capt. Reynolds.
" 29th	"MEXICAN"	Capt. Martin.
Aug. 12th	"MOOR"	Capt. Tyson.
" 26th	"BRITON" (Twin Screw)	Capt. Griffin.

From ENGLAND to CAPE TOWN. (VIA TENERIFFE.)

April 1st	"GOORKHA" (Twin Screw)	Capt. Moseley.
" 15th	"GERMAN" (Twin Screw)	Capt. Sylvester.
" 29th	"GREEK" (Twin Screw)	Capt. Chope.
May 13th	"GASCON" (Twin Screw)	Capt. Armstrong.
" 27th	"GUELPH" (Twin Screw)	Capt. Hague.
June 10th	"GAUL" (Twin Screw)	Capt. Wilford.
" 24th	"GAIKA" (Twin Screw)	Capt. Bremner.
July 8th	"GOORKHA" (Twin Screw)	Capt. Moseley.
" 22nd	"GERMAN" (Twin Screw)	Capt. Sylvester.
Aug. 5th	"GREEK" (Twin Screw)	Capt. Chope.
" 19th	"GASCON" (Twin Screw)	Capt. Armstrong.

Railway Arrangements.

HOMEWARD PASSENGERS LANDING AT SOUTHAMPTON.

SPECIAL ARRANGEMENTS have been made with the London and South-Western Railway Company for the Conveyance of Homeward Passengers from Southampton to London. On the homeward voyage, and before arriving at Southampton, the Captain's Clerk on board the ship will hand to each Passenger a Railway Ticket to correspond with the class in which the Passenger is travelling. Carriages for Passengers and their Baggage will be in waiting at the Southampton Dock Extension, where Passengers disembark, and these carriages will either be despatched as a Special Train to London, or attached to the first ordinary train leaving for London, as the case may be.

HOMEWARD PASSENGERS' BAGGAGE.—The quantity of luggage allowed free by the Railway Company is limited to 240lb. for 1st Class, 200lb. for 2nd Class, and 120lb. for 3rd Class. All in excess of these quantities must be paid for by Passengers themselves.

HOMEWARD PASSAGES.—The passage to England of persons residing in the Colony can be paid at the London or Southampton Office, where an Order will be issued, which is exchangeable for regular Passenger Ticket at either of the Company's Coast Agencies, and to save time and to facilitate arrangements the Union Company will send a cablegram at the lowest possible rate for those who desire to communicate with their friends in the Colony with a view to their passage home to England.

BAGGAGE.—All Baggage should be fully addressed Labels can be obtained at the Company's Offices.

D. E. & Co.

FLEET.

Ship.		Tonnage.	Captain.
SAXON	(Twin Screw)	10,300	(Building.)
BRITON	do.	10,248	Griffin.
SCOT	do.	7,815	Morton.
NORMAN	do.	7,537	Reynolds.
GERMAN	do.	6,850	Sylvester.
GASCON	do.	6,288	Armstrong.
GAIKA	do.	6,287	Bremner.
GOORKHA	do.	6,200	Moseley.
GUELPH	do.	4,917	Hague.
GREEK	do.	4,747	Chope.
GAUL	do.	4,745	Wilford.
GOTH	do.	4,738	Neilson.
MEXICAN		4,661	Martin.
MOOR		4,464	Tyson.
TROJAN		3,652	Kennedy.
SPARTAN		3,487	
ARAB		3,192	Bayldon.
NATAL		158	
TITAN		150	

READING ROOM.—The Merchants' Reading Room at South African House is open for the use of Merchants and visitors.

CHILDREN under Fifteen Years old to be charged ONE SIXTEENTH of the Full Fare for each year or part of a year of their age. Servants Second Class Fare.

BAGGAGE—Adults are allowed, Free of Charge, 20 cubic feet of Baggage, First and Second Class, and 10 Feet Third Class.

THE RATES for all Classes include the use of Bedding, Mess Utensils, &c. A FREE PASS BY RAIL IS GRANTED FROM SOUTHAMPTON TO LONDON OR TO PLYMOUTH.

RETURN TICKETS are issued at an abatement of 10 per cent. off two single fares.

For Freight and Passage, apply to

UNION STEAM SHIP COMPANY, LIMITED, CAPE TOWN.

[For Fares, see Over.

1

a new and important trading possibility. As more effective ways were found to fight pests and improve product quality, deciduous and citrus fruit farming became increasingly successful. Each year a substantial surplus of high quality produce was available at a time when fruit from the northern hemisphere's orchards had long since been harvested. The makings of a lucrative fruit trade were evident to all: a surplus in one area and a demand in another. The only problem was transportation.

In December 1888, an experimental venture of packing fruit boxes in a Union liner met with instant disaster when the ship was involved in a collision. The next step – a response to discussions that Currie had had during his South African tour – was taken by the Castle Line in February 1889. A small refrigerated compartment was fitted in a hold of the *Grantully Castle* and thirty tons of fruit – mainly grapes – were loaded, but the cork dust, which had been used as the insulation material, did not maintain a sufficiently low temperature and the consignment had to be destroyed on arrival in Britain.

More effective refrigerated chambers were fitted to later vessels but it was not until February 1892, when a consignment of peaches (ex the *Drummond Castle*) reached Britain in good condition, that the fruit export industry was set to become one of the main clients of the mailships. By the 1930s, such was the demand for South African fruit in Britain and Europe that a fleet of fast refrigerated cargoships was built shortly before World War II to carry thousands of tons of fruit to the waiting markets.

Barrels of wine and brandy ready to be loaded aboard the mailships were also a common sight on the wharf in Cape Town. Indeed, what had started as simply a contract to carry mail, was expanding into numerous and diverse avenues, particularly in respect of cargo. The reason was simple. Shippers preferred the mailships because they operated according to a strict schedule, thereby assuring specific delivery dates. Nevertheless, competition was increasing for the mail companies.

The Portuguese colonies of Angola and Mozambique were also requiring regular sea links with their mother country and, as had been the case with the Cape Colony and Britain, required a reliable mail service. It was not surprising, therefore, that a Portuguese mail steamer company should enter the southern African trade. The arrival in Table Bay of the *Rei de Portugal* in 1889 was the start of the regular service. This presaged serious competition to both Union and Castle intermediate liners, which frequently put in to Lisbon to load cargoes.

German lines also began to pose a threat to the supremacy of the Union and Castle lines, particularly when vessels of the Deutsche Ost-Afrika Linien (DOAL), already operating a service to East Africa, began calling at South African ports in 1892. With the Woermann Line, which was serving German West Africa (now Namibia) and the other German territories in West Africa (Togo and Cameroon), the two German lines could offer passages to Europe via some interesting ports of call around Africa, presenting attractive alternatives for prospective passengers of the mail companies.

Before the turn of the century, two further British companies had also begun services that had every prospect of making inroads into the clientele of the mailships and the intermediates. The *Viceroy*, a chartered ship, began a service – initially to Port Elizabeth – for Bucknalls, whose own cargo steamer, *Afrikander*, arrived in Table Bay in 1892. This was the forerunner of the comfortable and immaculately maintained 'City' ships of the prestigious Ellerman & Bucknall Line which operated on the South African trade until 1977, thereafter continuing in a consortium of container lines. The other arrival at the time was White Star's *Medic*, which inaugurated that company's colonial immigrant service to Australasia but nevertheless carried passengers to South Africa.

In the face of this growing competition, further discussions culminated in the Bucknall group joining the South African Conference, and in exchange for a subsidy, they agreed, as did the Clan Line, not to load cargo for the homeward passage. For their subsidy, the Clan Line was to receive £3 000 per annum for not loading homeward from the Cape, Natal or Delagoa Bay, and £4 000 per annum for not carrying passengers outward to any of the southern African ports. Nor was it to tender to carry any immigrants to South Africa or troops, except in the case of war. For any passenger carried by Clan, it would have to reimburse the mail companies half of the passage fare. However, Clan could charter its ships to either the Union or Castle lines for the carriage of homeward cargo. The mail companies benefited greatly by this and were able to continue their dominance of the trade.

Shortly before the advent of the *Scot*, the Union Line had been targeted as a potential client by the Belfast shipyard Harland & Wolff. To this end, Sir William Pirrie, chairman of Harland & Wolff, went to South Africa to learn first-hand the requirements for ships

2

3

on that trade. The navigational hazards presented by the bar at the entrance to the harbours at East London and Durban necessitated visits to both towns to determine a design that would best facilitate a vessel's entry to the ports, rather than it having to work cargo overside in the exposed roadstead. Climatic conditions, cargo types and loading techniques along the route, particularly at Port Elizabeth where lighterage was the only option at the time, also occupied his attention.

On his return to Belfast, Pirrie's company tendered successfully to the Union Line for the construction of three intermediate steamers (*Gaul*, *Goth* and *Greek*), which were built at cost in order to attract subsequent orders. Gustav Wolff, the other major partner in the shipyard, then bought a large shareholding in the Union Line to strengthen his negotiations for future Union contracts, all of which were indeed secured by Harland & Wolff. In 1895 Wolff joined the Board of the Union Line, filling – numerically – the place left by

1 *Publicizing the name of each ship's captain was a custom that continued well into the twentieth century, as many travellers booked their passage according to the captain with whom they wished to sail rather than the ship itself.*

2 *The launching of the* Norman *on 19 July 1894 – the first of eight ships that epitomized the Cape liners between 1894 and 1920.*

3 *On board the* Norman. *The poop, from which this photograph was taken, accommodated most of the third class passengers, the remainder being accommodated in the fo'c'sle. First and second class passengers lived in luxury amidships.*

1

2

the death of the line's chairman, Alfred Giles. This move cemented a relationship that was to last for a further sixty-two years. From 1900 until 1957, all mailships (apart from the *Armadale Castle*, *Balmoral Castle* and *Windsor Castle*, which came from yards on the Clyde), thirteen intermediates and sixteen cargoships were to be built in the Harland & Wolff yards. It was the fateful 'non-launch' of the *Pendennis Castle* in 1957 that severed the association, from which time no Union-Castle/British & Commonwealth ship was ever built by Harland & Wolff.

Following the remarkable success of the *Scot*, her owners began a programme for the construction of several ships to replace ageing vessels and, more particularly, to supplement their fleet to meet the steadily increasing demand for berths to South Africa, where the economy continued to grow at a phenomenal pace.

Enticed by the emotive language of the advertisements and by the lure of the African sun, many Britons headed for South Africa to start a new life for themselves. Others merely wished to enjoy the leisurely sea voyage and soak up some sunshine before returning home to Britain. Anyone reading *The Land of Gold, Diamonds and Ivory*, an account of southern Africa written in 1889 by J.F. Ingram and sponsored by the Union Line, could not help but be tantalized not only by the excitement of Africa, but also by the promised pleasures of the voyage itself:

The voyage to the Cape has been described by so many writers that any extended

RMS BRITON

Avoiding engine designs such as had led to the high coal consumption of the Scot, *and modifying the general plan of the popular* Norman, *the Union Line ordered what was to be the penultimate mail vessel to carry one of their traditional names. When she emerged from the Harland & Wolff yards, the* Briton *was indeed a splendid ship, resembling on a smaller scale the* Oceanic, *which Harland & Wolff had built for the White Star Line on the adjoining slipway.*

Apart from some of the ships on the North Atlantic run, the Briton *at 162 metres in length and 10 248 tons was the largest liner serving Britain, surpassing even the largest of the prestigious P&O ships at the time.*

She was one of the fleet of six Union-Castle ships which, in 1914, were hastily commissioned in Cape Town to carry troops of the Imperial Guard to Britain and thence to serve in France. She returned to the mail run in 1915 but it was not long before she was again called for trooping duties. She then carried troops to the Mediterranean, Nigerians from Mombasa to Lagos, and Americans to Britain. Before her return to peacetime service in 1920 she undertook voyages to New Zealand and the West Indies, mainly for the repatriation of soldiers.

After a period laid up at Netley, the Briton *was recalled to service at the conclusion of the strike of 1925. One voyage later she went to the breakers' yards in Italy.*

reference to it here would be superfluous. It has, in truth, been called the most delightful voyage in the world. After the Bay of Biscay, with its chronic 'lumpiness' is passed, the skies assume a more limpid blue, the water a richer tint, while the balmy airs that sweep the deck proclaim:

> that the piercing winds and the whirling snow have been left behind.

The glimpses afforded of the islands are pleasant interludes to the regular and well-ordered life of the ship, while each day presents its own panorama of tinted clouds and of sunlit sea.

No mention was made of the notorious Cape rollers, or the occasionally severe conditions off the Portuguese coast!

In its *Illustrated Handbook* of 1898, the Castle Line tried another sales tactic in its drive to secure passengers:

> The writer wishes to show that, although so rich in minerals, South Africa is not merely 'The Land of Gold, Diamonds and Ivory' [an obvious reference to the Union Line's publication, indicating the level of rivalry that still existed between the two mail companies] but that at some future date, it may – probably will – be as thickly populated with small tenant farmers as are a fruitful valley in Switzerland, or an irrigated plain in the Canary Islands . . .
>
> It should be borne in mind that emigration is no longer a bugbear to frighten children with. What was once a life-long separation is now a journey of two or three weeks, which debars no man from making an occasional visit to the old home and the old folks living there.

Another paragraph in the Castle Line's publication ran: 'The Rates of Passage Money include in all three classes a liberal table and the use of beds, bedding, cabin linen and furniture.' Elsewhere it eulogized Southampton as the line's port of departure for the Cape:

> All passengers may now join the boat at Southampton, where the train runs into the Docks [sic]. It is a most excellent point of departure, and the smooth waters of the Solent allow time for even the worst sailors to arrange their cabins in comfort, whilst the farewell views of the English Coast, as the vessel runs past the Needles, can hardly be excelled in beauty or interest.

The Union Line's boarding arrangements also involved a train from Number One Platform on Waterloo Station, whence the 'Union Special' would depart at 11:40 on sailing day and take passengers to the side of the ship in Southampton. However, its *Gazette* of July 1896 said: 'It does not appear to be sufficiently well known that outward passengers by the Union Company's steamers are put to no expense for Railway conveyance between London and Southampton or between Plymouth and Southampton or for dock charges at Southampton. These are included in the fare.'

Concerning the 'boat train', a certain Captain Charles Chapman had written in 1872:

> Stepping out of the train at Southampton, you are at once surrounded by many persons. Some are waiting for their friends; some looking on from curiosity; but by far the greatest number are porters, who (so to say) live in the Railway Station. At one glance, they reckon you up; they know who you are, what you are, where you are going, why you are going, and pretty nearly how much money you have in your pocket.
>
> If you are a tall, stout, military-looking man, with a sort of round face, florid complexion, true Saxon features, and a cigar; or if you are a rough, burly-looking fellow with a rough suit on and a rough coat over your arm, having a lady with you with winter garments, and two or three children with very light hair, the porter says to himself – 'They are for America,' and makes up his mind what to charge you for taking the luggage down to the North-German steamer that is just about to start. If you are a swell, with an expensive suit on, with a rich railway rug thrown over your arm, having with you a lady with a rich travelling dress, and very expensive lace about the wrists and neck, the porter will make up his mind that they are going to India and say they are for the P and O boat. Then again, if you happen to be an ordinary man, well dressed, with the little bag strapped over your shoulder, with your lady just middlingly dressed, with a servant who looks like the ordinary little slavey of Old England, and three or four children all looking very important, the very same porter will say they are for the Jersey boat or for the Continent. But if you happen to be just a middling man, not a swell, not having a very expensive costume, just comfortable, no more, the porter says again to himself – 'That man is for the Cape,' and he steps forward at once, and says, 'Going to the Syria, sir?'

Several rumours were in the wind at this time to the effect that the two rival companies were considering amalgamation. It seemed senseless that there should be competition between two lines operating in terms of the same contract, and a pooling of resources would assist greatly in the face of outside competition.

Both Union and Castle had orders for new ships. Besides the three 'G'-class vessels that had come out in 1893, a further seven Union Line intermediates came from Harland & Wolff, including the *Galeka* – the last vessel to be delivered to the Union Line – and the *Galician* which, although ordered by Union, was completed in 1900, shortly after the amalgamation of the two mail companies. Pride of place, however, went to the three mailships: *Norman* (1894), *Briton* (1897) and *Saxon* (1900).

The launch of the *Saxon* was reported in the *Belfast Newsletter* of 22 December 1899:

---

1 *The* Briton *fitting out at the Harland & Wolff yards, Belfast, prior to her maiden voyage in 1897.*

2 *The luxurious décor and fittings of the* Briton *can be gauged from this photograph of the first class library.*

1

2

3

LAUNCH OF A UNION LINER

The royal mail steamer *Saxon*, built by Messrs. Harland & Wolff for the Union Steamship Company, was successfully launched from the south end of Queen's Island at noon yesterday. The new vessel, which is the largest and most powerful that has yet been constructed for this well-known company, is 585 ft. 6 in. long by 64 ft. beam and 42 ft. 9 in. deep, and will have a gross tonnage of 12,970. The passenger accommodation will be very large, and a notable feature will be the size of the staterooms, making them exceptionally large, airy, and comfortable. The first class accommodation will be on the bridge, upper, and middle decks, and the second class on the middle decks. Besides the open berth steerage accommodation forward, there will be provision for a large number of third class passengers in the poop and after middle 'tween decks. A separate galley and pantry will be provided for the third class passengers. The first class saloon will be situated on the upper deck. It will be very handsome, spacious, and will have seating accommodation for a large number. The first class library and drawing-room, as well as the smoking room, will be on the promenade deck, and they will be very large and elegantly furnished. The entrance to the second class saloon will be provided with sofas, and will make a comfortable apartment for ladies who wish to have a sitting room on deck. Large promenade decks will be a feature in the new steamer, as they are in the *Norman* and *Briton*. The officers

4

5

6

will have well-ventilated rooms, conveniently situated on the boat deck. The *Saxon* is fitted with two sets of quadruple expansion engines, arranged on the balance principle to minimise vibration, and she is designed for carrying a large cargo or a considerable number of troops. All the twelve vessels built by Messrs Harland & Wolff for the famous Union line are twin screws, and each has been of special design, embodying all the latest improvements in naval architecture, and peculiar interest attaches to the launch of the *Saxon* as forming another link in the chain binding the mother country to her distant colonies. The putting of the *Saxon* into the water brings a number of incidents to a satisfactory and successful termination. She is the last boat launched this year by the Queen's Island firm, who easily head the list again this year with seven enormous vessels of an aggregate tonnage of 82,634 and 66,150 I.H.P. The builders commenced the year with the *Oceanic*, and they have concluded it with the *Saxon*, which will be by far the largest and finest vessel ever built for trading to the colonies. There is also another interesting fact to note – viz., that yesterday's event completes a stage in the history of the Union line, as the *Saxon* is probably the last launch under the old regime, the Union and Castle lines having declared their intention to amalgamate, so that succeeding ships (and we trust there will be many to follow in the near future) will, of course, come under the new arrangement. Miss Evans, daughter of Sir Francis Evans, M.P., chairman and managing director of the Union Company, gracefully christened the new vessel the *Saxon* as she began to glide down the ways. Subsequently a number of guests were entertained to luncheon in the Station Hotel by Messrs Payne and Kerr, on behalf of Messrs Harland & Wolff and the Union line respectively. Speeches were made congratulating the companies on their prosperous record, these being appropriately acknowledged by Mr Payne, Mr Kerr, and Mr John Boal.

A fourth mailship, the *Celt*, was ordered by the Union Line, but since she was launched after the amalgamation, she was named *Walmer Castle*.

In all of these mailships there were traces of the *Scot*: exquisitely decorated interiors, twin screws, two raked funnels and, apart from the three-masted *Briton*, two masts. However, they clearly represented an advance in design, in speed capability and in both passenger and cargo capacity.

Meanwhile, the Castle Line had been keeping Scottish yards busy. Since the maiden voyage of the *Dunottar Castle*, they had taken delivery of nine intermediate vessels and five mailships: *Tantallon Castle* (1894), *Dunvegan Castle* (1896), *Carisbrook Castle* (1898), *Kinfauns Castle* and *Kildonan Castle* (1899), the last making her maiden voyage as Her Majesty's Transport No. 44 to ferry troops and equipment to South Africa for the Anglo-Boer War, which had broken out in October 1899. It was a role in which the *Kildonan Castle* would serve for two years, sometimes carrying over 2 000 soldiers in a single voyage.

In response to the disenfranchisement of Britons in the Transvaal and mindful of the great wealth beneath the soil of that Boer Republic, the British Government protested at the treatment of its nationals and emphasized its objections on 9 September 1899 by sending 8 000 troops to Natal. Nevertheless, since the collective might of the Boers could outnumber the British forces, further reinforcements were sent from Britain and concentrated in the Natal interior.

On 28 September, the Transvaal mobilized its forces and began to send them to Natal, familiar terrain to many of the Boers who had fought the British there eighteen

---

1 *The* Saxon *– the last mailship delivered to the Union Line before amalgamation with the Castle Line. She is shown with black hull and funnels, the guise adopted at one stage during World War I.*

2 *In common with other mailships of her time, the* Saxon *had luxurious first class accommodation, as is evidenced by this cabin. (The hand basin was concealed in the cabinet on the left, the bottom section of which held the receptacle for waste water.)*

3 *Third class accommodation on board the* Saxon *was spartan, and passengers even had to supply their own bedding.*

4 *Baskets for sale on board the* Briton, *anchored off Madeira.*

5 *The basket (shown here on the* Briton, *circa 1899) was used to land or embark passengers at Mossel Bay, Port Elizabeth and East London. Its use at the latter two ports was only discontinued when the mailships could berth in the harbours.*

6 *The egg-and-spoon race on board the* Briton.

1

2

years previously. Reluctantly at first, and later with great patriotic fervour, the Orange Free State followed suit and mobilized on 2 October. Then came the Boer ultimatum, handed to a British agent on 9 October 1899, in which Britain was accused of breaking the London Convention of 1884 by interfering in the internal affairs of the Transvaal Republic on the question of franchise for foreigners and by massing troops close to the Transvaal borders. Among the demands in the ultimatum were that all British troops landed in South Africa after 1 June 1899 be withdrawn, and that those reinforcements already on ships bound for South Africa should not be landed. Unless assurances on these issues were given by the British Government within forty-eight hours, the South African Republic (Transvaal) would regard itself at war with Britain. In view of Boer statements regarding an envisaged Boer republic from Table Bay to the Limpopo River, the British indicated their disregard for the Boer ultimatum by strengthening their military position in Natal and the Cape.

Although the deadline contained in the Boer ultimatum passed and the Boers had lain siege to Kimberley and Mafeking, it was not until 20 October that the first battle took place – near Dundee, Natal – *inter alia* claiming the life of General Penn Symons.

At sea, on board the *Dunottar Castle*, was General Redvers Buller on his way to command the British forces in South Africa. Since leaving Madeira, where cables containing news of the war had been available, he and others aboard the Castle liner were ignorant of

3

the latest developments in South Africa. Two days before the ship was due to dock in Cape Town, the officer of the watch sighted a steamer that altered course to pass close to the mailship. The Cape-bound passengers crowded to the rail to watch, hoping for further news about the situation in South Africa. A gasp went up as they read the message written on a board on the small steamer: 'BOERS DEFEATED – THREE BATTLES – PENN SYMONS KILLED'.

All were shocked at the news of the death of General Penn Symons, but those hoping for the glory of battle were disappointed, for it could be inferred from the message brought by the steamer that the war was over. Little could they realize that it would take a further two and a half years and the deaths of thousands of soldiers and civilians for peace to come to South Africa.

The *Roslin Castle*, one of five ships to be chartered immediately after the outbreak of the Anglo-Boer War to convey British troops to South Africa, arrived in Table Bay on 8 November 1899. She was diverted to land the troops at Durban, whence they would move into the interior to attempt to halt the Boer invasion of Natal.

Over the following months, dozens of transports brought troops and equipment for the war, causing extensive congestion in the harbours of Cape Town and Durban. Compounding the congestion was the arrival of many sailing ships loaded with coal for use by the steamers on their return passage to Britain. One well-known photograph of Table Bay in 1900 shows the harbour filled to capacity, while fifty-four sailing ships and fifteen steamers lay at anchor in the roadstead. On 30 January 1900, the *Cape Argus* reported that thirty-seven ships were berthed in the harbour, including the mailships *Briton* and *Dunottar Castle*, the transport *Kildonan Castle*, which had arrived from Durban, and the intermediate steamer *Braemar Castle*. Among the seventy-eight ships at anchor were the *Roslin Castle*, recently returned from taking troops to Durban, the *Galeka*, *Tintagel Castle*, *Gaika* and the transport *Harlech Castle*. The newspaper further reported that:

> The Transport Officers at the Docks are again having a very busy time of it. Freight ships are coming to hand almost hourly, while more urgent transports carrying the 7th Division are arriving well up to time. The Union Company's Mail Steamer *Briton* yesterday landed the first detachment of the City of London Volunteers consisting of nine officers and 251 non-commissioned officers and men under the command of Colonel Cholmondeley.

Although living conditions on board the transports were comfortable for the officers, the

1 *The* Tantallon Castle *off East London.*
2 *Field guns being off-loaded from a mailship for action in the Anglo-Boer War.*
3 *The* Dunvegan Castle *at Gravesend, circa 1898.*

1

2

troops were expected to tolerate miserable, crowded conditions. There was little privacy, water was rationed, and for those soldiers transported on deck, tarpaulins were their only shelter from the biting cold of the North Atlantic or the tropical heat. In addition, seasickness was rife among the men, few of whom had travelled by sea before. Thus, arrival in Cape Town or Durban brought immense relief from the unpleasant conditions that had been endured for nearly three weeks.

Although the mail service between Southampton and Cape Town was not disrupted extensively, the continuation of the scheduled South African coastal service by the mailships was impossible, as they were turned at Cape Town to return to Britain as quickly as possible in order to bring the next contingent of troops. For a considerable part of the duration of the war, the *Pembroke Castle* and the *Arundel Castle* were employed on the South African coast conveying mail, troops and equipment to Durban. Once berths had been allocated to military personnel, ordinary passengers could take whatever berths remained; similarly, military cargo was given preference.

Among those brought to South Africa by Union or Castle liners were Lord Roberts, Lord Kitchener, Lord Methuen, Sir Jack French and Lord Milner. During the war, nearly half a million British soldiers were deployed in South Africa, most of whom had been conveyed specially from Britain to bring about the inevitable, yet extremely costly, victory which was concluded with the signing of the Peace Treaty of Vereeniging on 31 May 1902.

While there had been so much conflict in South Africa, discussions in England had paved the way for one of the most significant events in the maritime history of South Africa – the amalgamation of the two rival mail companies to form the powerful Union-Castle Company whose influence would be felt in the region for more than half a century.

3

4

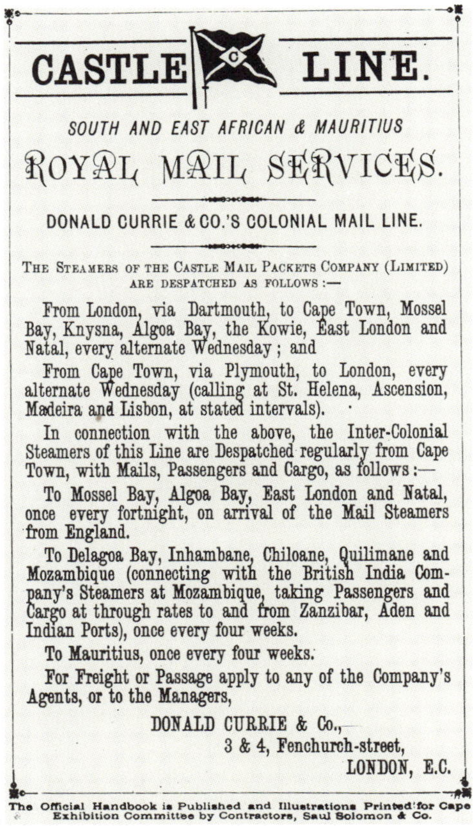

CASTLE LINE.

SOUTH AND EAST AFRICAN & MAURITIUS

ROYAL MAIL SERVICES.

DONALD CURRIE & CO.'S COLONIAL MAIL LINE.

THE STEAMERS OF THE CASTLE MAIL PACKETS COMPANY (LIMITED) ARE DESPATCHED AS FOLLOWS :—

From London, via Dartmouth, to Cape Town, Mossel Bay, Knysna, Algoa Bay, the Kowie, East London and Natal, every alternate Wednesday ; and

From Cape Town, via Plymouth, to London, every alternate Wednesday (calling at St. Helena, Ascension, Madeira and Lisbon, at stated intervals).

In connection with the above, the Inter-Colonial Steamers of this Line are Despatched regularly from Cape Town, with Mails, Passengers and Cargo, as follows :—

To Mossel Bay, Algoa Bay, East London and Natal, once every fortnight, on arrival of the Mail Steamers from England.

To Delagoa Bay, Inhambane, Chiloane, Quilimane and Mozambique (connecting with the British India Company's Steamers at Mozambique, taking Passengers and Cargo at through rates to and from Zanzibar, Aden and Indian Ports), once every four weeks.

To Mauritius, once every four weeks.

For Freight or Passage apply to any of the Company's Agents, or to the Managers,

DONALD CURRIE & Co.,—
3 & 4, Fenchurch-street,
LONDON, E.C.

The Official Handbook is Published and Illustrations Printed for Cape Exhibition Committee by Contractors, Saul Solomon & Co.

1 *The* Kildonan Castle *leaving Durban. She was the last Castle mailship to be built before the amalgamation. Under construction at the outbreak of the Anglo-Boer War, the liner was completed as a transport. On her maiden voyage in November 1899, she brought more than 3 000 soldiers to South Africa. As she was less than half the size of the Union-Castle troopships of World War II, which carried a similar number of troops, the hardships endured by those crammed on board must have been considerable.*

2 *A Union Line hospitalship at the Bluff in Durban, circa 1900.*

3 *At the time of her delivery for the mail service in 1880, the* Trojan *was the first vessel on the Cape run to have electric lights, albeit only in the first class saloon. On her maiden voyage in the same year, she continued to Durban to embark Princess Eugénie who had been in Natal to visit the site where the Prince Imperial was killed during the Zulu War. For nine years, the* Trojan *plied the mailship service before being relegated to the intermediate fleet. During the Anglo-Boer War she was requisitioned by the British Government for service as a hospitalship.*

4 *At one stage, the mail service provided by the Castle Line terminated at Cape Town, with coasters and intermediate liners providing a shuttle service along the southern African coast and to the Indian Ocean islands.*

1

3

Combined forces

1900-1919

2

By mutual consent, speed had been eliminated from the mail service as a factor to be promoted by either the Union or Castle line. Some commentators remarked at the time, and again subsequently, that because Donald Currie knew his ships could not better the record set by the *Scot* in 1893, he was only too pleased to settle with Union on the issue of speed. Nevertheless, the fierce competition between the Union Line and Donald Currie's Castle Line continued as the century drew to a close. Both lines adopted aggressive marketing campaigns, focusing particularly on the quality of service each offered to shippers and passengers.

In many respects, Currie had a clear advantage. He had gained international prominence through the cruises of the *Pembroke Castle* to the Baltic in 1883 when, *inter alia*, twenty-nine royal personages (including the reigning monarchs of three countries and the Princess of Wales) were received on board by Currie at Copenhagen. Such was the success of that occasion that a short history of the company published at the turn of the century enthused: 'Ships of war of every nationality lying in the harbour manned yards and played the National Anthems of the Royal personages aboard the *Pembroke Castle*.'

The *Tantallon Castle* had been present at the opening of the Kiel Canal in 1895. Again Currie had stolen the limelight, having entertained the Danish Royal Family on board en route to Kiel, and also when at Kiel, the liner's movements 'had been recorded in all newspapers side by side with those of the Emperor of Germany's yacht and the many stately war vessels gathered together from all parts of the world'. Currie's was a personal, flamboyant campaign for publicity, aided greatly by his outgoing and entrepreneurial character, as well as his own personal fortune. To the public at large, Currie and his Castles were inseparable. Unfortunately, until the advent of the *Kinfauns Castle* and the *Kildonan Castle* in 1899, Sir Donald and his advisers could not design ships to compare with those recently launched by their rival company and had lagged behind for several vital years.

3

The Union Line, on the other hand, had scored with the highly successful *Norman* and *Briton*, and now the 12 000-ton *Saxon* was nearing completion. In addition, the G-Class intermediate vessels, which had considerable cargo capacity for their size, were doing well. Yet despite these positive factors, the Union Line was still struggling financially as it had used most of its resources to meet the high cost of its recent building programme, which had included not only the mailships, but also the ten G-class ships.

This is how the official Union-Castle chronicler, Marischal Murray, described the events that ultimately led to amalgamation:

> In terms of the mail contracts, amalgamation of the Union and Castle Lines was, and remained, forbidden, except with the approval of the Cape Government. There was, however, no reason why one company should not endeavour to obtain entire control through acquisition of shares in the rival concern. A number of shareholders had investments in both companies. Sir Donald himself held Union shares. Through nominees, it might be possible to acquire still more. Currie, moreover, could approach the Union Line with attractive offers, for his resources – not necessarily those derived from shipping only – allowed of generosity.
>
> In the event it was, paradoxically, the action of the Cape Government itself which precipitated the amalgamation of the Union Line and the Castle Line. Amalgamation had consistently been forbidden with the idea that the two Lines should always be in competition. Each successive contract had produced improved facilities for the Cape Colony. A new mail contract was due in 1900. It was the natural desire of the Colonial Government, encouraged by merchants and the Chambers of Commerce, on this occasion to secure an even better service. The Government accordingly announced that the new mail contract would not be divided between the Union Line and the Castle Line, as had always been the case [since 1876], but would be put up for public tender, and would also have to be tendered for as a whole. In other words, the contract would be awarded to one Company only.
>
> If either Union Line or Castle Line alone were to be responsible for the performance of the mail service, this would certainly entail the construction by the company of four or five new mailships. Either line, moreover, might be expected to offer better terms than its rival. Last, but not least, the colonists anticipated that other British – or, it was whispered, even foreign – lines would tender, and thereby stimulate competition to the utmost.
>
> Tenders were invited. Neither Union Line nor Castle Line submitted offers for the service: they declined to compete against each other. No offers came from any outside line. A certain Mr H.T. Van Laun of the City of London guaranteed to run mailships

1 *The* Kildonan Castle *approaching Durban.*
2 *Sir Owen Philipps, later Lord Kylsant, chairman of Union-Castle from 1912 to 1931.*
3 *The* Pembroke Castle *was employed mainly as an intermediate ('extra') steamer but made several voyages on the mail service. She is probably best known for the voyage she undertook shortly after her delivery in September 1883, when Donald Currie invited Prime Minister Gladstone, Alfred Lord Tennyson and several other dignitaries on a cruise to Norway and Denmark, where he also entertained on board twenty-nine members of Europe's royal families. Gladstone received a royal reprimand from Queen Victoria for his participation in this voyage, since he had not first sought her permission.*

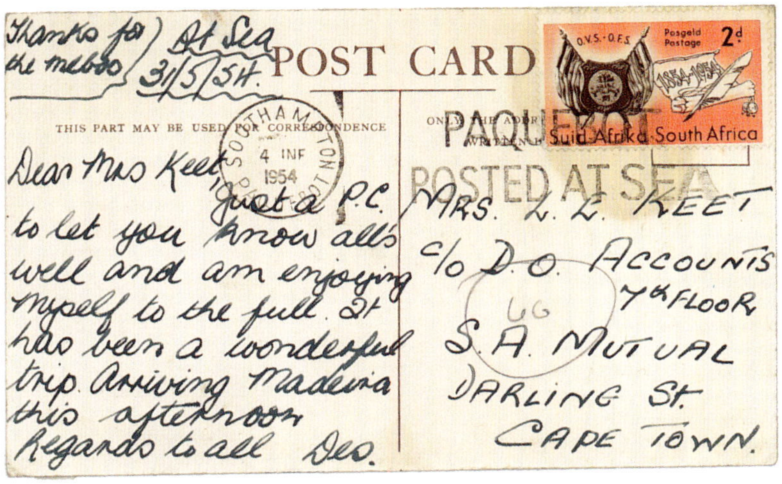

OCEAN POST OFFICES ON BOARD THE MAILSHIPS

Even at the turn of the century, the large mailships carried about 700 passengers as they sailed between Southampton and Cape Town. Although there were a few organized activities on board, passengers had a considerable amount of time on their hands, and this was often spent writing letters to friends and relatives.

The call at Madeira was an ideal opportunity for letters written to those left behind to be transferred to the mailship heading in the opposite direction. At first, this was a relatively casual arrangement but later it was to develop into a formally structured postal service with its own unique franking system. Envelopes or postcards 'posted' at sea are now greatly sought after by collectors, who pay handsome sums for clearly franked postcards of the ships on which the cards were written.

The text of one such card, written on Tuesday 22 May 1894, is quoted by P. Cattell in his book Union-Castle Ocean Post Offices*:*

> *South Atlantic Ocean. On board Hawarden Castle.*
>
> *Dear Aunt*
> *We shall reach Madeira tomorrow after making one of the quickest passages on record – this card will not be landed, but will be taken off to a passing Mail Steamer which has already left Madeira for home. Please save this.*
>
> *With best wishes,*
> *Willie*

These ocean post offices were not peculiar to Union-Castle. The system was adopted by several of the major liner companies, where outward-bound ships crossed their homeward consorts en route.

Because of the severe dislocation of the South African mail service during World War I, this quaint practice of the Cape run was suspended. However, as late as the mid-fifties, special franking still applied. A typical example is the postcard, reproduced above, written on board the Edinburgh Castle *on 31 May 1954. Note the words 'paquebot posted at sea' franked across a South African stamp and the Southampton postmark dated 4 June 1954.*

to Cape Town in fourteen days in return for an annual subsidy of £158 000. Mr Van Laun was not a shipowner and his prospects of becoming one seemed nebulous. In the circumstances the Cape Government fell back on the two companies which had served the Colony so well for many years, and agreement was reached on the basis of terms submitted by the Union Line and the Castle Line respectively. Once again the mail contract was divided, as before. In the new agreement, however, there was one most significant omission: there was no clause limiting the power of the two companies to amalgamate. Fusion of Union and Castle – should this be judged desirable – had for the first time become a practical possibility.

The initiative came from Sir Donald Currie. To the directors of the Union Line he offered seats on the Board, or 'Council' of an amalgamated company; to the Chairman, Sir Francis Evans, he offered a partnership in Donald Currie and Company, which firm would manage the new concern in the same way as it had been managing the Castle Line.

A stage had now been reached where the rapid strides recently made by the Union Line were, in effect, to no purpose, for the majority of the Company's shares were held by those who were not unsympathetic to Donald Currie's point of view. Currie, thus, was in a strong bargaining position. Instead of dictating terms, however, he preferred to come to an amicable arrangement with his opponents. In addition to the offers already mentioned, he gave assurances that in the event of an amalgamation the staff of the Union Line would be treated with fairness and generosity.

In December 1899, the public learned that the two Boards had agreed on the terms whereby the Union Line and Castle Line should be amalgamated. Briefly, these were as follows:

– The Castle Mail Packets Company were to take over the fleet, property, assets and liabilities of the Union Steamship Company, the name of the former being changed to that of the Union-Castle Mail Steamship Company;

– Donald Currie and Company, Managers of the Castle Line, were to become Managers of the Union-Castle Line, Sir Francis Evans, Chairman and Managing Director of the Union Line, now being associated with them in the management of the joint undertaking;

– The existing directors of the Union Line were to join the Council of the Union-Castle Line.

Meetings were held on February 13 1900, so that the shareholders of the respective companies might give their approval. At the meeting of the Union Line Sir Francis Evans stated that, apart from the conditions already set out, he had obtained for the Union Company a bonus of some £350 000, this in view of the fact that additions to the Union Line had been more rapid in recent years than those of the Castle Line. In round figures, the tonnages of the respective fleets totalled Union 114 000; Castle 107 000.

At amalgamation, the fleets of the two mailship companies were as follows:

UNION LINE: MAILSHIPS		CASTLE LINE: MAILSHIPS	
Arab	*Saxon*	*Carisbrook Castle*	*Kildonan Castle*
Briton	*Scot*	*Dunottar Castle*	*Kinfauns Castle*
Mexican	*Spartan*	*Dunvegan Castle*	*Norham Castle*
Moor	*Trojan*	*Garth Castle*	*Roslin Castle*
Norman		*Hawarden Castle*	*Tantallon Castle*

The Union Line had ordered the *Celt* shortly before the amalgamation, but since the vessel was launched only in 1902 she bore the name *Walmer Castle*, the suffix -Castle appearing on all subsequent vessels ordered by Union-Castle. Each company had ten intermediate ships. Murray's text continues:

> The shareholders of the two companies gave their approval. Amalgamation was achieved. Much that was picturesque and exciting was now to go out of South African shipping, but to take its place, a fleet was eventually to evolve, second to none in the mercantile marine of Britain. On March 8 1900, the Union-Castle Mail Steamship Company Limited was registered.

Murray next recounts the occasion of the first unfurling of the Union-Castle house flag:

> The new flag was hoisted on Saturday March 17 1900. The *Dunottar Castle* (Captain Rigby) was to sail from Southampton on that day with a long passenger list which

included the Duchess of Teck and Lady Roberts, wife of the Field Marshall [sic]. In a speech made at a luncheon given on board for a party of journalists, Sir Donald Currie announced that during the afternoon, the ceremony would take place. It symbolised, he added, the unity of the two companies, Union and Castle, and he hoped that unity in South Africa would soon be achieved. Shortly afterwards the Castle Line Express from Waterloo drew in with its distinguished passengers, who were met at the gangway by Sir Donald Currie. After luncheon, certain chosen guests, including Princess Adolphus, Duchess of Teck, Lady Roberts, Sir Francis Evans, and others were escorted to the promenade deck aft, where the ceremony of breaking the flag took place. A charge from the ship's small gun was fired, and to the accompaniment of cheers, the flag was run up to the masthead of the *Dunottar Castle*. Simultaneously, the flag was broken at the masthead of the intermediate steamer *Gaika* (Captain H. Strong) which was lying astern and which soon afterwards steamed out, her masts and rigging crowded with troops who sent up cheer after cheer as they passed the first mail steamer to fly the house-flag of the Union-Castle Line.

Although the Anglo-Boer War had brought much conflict, misery and entrenched bitterness to South Africa, it had also brought significant, albeit short-term, growth to the newly formed Union-Castle Line.

Following the signing of the Peace of Vereeniging on 31 May 1902, South Africa required substantial overseas assistance for reconstruction, especially as so much of the agricultural production of the interior had been devastated by the war. Peace in the country encouraged immigration, even among many former British soldiers who had served in South Africa during the war. These factors stimulated trade to the country and resulted in the mailships sailing for South Africa with their holds filled and their passenger accommodation in great demand. But the boom did not last long.

The amalgamation of the two fleets and a recession on the trade dictated the need to rationalize sailings and to restructure the fleet according to the requirements of the new company. It therefore came to pass that, of the mailships in service at the time of amalgamation, only five were operating on the mail service four years later. One had been scrapped, nine had been sold and two had been transferred to the East African service. There had also been two major losses.

The Union-Castle Company was barely two months old when the mailship *Mexican* sank after colliding with the freighter *Winkfield* near Cape Town. The following are

Her lifeboats still black from the days when Union Line vessels were entirely black, the Mexican *is shown here off East London. She sank after a collision with the steamer* Wakefield *off Cape Town on 6 April 1900.*

1

2

extracts from the reports published in the 12 April 1900 edition of *Lloyd's Weekly Shipping Index*:

APRIL 6 *Mexican* in collision Thursday morning with *Winkfield* 80 miles from Cape Town. *Mexican* abandoned, sinking. All hands saved and will be forwarded by *Guelph* and *Tantallon Castle*. Most of letter mails were saved. *Mexican* was going half speed owing thick fog.

CAPE TOWN: APRIL 6 The Post Office tonight issued a notice to the effect that all the *Mexican*'s mails were saved, except one bag of registered letters for London and one of English letters, with general addresses, and 145 bags of newspapers. The Army letters were all recovered in good condition.

CAPE TOWN: APRIL 6: 10 A.M. The Union-Castle liner *Mexican* which left with mails on Wednesday afternoon has been run into and sunk by a cattle-boat. [Other telegrams indicated that the *Winkfield* was a troop transport.] Her passengers, which included Sir Charles Hunter returned safely in the cattle-boat today.

CAPE TOWN: APRIL 6: 10:45 . . . it appears that Wednesday night was very foggy. The *Mexican* subsequently blew her foghorn for three hours and went at half speed. She heard another foghorn at intervals, but saw no sign of a ship until at 2 on Thursday morning when she collided with the *Winkfield* . . . The *Mexican* was not seen to sink by those on board the transport.

3

LONDON: APRIL 7 The owners of the *Winkfield* have received the following telegram from Cape Town – Have been in collision with Union Liner *Mexican* in fog 80 miles off port. Crew and passengers saved. Tried towing her, finally abandoned, reported sinking condition. Our bow and stem crushed in; serious. No lives lost. Shall I appoint a Lloyd's Agent?

LONDON: APRIL 11 A Central News telegram from Cape Town dated April 9 states that H.M.S. *Tagus* which went in search of the *Mexican*, has returned. Her Commander states that the *Mexican* has undoubtedly foundered. From wreckage found near the scene of the collision, it is evident that the boilers of the liner burst shortly before she sank.

The second loss was that of the *Tantallon Castle*. Among the passengers on board on her southbound voyage in May 1901 was a group of nurses who were to join the staff of the Uitvlugt Hospital, Maitland Camp, near Cape Town. (The hospital cared for convalescing soldiers during the Anglo-Boer War.) In a letter to her family in Britain, one of the nurses, Lucy Nottage, described the scene on the mailship before and after the fateful stranding on Robben Island, Table Bay, on 7 May 1901. The following extracts from the letter also provide some interesting insights into communication at the time:

. . . by the time you receive this, the wreck of the "Tantallon" will be an old story, but it is still fresh in my mind . . . You will have had all the latest news home by the "Saxon". I had written all my experiences since leaving Madeira and posted them

FRESH MILK AT SEA

Apart from highlighting the degree to which the agencies were dictated to by head office, the text of the following letter, dated 6 December 1902, from Fenchurch Street to the Cape Town agency alludes to the conditions under which passengers travelled. The more affluent were able to improve their standard of living through the provision of such commodities as fresh milk, whereas those in steerage often experienced great hardship when travelling by sea.

The cow which was put on board the "Briton" at your port on her last homeward voyage for the use of Dr Jameson is being returned in the ship with the instruction that if she continues to give sufficient milk, she will be made use of in the homeward passage, and the English cow will be landed in the ordinary course at East London, but if the Cape cow is not giving sufficient milk (she is at present giving very little) she can be landed at your port and sold on our account, in which case the English cow will not be landed at East London, but brought back for the use of passengers.

Two cows are being put aboard by Lady Farrar for use of herself and her family during the voyage.

Two other letters from the Union-Castle Mail Steamship Company, London, to the Cape Town agency also concerned a cow, this time on the Norman*:*

November 21st, 1907

Dear Sirs,

As we are not putting a new cow on the NORMAN this voyage, the old one will require to do the round trip, and will not be landed at Cape Town as hitherto.

For your information, we may say that as the whole question of continuing to put cows on board our mail steamers is under consideration, it would be well for you not to make any forward arrangements for the sale of same in the meantime.

Yours truly

THE UNION-CASTLE STEAMSHIP COMPANY LIMITED
For Donald Currie & Co

SIGNATURE INDISTINCT

Someone had second thoughts about the issue of the cow on the Norman*:*

23 November, 1907

Dear Sirs,

COW ON R.M.S. NORMAN.

Referring to ours of 21st. instant respecting the cow on board the NORMAN, we find that this cow is only giving a moderate supply of milk, and as it is possible that she may further deteriorate in this respect were she to be brought home, we think it well that you should sell her at one of the South African ports, provided you can get a reasonable price, and we shall send by the KINFAUNS CASTLE some bottled milk to take the place of the cow on the voyage home.

Yours truly

THE UNION-CASTLE STEAMSHIP COMPANY LIMITED
For Donald Currie & Co., Managers

1, 2 *The* Tantallon Castle *aground on Robben Island in 1901. These two photographs, taken over a period of a week, illustrate how quickly she succumbed to the might of the sea. In the first photograph, a person can be seen descending a ladder to the lifeboat below, while the sky hints at the gathering storm which later smashed the ship to pieces.*

3 *Coaling ship was an arduous task. In the early days, sacks of coal were lugged aboard and their contents tipped into the bunkers. Despite special awnings, coal dust flew everywhere, to the dismay of the seamen who would have to clean the ship before sailing. To ensure that the vessel did not run out of fuel in those unpredictable days of steamships, surplus sacks of coal were stowed in any available space, even on top of cargo in the holds. The* Saxon*, alongside in Cape Town, is preparing to load the surplus coal. On the wharfside, cab drivers, perched precariously at the back of their vehicles, await passengers.*

1

by 8 o'clock on Monday night. (We were then expecting to get into Cape Town at 12 midday at the latest.) We had a nice concert again that evening and I retired to bed about 11 pm (very late for me) and with my usual propensity, slept well. Some of the others, however, were wakened by 3 am by the continual blowing of a foghorn; it seems that a fog had enveloped us and another vessel was in front, which we were afraid of running down. The fog and the screeching continued at intervals until 10 am Tuesday morning when suddenly it lifted and we sailed until 11.30 in beautiful sunny weather and were able to discover and safely get ahead of the other vessel which we passed at a distance of 5 miles though she was out at sea where, evidently, we had much better have been. While it was sunny and bright, I for the first time went up the forecastle, and while there, thought we could see Cape Town (we were only then 36 miles from it) but upon enquiry, the man told us it was a bank of fog and not land at all. However, a sailor went up the rigging and could see Cape Town quite distinctly over the fog . . . By this time, the engines had been reduced to half speed and after that at four miles per hour [sic], in spite of the entreaties of the passengers who wished to go faster . . . We had lunch and nobody suspected danger and in the afternoon, having nothing else to do, and being too excited by the nearness of the journey's end . . . most of the people were idling about on deck, and many laughing and talking, when all of a sudden, at 3.20 pm, a slight grazing sound like a little boat being dragged onto the beach, that was all. The next thing I saw was the poor Captain on the bridge, flinging his arms about, looking agonies, and with that, the electric bells down to the engine room. Immediately, everyone rushed for the side of the ship, more to see what was up than with any thought of danger . . . The engines were reversed, but to no purpose. She would not move.

The next thing, all the boats were got out, and guns fired, and after waiting in some suspense, a little boat put off with an officer and a few men. Nobody could tell where we were, only that we were aground. Presently, our signals of distress brought a little tug out to us. She was the little mail from Robben Island, the leper island, where we had struck. She had been unloading a vessel on the other side of the island when our distress signals were heard. Even then, I did not think we should have to leave our vessel, but when the parleying had been done, we were taken in small boatloads to the little tug which was lying about half a mile from us. During all this time, the foghorn was screeching at intervals for fear of other vessels running near us or the other little tug . . . The mothers and babies were got off first . . . There were only 320 passengers – I thought there were many more . . . The hospital nurses went last (among the women); then came the men after . . . doing everything they possibly could to help us . . . We were very thankful to see them come on board at last, for when we left the ship, she was lying quite on one side and was going over very quickly. Of course we had to leave everything . . . However, after waiting for another tug to come to take the mails, we set off at 6 pm and still we had qualms of the other tug running into us . . . We

2

3

4

5

6

finally reached Cape Town at 8.20 pm, having been all that time coming 8 miles . . . We had the Governor of Natal with us, Sir Henry MacCullin, and various other nobs, and to think of them entering Cape Town in that unceremonious manner was too funny. We landed and went to the Union-Castle Office where they made arrangements for 80 passengers to sleep on the "Saxon" which was sailing the following day and taking Sir Alfred Milner home – and the mails . . . They gave us supper, and we shared a cabin with a lady who lent us all the necessary toilet requisites, for we simply had nothing . . . After breakfast, we had to run to the other part of the Docks to sort out our luggage which we had despaired of getting at all, and you should have seen the variety of articles, for . . . all the things that had been left in the cabins were tied in sheets and sent ashore; everything was splendidly managed . . . I very much wanted to cable home, but each time I suggested it, people looked at me as though I was a sort of mild lunatic, for everything concerning us would be known at the office in London, so I left it . . . I only hope you heard the true report . . .

Nurse Nottage added several paragraphs in which she described how Lady Hely-Hutchinson, the wife of the governor, had entertained the shipwrecked passengers. A further paragraph read:

Today we heard that there is no hope for the "Tantallon"; she is going to be a complete wreck. Two very large vessels [actually, three Union-Castle liners – *Braemar*

1 *The* Walmer Castle *leaving Durban.*
2 *The launching of the* Kenilworth Castle *at the Harland & Wolff yards, Belfast, on 5 December 1903. She was the first mailship to be ordered from the yard by Union-Castle after the amalgamation.*
3 *An open bridge with canvas awnings as the only protection from the elements afforded little comfort to the mariners of yesteryear. As late as 1910, officers on some of the mailships still had to brave icy wind, driving rain and spray.*
4 *Union-Castle complied strictly with all regulations pertaining to safety at sea. Lifeboat drills, such as this on board the* Saxon, *circa 1903, were common, and apart from their obvious safety function, relieved the boredom.*
5 *Designed for the warm climatic zones through which the ships travelled, the wide, open promenade decks, which ran for more than half the length of a ship, were a welcome feature of the Cape liners that entered service from 1890. Even the later vessels with more adequate ventilation systems boasted these wide decks, which were always kept immaculately clean and served as a gathering place for passengers in fair weather. It was here that many passengers took their beef tea in the morning, played deck quoits, or simply sat and read or gazed at the endless sea.*
6 *The unsung heroes of the mail service were the engineers, stokers and greasers whose efforts to keep the ships to their tight schedules were momentous. Even in the later years, when semi-automation made life much easier for the engineers, there was still great pressure on them to keep the ships running to time.*

THE NORHAM CASTLE

The Norham Castle *was one of a trio of ships that Donald Currie built in 1883 to compete with the speed of the Union Line's* Moor, Athenian, Mexican *and* Tartar, *which had come out only months earlier.*

The Norham Castle *and her sister ships,* Roslin Castle *and* Hawarden Castle, *all of which came from different yards, had a narrower beam than previous ships of similar length. Their 158 first class passengers accommodated in the poop, and the eighty-four second class passengers, found the ships most uncomfortable in a beam sea, particularly in the Cape rollers. It may have been an experience in one of these ships which prompted the financier, Sir Lionel Phillips, to write that 'sea travel is an interminable penance, rolling nearly all the time, oil lamps giving off fumes . . .'*

Eclipsed by faster ships, all three vessels were sold in 1904. The Hawarden Castle *went to the Booth Line. As the* Cyril, *she sank after a collision with another Booth liner in the Amazon River. The* Roslin Castle, *which had been extensively lengthened, re-engined and refitted by Barclay Curle to remedy defective steering, was bought by German shipowners who fitted her out as a storeship for the Russian fleet. As such, and under the name* Regina, *she grounded on the Mozambique coast in 1905. Refloated, she was towed to Durban and thence to Genoa where she was scrapped.*

The Norham Castle *became the* Martinique, *belonging to the Cie Générale Transatlantique and remained in their service until 1933 when she went to the shipbreakers. That she lasted as long as she did is miraculous, for while she was a Castle liner she had suffered two serious breakdowns as described in the extracts below.*

The Cape Argus, *19 March 1901.*

The Union-Castle mail steamer Norham Castle, *outward bound and due to arrive at Cape Town on the 20th instant, has been towed into Ascension by the New Zealand steamer* Tongariro. *It appears that the* Norham Castle *was disabled 500 miles north of Ascension by the bursting of the crown of her high pressure cylinder. One man was badly scalded.*

The Cape Argus *of 4 April 1901 published a fascinating account of the incident written by a passenger who, besides providing a wonderful insight into the hazards of ocean travel at that time, described some aspects of the transport of soldiers to the Anglo-Boer War.*

We sailed from Southampton for Cape Town on 2 March 1901. In addition to the considerable number of passengers, there were on board 330 troops – Imperial Yeomanry. All went well until Thursday the 14th. We had a disagreeable trip across the Bay of Biscay and the Norham Castle *did roll! However, Madeira was in due course reached where many passengers left us. The usual games, drill for the soldiers, a certain amount of music, eating, sleeping and novel reading passed the time uneventfully until the morning of the 14th, when, about 4 a.m., a great explosion took place. The top of the triple-expansion cylinder blew off with a loud report; then there was a hissing of escaping steam which severely scalded one man, others having the most miraculous escapes. Great was the excitement among the passengers who, in night costume, rushed to and from to find out what was wrong. There was no panic, but an immense feeling of relief when it was ascertained that no lives were lost.*

. . . The engineers exercised their best talent to disconnect the broken cylinder and put the engines in working order with two cylinders only.

Meantime, sails were set forward to keep the vessel from drifting out of the track of steamers, and we were flying signals of distress. We were fortunate in having splendid weather, and had it not been for the horrible uncertainty of what might have occurred, and the anxiety of our friends if we were reported overdue, we would have enjoyed ourselves for the water was smooth. With 600 persons on board, it is always a question of the matter of provisions and water, especially water. We had to exercise patience, trust in those in authority, and wish for good luck. The soldiers took advantage of the steadiness of the ship to practise firing with ball cartridge at boxes thrown overboard . . .

We tried to be philosophical, and ate, and listened to the ship's band which played in the afternoon. One pair fished, catching two sharks, seven or eight feet long; another set played quoits; some did a mild gamble at cards, and it was as well the weather permitted all the usual amusements to go on. We relied on the man at the masthead spotting a relieving vessel and about 5 p.m., thirteen hours after the breakdown, the cry of 'Vessel in Sight!' was passed along. This turned out to be the S.S. Tongariro, *for Cape Town with 1,000 troops who responded in a truly British manner to our cheers of welcome. It was a thrilling moment. Our Captain and the Commanding Officer of the Imperial Yeomanry went on board the other steamer and agreed we should be towed to Ascension Island, 520 miles distant while our engineers tried to repair our engines. The* Tongariro *stood by all night, and in the morning, had our steamer in tow. The sea was calm, the weather fine, and it was such a feeling of relief to know we were no longer drifting . . .*

During the afternoon of our breakdown, sports were held on the quarterdeck, both soldiers and passengers enjoying the fun, and in the evening a successful concert was held. We were all sound asleep after the evening's amusement until 2.30 a.m. when the foghorn was vigorously sounded, notifying the Tongariro *that the tow lines had broken.*

We were once again drifting, though this time but a short distance from our friendly escort. At 7.30 a.m. we were off again with little wind to impede our way, a smooth sea and everything in our favour.

In the evening, the soldiers held a concert forward, which from the enthusiastic applause was evidently appreciated. Tommies prefer to sing in their own quarters to taking part in entertainment on the saloon deck. Sunday followed with the usual Service, and we enjoyed the steadiness and peaceful feeling of being towed in a calm sea.

Kit parade took place in the afternoon – every inch of the quarterdeck being used – in fact the soldiers rather encroached on the passengers' rights, the latter having to quarter themselves for the time being on the Madeira egg-baskets stored at the end of the ship, causing sundry complaints resulting in orders being given for future parades to be held elsewhere. The other extreme was now gone to and the soldiers confined to a space quite inadequate to their requirements. A happy mean was being reached by the time we left the Norham Castle. *I believe in every opportunity being given soldiers on ships preparing for the duties that await them on shore.*

Next morning, the passengers woke to find themselves off the island of Ascension which from the sea looked larger than expected. The tow rope again broke as we neared the anchorage. During the day, the mailbags were trans-shipped, and at 4.30 p.m., the Tongariro *left for Cape Town, being given a hearty cheer by all our ship's company.*

On Saturday 23rd March, our engines being temporarily repaired with the assistance of H.M. artificers, and the trial trip proving satisfactory, we started about 2 p.m. on our voyage to St Helena – glad to be able to proceed, but sorry to leave the hospitable friends we had made ashore. The sea being smooth, we steadily steamed at 10 knots, congratulating the engineers and our own good fortune in being able to proceed . . .

On arrival at St Helena and when the engines were reversed, the concrete packing around the damaged cylinder gave way and until effectively made good, the Norham Castle *was again helpless, this time fortunately at a safe anchorage.*

On 28th March, the Carisbrook Castle *came in sight, bound for Cape Town, and it was arranged for the* Norham Castle*'s passengers to be trans-shipped, which was accordingly done with the aid of boats from H.M.S.* Thetis.

The length of the passage of the Norham Castle *from Southampton to Table Bay on that occasion was thirty-four days and fourteen hours, of which eight days and sixteen hours were spent at anchor, one day and eight hours drifting, and two days and eighteen hours under tow, bringing the total delay to twelve days and nineteen hours.*

Following the disappearance of a 10 000-ton passenger liner the Waratah, *off the South African coast in 1909, an earlier incident involving the* Norham Castle *was related in a letter to the press from a Mr Hermann Flugge:*

In January 1888, we left Cape Town [on board the Norham Castle*] with only 12 Passengers, and, after being at sea for a day and a half, we had the misfortune to break our propeller, and the worst was that the screw smashed our rudder, so that we were helpless.*

Our gallant Captain rigged up a yard and sails, and we were drifting for weeks, and the Norham Castle was given up for lost here and at Home [Britain].

Not one but half a dozen ships came in sight, but as soon as we signalled our distress, the vessels turned out of our course . . . I remember when our Captain assembled every soul on board in the saloon. 'Our vessel is safe from sinking,' he said. 'With the rigged-up sails I hope to reach St Helena. Should this fail, we are drifting into a current which, after three or four months, will bring us to the coast of Brazil. From the day that we miss St Helena, only half rations will be served.'

Fortunately, one of the sailing vessels we sighted, which passed St Helena, and was questioned there as to the lost Norham Castle, *reported having sighted a steamer in distress, and gave as far as possible our whereabouts. A whaler, lying at that time in Jamestown, was despatched to our rescue.*

Three weeks we had drifted, and if not rescued, would perhaps have drifted as many months without our fate becoming known to any living being.

Can not a similar mishap have happened to the Waratah? *No wreckage has been found up to date, and I advise all those who have friends on the vessel not to give up hope till it is definitely proved that the* Waratah *has gone to the bottom.*

The Norham Castle *had also been involved in a dramatic rescue off the Natal coast.*

In the early hours of 7 February 1895, the four-masted steel sailing vessel Fascadale, *on a voyage from Java to Lisbon with a cargo of sugar, went aground south of the Mbizana River near Port Shepstone. She ended up some 114 metres from the shoreline, which the crew attempted to reach but were foiled by the heavy sea running at the time. Two men were lost in the attempt. The unfortunate vessel was sighted by the officer of the watch on the* Norham Castle *and presently, to secure a lifeline to the stranded vessel, a lifeboat under the command of Chief Officer Frank Whitehead was launched. Near the wreck, Whitehead dived into the sea with a lifeline and struck out for the* Fascadale. *On the way, he encountered a crew member from the sailing ship, who likewise had plunged into the sea to meet him and assist him with the lifeline.*

Owing to the combined efforts of these two men, eighteen lives were saved by means of the lifeline. Six other men eventually swam ashore. Loss of life was limited to four crewmen, two monkeys, six cockatoos, a dog and a cat.

Whitehead and a seaman called Ferries were awarded the Board of Trade's Sea Gallantry Medal, the former also receiving the Castle Mail Packet Company's Gallantry Medal, the Lloyds Silver Lifesaving Medal, the Liverpool Shipwreck and Humane Society's Silver Medal, a pair of binoculars and largesse. Captain Duncan of the Norham Castle *was awarded the Liverpool Silver Medal and largesse. Largesse also went to the crew of the lifeboat.*

Castle, *Avondale Castle* and *Raglan Castle*] tried to tow her off, and one only escaped being wrecked herself, so they have had to abandon her and Captain Travers and crew came off last evening. Everyone shows the greatest sympathy for the Captain. He is getting old now, and to think this should have happened after all his experience is too dreadful . . . Every scrap of luggage has arrived, even the bicycles . . .

Captain de la Cour Travers had commanded the *Scot* on her maiden voyage, as well as on that memorable record-breaking passage in 1893. Therefore, as Nurse Nottage wrote, it was indeed tragic that, in its final stages, his otherwise exceptional career should have been marred in this way.

In the final paragraph of her letter, Nurse Nottage mentioned 'frightful weather, bucketsful of rain' associated with a storm. That storm was responsible for the heavy swell that battered the wrecked mailship for several days and smashed it to pieces.

Still in service were the *Briton*, *Kildonan Castle*, *Kinfauns Castle*, *Norman* and *Saxon*. The *Walmer Castle*, originally laid down as the *Celt*, had also joined the fleet in 1902. Although similar to the *Saxon* in that she had eight double-ended and two single-ended boilers with fifty-four furnaces, the *Walmer Castle* was far less efficient in terms of her coal consumption. Even when using the best Welsh coal, a startlingly high 240 tons per day were required to maintain her service speed of 15 knots. (The larger *Arundel Castle*, which entered service in 1921, used only 200 tons per day.)

Since the building of the *Norman* in 1894, all of the Union Line orders had gone to Harland & Wolff, while Sir Donald Currie had preferred Scottish yards to build his ships. Because both mail companies had been satisfied with their ships, Union-Castle decided after amalgamation that future orders should alternate between Belfast and Scotland. Therefore, when new ships were required to replace obsolete tonnage, Fairfields of Glasgow was awarded the contract for the construction of the splendid liner *Armadale Castle*, while Harland & Wolff built her sister ship, the *Kenilworth Castle*, both similar in some ways to the *Walmer Castle* and her predecessor, the *Saxon*. There is no doubt that the Harland & Wolff design, initially adopted by the Union Line for the *Norman* and modified for the *Saxon* and *Walmer Castle*, was far superior to anything that the Castle Line had devised; even the *Kildonan Castle*, the last vessel ordered by the Castle Line, could not match the Union ships for design and efficient layout. Therefore, the design of the next four mailships ordered by Union-Castle reflected the *Norman* prototype.

To take advantage of the increasing number of immigrants to South Africa, each ship carried nearly 800 passengers – a remarkable figure when one considers that the capacity of the 1960 *Windsor Castle* was only 782. That the *Armadale Castle* and her consorts of the time carried such a great number of passengers can be ascribed to the small size of the cabins and there being many six-berth cabins. The catering department on those ships performed miracles daily to ensure that all had enough to eat.

For the maiden voyages of the *Armadale Castle* and *Kenilworth Castle*, Union-Castle issued a special lavishly illustrated album. The following extracts from that album describe aspects of the accommodation on board those ships:

The first class cabins are located on the Promenade, Upper and Main Decks, and are mostly two-berth cabins. Single cabins and groups of state rooms are provided with sliding doors, by means of which two or more of them can be made en suite or to communicate so as to provide accommodation for families. All these state rooms are fitted with chests of drawers or wardrobes, and special attention has been given to the lighting and ventilation. The seats and sofas in each room are tastefully upholstered.

The first class Entrance Hall in each steamer is on the Promenade deck with fine double staircases of oak, leading down to the vestibules and saloons. It is panelled in pure white and supported by oak pillars and the floor is laid with non-slipping rubber tiles of a bold black and white design . . .

The Reading Room at the forward end of the Promenade Deck is approached from the Entrance Hall by two short corridors. It is a lofty apartment with large square windows on three sides, looking ahead and to port and starboard. An ornamental Cupola in the centre of the ceiling, supported by four carved Corinthian pillars

The Norham Castle *at Gravesend before she was re-engined. She was on the mail service for thirty-one years.*

MAINTAINING THE SCHEDULE

Punctuality was an essential condition of the Ocean Mail Contract. The following exchange of telegrams between Cape Town and London illustrates the concern Union-Castle had for keeping to the prescribed mail schedule:

Cable Cape Town – London 7 Feb 1906

STIFF GALE; IF WALMER WILL NOT LEAVE UNTIL TOMORROW, SHOULD ARRIVAL AT SOUTHAMPTON BE LATE IN PROPORTION?

Cable London – Cape Town 7 Feb 1906

REFERRING TO YOUR TELEGRAM OF 7TH INSTANT; TELL THE CAPTAIN WALMER CASTLE IF YOU LEAVE TOMORROW MORNING (THURSDAY) ARRIVE SOUTHAMPTON SATURDAY AFTERNOON

The Walmer Castle *in fact managed to leave at 17:00 on 7 February 1906.*

COUNTING THE COST

As an accelerated mailship service between Cape Town and Southampton was required in 1910, before committing themselves to an upgrading programme the Union-Castle management debated the options open to them and the costs involved. Some suggestions recommended that the ships arrive in Southampton at 10:00 on a Friday morning, which would require an average speed for the voyage of 14,9 knots. Others recommended an arrival time of 14:00, which would require an average speed of 14,5 knots. The engineering superintendent then presented the following cost analysis:

	ARRIVAL FRIDAY 10:00	ARRIVAL FRIDAY 14:00
Extra costs of lubricating oil, stores and upkeep due to greater wear and tear	*£8,000 p.a.*	*£6,500 p.a.*
Additional dry-docking of the lower-powered ships to ensure they maintained the schedule	*£3,000 p.a.*	*£3,000 p.a.*
*Additional stoke-hold labour**	*£ 900 p.a.*	*£ 750 p.a.*

** One of the reasons cited for this additional cost was that the coal bunkered in Cape Town was largely Natal coal, which produced more ash and clinker than Welsh or Tyneside coal. Therefore more tending of the fires in the boilers would be necessary.*

Extra coal consumption:

SHIP	NUMBER OF VOYAGES PER ANNUM	COAL CONSUMED TONS PER ANNUM	
Balmoral Castle	*6*	*2,028*	*1,440*
Edinburgh Castle	*6*	*2,028*	*1,440*
Armadale Castle	*6*	*2,028*	*1,440*
Kenilworth Castle	*6*	*2 028*	*1,440*
Walmer Castle	*6*	*1,740*	*1,230*
Saxon	*6*	*1,740*	*1,230*
Briton	*6*	*1,452*	*1,104*
Kinfauns Castle	*5*	*1,872*	*1,368*
Kildonan Castle	*5*	*2,004*	*1,512*

also gives light and air to the room. At the after end is the handsome bookcase, containing some hundreds of specially chosen books suitable for all lines of thought. Round the room are sofa seats, arranged in little bays with tables in the centre. Writing tables with Queen Anne chairs stand here and there. The sofa seats are upholstered in tapestry of a quaint old Flemish design with chintz covers, the prevailing colour of the whole being a quiet tone of green. A handsome carpet and curtains of subdued colour at the windows give an air of comfort and privacy to the room. On the *Armadale Castle*, the walls are panelled in satin-wood, and on the *Kenilworth Castle*, in oak, interlaid . . . The Smoking Room . . . has a Bar and Lavatories attached. There are large square windows on both sides, and from the centre of the ceiling, rises a dome . . . This room is fitted with a powerful electric fan which draws out and perpetually renews the air . . .

The First Class Dining Saloon . . . will accommodate at one sitting 187 passengers, and underneath is an auxiliary First Class Children's Dining Saloon . . . The walls of the Dining Saloon in the *Armadale Castle* are panelled in mahogany, finished in dull polish; the *Kenilworth Castle* being in oak. The ceiling and dome are painted white, the base of the latter having a handsome carved wreath around it. There are two long and fourteen small tables in the Saloon, and all are provided with revolving chairs, which, by an ingenious arrangement, can be moved towards or away from the tables as required. The floor is polished teak, spread with Wilton carpet . . .

The Second Class cabins are unusually comfortable; a special mention may be made of those on the Promenade deck, fitted for two passengers only, and each containing a wardrobe.

The Third Class sleeping accommodation is aft, and the berths are erected in two tiers only. The cabins are for two, three, four or more passengers and are well lighted and ventilated and comfortably fitted. There are two saloons, one on the Upper and one on the Main Deck, with a separate pantry. One of the special features provided is a very comfortable Third Class Smoking Room. In addition, the spacious entrance on this deck to the Third Class Accommodation has seats round it, and makes a pleasant sheltered lounge. An extensive library is also provided for the use of Third Class passengers.

The sanitary accommodation has received special consideration, and is of the latest and most improved description. An ample number of baths supplied with hot and cold water is provided for each class of passenger. A continuous water service is supplied throughout the ship, and this is quite separate and distinct from the water supplied for other than passengers' use. All the accommodation is heated and ventilated, and is so arranged that a proper temperature can be maintained. Electricity is largely brought to bear in ventilating the Saloons, Corridors, Sleeping Cabins, etc., by means of a large number of electric fans. The large pantries are fitted with steam carving tables.

The store rooms are commodious, particularly the Cold Rooms where there can easily be stored 60,000 lbs of fresh meat, 6,000 head of poultry and game, 10,000 lbs of fresh and dried fish, and innumerable other items such as fresh butter, bacon, ham, cheese, fruits, vegetables, salads, etc. . . .

A commodious and well-equipped Hairdressing Saloon, with electric rotary hair brushing machine, shampooing apparatus, etc., a Printing Room, Hospital, Dispensary, Mail and Specie Rooms are arranged in various parts of the ship . . .

During the latter stages of the Anglo-Boer War, shipowners had begun to plan for an anticipated expansion of the Britain-South Africa trade. Representatives of Union-Castle, the Clan Line, Bucknall Line and Harrison Line had reached agreement on a wide-ranging freight policy for operations between Britain and South and East Africa. In essence, the agreement gave Union-Castle carte blanche for the carriage of freight between Southampton and London on the one hand and South African and Mozambique ports on the other, while the other lines would use Liverpool and Glasgow as their British ports. A clause was also introduced granting Union-Castle the right to charge higher freight rates on cargo carried by the mailships. This agreement had been reached because the mail contract stipulated a maximum voyage duration and demanded punctuality; the mailships could therefore offer the fastest shipment of cargo and virtually guarantee a specific delivery date – an advantage that the company was keen to advertise at every possible opportunity.

A Union-Castle brochure, published in about 1903, contained the following honey-toned sales pitch:

> The voyage to South Africa has long been known as one of the most agreeable that a pleasure seeker or invalid can make, and the increase in traffic during the last decade has enabled the Company to establish a fleet of vessels equal to those of any other line in existence . . .
>
> Very rough weather is seldom experienced on the Cape route, and is more likely to be met with in our home waters than elsewhere. As a rule, even the dreaded Bay of Biscay is smooth. However dangerous a westerly gale may be to a sailing vessel caught on a lee shore, the storm must indeed be high if a modern mailboat cannot put her nose to the wind and force her way, steadily and quickly, to the outside of the cyclone. The vast expanse of ocean lying between the Bay and South Africa is remarkably calm, and the storms which sometimes convulse the North Atlantic, are almost unknown in these milder latitudes.

Unfortunately, when the boom period that was expected to follow the end of hostilities in South Africa did not materialize, there was a drop in the demand for both cargo space and passenger berths. In 1904, to counteract the effects of the recession that occurred on the Britain-South Africa trade, the nine major participatory freighter operators – Union-Castle, the Clan Line, Bucknall Steamers, Bullard King, John T. Rennie, the Ellerman-Harrison Line, Houston's, the South African Line and the International Line – held discussions that culminated in the South and East African Cargo Contract Agreement, a modification of the agreement concluded in 1902. Although it was agreed that £12 000 per annum would be paid to two other shipping operators not to load homeward (some called this a bribe to avoid additional competition), the agreement, like its predecessor, favoured the mailship company, which continued to be the dominant participant in the trade, not only in terms of the amount of cargo it carried, but also in terms of the substantial influence it enjoyed in official circles, mainly because of the mail contract. This dominance, however, was soon to be weakened by the loss of its two central pillars.

Sir Francis Evans, the former chairman of the Union Line and managing director of Union-Castle, died in January 1907. Apart from having helped pave the way for the amalgamation of the Union and Castle lines, and in the process gained for Union Line shareholders a substantially better deal than Sir Donald Currie had proposed, Sir Francis had contributed a wealth of experience that had proved crucial to the success of the new company in the early and difficult years of combined operations. It is thought that Currie's flamboyance possibly obscured the substantial and vital role Sir Francis Evans played in those few years of partnership prior to his death.

On 13 April 1909, at the age of eighty-three, the main force behind the company also passed away. Sir Donald had worked almost to the last, but as failing health had meant

The Briton *in Union-Castle colours.*

1

2

3

4

fewer days spent in the office, his family persuaded him to reside in semi-retirement at Sidmouth in Devon, the place of his death. There is no doubt that the passing of these two men within so short a period stemmed the continued prosperity of the company.

Currie's son-in-law, Frederick Mirrielees, took over as chairman, but without the powerful influence of the charismatic Sir Donald who, respected by Boer and Briton alike, had enjoyed the ear of government both in South Africa and Britain, Union-Castle faltered. There followed one of the darkest periods in the company's history, a situation aggravated by the recession in the South African trade.

Only after 1908, when the South African mining and industrial sectors began to expand once more, bringing about a healthier economy, did competitive bustle return to the shipping services, particularly on the Britain-South Africa trade. Another encouraging factor for the shipping industry was the advent of Union, in whose wake it was predicted the country's enormous potential for economic expansion would be realized.

In anticipation of an immigration boom for South Africa, Union-Castle either sold or scrapped several obsolete vessels to make way in 1910 for another pair of mailships – the *Balmoral Castle* and *Edinburgh Castle* – slightly larger than the earlier pair, but still based on the *Norman* prototype. Like the previous pair of sister ships, one of the new vessels – the *Edinburgh Castle* – came from Belfast and the other from the Fairfields shipyard.

Towards the end of 1911, there was much speculation that Sir William Pirrie, chairman of Harland & Wolff, and Sir Owen Philipps, chairman of Royal Mail and King Lines, were to open negotiations for the acquisition of Union-Castle, which at that stage was continuing to experience financial difficulty – a hangover from both the recession in the pre-unified South Africa and the deaths of Currie and Evans. Among the Union-Castle directors was Gustav Wolff, Pirrie's partner in Harland & Wolff, and, one suspects, an informant for Pirrie regarding the affairs of Union-Castle. Earlier speculation concerning the acquisition of Union-Castle proved correct, for through their involvement in the Elder Dempster Line, Pirrie and Philipps made a virtual take-over offer to the Union-Castle board who, in April 1912, accepted, and almost immediately installed, Philipps as its chairman. With this take-over, and taking into account their existing shipping interests, the two men now controlled forty-four ships, effectively the largest British fleet at the time. In addition, the link with Harland & Wolff meant that most new orders from all companies within the group went to the Belfast shipyard, while the repair yards of

1 *The* Edinburgh Castle *prior to her launch on 27 January 1910 at Belfast.*
2 *At the behest of Mrs John Currie, wife of Sir Donald's nephew who was a partner in Donald Currie & Company, the champagne bottle breaks on the bow of the* Edinburgh Castle *on 27 January 1910.*
3 *Harland & Wolff designers ensured that the early twentieth-century mailships had splendid interior décor. The two-funnelled* Edinburgh Castle *was no exception, as confirmed by this photograph of the dome and well above the first class saloon and lounge.*
4 *Lighters being towed from the side of the* Balmoral Castle *in the anchorage off Port Elizabeth.*

1

A FIRST CLASS VOYAGE

Extracts from letters written by Martin Leendertz to his parents while he was on board RMS Briton*:*

6 OCTOBER 1912

. . . We left Table Bay about 5.30 p.m. on the Wednesday and had to wait for a bag of late mails which was conveyed to us by a motor launch. We rolled a little while waiting off the breakwater, and I saw the last of you, although I have an idea that Freddy waited on the promenade to see the Briton go out. I felt quite well on leaving Table Bay, and as dinner was announced before passing Robben Island, I went down and had an excellent meal – not too much but just a pick of the many good things offered . . . The ship's band of six – piano, cello, cornet, clarinet and 2 violins – almost the same composition as at Wolfram's – played music on the promenade deck. I slept well but during the night, the waves became bigger, and she rolled more. I thought I would be alright in the morning, but should not have got up. I did, and got sick, and then lay down on the sofa for the rest of the day, reading or sleeping. That was the only time I had to succumb . . .

On Monday . . . there was a boat drill in the morning when all the covers had to be taken off the 16 lifeboats on the boat deck – there are also 4 aft, making 20 in all – as many as the ill-fated Titanic, four times the Briton's size . . .

One [could] feel one was getting near the Equator, as it was boiling hot on the boat deck which is not shaded, but on the promenade deck it is cool enough. In the evening there was a dance, for which all the ladies participating 'dressed' in the usual manner . . .

On Tuesday, we got ocular evidence of approaching the tropics as every one connected with the ship – officers, engineers, stewards and bandsmen – appeared in white uniforms, but although the weather is warm, the change is not great. The passengers are getting into flannels too, now.

We get ices at lunch, and the food up to the present, has been splendid – an excellent variety, excellently cooked . . .

The Briton beats the old Mexican for steadiness [the Leendertz family had immigrated to South Africa on the Mexican*], the mileage run, as posted up each day at noon, having been: 289, 379, 383, 384, 386, 386, 389, 369, 378, 364 miles. The first day was not a full day, and the others are increasing because as the coal gets consumed, the ship is somewhat higher out of the water and therefore, easier to propel. Why there was the drop from 389 to 369 I do not know, unless it is the effect of a current from the north – it was when we were approaching the coast near Liberia . . .*

On Thursday morning we passed a German cargo boat close and soon afterwards a sailing ship, for which we turned back to read her signals. She stated that she had had her second officer killed through an explosion. We have of course passed the mail boats going the other way, but at early hours when most were asleep . . . We are again getting into a cooler zone and the staff have their black uniforms on again . . .

We were in wireless communication with Slangkop until our first Saturday morning at sea, and then we were cut off from the rest of the world, until approaching the coast of Africa again, when we got into touch, first of all with the Monrovian wireless station; a day after with that at Dakar, and then with that at Las Palmas, so that there are more such stations than I knew of, but they do not seem to be so powerful as the two in S.A. We also communicated with the Saxon and the South American 15,000-ton new mail steamer Arlanza.

14/10: . . . We have a well-stocked library in the first class, of which the second class are allowed to have the run from 10.30 to 11 a.m. in order to select a volume. I have not made much use of it until a few days ago as there were a number of papers and magazines lying about in the smoking room, which is our lounge, reading and refreshment room combined, as the Briton, being an older boat, is not so well provided as the latest mail boats which have a separate smoking room, ladies' room and library in the second class, but I cannot complain about the Briton as she has proved very comfortable and has a roomy deck.

The passengers fraternised pretty quickly and are now like a big family party. Most have formed card groups and play bridge almost all day and night in calm weather on the deck.

We had a concert in the first class saloon, but as most dressed for it, I did not want to go, but heard all I wanted to from the alley way through the open windows . . .

The other afternoon, there were games and sports on deck which caused much amusement, although I do not go in for that sort of thing, and prefer a quiet holiday in every sense . . .

We get fruit at every meal, of which I always help myself. We had some splendid apples, also bananas, oranges and lemons, and we get nuts at dinner, fine cake and in fact anything one can desire in the way of food. There is no meal after 6 p.m., but at 10 we can get biscuits and cheese which is sufficient . . .

A second letter was written after departure from Madeira and dated 17 October 1912.

. . . We arrived at Madeira at 6.45 in the morning [Tuesday] – the most delightful incident in my trip so far . . . At daybreak I heard the engines still pounding as usual – I generally awake at 5.30 owing to the decks being washed and I get the first light of day through the porthole, being on the starboard side. A little later they slowed down and then for the first time in 13 days stopped, quite a pleasant sensation because my cabin is right above them . . . It was 6.30 and I looked through the porthole. We were just slowly passing the Russian 4-funnelled battleship Rossia and a couple of boats with diving boys in them. I dressed about half an hour later, and on the other side of the ship lay Funchal in all its beauty with the sun just rising. It was a scene I shall not soon forget.

Soon afterwards, passengers started leaving for the shore . . . There was a busy scene aboard – the promenade deck was littered with Madeira chairs and the usual goods – lace, baskets, fruit, photos, jewellery, coral, etc – all of which had to be hoisted up by their swarthy proprietors out of their own small boats by ropes and then let down again after a couple of hours . . .

After 10 o'clock, all the litter had been removed from the deck and the diving boys and men came offshore again and made a hideous row shouting for tickeys. At 10.20 we were off, more was the pity and soon headed for the open sea. I always thought there was one island there, but there are several, and up till 2.30 we were passing them, the last being extremely rocky and precipitous, with a lighthouse high up . . .

Friday Oct. 18. . . . We are now, of course, in the English Channel, and taking it easy. We could easily get to Southampton this evening, but are not due until early on Saturday morning, so we are not going full speed. An engineer told me that if the Briton were pressed, she could knock two days off the 16⅓ days, so you see we are not being hustled, which also explains why there is a drop in our daily mileage.. He said that many old travellers preferred the Briton, Saxon and Norman to the newer boats because they are so well constructed and money has been spent on their engines and hull more than on ornamentation and fine passenger apartments like in the later boats. . .

This morning, the mails were got out of the mail room and stacked on the first-class promenade deck so as to be ready for tomorrow.

Saturday October 19. 7.30 a.m.. We arrived at Southampton about one o'clock this morning . . . I woke up during the night and thought the moon was shining, but when I got up, I saw it was one of the arc lamps of the docks; that we were safely moored and they were actually already starting to unload cargo. Time 3.30 a.m. They have hydraulic cranes, so that there was no clatter, but still there was so much walking overhead that further sound sleep [was] impossible and I got up at 6.30 . . .

This morning, the weather is glorious, even if the breeze is nippy, but the sun is just up. I am quite pleased with Southampton docks as there are 5 or 6 big liners nearby and plenty to see. Of course, I cannot say anything about the town as I have not seen it yet, and I want to post this letter early because the outgoing mail leaves this afternoon . . .

There is a great deal of bustle on board as nearly all the passengers are going on to London by the 8 o'clock boat train.

2

3

Harland & Wolff reaped considerable benefits from this large pool of ships, particularly as the repair facilities that Union-Castle had developed at Southampton were transferred to the control of Harland & Wolff.

In the recently unified South Africa there was agitation for the mail contract to have more local flavour. It was felt in some quarters that the attitude of Union-Castle officials towards South African Government officials and merchants had been too aggressive, in response to which there were suggestions – supported by such influential personalities as General Louis Botha and the minister of transport, H. C. Hull – that the South African Government should establish and operate its own mailship company; others suggested that, to make the mail contract really competitive, overtures should be made to operators other than Union-Castle. The efficient Deutsche Ost-Afrika Linien which had begun to call at Southampton en route to South Africa was regarded as a particularly suitable candidate for the mail contract, although it would have to provide larger and faster ships.

The Fenchurch Street head office of Union-Castle believed it unlikely that the contract would be awarded to others; nonetheless, the new management reacted swiftly to the groundswell of opinion in South Africa and, as one observer phrased it: 'There is now an opportunity which may never occur again of putting matters on a really firm and friendly footing, and this should not be lost.'

Learning from the style of Sir Donald Currie, Philipps immediately contacted the South African Government to negotiate a new mail contract and in May 1912 he travelled to South Africa to meet officials from various governmental as well as private institutions. His wide-ranging discussions confirmed the need to make positive overtures to the recently formed government which, as a gesture of goodwill to the South African farming community, still suffering from the aftermath of the Anglo-Boer War, was anxious to encourage and improve agriculture. Philipps therefore struck the right chords when he proposed that amendments to the mail contract should provide for the carriage of pedigree livestock from Europe or Britain to South Africa, free of freight charges. Other provisions included reduced rates for South African agricultural exports such as maize, wool, skins and forest products. To boost the burgeoning fruit industry, Philipps proposed favourable freight rates and agreed to build bigger and faster ships with enlarged refrigeration capacities.

Such proposals were received with great enthusiasm by the South African Government which, in the absence of any other serious contender for the mail contract, awarded it to Union-Castle for a further ten years.

Although two intermediate liners, the *Llandovery Castle* and *Llanstephan Castle*, were completed in 1914, the travelling public and the South African Government would have to wait until 1921 before larger and faster ships entered the mail service.

---

1 *Symbolic of the leisurely life at sea, and indeed of the pace of life in the early 1900s, the ship's orchestra provided music for all occasions: background music for dinner in the first class saloon, evening entertainment or music for dances and, until piped music became available in later years, they were also on hand to play the mailship away from the quay in grand style.*

2 *It was intended that His Royal Highness Prince George, Prince of Wales, should open the first session of parliament in the Union of South Africa in October 1910, but owing to the death of King Edward VII in April of that year the prince's place was taken by the Duke of Connaught, brother of the late king. Union-Castle's latest mailship, the* Balmoral Castle, *had been made available to convey the royal party to Cape Town, and to that end the liner was already in Portsmouth where naval artisans had made appropriate alterations to her accommodation. In keeping with her royal yacht status, her hull was painted white and her funnels yellow.*

On 11 October 1910, with the Duke and Duchess of Connaught and their daughter Princess Patricia aboard, the Balmoral Castle *steamed slowly out of Portsmouth harbour. She was manned almost entirely by Royal Naval personnel, although some of her officers and crew had been retained. This photograph shows her in Cape Town. At the masthead is the Royal Standard of the Duke, on the jackstaff the Union Jack, and on the mainmast, the white ensign. She also displays a yard specially rigged on the foremast in Portsmouth to enable proper naval signalling procedures. On the fo'c'sle, are men in Royal Naval uniform, while a signalman using semaphore can be seen forward of the mast.*

Having delivered the royal party safely back to England, the Balmoral Castle *took her normal schedule on the mail service early in 1911.*

3 *The writing room and library on the* Balmoral Castle.

1

2

PHILIP BROTHERS

ARE RECEIVING

EX "WALMER CASTLE,"

LARGE ADDITIONS TO THEIR

SUMMER GOODS.

AMONGST OTHERS A GREAT VARIETY OF

DOLLY VARDEN and other Fashionable STRAW HATS
Newest Designs in FRENCH MUSLINS
SILK DRESSES, latest Designs
LUSTRES and other Dress Materials
BLACK LACE SHAWLS
LACE COLLARS and SETS
Dress Trimmings and Ribbon Velvets.

No. 6, ADDERLEY-STREET,

Opposite the Railway Station.

3

4

5

During World War I, several mailships were commandeered for special duties throughout the war, and although the others continued the mail service, augmented by the drafting of some intermediate vessels to fill the vacuum left by the absence of most of the mailships, severe dislocation of the regular service was unavoidable.

To counter the threat of war in Europe, British and Allied forces were gathered from many parts of the world. To convey the troops and their equipment from South Africa to Europe, six Union-Castle ships – the mailships *Balmoral Castle*, *Kenilworth Castle* and *Briton*, and the intermediates *Dunluce Castle*, *Goorkha* and *Guildford Castle* – were being refitted in South African harbours. Late in August 1914, they were all in Table Bay harbour to embark more than 5 000 officers and men of the Imperial Garrison for transport to France, via Southampton. Three hundred and seventy-six women and children, the families of the soldiers, were also among the passengers. On 27 August, under escort of HMS *Hyacinth* and HMS *Astrea*, the convoy left Cape Town. A contemporary painting shows HMS *Hyacinth* leading a column of three vessels; to port steamed the other three liners and HMS *Astrea*, which returned to Cape Town when its escort duties were taken over at St Helena Island by HMS *Leviathan*.

Having arrived in Britain during the latter half of July with several distinguished passengers aboard, including Viscount Gladstone, the first governor-general of South Africa,

1 *The* Walmer Castle *arriving in Cape Town.*

2 *Until World War II, when the South African industrial sector began to find its feet, the retail trade relied overwhelmingly on British and European sources for its wares. Emphasis was placed on the recent arrival of goods aboard a mailship, implying the modernity of goods offered for sale. This newspaper advertisement appeared in 1901.*

3 *Officers versus the passengers at cricket. The rules were adapted to the conditions.*

4 *The* Kinfauns Castle *at East Pier, Cape Town, after the war. (When delivered in 1899, she was the first Castle liner to have twin screws.)*

5 *The black-painted* Kenilworth Castle *steams slowly up the Thames in February 1917. Her lifeboats are lowered in anticipation of a submarine attack.*

1

2

the *Armadale Castle*, which was loading for South Africa in Southampton, was taken over by the Admiralty two days before war was declared. Immediately there began a rapid conversion job to turn the Cape mailship into an auxiliary cruiser.

Within a week, the first class cabins on the upper deck and all public rooms had been gutted. Most of the third class accommodation was to be set aside for naval ratings, while the rest of that part of the ship would become shell magazines. Extra steel plates provided protection for the engine room, where steel wire mesh was fitted to the deckhead to prevent steel splinters from fouling the engines. The deck had to be strengthened for the installation of eight 4,7-inch guns, two on the fo'c'sle, two on the poopdeck and four in the well-decks. Any obstruction to the operation of the guns had to be removed; therefore many metres of railings, several ventilators and some rigging were cleared. Canvas-covered mattresses provided a measure of protection for those on the bridge. Magazines and ammunition lifts were installed in the holds, and surplus equipment was left in warehouses in the Southampton dockyard. On 11 August 1914, HMAMC *Armadale Castle* left Southampton for Simon's Town, whence she would operate in the campaign to capture South West Africa (now Namibia) from the Germans who had colonized the territory in the late nineteenth century.

Her first assignment was to bombard the wireless station at Swakopmund, just to the north of Walvis Bay. On 2 October, she landed units of the Kimberley Rifles and of the Kaffrarian Rifles at the small desert port of Lüderitzbucht (Lüderitz) where, because of the shallow draught restrictions, she lay well offshore while the troops were ferried ashore by a fleet of coasters and other smaller craft. Another assignment took her to Cape Cross, north of Swakopmund, to annihilate the wireless station. One of the shells from her 4,7-inch guns hit a petrol dump. From her, General Louis Botha, the erstwhile Boer hero and more latterly the first prime minister of South Africa, landed at Walvis Bay in February 1915 and after the surrender of the German forces, Governor-General Buxton travelled in her from Cape Town to Walvis Bay and thence to Windhoek to receive the defeated German commanders.

Once the South West African campaign had been completed, the *Armadale Castle* moved to the Indian Ocean in support of the capture of German East Africa (now Tanzania). A special assignment – the carriage of £7 million of gold to Canada – preceded engagements in the North Atlantic patrol and thereafter she performed escort duties for convoys moving between West and southern Africa.

Another mailship used in the South West African campaign was the three-masted *Kinfauns Castle*, which had been commandeered by the Admiralty immediately the war had broken out. With the same armaments as the *Armadale Castle*, the *Kinfauns Castle* was sent to Port Nolloth on the west coast of South Africa to cover the landing of troops there for the invasion of South West Africa.

To assist in the hunt for the German cruiser *Königsberg*, known to be somewhere along the East African coast, HMAMC *Kinfauns Castle* was fitted with a seaplane and despatched to the area around the mouth of the Rufidji River in present-day Tanzania. The German cruiser was spotted by the pilot of the plane, a sighting which led to the destruction of the warship.

Laid up at Netley, the *Norman* was hurriedly pressed back into service to assist in the landing of troops in France as part of the initial wave of Allied response to the threat in Europe. She continued for much of the war on the mail service but was refitted for service as a troopship for the last twelve months of the war.

The *Saxon* was the last mailship to leave Cape Town before the outbreak of World War I. Among her passengers was the German consul-general from Cape Town, Baron von Humboldt. A tricky diplomatic wrangle ensued as the authorities pondered the course of action to be taken against the representative of a hostile country. Finally, it was decided that the baron should be landed on the Isle of Wight and detained in the Sandown Hotel.

The *Saxon*, the *Balmoral Castle* and the *Walmer Castle* continued the mail service for much of the war before being used for trooping; a similar wartime career befell the *Briton*, which also spent a short period on the mail service in 1915 before trooping, which took her to the Mediterranean, East and West Africa, the West Indies and New Zealand. On the voyage to New Zealand, she became the first Union-Castle liner to pass through the Panama Canal.

Sailing on the last scheduled voyage in the mail service, the *Edinburgh Castle* was ordered to divert to Gibraltar to embark troops for conveyance to Britain. Carrying more people than permitted, the *Edinburgh Castle* left Gibraltar under escort of HMS *Minerva*

3

4

1 *During the initial stages of World War I, Union-Castle ships, like most British merchantmen, were painted grey. Later, when the threat of action by raiders seemed to abate, the familiar Union-Castle colours again appeared. The presence of the German raider* Möwe *in the South Atlantic early in 1916 forced ships' crews to reach for the brushes to paint the hulls and funnels black. By the end of 1916, most ships had been camouflaged with 'dazzle-paint', as shown here on the* Kildonan Castle *in Portsmouth.*

2 *It was the custom every voyage for Union-Castle to distribute a passenger list to those people travelling on a ship. It was also customary for the South African press to publish the names of passengers who had just arrived on a mailship or who were about to sail for England.*

3 *While operating as a substitute mailship, the* Galway Castle *ran aground on Orient Beach, East London, on 12 October 1917. Efforts by tugs and other craft at subsequent high tides met with success and she was refloated some days later.*

4 *HMAMC* Edinburgh Castle *seen intercepting a merchantman on 19 May 1916.*

1

which, during the passage to Southampton, captured and sank the Austrian steamer *Bathori*, whose crew was transferred to the mailship. Barely two weeks after arrival in Britain, the *Edinburgh Castle*, refitted as an auxiliary cruiser, left for patrol and escort duties in the South Atlantic. During the latter stages of the war, she carried troops across the North Atlantic.

The closest any of the mailships came to disaster during the war was an unfortunate and freak accident involving the *Kenilworth Castle* while homeward bound from South Africa in June 1918. Escorting a small convoy that included the two-funnelled mailship, were the cruiser HMS *Kent* and the destroyer HMS *Rival*. When the cruiser turned to leave the convoy to head for Plymouth, she found herself on a collision course with the *Kenilworth Castle* which, in order to avert disaster, immediately altered course, only to collide heavily with the stern of the destroyer. Depth-charges on HMS *Rival* exploded, ripping a huge hole in the bow of the Union-Castle vessel which began settling by the head. Confusion reigned on the liner as it was thought that she had been torpedoed. Several lifeboats were lowered and two were swamped, precipitating their passengers into the cold waters of the English Channel. Fifteen people were drowned. Down by the head, the *Kenilworth Castle* made Plymouth where extensive repairs were carried out before the ship could return to service.

Of the *Kildonan Castle*, which initially had been a hospital ship and thereafter refitted as an auxiliary cruiser, Marischal Murray wrote in his *Ships and South Africa*:

> While the *Kildonan Castle* was in Glasgow in January 1917, rumours went round that she was shortly to be employed in work of a highly important nature. No one knew what was in the wind, but arrangements were made for the accommodation of a number of passengers . . . and a special staff of stewards arrived from the Union-Castle Company under Chief Steward Matthews.
>
> Putting to sea under sealed orders on January 17 1917, the *Kildonan Castle* eventually found herself at Oban, and in that remote harbour she embarked a body of men who were to undertake one of the gravest missions of the war . . . The passengers who now joined . . . formed the Allied Mission to Russia, which represented an eleventh-hour attempt to prevent the collapse of the great Empire . . .
>
> Provided with a powerful escort, the *Kildonan Castle* put out from Oban on January 20, and five days later, she arrived safely at Port Romanoff, Murmansk, the only ice-free port in North Russia at that time of the year . . . For a month, waiting the return [of the mission], the *Kildonan Castle* lay in Port Romanoff. The cold was intense – sometimes it was forty degrees below zero – and the ship was frozen fast and had to be broken out occasionally by ice-breakers . . . After a month, the Mission returned from Petrograd . . . [and] . . . the *Kildonan Castle* made her way home . . . [to] . . . anchor in Scapa Flow on March 2. There Admiral Sir David Beatty boarded her, and was locked up for some time with members of the Mission. Shortly afterwards, all the members disembarked and the *Kildonan Castle* was once again put on the Northern Patrol. Within a few weeks, Russia was in the throes of Revolution.

There were several other interesting assignments in store for the *Kildonan Castle*, including another trip to northern Russia and one much later (in March 1920) to Vladivostok to repatriate 1 800 Yugoslavs who, through a series of unfortunate incidents, had found themselves in the extreme east of revolution-racked Russia.

Although all the mailships survived the war, which had seen the first offensive submarine operations in history, eight other Union-Castle ships (including the *Leasowe Castle*, which Union-Castle was managing for the British Government) had been lost in those offensives. In addition, one ship had been mined and a further six had been seriously damaged during the war, while 440 Union-Castle personnel, ashore and afloat, had lost their lives.

Because many of the mailships were engaged in postwar repatriation and thereafter underwent extensive refits before they could regain their prewar standard of accommodation, the mail service was only normalized in 1919 when the mail fleet consisted of the *Armadale Castle*, *Balmoral Castle*, *Briton*, *Edinburgh Castle*, *Kenilworth Castle*, *Kildonan Castle*, *Kinfauns Castle*, *Saxon* and *Walmer Castle*.

In the aftermath of the 'War to end all Wars', thousands of people sought pastures new and the mailships sailed with their full passenger complements. The dislocation of shipping services between South Africa and her overseas suppliers of both capital and consumer goods had forced the country's industrial sector to expand to provide many of the commodities that formerly were imported. The immediate postwar period saw a further upturn in industrial output, and the agricultural sector too was being stimulated by expanding export potential. It was not surprising, therefore, that ships on the South African trade were loaded to capacity. To augment the fleet for the anticipated postwar immigration boom to South Africa, the *Norman* and the *Carisbrooke Castle*, originally intended for lay-up, were drafted back into service. With the South African economy expanding and immigration proceeding at a remarkable pace, five other British operators, as well as Dutch and German lines, presented considerable competition for Union-Castle. The time was ripe for the mail company to take bold steps to ensure that it retained its dominance on the South African run.

2

4

Between the wars

1919-1939

3

All the ceremony of the punctual departure returned when the mail service was resumed shortly after the war. Sailing time from both Southampton and Cape Town was changed to 16:00 each Friday afternoon, a time that would become an institution for Cape Town until the mid-sixties, while the departure day from Southampton changed to Thursday in 1938.

How different were the farewells to those of scarcely a year before. Crowds gathered and bands played as the ships left on voyages that promised a happy, relaxed holiday atmosphere. 'Sail in Comfort' and 'It's Fun to Travel' were some of the slogans adopted by the Union-Castle advertisements in a campaign to attract passengers. However, the onset of the new era was slightly marred for Union-Castle by an embarrassing incident that occurred in 1919. General J.B.M. Hertzog, the South African opposition leader, and several supporters were to travel to Britain aboard the substitute mailship *Durham Castle* to hold talks with the British Government concerning South African independence. Incited by opponents of Hertzog, the crew refused to sail with him on board, and it was only after protracted negotiations that they finally agreed to continue the voyage. This incident had repercussions later when the official history of the role played by the Union-Castle Line in World War I was published.

Because the book did not sell as well as anticipated, the company decided to donate the remaining copies to schools. Unfortunately, Hertzog came to hear that the book contained a reference to the strike. The offending passage concerned the wartime exploits of a much-respected Union-Castle master,

1 *Fancy dress on board the* Armadale Castle, *circa 1904.*
2 *The* Windsor Castle *in rough weather.*
3 *Robertson Fyffe Gibb, chairman of Union-Castle from 1932 to 1939.*

1

2

3

4

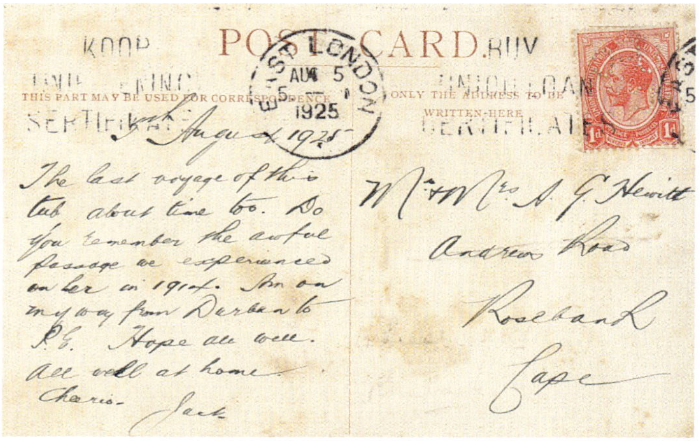

POST CARD.

THIS PART MAY BE USED FOR CORRESPONDENCE

ONLY THE ADDRESS TO BE WRITTEN HERE

EAST LONDON AU 5 1925

KOOP UNION-KING CERTIFICATES — BUY UNION LOAN CERTIFICATES

5th August 1925

The last voyage of this tub about time too. Do you remember the awful passage we experienced on her in 1914. Am on my way from Durban to P.E. Hope all well. All well at home. Cheerio – Jack

Mr & Mrs A. G. Hewitt
Andrews Road
Rosebank
Cape

5

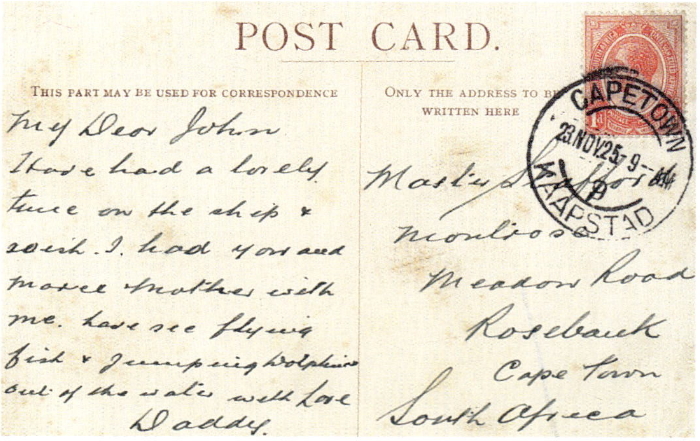

POST CARD.

THIS PART MAY BE USED FOR CORRESPONDENCE

ONLY THE ADDRESS TO BE WRITTEN HERE

CAPETOWN 23 NOV 25 KAAPSTAD

My Dear John
Have had a lovely time on the ship & sick. I had yours and more another with me. have see flying fish & jumping dolphins out of the water with Love
Daddy.

Master [illegible]
Montrose
Meadow Road
Rosebank
Cape Town
South Africa

6

COMMODORE BETTS LOOKS BACK

These comments are attributed to Commodore Morton Betts, who addressed the Port Elizabeth Rotary Club in October 1935. (Commodore Betts first visited South Africa in June 1895. At the time of this speech he commanded the *Warwick Castle*, which had just distinguished itself as the first mailship to berth in Port Elizabeth harbour.)

After several voyages to Australia and visiting all the principal ports there, I was very disappointed with the ports out here. Cape Town seemed small, gloomy and out of date. Here – Algoa Bay – steamers and sailing ships were anchored in the open ocean with no protection from the elements and it was not safe to leave the ship for a few hours to visit the town. Then there was East London with its narrow and shallow entrance and a small rickety wharf on the east side of the river. This reminds me that I was then serving in the Greek *of 4,747 tons which with three others was built expressly for the purpose of crossing the Bar at East London. On the voyage out, a discussion arose in the smoking room one evening about the possibility of a ship of that size entering the port. The Chief Engineer assured the passengers that the ship had been specially built for the purpose and had rollers fitted to assist in crossing the bar . . . [When] we did get inside at East London . . . [we] had to remain there for five days as the Bar was impassable owing to bad weather.*

Durban again, was very disappointing, a shallow channel with a bar that was often impassable, and a miserable old wharf at which we had to use our own cargo gear – no cranes . . .

However, with all these disabilities, we used to handle a lot of cargo – our ships always came out with good cargoes, but went home with very little, and in fact I made several homeward voyages with empty holds in those days. Today . . . the position is reversed. I have not sailed with a full ship from home for many years, but [I] have gone home full to the hatch-coamings with the produce of South Africa . . .

I have often thought of the cargoes we used to bring out here: hundreds of baskets of eggs on deck from Madeira, eggs in long flat cases from Russia and Holland, shipped at Southampton and also carried on deck . . .

Another voyage we had some very big 14-ton cases of electrical plant for Johannesburg which had to be landed at East London . . . We had to discharge them with the ship's gear in the roadstead, with a tug astern to keep the ship head on to the swell . . . one day, [we] had to go to sea with one of these big cases lashed to the deck as the weather was bad, and had to wait several days for another chance to continue the discharge . . .

The importation of carnations built up a big industry in Natal. In the first place, they were shipped on deck all a-blowing and a-growing in cases about 8 feet by 2 feet 6 inches and 15 inches in depth, with special soil, and we watered them during the voyage . . .

There were all sorts of people coming out. Apart from the big men who made names for themselves as financiers or builders of big industries there were . . . men and women of all trades and professions . . . We used to carry a lot of Russian and Polish Jews in the steerage, a form of open berth accommodation for men. The fare was ten pounds from England to Cape Town . . .

I feel I have made history in Port Elizabeth by being in command of the first mailship to go alongside in the new dock . . .

7

8

Captain Dyer (who had been in command of the *Durham Castle* at the time of the dispute). It read: 'He [Captain Dyer] is still in command of a Union-Castle liner, the one, by the way, whose crew a short time ago refused to carry Hertzog and his delegates from the Cape to England.' So great was the offence taken by Hertzog that the South African Department of Education prohibited the distribution of the books to schools.

A subsequent Union-Castle memorandum indicated that the context of the passage implied that the author – and therefore Union-Castle, since it had sponsored the publication – had found the strike a patriotic and commendable gesture on the part of the crew, a perception which negated the apology offered to Hertzog at the time of the incident. The memorandum concluded with a most remarkable statement, showing the lengths to which the company was prepared to go to placate influential people in South Africa: 'In this respect, it would be best if the Company and its staff regard itself as a Government Department and the staff as Civil Servants.'

In the midst of World War I, Union-Castle had placed an order with Harland & Wolff for the construction of the largest ship of the time on the South African trade, though after keel-laying in 1915 four years were to elapse before the *Arundel Castle* went down the slipway of the Belfast shipyard. The following is an extract from the *Belfast Newsletter* of 13 September 1919:

GREAT LINER LAUNCHED AT QUEEN'S ISLAND

Palatial South African Mail Steamer

THE PERFECTION OF SHIPBUILDING

An interesting event took place at Belfast yesterday when Messrs Harland & Wolff Ltd., launched the splendid passenger steamer *Arundel Castle*, at present being constructed by them to the order of the Union-Castle Mail Steamship Company Ltd., London, for their South African mail and passenger trade. There was no formal ceremony in connection with the launch, but Lord and Lady Pirrie were present, and were deeply interested in the proceedings, while crowds of people gathered at the various vantage points on both sides of the river to watch the event. The *Arundel Castle* is the largest steamer which has been launched in Belfast since December 1914, when the *Belgenland* was built. The launch, which was most successful, only occupied a few

1 *The* Arundel Castle *was launched in September 1919 after four years on the stocks, a delay enforced by World War I.*

2 *The semi-enclosed wheelhouse of the* Arundel Castle.

3 *The* Arundel Castle *and the* Windsor Castle *were designed to carry the largest complement of passengers on any liner built for the South African mail service, though once completed, their passenger capacity was only 870. To provide for their safety, twelve lifeboats were positioned abaft the fourth funnel but the launching gear – an arrangement of giant davits – was cumbersome to operate and it is debatable whether the boats could have been launched in a crisis. They were replaced by more modern gear during the vessels' refits in the late thirties. Also shown in this photograph are the H-girder derricks, unique among Union-Castle ships to the two four-funnellers.*

4, 5 *Postcards typical of the thousands written on board the liners over the years and conveying the sentiments of passengers from all walks of life.*

6 *Early harbour development at East London. Note the narrow entrance, the sandbar on the left and also the 'rickety wharf' (here still under construction) to which Commodore Betts referred.*

7 *The first class reception room on the* Windsor Castle.

8 *A first class double cabin on the* Windsor Castle.

1

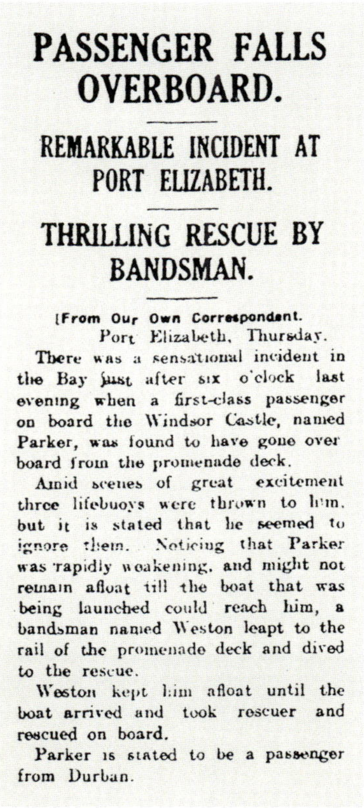

PASSENGER FALLS OVERBOARD.

REMARKABLE INCIDENT AT PORT ELIZABETH.

THRILLING RESCUE BY BANDSMAN.

(From Our Own Correspondent.
Port Elizabeth, Thursday.

There was a sensational incident in the Bay just after six o'clock last evening when a first-class passenger on board the Windsor Castle, named Parker, was found to have gone over board from the promenade deck.

Amid scenes of great excitement three lifebuoys were thrown to him, but it is stated that he seemed to ignore them. Noticing that Parker was rapidly weakening, and might not remain afloat till the boat that was being launched could reach him, a bandsman named Weston leapt to the rail of the promenade deck and dived to the rescue.

Weston kept him afloat until the boat arrived and took rescuer and rescued on board.

Parker is stated to be a passenger from Durban.

2

minutes. Punctually to the time arranged – 11.45 a.m. – the huge hull, on No. 3 slip, was set in motion, and moved majestically down the ways, taking the water gracefully. She was afloat in something under a minute, and a number of powerful tugs then took her in charge and brought her to her station alongside the fitting out wharf. It is interesting to note that shortly after the *Arundel Castle* left the slips the number of her successor was hoisted, thereby intimating that the building of another vessel is to be begun immediately.

HIGHEST PRODUCTION IN NAVAL ARCHITECTURE

The *Arundel Castle* is the embodiment of all the latest improvements in naval architecture and marine engineering, and marks a great advance on the previous vessels of this well-known line. Accommodation is provided for 273 first class, 224 second class, and 566 third class passengers – in all 1,063 passengers – and very careful thought and consideration has been given by the owners and builders to ensure that the passengers may have the utmost comfort and enjoyment on this favourite ocean route. The vessel and machinery are being constructed under Board of Trade Survey for passenger and safety certificates, also to the requirements of the British Emigration Survey and the Home Office. Its dimensions are 650 feet long by 71 feet beam, and the gross tonnage over 18,000 tons. The *Arundel Castle* will be a two-masted fore and aft

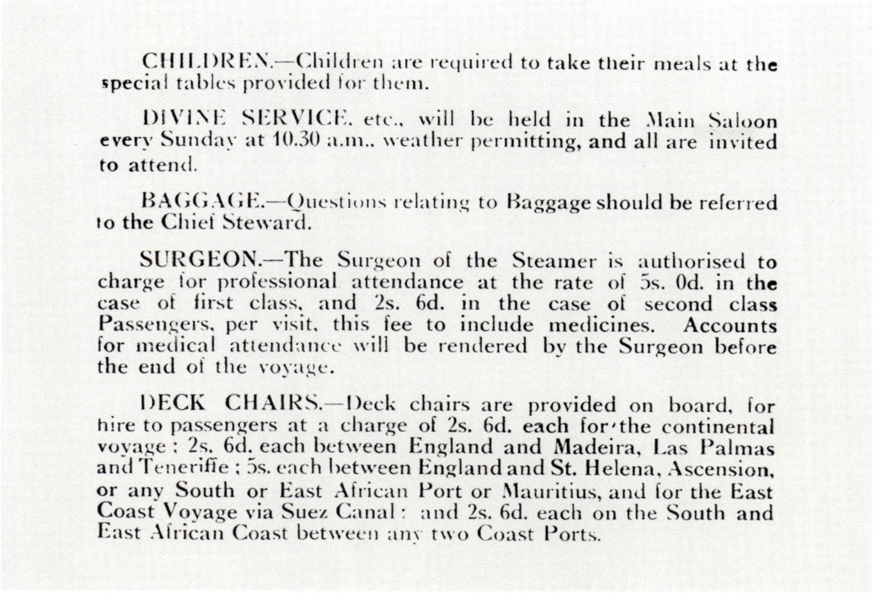

CHILDREN.—Children are required to take their meals at the special tables provided for them.

DIVINE SERVICE, etc., will be held in the Main Saloon every Sunday at 10.30 a.m., weather permitting, and all are invited to attend.

BAGGAGE.—Questions relating to Baggage should be referred to the Chief Steward.

SURGEON.—The Surgeon of the Steamer is authorised to charge for professional attendance at the rate of 5s. 0d. in the case of first class, and 2s. 6d. in the case of second class Passengers, per visit, this fee to include medicines. Accounts for medical attendance will be rendered by the Surgeon before the end of the voyage.

DECK CHAIRS.—Deck chairs are provided on board, for hire to passengers at a charge of 2s. 6d. each for the continental voyage; 2s. 6d. each between England and Madeira, Las Palmas and Tenerife; 5s. each between England and St. Helena, Ascension, or any South or East African Port or Mauritius, and for the East Coast Voyage via Suez Canal: and 2s. 6d. each on the South and East African Coast between any two Coast Ports.

3

4

schooner rigged, with a straight stem and a cruiser stern, a novelty which will distinguish her from the earlier vessels of the fleet. The hull is a very strong structure, with lower, middle, and upper decks, continuous all fore and aft, and orlop deck forward and aft of boiler spaces, with bridge and poop decks joined, topgallant forecastle, promenade and boat decks, and navigating bridge. She is sub-divided into twelve watertight compartments by eleven watertight bulkheads, and the double bottom extends right fore and aft.

PASSENGER ACCOMMODATION

The accommodation for passengers will be of the most sumptuous character in the first class, elegant and comfortable in the second class, while the third class accommodation will be spacious and popular. The first class dining saloon, reception-room, and children's saloon are situated amidships on the middle deck. The reading room on the boat deck will doubtless be a favourite resort of voyagers, and will have large vertical sliding windows. The lounge is at the fore end of the promenade deck, and the smokeroom is also on the promenade deck. A verandah will be arranged on this deck for open air assembly or conversation. There will also be a gymnasium on the promenade deck for seniors and a separate one for juniors, while a new feature will be the swimming bath, also situated on the promenade deck. The first class staterooms on the bridge deck are single berth and two berth cabins, with vertical sliding windows, beds or "cot" type enamelled white, separate folding lavatories, chests of drawers, and wardrobes for each passenger, together with mahogany furniture. The staterooms on the upper deck are arranged on the tandem principle, giving the maximum light and air and avoiding inside rooms. They are furnished with "cot" bed and pullman beds. The second class dining saloon is on the middle deck with second class children's saloon forward. The smokeroom and library are on the bridge deck. There is also a verandah on the promenade deck for second class passengers. The second class staterooms are situated on the upper and middle decks. As already indicated the third class passengers are very well provided for. There is a large general room on the poop deck, and immediately abaft this is the smokeroom. The dining saloon is on the upper deck. There will be a crew of about 400, the accommodation for whom will be arranged on the latest principle. The vessel has a large cargo and refrigerated capacity.

LATEST TYPE OF MACHINERY

The vessel is propelled by twin screws, which are driven by two sets of geared turbines, each set consisting of a high and low pressure turbine. The steam required for the machinery is generated at a pressure of 220 lbs per square inch in eleven large cylindrical boilers working with natural draught. All the auxiliary machinery is of the most up to date type, and is worked independently of the main engines. A very complete electrical installation will be fitted on board the *Arundel Castle*. There will be four turbo generators situated in the engine room and in addition to this a Diesel engine driving a 75 kilowatt dynamo is installed well above the water line for supplying light and power in case of emergency. The steering gear is of the builders' latest quadrant type, operated by two electric motors. It is controlled by electric telemotor from the wheelhouse and by hand gear from the docking bridge aft. The watertight doors will be electrically operated, and can be controlled by the captain from the bridge. The vessel will have a submarine signalling apparatus and wireless telegraphy.

LARGEST VESSEL OF THE YEAR

It will be seen from the foregoing that in this magnificent ship a great advance is being made in the size and type of South African liners, this being the first of similar vessels under construction for the Union-Castle Line . . . She is likely to be the largest vessel of the year . . . With her large and spacious accommodation and novel features . . . the *Arundel Castle* will worthily uphold the traditions of the line, and indicate to our South African colonists the determination of her owners to provide for their growing requirements and do everything in their power in the future, as in the past, to strengthen the links of commerce and mutual interest that bind together our great Empire, which they and we have so lately and successfully striven to maintain.

The new liner, the first four-funneller on the regular South African trade, brought crowds to watch her berth when she arrived in South African ports for the first time in 1921. Many who could not be at the docks at the time of her arrival found their way to the wharf during the course of the day to marvel at the great liner which, at 19 023 tons, was almost half as big again as the *Balmoral Castle*, the previous Union-Castle flagship. As she was almost the first new mailship for eleven years, the *Arundel Castle* was booked to capacity in both directions for several subsequent voyages as people rushed to experience the latest comforts in ocean travel.

A new wave of excitement again brought crowds to the docks the following year when her sister ship, the Clyde-built *Windsor Castle*, arrived on her maiden voyage in 1922. HRH The Prince of Wales had performed the launching ceremony on 9 March 1921, the first such occasion involving a merchant ship at which royalty had officiated since Prince Albert launched the *Great Britain* in 1843.

1 *The labours of the stokers produce clouds of smoke and steam as the* Arundel Castle *sets course for England.*
2 *An article thought to come from the* Cape Argus, *circa 1924.*
3 *An extract from the preamble to the passenger list for the maiden voyage of the* Windsor Castle *in 1922.*
4 *An early postcard of the* Arundel Castle.

1

THE ENGINE ROOM

Since the advent of steam propulsion, ships have required the services of the Engineering Branch, whose function it is to ensure that all machinery – and, most importantly, the engines – on the ship operate efficiently.

The last coal-burning passenger ship built for the Union-Castle Line was the intermediate *Llandaff Castle* in 1926 which, with the *Llanstephan Castle* and the *Llandovery Castle II*, were converted in 1939 to burn oil in their furnaces. The largest of the Union-Castle coal-burners, the *Arundel Castle* and *Windsor Castle*, had eleven boilers which consumed some 8 000 tons of coal during a round voyage to South Africa until their conversion to burn oil in 1937. Apart from a few obsolete ships that were used as depot or accommodation ships during World War II, the last fully operational coal-burning passenger liner belonging to the Union-Castle Line was the *Gloucester Castle* which, while a substitute liner on the mail service to South Africa, was sunk by gunfire from the commerce raider *Michel* in July 1942.

In the depths of the engine room on the coal-burners laboured the 'black gang', whose task it was to keep the ship operating efficiently. The engine room leading hand – colloquially known as the 'donkeyman' – is the equivalent of the bosun, and is a key man in the efficient operation of an engine room. Beneath him in the hierarchy are the greasers, or in the days of coal-fired boilers, the firemen. Stripped to the waist, smeared in coal-dust, ash and sweat, and, despite wearing protective gloves, with their hands seared by heat from the furnaces, the firemen would work in the hot, poorly ventilated and badly illuminated stokehold, shovelling coal from the bunkers into the furnaces. Because of the nature of their work and workstation, the firemen were mainly small, sinewy men, who came traditionally, though not exclusively, from Merseyside. As was the case of the Deck Branch, the firemen worked in watches.

At the lowest rung of the stokehold hierarchy were the 'bunker rats', youths who had the task of keeping the firemen supplied with coal from the dark bunker spaces. They would dump wheelbarrow loads of coal on to the steel deck adjacent to the furnace doors for the fireman to shovel into the furnace; if his 'rat' was tardy in bringing the coal, the fireman would rattle his shovel on the gratings, and yell for the coal.

Before a furnace door could be opened, a draught lever had to be pushed to prevent a searing flame from shooting across the stokehold. The fires had to be raked out evenly across the bottom of the furnace, and the new coal spread uniformly on top of the nearly white-hot coals. With the depth of coal limited to about ten centimetres, this operation required great skill. Since the furnace doors were only slightly wider that the shovels, any miscalculation could result not only in the spilling of coal, but also in an agonizing jar to the arms of the fireman.

Besides feeding the hungry furnaces with nearly 50 tons of coal per four-hour watch, the firemen would have to clean the furnaces. The slice-bar, a thin skewer-like implement, was thrust along each track of the grate, forcing out clinker and other impurities into the ash trap below the furnaces. At the end of each watch, the ash traps were hosed down and the waste was loaded into canvas bags to be hoisted to the deck for dumping overboard. In more sophisticated ships, this waste matter was emptied into a metal receptacle connected by piping to a vent in the ship's side. Water pressure through the vent then forced the waste outboard into the sea. The entire operation was known as 'shooting the ashes'.

Raking, firing and slicing went on continuously to maintain a good 'head of steam' (the steam pressure required for optimum operation of the ship), particularly when the safety of the ship could not be jeopardized through a lack of power at crucial times, such as when the ship was in busy sealanes or manoeuvring in harbour. Since the steam pressure had to be maintained in all conditions of the sea and weather, from the violent rolling in the Bay of Biscay or off the Cape in winter, to the stifling humidity of the tropics, one can appreciate the taxing nature of the work in the stokehold.

When marine engines evolved gradually to use oil or diesel, the lot of the firemen became easier. Although there is still considerable heat in a modern engine room, the work is much less arduous, and by the latter years of the mail service, great strides had been made in the automation of many aspects of marine propulsion, thus reducing the number of engine room hands required and limiting their work to greasing, cleaning and assisting the engineers with maintenance work.

2

3

4

RMMV CARNARVON CASTLE

In 1923, Union-Castle placed an order with Harland & Wolff for a turbine steamer, a modified version of the Arundel Castle. *Responding to the advantages of the economical operation and the increasing popularity of marine diesel-power, Union-Castle changed the specifications of the proposed vessel to become the first motorship not only for the mail service, but also on the regular South African trade. Her two massive eight-cylinder, double-acting four-stroke diesels – each providing 6 500 BHP for a service speed of 17 knots – generated intense heat and noise, causing considerable discomfort to her engineers. Her engine room was described by one prominent maritime expert as 'the repository for 1,500 tons of revolving scrap-iron'.*

Her profile – two squat funnels and a low superstructure, which was an aesthetic improvement on the profile of the Arundel Castle *– drew much favourable comment. The South African press was intrigued by the diesel engines, which consumed about 60 tons of fuel daily – a stark contrast to the heavy consumption of about 200 tons of coal that the steamers used each day. Her cargo capacity and the standard of passenger accommodation were similar to those of the* Arundel Castle. *The* Carnarvon Castle *could carry 310 passengers in first class, 275 in second class and 266 in third class, a few more than the four-funnellers. Overall, the* Carnarvon Castle *and her two later sisters represented a welcome change from the griminess of the coal-burners.*

1 *The delivery of the* Carnarvon Castle *caused great excitement in maritime circles, for she was the first motorship on the regular Cape service. Although the engine room was very different to her coal-fired predecessors, it was still a complex maze of pipes and machinery. This photograph of the manoeuvring platform was taken in August 1926. In later years, there were several modifications to her engines.*

2 *The* Carnarvon Castle *sliding down the ways at Belfast on 14 January 1926, after being named by Lady Suffield, the daughter of Lord Kylsant.*

3 *Fitting the second funnel on the* Carnarvon Castle.

4 *The* Carnarvon Castle *sailing after her first call in Durban. Her squat funnels represented a great change from the tall stacks of the steamers.*

1

THE LOWER DECK

The British Merchant Service distinguished clearly between the status of officers and that of ratings (also known as 'members of the lower deck'). Most Union-Castle officers were 'company men' who had moved up from cadet or junior engineer status. In the latter decades, many of the ratings were drawn from huge centralized seamen's 'pools' that had been established during World War II to enable men from ships that had been sunk – or others wishing to go to sea – to register for allocation to any ship as berths became available. Despite the allocation system, there were scores of old hands who had gone to sea in Union-Castle ships at a tender age and become wonderfully loyal company men, retiring perhaps forty years later, knowing no other line.

Shortly before a mailship's departure from Britain, each crew member would be signed on to the ship's 'articles' – the official contract between master and crew that governed the conditions of service for all on board. At the conclusion of the voyage, the duration of which was usually six weeks, the articles would be terminated.

In terms of a ship's articles, the master was ultimately responsible for the good discipline of the crew and had the authority to deal out punishment as laid down by the Merchant Shipping Act. Transgressors were usually fined a day's pay for minor offences, but a far more serious penalty for a misdemeanour was a negative entry in a seaman's discharge book at the time of the closure of the articles. The standard entry for good conduct and ability was 'VG' (Very Good); anything less (even 'G') would adversely affect the seaman's prospects for future employment.

In earlier days, fines could be imposed for a wide range of offences, as the following extract from the Articles of Agreement *dated 1874 shows:*

OFFENCE	FINE (DAYS' PAY)
1 Not being on board at the time fixed by the agreement	2
2 Not returning on board at the expiry of leave	1
3 Insolence or contemptuous language or behaviour towards the master or any Mate	1
4 Striking or assaulting any person on board or belonging to the ship	2
5 Quarrelling or provoking to quarrel	1
6 Swearing or using improper language	1
7 Bringing or having on board any spiritous liquor	3
8 Carrying a sheath-knife	1
9 Drunkenness – First offence : 2 days' half allowance of provisions	
Drunkenness – Second offence	2
10 Neglect on the part of the Officer of the watch to place a look-out correctly	2
11 Sleeping or gross negligence while on look-out	2
12 Not extinguishing lights at the times ordered	1
13 Smoking below	1
14 Neglecting to bring up, open out and air bedding when ordered	Half
15 [For the cook] Not having any meal ready at the appointed time	1
16 Not attending Divine Service on Sundays unless prevented by illness or duty of the ship	1
17 Interrupting Divine Service by indecorous conduct	1
18 Not being clean, shaved and washed on Sundays	1
19 Washing clothes on a Sunday	1
20 Secreting contraband goods on board with intent to smuggle	1 month
21 Destroying or defacing the copy of the Agreement which is made accessible to the crew	1
22 If any Officer is guilty of any act or default which is made subject of a fine, he shall be liable to a fine of twice the number of days' pay which would be exacted for a like act or default from a Seaman and such fine shall be paid and applied in the same manner as other fines.	

In time, the Articles of Agreement were modified, but despite the more recent unionization of seamen, strict control is still necessary to ensure the safety of the ship and all on board.

Accommodation was always very spartan for members of the lower deck, except the senior ratings, such as the bosun, the engine room leading hand and the more senior stewards who had their own cabins and mess. Watchkeeping quartermasters were berthed three to a cabin, while the seamen were accommodated seven to a cabin along the starboard side of the fo'c'sle. The engine room crew occupied similar quarters on the port side. Accommodation for the stewards, laundrymaids and other members of the catering department was scattered below decks fore and aft, depending on the function of the particular crew member.

In the fo'c'sle, facilities were crowded and largely communal, leaving little privacy for the crew, a factor that negatively influenced the number of men wishing to go to sea. This is in stark contrast to the luxurious accommodation with private facilities provided by present-day shipowners for even the lowliest of the lower deck.

To cater for the crew a special galley was provided in the fo'c'sle space, manned by a cook and two assistants. The men were waited on at table by deck boys, known universally as 'Peggies'. Generally the food was good.

One of the highlights of the voyage was the 'Sods Opera' – a variety show produced entirely by the lower deck, and only performed for them. Planning reached fever pitch during the evenings prior to the show, which received tumultuous acclaim from its audience. One man who must have done well on those occasions was the fifties singer, Tommy Steele, once a crew member on the liners.

Towards the end of the mail service days, ships had a pub for the crew where they could relax during their off-watch periods. Prior to this facility, crew members were permitted only one bottle of beer per day, and it is possible that the pubs were introduced with the twofold purpose of avoiding clandestine drinking and of being an added inducement to attract potential recruits during the drift away from sea-going careers in the sixties and seventies.

2, 3, 4

5

6

1 The ubiquitous soot from the funnels made cleaning the decks and canvas awnings a full-time occupation for day-watch men. Among the party in this photograph are two young deck boys, probably about fifteen years of age. (Circa 1903.)

2 Land in sight viewed from the Edinburgh Castle*, 1927.*

3 On board the Edinburgh Castle *at Madeira, 1927.*

4 Lifeboat drill, 1930.

5 The Winchester Castle*, fitted out and being moved on 1 September 1930 for a final paint before her sea trials.*

6 The Warwick Castle*, the third motorship for the mail service, seen here shortly after her launch.*

1 2

Numerous dignitaries travelled in the Union-Castle liners: the governors-general arrived in and left South Africa on the mailships, while notable among the South African officials who used the liners was the prime minister, General Jan Smuts, who in 1921, with members of his cabinet, travelled on the *Arundel Castle* on the northbound leg of her maiden voyage to attend the Imperial Conference in London. For their return journey, however, in August of that year, they boarded the less auspicious *Saxon*. Other notable passengers on that voyage were the former mining magnate and politician, Sir Lionel Phillips, and the French Duc d'Orléans. A fire broke out in the coal bunkers shortly after the liner had left Madeira. It soon gained considerable hold and cabins had to be evacuated and flooded to prevent the woodwork from catching fire. For two days, passengers and crew kept up a brave façade while the vessel, with smoke pouring from her sides as the lavender paint on the hull blistered and burnt, steamed at full speed for Freetown in Sierra Leone. Once the ship had berthed, the fire was brought under control, but the stranded passengers had to wait for the next southbound mailship, the *Kenilworth Castle*, to be diverted to Freetown before they could continue their journey. As for the *Saxon*, all her bunkers had to be cleared of burnt coal and replenished before she could sail for Cape Town, escorted by the *Armadale Castle*.

Lord Pirrie, chairman of Harland & Wolff, died in 1924. Against the wishes of Lady Pirrie, Owen Philipps (by then Lord Kylsant of Carmarthen) immediately took over as chairman of the shipyard which, by that stage, was controlled by the Royal Mail Group, comprising the Royal Mail Line, Union-Castle, Elder Dempster and Harland & Wolff.

The growing animosity between the chairman and Lady Pirrie over the management structure of Harland & Wolff was compounded by his discovery that Pirrie's estate was practically insolvent, as most of his investments had been in ailing shares, backed by several large loans. In addition, the shipyard had been benefiting artificially from the Trade Facilities Act, in terms of which shipowners could obtain government loans for building new vessels. Among other companies, Union-Castle had utilized the loan facilities to order the *Carnarvon Castle*, a fine replacement for the ageing *Kinfauns Castle* and *Kildonan Castle*. Orders had also been placed for four intermediate liners (*Llandovery Castle*, *Llandaff Castle*, *Llangibby Castle* and *Dunbar Castle*) and, for the mail service, two sister ships for the *Carnarvon Castle* (*Winchester Castle* and *Warwick Castle*).

The press became very excited at the arrival of the new ships in South Africa. The *Cape Times* of 10 November 1930 wrote: 'Today for the first time in the history of Table Bay, two 20,000-ton motor mail vessels will be seen in the docks at the same time . . . The magnificent new vessel, *Winchester Castle*, on her maiden voyage from Southampton, will dock shortly after 6 a.m., to be followed by the *Carnarvon Castle* from Coast ports.' (At that time, the outward-bound ship from England docked at daybreak on a Tuesday, while the down-coast mailship arrived from Port Elizabeth at about 11:00.)

Time would show that the extensive outlay of capital for the construction of so many ships for several of the companies within the Royal Mail Group was an error of judgement, for when the British Government repealed the Trade Facilities Act in 1928, shipowners withdrew orders. This left many shipyards, including Harland & Wolff, in severe

3
4

5
6

7
8

financial difficulties, aggravated by the looming depression. To try to rescue Harland & Wolff, Kylsant announced that the shipyard would invite public shares, and various balance sheets were issued that made the beleaguered company appear stronger than it was in reality. The injudiciously managed share issue and several other unsound investments, notably in the ailing White Star Line, led to the collapse of the Royal Mail Group. Kylsant was disgraced and for his part in the debacle received a short jail sentence.

Besides the financial turmoil at Harland & Wolff brought about by the collapse of the Kylsant empire, Union-Castle found itself with an enormous debt to repay for ships ordered since 1924 and with its reputation in serious jeopardy. Fortunately, within its executive were two men of exceptional ability and tenacity. One was Sir Robertson Gibb who, after some forty-nine years of loyal service since joining the Union Line in 1883, was elected chairman in 1932. The other was Vernon Thomson, who assumed the dual positions of deputy chairman and managing director and whose influence and energy contributed significantly to the successful resurrection of the company. The task was daunting, but steadily, through almost dictatorial management, Union-Castle regained its good public image as well as its financial independence.

That the Gibb-Thomson combination succeeded in revitalizing Union-Castle was astonishing, for competition on the South African trade was increasing. Both the Deutsche Ost-Afrika Linien and the Italian company, Lloyd Triestino, had built fast ships capable of overtaking the slower mailships, and the South African Government had already made a move to negotiate various contracts with the two lines. For a time – particularly when a thirteen-and-a-half-day schedule was being called for – it seemed that even the mail contract, due for renewal on 1 January 1937, could go to non-British ships.

In 1934, having assessed the situation, Union-Castle responded to the threat by announcing a two-pronged plan to modernize its passenger fleet. The oldest vessels would be replaced by three larger and faster mailships capable of 20 knots, while the five most recent mailships would be re-engined and their hulls redesigned to enable them to maintain the faster schedule.

At the same time, because Harland & Wolff was by far the largest employer in Northern Ireland, the Ulster Government needed to support the ailing shipyard to prevent widespread unemployment. Ulster therefore negotiated special financial arrangements

1 *A Union-Castle advertisement, 1926.*
2 *The* Armadale Castle *in Durban. In 1904, she had been the first Union-Castle mailship to cross the bar in the harbour.*
3 *Departure day in Durban, circa 1934.*
4 *The departure of the* Winchester Castle *from Durban, circa 1934.*
5 *The second class smoking room on board the* Winchester Castle*, circa 1931.*
6 *On board one of the four-funnellers, circa 1932.*
7 *The third class lounge on board the* Winchester Castle*, circa 1931.*
8 *Vans landed from the* Warwick Castle *in Port Elizabeth.*

1

2

3

4

with the Midland Bank to provide Harland & Wolff with the assistance necessary to tender successfully for the construction of six Union-Castle vessels:

* two mailships – the *Stirling Castle* and the *Athlone Castle* (a further ship, the *Capetown Castle*, would follow in due course);
* two refrigerated ships, the *Roslin Castle* and the *Rothesay Castle*, forerunners of a fleet of six fruitships; and
* two intermediate liners, the *Dunnottar Castle* and the *Dunvegan Castle*.

Despite the close co-operation between the two companies, Harland & Wolff was receiving no hand-outs from Union-Castle. Vernon Thomson scrutinized every detail of the contracts and plans for each ship before he would commit the company to the order.

The specifications for the first two new mailships included powerful ten-cylinder Burmeister-Wain engines which would push the ships along at 20 knots. But the newcomers represented advances in both style and operation. Whereas the *Carnarvon Castle* and her two sister ships had a straight stem, squared superstructure and two squat funnels, the new ships were to have the famous clipper-like Tobin bow, so called after the marine architect, T. C. Tobin, who had also been responsible for the dumpy profile of the three earlier ships and several vessels of other companies. There was to be a sleekly-slanted funnel and, just below the boat deck, a covered promenade deck that would extend from the rounded forward end of her superstructure to the stern, a feature that later proved greatly popular with passengers. The stern itself was also similar to that of the *Carnarvon Castle*.

5

THE WINCHESTER CASTLE RUNS AGROUND

On the night of 16 February 1936, a dense fog having settled over the English Channel, the Winchester Castle *was approaching Southampton at reduced speed.*

As they peered out into the gloom, the coastguards at Fortune's Well, near the Portland Lighthouse, were startled to see the lights of a liner close inshore. They rushed out of the coastguard station, flashing lights to alert the officers on board the liner, but to no avail. The Winchester Castle *shuddered to a halt as she grounded on the rocks.*

Several extracts from Lloyd's List and Shipping Gazette *continue the account:*

> *Feb. 17 – The owners of the motor vessel* Winchester Castle *have received the following messages from the Master: –*
>
> *Dated Feb. 16 – 10 15 p.m.: Ashore. Position unknown; no danger at present.*
>
> *Dated Feb. 16 – 11 5 p.m.: Ashore west of Portland. Waiting for tugs. No immediate danger. Suggest going into Portland when afloat. No. 1 6 ft. 6 in. No. 2 2 ft. 4 in. not gaining; other holds dry; anticipate ship safe when afloat.*
>
> *Dated Feb. 17 – 1 37 a.m.: 0 55 a.m. GMT. Ship afloat. Proceeding to Weymouth Bay to land passengers. Shall arrive 3 a.m. GMT.*
>
> *Dated Feb. 17 – 4 41 a.m.: Anchored Weymouth Bay 3 14 a.m. Awaiting tugs which you informed were on the way.*

The mailship resumed her passage to Southampton where she berthed that afternoon. On 19 February, the Lloyd's List *correspondent in Southampton reported:*

> *When the motor vessel* Winchester Castle *was docked in the Trafalgar Graving Dock here today, following the discharge of the bulk of her cargo, it was revealed that she suffered more damage than was at first anticipated as a result of grounding on rocks near Portland on Sunday night . . . Forefoot for about 20 to 25 feet has been bent and twisted to port and plates near keel on both port and starboard sides have been buckled and cracked for about 100 feet. Repairs which will be put in hand immediately, will be undertaken by Messrs Harland and Wolff. The scheduled sailing of the* Winchester Castle *for Cape Town on Feb. 28 will be impossible. Bales of wool and skins affected by seawater in No. 1 hold were discharged after vessel was dry-docked.*

The ship was indeed fortunate. Severe storms had swept in from the Atlantic only hours before the ship had grounded, but had not caused abnormal sea conditions in the Portland area.

At the subsequent inquiry, there were several acrimonious exchanges between the officers who had been on watch at the time of the stranding and counsel for the master, Captain W. Kerbey. The officers alleged that Captain Kerbey had frowned upon the use of modern navigational aids, a problem which had led to the stranding of the liner. Captain Kerbey had his master's ticket suspended.

Although the general configuration of public rooms was also similar to that in the *Carnarvon Castle*, the luxurious fittings of the new ships surpassed anything seen previously on the Cape run. The accommodation too had been improved, but nowhere was it more marked than in the large cabin class cabins – most of which had portholes. This represented a major upgrade from the rather austere facilities of former years in tourist class – a term abolished in the new liners.

A passenger complement of close to 300 in the very comfortable first class accommodation and 490 in cabin class was less than that of earlier ships; significantly greater than that of the *Carnarvon Castle* class, however, was the cargo capacity of just over 15 000 d.w.t. in the new ships. This also included substantially more space for refrigerated cargo, mainly for the rapidly expanding South African fruit export industry.

The first of the new liners down the slipways at Queens Island, Belfast, was the magnificent *Stirling Castle*, launched on 15 July 1935. She was soon joined by the almost identical *Athlone Castle*, launched on 28 November 1935 by Princess Alice of Athlone, whose husband, the Earl of Athlone, had been governor-general in South Africa from 1923 to 1931. Once commissioned, the *Athlone Castle* undertook a shake-down cruise from Belfast to Southampton. As was the custom, many guests and Union-Castle shore personnel were the guinea pigs for the catering department on this voyage, during which the Union-Castle vessel passed another liner also on a shake-down cruise – the *Queen Mary*. The chairmen of Union-Castle and Cunard, as well as the two masters, exchanged greetings as the two liners drew abeam.

The entry of the *Stirling Castle* and the *Athlone Castle* to the mail service introduced an era of faster and more elegant travel between Southampton and South Africa. It was therefore inevitable that, unable to keep to a faster mail schedule, and now obsolete, the *Armadale Castle* and the *Kenilworth Castle* were withdrawn and scrapped.

Any fears that the new mailships might still be too slow were quickly allayed in 1936 by the sensational voyage of the *Stirling Castle*. To much acclaim, she shattered the Southampton-Cape Town record set by the *Scot* in 1893. Under the headline 'Cape Town's Big Welcome', this is how the *Cape Times* of 4 September 1936 recorded the ship's arrival after the record-breaking passage:

> An enthusiastic welcome was given to the Union-Castle liner *Stirling Castle*, which docked today after accomplishing the voyage from Southampton to the Cape in 13 days 6 hours and 30 minutes, breaking the forty-three-year-old record held by the *Scot* by 1 day 12 hours 27 minutes, thus inaugurating the new fast mail service to the Cape . . .
>
> Sirens blew, flags dipped and bands played, while the air hummed with wireless messages of congratulations . . .
>
> The deep blare of the *Warwick Castle*'s foghorn, prolonged for several minutes, could be heard ten miles away . . .
>
> Of the many interesting people aboard the mailship, none caught the public fancy more than the Band of the Gordon Highlanders who are on their way to the Empire Exhibition. After being welcomed by Lieutenant-Colonel Hearne aboard the ship, the Band marched through the city to the admiration of a large crowd of cheering people . . .
>
> The early arrival of the mailship provided the post office with the job of handling in-coming and out-going mail on the same day . . .
>
> Even greater had been the enthusiasm in the midnight hours as the *Stirling Castle* raced at 19 knots towards her goal. A mile or two from the finishing line, she was met by a small squadron of whale catchers which set up a tremendous din with their high-pitched steam whistles. As the great liner rushed by, she swept across the imaginary line between Robben Island and Green Point lighthouses to end a remarkable voyage . . . The last half hour in the ship was one of intense excitement. In spite of the late hour and the inclement weather, most of the passengers remained on deck to see the finish. The rails were lined with hundreds of passengers, clad in greatcoats and muffled up because of the cold . . .

1 *Laying the keel plate of the record-breaking* Stirling Castle *on 1 May 1934.*
2 *The* Stirling Castle *after her launching.*
3 *The podium ready for the ceremony to launch the* Stirling Castle *on 15 August 1935.*
4 *A publicity poster of the kind that would have appeared on railway station billboards.*
5 *Regular maintenance of paintwork was essential to keep the liners looking fresh and clean. Here shoreside workers paint the stern of the* Athlone Castle.

1

2

Having arrived during the night, the ship anchored in Table Bay to berth at daybreak.

After the South African coastal passage, the *Stirling Castle* raced back to Southampton in a time of 13 days, 8 hours and 38 minutes, a record for the northbound trip. The remarkable vessel achieved yet another record on the following southbound voyage when she clipped an hour and ten minutes off her own record. Within a year, the record was shattered yet again. Not to be outdone by her younger consort, the *Carnarvon Castle* sped to the Cape in just over twelve and a half days.

In terms of the mail contract, effective from 1 January 1937 and with a duration of ten years, an accelerated schedule of thirteen and a half days was to be introduced towards the end of 1938. The *Stirling Castle* and the *Athlone Castle* had sufficient reserve power to keep to the schedule, but the two four-funnellers, as well as the *Carnarvon Castle*, *Winchester Castle* and *Warwick Castle* needed to be modernized and re-engined. A downturn in the South African trade in the latter half of the thirties allowed these five ships to be withdrawn from their regular service over a period of two years and to be upgraded at the Harland & Wolff yards in Belfast.

The *Arundel Castle* was the first to undergo major reconstruction. Her eleven coal-fired Scotch boilers were replaced with four oil-fired water-tube boilers and six modern steam turbines, enabling her to have a service speed of 19 knots. When she emerged from the yards, her profile represented a radical change: she now had two raked funnels instead of four and her straight stem had been altered to a clipper-like bow. Similar alterations were made to the *Windsor Castle.*

3

4

The original four-cycle engines of the three motorships were replaced with two-cycle machinery. To achieve a faster speed, the *Carnarvon Castle*'s bow needed to be altered, while the other two retained their straight stems.

Few alterations were made to the accommodation of any of the ships, a point raised by several critics of Union-Castle. Nevertheless, with the wisdom of hindsight, it was probably the correct decision, for within a few months of the last of the modernized vessels returning to service, all the mailships were requisitioned by the Admiralty, gutted of their luxury fittings, and sent to sea for wartime duties.

Harland & Wolff had been doing well out of Union-Castle. Since 1936, further

1 *The* Stirling Castle *leaving Cape Town's Victoria Basin, circa 1936.*
2 *The first class lounge on the* Athlone Castle.
3 *The last occasion on which the two four-funnellers were together before their major refits and their conversion to oil-fired engines. This photograph, taken in Cape Town on 8 December 1936, shows the* Windsor Castle *coaling at East Pier with the* Arundel Castle *outward for the South African coast. On her return to Cape Town from the coastal voyage on 21 December, the* Arundel Castle *became the first mailship to enter the Duncan Dock.*
4 *The* Arundel Castle *arriving for the last time as a four-funneller in Durban harbour, December 1936.*

1

2 3

4

orders had been placed for four intermediate vessels, a small cargo ship for the European feeder service and four refrigerated ships. Pride of place, though, went to the order placed in 1935 for another mailship – a larger, modified version of the two delivered in 1936.

A letter to the *Cape Times* written in January 1927 makes interesting reading. The main body of the letter advocated that Union-Castle advertisements should indicate the names of the masters of the ships so that prospective passengers could choose their ship according to their 'favourite Captain'. However, the concluding paragraph of the letter was almost prophetic:

> Finally, I think it would be a graceful recognition of the country that has poured so many millions of sovereigns into the coffers of the Union-Castle Company if they named their next mail boat the *Capetown Castle*. There is greater affinity between Cape Town and the Union-Castle Company than exists between them and, for instance, the villages of Carnarvon, Llandaff, Llandovery and Llanstephan. In this land, there is only one real castle, and no mailboat plying between England (not Wales) and the Union has received the name of our one and only South African stronghold.
> AN OLD VOYAGER, MOSSEL BAY.

Possibly recalling that letter of 1927, Union-Castle management took the unprecedented step of opting for a South African name for the new mailship. They chose *Capetown Castle*. She was followed by the intermediates *Durban Castle* (1938) and *Pretoria Castle* (1939). As might have been expected, the move was not well received in some quarters and engendered much public debate, antagonists arguing that traditional Union-Castle names came from British castles, not the 'forts of colonial Africa' as one person put it.

However, it was the *Capetown Castle*, duly named by the mayoress of Cape Town, Mrs J.D. Low, that moved down the Harland & Wolff slipway in September 1937. To mark the occasion, a special luncheon was held in Cape Town's city hall and the ceremony, broadcast live by the BBC, was relayed to the guests over a public address system. Union-Castle employees in the Cape Town office gathered in the manager's office to listen to the broadcast.

The *Capetown Castle* had arguably the most attractive lines of any contemporary

1 *One of the finest photographs of the* Arundel Castle, *taken on 21 September 1937 during her trials on Belfast Lough at the conclusion of her refit.*
2 *The bow of the* Carnarvon Castle, *photographed on 17 January 1938 during her refit at Belfast. She emerged from the refit with a clipper bow, re-vamped engines, improved accommodation and a single funnel.*
3 *The* Warwick Castle *after her refit.*
4 *The* Windsor Castle *refitting at Belfast on 14 May 1937, two days after the coronation of King George VI, hence the bunting.*

1

2

motorship of that time, and was dubbed the 'Queen of the Southern Seas' in a maiden voyage publicity pamphlet that continued:

> In all her public rooms and staterooms alike, she is an example of the great advances which have been made in recent years in counselling the comfort and convenience of the travelling public. Likewise, she represents the peak of the building and re-conditioning programme which the Union-Castle Line has been through in recent times with the object not only of providing a faster service, but also of meeting the ever-growing needs of the South African trade.
>
> Never in the eighty years during which this famous Line has served South Africa, has its policy of keeping abreast or ahead of immediate needs been so firmly accentuated as it has been since 1926 . . . The fact that the *Capetown Castle* is the latest, if not the most majestic unit of the fleet of fourteen new vessels commissioned since that date, with four more approaching completion, speaks for itself . . . Outstanding in size and distinguished alike in design and equipment, she supplies a more intimate link with South Africa than any of her predecessors have done, for the reason that she is the first *Castle* boat to carry a South African name.

At 224 metres, she was also the longest motorship – more than 6 metres longer than the Cunarder, *Britannic*, and 13 metres longer than Shaw Savill's *Dominion Monarch*, which was delivered the following year. Unfortuntely, since the engines of the *Capetown Castle* were similar to those of the slightly smaller *Athlone Castle*, time would show the latest Union-Castle liner to be underpowered to the extent that her fuel consumption far exceeded that of any of the other mailships.

The maiden voyage of the *Capetown Castle* in April 1938 was an eagerly awaited event

THE BOYS' CLUB ON BOARD THE STIRLING CASTLE

Out of concern for the welfare of deck boys and galley boys who went to sea in their mid-teens, the masters of several liners established clubs for them. A small venue was set aside for their use and decorated by the lads, who could then spend what little leisure time they had with their peers in the 'Glory Hole', as the clubroom was called. Physical education, carpentry, boxing, model-making and several other pastimes were encouraged. And when the ship was in port for a few days, excursions ashore were arranged for the youths. Captain A.O. Morgan, master of the Stirling Castle, *established the first such club on a Union-Castle mailship in 1937. Once the minimum age of new entrants to the lower deck was increased to eighteen the clubs ceased to serve a need.*

1 *The* Capetown Castle *takes shape in Belfast in August 1938.*

2 *The* Capetown Castle *berthing in Cape Town with the first line ashore. The ensign has been lowered from the gaff and run up at the stern, and the ports are open for the gangways.*

1

UNION-CASTLE
LINE
TOURS
TO ENGLAND
DURING THE ENGLISH SUMMER 1936
FROM: | R.M.S. ARUNDEL CASTLE | R.M.S. WINDSOR CASTLE
Durban | 11th June | 25th June
East London | 12th June | 26th June
Port Elizabeth | 13th June | 27th June
Capetown | 19th June | 3rd July
AT GREATLY REDUCED FARES
ASK FOR PARTICULARS FROM THE UNION-CASTLE LINE AT CAPETOWN,
PORT ELIZABETH, EAST LONDON, DURBAN & JOHANNESBURG, OR AGENTS

2

3

4

in the city of her name, but it turned out to be something of a damp squib. The *Cape Argus* of 13 April wrote:

Cape Town gave a quiet welcome to the big mailship named in her honour when the *Capetown Castle*, 27,000-ton flagship of the Union-Castle fleet, glided slowly into dock on her maiden voyage before dawn today. On board were many distinguished passengers, including Sir Robertson F. Gibb, the Chairman of the Line.

The new liner arrived in Table Bay at two o'clock this morning, four hours ahead of schedule, after a fast passage of 13 days 9 hours from Southampton. She was ablaze with lights as she moved towards the New Basin [Duncan Dock] entrance shortly after six o'clock. Owing to the early hour – it was still quite dark – there was only a small crowd on the quayside and fewer passengers were about on the decks.

Despite the disappointingly poor turnout to greet the liner, all kinds of accolades were passed to the designers of the new liner when she arrived. The pilot found her 'easy to manoeuvre' while her master, Commodore Bertie Barron, commented that she 'handles like a live thing'.

The vessel's maiden voyage was also notable for the introduction of the first 'talkies' on the Cape run. They were: *The Housemaster*, *Sweep Devil* and *Sailing Along*. The ship was fitted with a full-size cinema screen and there was a double projector to avoid stoppages while the reels were changed. Shaw Savill's *Ceramic* and the Canadian-Pacific liner *Empress of Britain* had similar equipment, but their cinema shows comprised only travelogues.

The new ships and faster service once more heralded the end for older vessels in the fleet. The now obsolete *Edinburgh Castle*, the first mailship to be fitted with wireless back in 1921, bowed out with dignity early in 1939. Although she sailed outward from Southampton on the mail service, it was as an intermediate that she made her homeward passage. A contemporary newspaper account described her last departure from Cape Town:

Prolonged blasts from the sirens of tugs, the *Athlone Castle* and the *Capetown Castle* yesterday bade farewell to the Intermediate liner *Edinburgh Castle* when she left on her last voyage. A fairly large crowd saw her off.

At 10 a.m., the ship was pulled stern first from No. 7 Quay, turned in the Victoria Basin, and soon afterwards, she steamed out of the entrance, leaving Table Bay where she had been a regular visitor for twenty-eight years, for the last time. The liner carried 100 passengers and her holds were full.

Reprieved from the scrapyard in September 1939, the old ship served a useful purpose during World War II. However, her master on that final voyage from Cape Town, Captain H. A. Causton, was to meet his death the following year when the *Dunbar Castle*, on which he was serving, was mined near the mouth of the Thames – one of the many millions to lose their lives tragically in the second Great War, which also took a heavy toll of the Cape mailships.

1 *The* Athlone Castle *at the Point in Durban, circa 1938.*
2 *One of several publicity posters aimed at attracting South African visitors to Britain.*
3 *A children's fancy dress competition, circa 1938.*
4 *Former passengers will recall the ships' letterheads, entertainment programmes and many other items of Union-Castle memorabilia.*

1

5

The Second World War

1939-1945

2

When, on 3 September 1939, Prime Minister Neville Chamberlain made the inevitable, yet shattering, announcement over the BBC that Britain had declared war on Germany, a relatively small percentage of British merchant seamen were listening. Most were at sea or in distant ports, some oblivious of the latest developments that were shortly to result in world conflict on a scale never before experienced.

On board the Union-Castle liners, the radio officers had tuned in to as many news bulletins as possible to keep the passengers informed, and the masters of the ships passed important news items to crewmen on the lower deck, for they were the men who would soon have to face all the perils of warfare at sea – aerial attacks, mines, torpedoes, shelling from raiders or warships, and the silent hunters of the submarine packs.

Two days before the outbreak of war, a cryptic article appeared in the *Cape Argus*:

THE CARNARVON CASTLE
NOTICE TO COAST PASSENGERS
Passengers booked from Cape Town for coast ports in the Carnarvon Castle *which is due from England next week, have been informed that they will not be able to travel in the ship.*

She was about to be commandeered by the Admiralty.

According to *Lloyd's Weekly Shipping Index*, the Union-Castle liners on that dreadful Sunday were spread out along the usual mailship route as follows:

ARUNDEL CASTLE Southampton, having arrived from Cape Town on 1 September.
ATHLONE CASTLE Two days outward from Cape Town, bound for Southampton.
CAPETOWN CASTLE In Port Elizabeth harbour, preparing to sail later that afternoon for East London and Durban.

CARNARVON CASTLE	At sea, four days' steaming from Cape Town, where she would dock on Thursday 7 September.
STIRLING CASTLE	In Southampton, loading to sail for Cape Town on 7 September.
WARWICK CASTLE	Six days out from Southampton, where she would arrive on Friday 8 September, bringing with her the news that she had been shadowed by submarines in the English Channel. (The *Chloris*, which also docked that day, reported a similar experience.)
WINCHESTER CASTLE	At sea, having sailed from Southampton on 31 August, bound for Cape Town.
WINDSOR CASTLE	In Port Elizabeth harbour, preparing to sail for Cape Town that afternoon. (As it was the wool season, the ship was spending a second day in Port Elizabeth loading hundreds of bales destined for Britain.)

Another mailship, the veteran *Edinburgh Castle*, which had sailed on its last voyage in the mail service the previous year, lay at anchor off Netley in reserve.

Fearful of the ravages of war, many people who had intended travelling during the next few months immediately cancelled their bookings, while for those already abroad, the declaration of war meant a scramble to obtain a berth at the earliest opportunity so that they could return to their home country. There were two factors compounding the problem. Firstly, in the allocation of berths, priority had to be given to military personnel being recalled to Britain, or being sent posthaste to various places in the Empire. The second problem was that some of the passenger vessels had been withdrawn from their usual service almost immediately war broke out. Union-Castle offices in both Britain and South Africa were inundated with enquiries regarding available passages and refunds for cancelled tickets.

For those fortunate enough to obtain a passage, the voyage was fraught with anxiety, for at any moment the unprotected ship might be at the mercy of a submarine, raider or aircraft. No decklights or navigational lights were displayed and portholes had to be tightly covered at night; no smoking was permitted during the hours of darkness lest the minutest of glows should betray the position of the ship. Everyone had lifejackets and gasmasks at the ready, while most had within easy reach a small bag with their most important possessions. Lifeboats were made ready and boat drills became daily events. Volunteers among the passengers were assigned to augment the lookouts for submarines or aircraft. Inevitably, with such a high degree of anxiety prevailing, there were many false alarms sending seamen and passengers alike scrambling from their bunks to dash to their boatstations.

On the *Athlone Castle*, which had left Table Bay only two days prior to Chamberlain's announcement, considerable consternation was turned to good use as passengers voluntarily took up paintbrushes to help transform the ship to its wartime grey. (Paint had already been issued to ships in readiness.)

The frenetic rush for berths at the outbreak of the war was short-lived. As the world waited for the onslaught, the number of passengers dropped drastically. On her last southbound voyage on the mail service before her requisitioning in mid-1940, the *Warwick Castle* carried ten first class passengers, a dozen naval officers travelling to South Africa to join HMS *Gloucester* and a handful of tourist class passengers.

The *Edinburgh Castle* was one of the first vessels to be appropriated by the Admiralty, and after a cursory refit, she sailed to Freetown, Sierra Leone, where she became an accommodation ship for many of the military personnel stationed there during the war, a very different role to her commissioning as an auxiliary cruiser for the 1914-1918 conflict.

Most of the intermediate ships were also requisitioned. The *Dunnottar Castle*, in London in mid-August, was sent to Belfast even before the outbreak of war to be converted to an armed merchant cruiser (AMC). Her passengers were hastily re-routed to Southampton in time to board the outward-bound *Carnarvon Castle*. The sister ship to the *Dunnottar Castle*, the *Dunvegan Castle*, was in East London on that Sunday. Telegraphed to the latter ship as she was about to sail for Durban were orders that she should return to Britain immediately. There she too would become an armed merchant cruiser, a role which, in August 1940, took her into the North Atlantic where a submarine sighted and torpedoed her. The *Pretoria Castle* (in post-war years to be renamed *Warwick Castle*) underwent two conversions, first to an armed merchant cruiser and later to an aircraft carrier.

3

4

It was inevitable that the regular mail service would be disrupted and that its eight ships would be requisitioned by the Admiralty. Their speed of 20 knots and their passenger capacity would be invaluable in the carriage of troops. All eight mailships spent considerable time in waters away from their usual run, some being sent to the Far East, Australia and even the Pacific Ocean.

THE ARUNDEL CASTLE

For several months after the outbreak of war local folk in South African ports observed the familiar profile of the two-funnelled *Arundel Castle*, then already painted grey but continuing the mail service.

Later, she was present at the North African and Sicilian landings but luckily escaped damage. Good fortune also accompanied her in November 1943 when, transporting troops in the Mediterranean, she was attacked by the Luftwaffe and by so-called 'pilotless missiles'. From that encounter the *Arundel Castle* again emerged unscathed, her gun crews managing to down two of the attacking aircraft.

One of her more special assignments was a voyage to Gothenburg in Sweden, where

1 *The* Capetown Castle *under attack in the Irish Sea, October 1940.*

2 *As the senior Union-Castle master during World War II and for his own major contribution as master of troopships, Commodore Sir Ernest H. Thornton, RD, RNR, was the only Union-Castle employee to receive a knighthood after World War II.*

3 *Two days out from Cape Town after war had been declared, passengers on board the* Athlone Castle *help to make sandbags.*

4 *Crew and passengers begin painting the* Athlone Castle *grey while the liner is at sea.*

1

she embarked Allied prisoners of war in exchange for injured German prisoners, an exchange arranged by the Swedes who had persuaded both sides to honour an agreement to grant the *Arundel Castle* diplomatic immunity for the voyage. To prevent the liner from being attacked in the course of her passage, the word PROTECTED in huge lettering and the Union Jack as well as the French flag were painted on the side. At night the ship was fully illuminated, while floodlights were trained on the insignia on her sides so that submarine commanders would let her pass unimpeded. A similar voyage in 1944 took the ship to Marseille.

But the most interesting voyage was one that took place after the armistice had been concluded. Indeed, compared to those anxiety-laden sorties of the war it was more of a pleasure cruise for her crew. It was also to earn the ship a Union-Castle record. On 6 December 1945, a bitter wind carrying her smoke parallel to the sea, the *Arundel Castle* steamed slowly out of port en route for Gibraltar, from where an extended repatriation schedule would take her to several Mediterranean ports, the Suez Canal, India, Indo-China, Malaya, Japan, Ceylon (Sri Lanka) and finally to West Africa. (On board for her return passage to Britain were soldiers from Ceylon who would participate in the Victory Parade in London.) In all, she was away for 160 days, during which time she covered 45 225 nautical miles.

In April 1948, the *Arundel Castle* began service as an immigrant ship on the South African run; however, within fifteen months she was again called on by the Government for trooping duties associated with the Palestinian crisis. A further spell carrying immigrants to South Africa meant that she returned to the mail service only in September 1950, the last of the Union-Castle ships to rejoin the normal mail schedule.

THE ATHLONE CASTLE

Commandeered almost immediately upon her arrival in Southampton from South Africa in 1939, the *Athlone Castle* had several unusual incidents in her six years of carrying troops and government passengers. July 1940 saw her narrowest encounter when, west of Ushant, the convoy of which she was part was subjected to aerial attack for about two hours, during which time she was the frequent target of machine-gunfire, while bombs splashed into the sea around her, one barely a hundred metres ahead of her bows. There was slight damage but, miraculously, no casualties.

Then followed the first great convoy around the Cape, in which the *Athlone Castle* (commodore ship of Vice-Admiral R. Hill) was accompanied by five of her peacetime consorts: the *Arundel Castle*, *Capetown Castle*, *Durban Castle*, *Winchester Castle* and *Windsor Castle*. Back in Britain in December 1940, she was lying in Liverpool harbour when the city came under attack by bombers. Since the harbour area was one of the prime targets of the raid, many ships were damaged, including the *Athlone Castle*.

In 1941 and 1942 there were trooping voyages to South Africa, India, Australia, New Zealand and America. She was also among the dozens of great liners from which the troops

2

landed at Casablanca, Algiers and Oran in late 1942 for the North African campaign.

After an absence of nearly three years, the *Athlone Castle* returned to Table Bay in July 1945 to a tumultuous welcome. Crowds thronged to the harbour as the liner, still in her wartime grey, came alongside A Berth. In her rigging, in the lifeboats, in every possible niche aboard, soldiers, sailors and airmen waved ecstatically at the sea of faces on the quay. They had every reason to be joyful, for those 3 000 men who arrived that day comprised the first contingent of repatriated South African prisoners of war.

By the time she returned to her normal peacetime role after a refit in 1947, she, of all the Union-Castle ships, had sailed the greatest distance on war service – more than half a million nautical miles in all the oceans, carrying 148 113 troops and government passengers, as well as foodstuffs and other essential cargoes.

THE CAPETOWN CASTLE

The newest mailship on the Cape run at the time, the *Capetown Castle* was also the last to reach Cape Town before the outbreak of war. Her speed allowed her to continue operating as a mailship for a while, often sailing without escort, but inevitably the Admiralty eventually requisitioned her as a troopship.

Like other Union-Castle ships involved in war service, a plaque mounted on the bulkhead of her Long Gallery detailed her wartime exploits. (Additional notes elucidating certain incidents are in square brackets and were not part of the wording on the plaque.)

1 *Fitted with hut-like structures on the poop, the veteran* Edinburgh Castle *lay at Freetown for the duration of the war. Exposure to tropical conditions and little maintenance during those years took their toll of the old ship, and on 5 November 1945, rather than risk a tow to scrapyards, she was sunk by gunfire from the frigate HMS* Fal *and the corvette HMS* Porchester Castle.

2 *The* Arundel Castle *arriving in Liverpool in March 1943 after her remarkable voyage to Sweden.*

1

2

1939 Rescued nineteen survivors of torpedoed *Clan Chisholm* from North Atlantic. [The *Clan Chisholm* had been homeward bound from India, and had joined a convoy at Gibraltar for the last leg of her voyage. On 17 October 1939 she was torpedoed by U48 while well west of Cape Finisterre. The lascar seamen rescued by the mailship had been in a lifeboat for several days.]

1940 5 FEB. Requisitioned by H.M. Government for war service as a troop transport, and remained continually in Government service throughout the war.

OCTOBER Attacked and bombed by enemy aircraft off Northern Ireland, but with minor casualties. [The aircraft had attacked her from a height of only about 100 metres, but all four bombs fell astern of the *Capetown Castle* which was rocked by the explosions. Thereafter, the plane raked the ship with its machine guns, but caused only minor injuries. It is thought that the plane, which appeared to lose height as it flew away, may have been hit by the liner's anti-aircraft guns.]

1942 AUGUST Rescued twenty-two crew of the torpedoed S.S. *Maldanada* in the neighbourhood of Bermuda. [The Uruguayan freighter had been sunk four days earlier. The *Capetown Castle* sighted one lifeboat, from which eleven men were rescued, and was directed by an American aircraft to a second lifeboat containing another eleven crewmen.]

3

1943/1946 Continued under requisition to H.M. Government, and during this period, made trooping voyages to African, Indian, American and Italian ports.

1947 9 JAN. Returned to peacetime duties after one hundred and eighty-four thousand miles on wartime service during which time one hundred and sixty-four thousand troops and Government passengers were carried.

One particularly interesting voyage undertaken by the vessel occurred in 1942 when, carrying German prisoners of war from Suez, she headed for the Cape, ostensibly to follow her prewar route from there to England. That was not to be. To avoid German submarines that had been operating most successfully in the South Atlantic and off the bulge of Africa, on her arrival at Cape Town she was diverted first to Saldanha Bay and then, under sealed orders, across the South Atlantic, through the Magellan Straits – at times blanketed in thick fog – northwards along the Pacific Coast of South America and through the Panama Canal to New York. The final leg of the voyage was across the Atlantic to Britain. Thereafter, she spent much of the latter part of the war carrying American troops to Britain and later to Europe.

It has been estimated that between 1939 and 1946 approximately 9 116 826 meals were served to persons on board the *Capetown Castle*, excluding the crew; 67 million cigarettes were issued, as were 34 422 pounds of tobacco, and 1,3 million bottles of mineral water.

THE CARNARVON CASTLE

In September 1939, the *Carnarvon Castle* arrived in Table Bay on the usual mail service from Southampton, four days after war had been declared. All 'through' passengers to other South African ports were disembarked at Cape Town, her fittings and furnishings were removed and she sailed to Simon's Town, a Royal Naval dockyard at the time, where she was converted to an armed merchant cruiser. Her main armament was eight 6-inch Mark VII guns with a range of about 8,5 nautical miles, considerably shorter than the raider she would engage in the not-too-distant future. Two 3-inch high angle anti-aircraft guns and six Lewis machine-guns completed her armoury. Commanded by Captain H.W.M. Hardy, RN, she was manned by Royal Naval personnel and Royal Naval Volunteer Reservists from South Africa.

By the end of September 1940, German surface raiders (battleship *Graf Spee* and three converted merchant ships – the *Atlantis*, *Thor* and *Pinguin*) had collectively sunk or

1 *The* Athlone Castle, *the commodore ship of the convoy, leaves Cape Town's Victoria Basin on 12 February 1941.*

2 *Bombs splash ahead of the* Athlone Castle *while she is in convoy west of Ushant in July 1940. The ship off the starboard bow is probably the P&O liner* Strathnaver.

3 *The* Capetown Castle *passes the submarine net as she leaves the safety of Table Bay harbour on 2 November 1940.*

1

2

captured thirteen ships in the South Atlantic and Indian Oceans. (Although the *Graf Spee* had been lost off Montevideo in December 1939, the others continued the effective harassing of shipping, which included the mining of the Agulhas Bank by the *Atlantis* in May 1940.) To counter this threat, the HMAMC *Carnarvon Castle*, among others, was ordered to patrol the South Atlantic.

On 4 December 1940, the *Carnarvon Castle* intercepted a Brazilian ship and took off twenty-two Germans. The following day, when about 550 miles south of Rio de Janeiro, she engaged the *Thor*, which had left Kiel on 6 June 1940. The main armament on the German vessel was six 5,9-inch guns of 1913 vintage and torpedo tubes, while her fire-control system was also almost obsolete.

Among the Royal Naval officers on board the *Carnarvon Castle* was Lieutenant-Commander P. N. Illingworth, who described the action in terms rather flattering to the British ship:

> On 5th December, while in the South Atlantic, and about 700 miles north east of Montevideo, we sighted a large vessel at dawn. Only mastheads were showing. The *Carnarvon Castle* immediately put on all possible speed, and at about 0700 hours, the vessel which was known to be an enemy raider, was "hull up" and steaming at approximately a little more than 17 knots. At this time, the *Carnarvon Castle* had been doing over 19 knots, faster even than she had steamed on her trials after alteration to her engines.
>
> At 0800 hours, the distance between the two vessels was about 17,500 yards, and visibility was very poor owing to the morning haze.
>
> As the raider failed to respond to all signals to heave to, a shot was fired at her which we observed to fall ahead of her port bow. The raider immediately replied with

3 

4 

her two after guns, port and starboard, and these shots passed over the *Carnarvon Castle*. The enemy ship was then observed to be turning 50 degrees to starboard, with the object of bringing her full starboard battery to bear. At the same time, she ran up a large battle ensign at the foremast.

In the meantime at 0803 hours, Captain Hardy had ordered action and the *Carnarvon Castle* was using every gun from her six-inch starboard battery, well trained forward, and, firing salvoes, turned towards the enemy as she also turned on her new course.

In the first few minutes the raider was hit by a salvo and apparently the whole of her starboard battery was silenced. [The raider was not hit at all by the fire from the British ship. The starboard battery did cease firing for a time, only because the guns were in danger of overheating.] In addition she appeared to be on fire forward. [She was making a smoke screen, and, as she had not been hit, there was certainly no fire aboard.] The *Carnarvon Castle* had also been hit several times and through a shot hitting the funnel casing, had developed a small fire in the store lockers.

At this time the raider was observed to be making smoke screens from vents forward and aft of her bridge. The smoke screens naturally made visibility still worse than it had been, but at first accentuated certain points of the vessel notably her heavy cross-trees and masts and bows which were above the screen. At this time the *Carnarvon Castle*'s electrical control gear for the guns had been shot away and she was firing independently with guns worked by hand control only. She had also had a fair number of casualties, both killed and wounded.

The raider now turned, in her smoke screen, towards the *Carnarvon Castle* which was steaming at her best speed, and rapidly closing range. In order to have fullest advantage of her whole starboard battery, she was keeping her course 'open' from the enemy.

Orders were given to alter course on a 20 degree starboard swing towards the enemy, when the track of two torpedoes, fired by the raider, were seen from the bridge. One of the torpedoes was observed to pass very close to the bows, in fact just missing, and the other some distance away astern. The *Carnarvon Castle* was then heading up the 'lane' caused by the wake of the torpedoes, and had closed to under 8,000 yards from the enemy, whom she was hitting continually. [See above.] The raider was by this time nearly completely turned round on the same course as the *Carnarvon Castle*. She had brought her port battery to bear, and was again firing salvoes, which were often hitting the *Carnarvon Castle* both fore and aft, and with very destructive effect on her upper works and boats. A lot of what were apparently anti-personnel shells were being fired with particular attention to the *Carnarvon Castle*'s bridge. [There were no specifically 'anti-personnel shells' on the raider; it is more likely that shells, standard for the armament carried by the raider, were striking the vicinity of the bridge which was then showered with shrapnel.] At this time the raider was firing two salvoes to one of the *Carnarvon Castle's* and the latter's speed was dropping all the time owing to fires which had broken out, necessitating large fire parties.

From this time on to about 0930 hours the raider put on full speed, which was vastly superior to the *Carnarvon Castle*'s and would appear to have been not less than 23 knots. [It is unlikely that the *Thor* could do more than 18 knots.] She continually threw out smoke screens and eventually was lost in the haze and became out of range. The action had lasted 90 minutes and the *Carnarvon Castle* had fired over 600 shells. It was observed that all the raider's shells had entered the *Carnarvon Castle* at an angle from the bow, thus proving how aggressively she had fought her battle and had at no time turned away.

The enemy raider was positively identified from sketches made from the *Carnarvon Castle*'s bridge during various stages of the battle, and it was discovered how very much more powerful she was than the latter.

It is understood the enemy's armament was eight 5.9-inch guns, 4 to a broadside, range 21,000 yards, 2 torpedo tubes in the bows, 3-inch armoured decks [She was not specially armoured in this way.] and extra armour around the engines. Heavy anti-aircraft battery and one E-boat stowed aft of the bridge and deck housing were observed. [The apparent inaccuracies that have been indicated in the account by Lieutenant-Commander Illingworth do not reflect upon either his professional expertise or his judgement; rather, they are no doubt a product of the intensity of the action and of the amount of reliable information available to the *Carnarvon Castle* at the time of the report.]

The former mailship was very fortunate to have survived the engagement. Not only had she been damaged by the thirty-eight direct hits, but any of the fires that had been started by the shelling could so easily have destroyed her. In addition, Captain Otto Kahler of the *Thor* may have erred too much on the side of caution by disengaging when he did, for had he continued shelling, there is every prospect that the *Carnarvon Castle* would have been irreparably damaged or even sunk. The *Carnarvon Castle* put in to Montevideo for temporary patching, after which she sailed to Cape Town for permanent repairs.

Two of the factors that made the Union-Castle liner a household word in South Africa were, firstly, that although two intermediates (the *Dunbar Castle* and *Dunvegan Castle*) had both been sunk by this time, the *Carnarvon Castle* was the first of the popular mailships to be engaged in action. Secondly, there is no doubt that the endurance and courage displayed by the ship's company caught the imagination of the South African

1 *HMAMC* Carnarvon Castle *berths in Cape Town after her engagement with the raider* Thor *in December 1940.*
2 *NCOs enjoy a meal on board the* Carnarvon Castle *on one of the vessel's many voyages as a troopship.*
3 *Damage inflicted by the* Thor *to the promenade deck of the* Carnarvon Castle.
4 *Plates from the German pocket battleship* Graf Spee*, which was scuttled at Montevideo in 1939, were used to effect temporary repairs to the damage inflicted on the* Carnarvon Castle *by the* Thor. *One of the vessel's six-inch guns can be clearly seen.*

1

public. From an unpublished source in the Union-Castle archives, comes the following:

> In one instance, an enemy shell failed to explode immediately and ricocheted on to the deck near a gun crew. A Petty Officer pluckily took it in his arms and hurled it overboard. On two occasions, the forward gun crew were knocked almost senseless by blasts, but all those who were capable of doing so, scrambled to their feet and returned to their posts.

Six of her crew died in the engagement and thirty-two were wounded, while two DSOs, one Conspicuous Gallantry Medal, five DSMs, and fourteen Mentioned in Despatches were awarded.

Until 1943 – a remarkably long time, when one considers the relatively low success ratio of the AMCs – the *Carnarvon Castle* continued her patrols, initially in the Atlantic, and then, for the period October/November 1941, she formed part of Operation Bellringer, in which a convoy of five French Vichy ships trying to return to France from Madagascar were captured off the South African coast.

Her appearance was changed during a refit in Norfolk, West Virginia, in early 1942. A radar and signal mast was fitted atop the wheelhouse and unnecessary deckfittings were removed, as was the topmast of the foremast. Again she patrolled the South Atlantic, and later moved to the Atlantic Narrows to intercept blockade runners, one of which she managed to stop and divert to Gibraltar.

In 1944, she was sent for another refit, this time to New York. She emerged as a troopship to carry American troops across the Atlantic to Britain for the Normandy landings, and also to the Mediterranean. When hostilities ended, she made repatriation voyages to East Africa, India and South Africa.

THE STIRLING CASTLE

Requisitioned for trooping, the *Stirling Castle* was virtually gutted, and with her public rooms as well as some of the holds fitted with tiers of bunks, and her cabin partitions removed to increase the number of berths for troops, she emerged from the yards with a capacity to carry nearly 5 000 men.

The early part of 1941 did not favour her. Inwards from Table Bay on the evening of 14 February, she ran aground just north of Toward Point in the Firth of Clyde. Everything possible was done to refloat her immediately but it took three tugs to pull her off on the high tide of the following morning. An inspection at Glasgow revealed no damage.

Only weeks later, the *Stirling Castle* was involved in yet another accident. Convoy WS7 was proceeding down the Clyde during the early hours of 25 March. The cold wind, driving rain and poor visibility, as well as the darkness, made the manoeuvre far from easy for all concerned, although it obviously prevented aerial observation. Also steaming down the Firth that night were the battleship HMS *Revenge*, the cruiser HMS *Edinburgh* and six other warships, including three Tribal-class destroyers – the heavy escort for the convoy of troopships bound for Port Said via the Cape of Good Hope. (Of this escort, all except the battleship would be sunk within eighteen months.)

In single line ahead and astern of the *Stirling Castle* were several other troopships. Out of the gloom, a large ship suddenly appeared very close to the starboard bow of the *Stirling Castle* and continued as if she were moving across the bow of the Cape liner. Captain E.E. Spradbrow immediately ordered the helm hard to starboard and the engines hard astern, a manoeuvre that enabled the *Stirling Castle* to miss the other liner – identified by now as the P&O transport *Strathmore* – by no more than 5 metres. To allow the *Strathmore* to regain her position in the convoy, Spradbrow continued at dead slow ahead. Suddenly, the Union-Castle liner shuddered and skewed off course. Most of her company thought a submarine had penetrated the defensive ring of destroyers and had torpedoed her. In reality, another P&O liner, the *Strathaird*, had struck the *Stirling Castle* heavily on the port quarter. The crew went to boatstations but was recalled after it had been ascertained that the vessel was not taking water as all damage had been above the waterline.

While the *Strathaird* had to put back to Glasgow for repairs to a 3,5-metre gash in her bow, the *Stirling Castle* continued with the convoy to Durban, where her damage was fully assessed and repaired. She had suffered an 8-metre gash in her port quarter, two shell plates had been crushed, and one dented. Eleven side frames, two deck plates, twenty-five deck beams, guardrails and stanchions had been buckled, and parts of her teak promenade deck had been smashed.

As the American troops were being moved across the Atlantic for the invasionary force, the *Stirling Castle* was one of scores of troopships in the 'Atlantic Bridge'. On one voyage alone, nearly 6 000 men were crammed into her troop decks, almost ten times as many as her peacetime passenger complement.

She rejoined the mail service in 1947.

THE WARWICK CASTLE

The *Warwick Castle* was one of the Union-Castle liners that carried troops to the Far East. In the face of the Japanese advance on Java in February 1942, she quickly left the area and returned to more familiar waters off the British coast. While manoeuvring in thick fog, the bridge party was appalled to see the dull outline of another liner immediately ahead. Despite efforts to prevent a collision, the *Warwick Castle* rammed the other ship aft of the bridge. Within minutes, it was established that she had hit one of her former consorts on the mail service, the *Windsor Castle*. Although no serious damage had been done to either ship, there were several dents and buckled plates to straighten.

Late in October 1942, huge convoys began to leave Britain bound for the Mediterranean. Among the ships in those convoys were the Union-Castle liners *Winchester Castle*, *Durban Castle* and *Warwick Castle*. The latter was carrying American troops for the landing at Oran, Algeria. There were sporadic attacks on the transports as they lay off the beaches, but as soon as their troops and the equipment were ashore, the ships turned and headed at full speed for Gibraltar, where a convoy was marshalled for the final leg of the passage back to Britain to embark reinforcements for the North African campaign. Having survived the onslaught of the German bombers and submarines in the Mediterranean, the ships had to run the gauntlet of the submarine ring around the approaches to Britain. In his book *Ships that Pass*, George Young picks up the story:

> It may have been a shortcoming in the organisation of the North African landings in 1942 that the flotilla of merchantmen which delivered the forces without incident to the landing beaches and ports, suffered severely from depredations by U-boats on their return voyage to Britain. Having been caught off their guard by the landings, the Germans mustered all their U-boats to waylay the passenger liners on the return passage, and the *Warwick Castle* was among those taken in the net. P & O lost their *Viceroy of India* at about the same time.
>
> The Cape liner was a unit of a convoy (MFK1) which left Gibraltar for Britain at 4 p.m. on November 12, 1942, just four days after the successful North African landings. West of the straits, the liners had to reduce speed to enable the escorting destroyers to maintain station, a westerly gale having thrown up an enormous sea and heavily punishing the ships. All went well for some hours until a U-boat, after waiting a long time for its quarry, darted into the tail-end of the convoy and picked off the *Warwick Castle*. The torpedo hit immediately below the bridge and opened up both the cargo spaces and the engine room, flooding both. The weight of the sea in the forepart caused the bows to break off, and the section sank in a cauldron of surging waves.
>
> While boats were being lowered into the wild weather, destroyers darted through the heaving seas in an effort to locate and sink the U-boat. Then the destroyer HMS *Achates* came close up alongside the doomed *Warwick Castle* to embark survivors from boats and rafts, and this action saved many. The liner was sinking quickly forward, the saloon deck being already submerged when members of the crew on the boat deck were still pitching rafts over the side. Captain Shaw (the Master of the *Warwick Castle*) and his two executive officers leapt for these rafts.

Because of the heavy sea running at the time, the commander of HMS *Achates*, Lieutenant-Commander Johns, had a difficult time bringing his ship close to the sinking liner. The first lieutenant, Lieutenant Paton Jones, dived into the sea to rescue an exhausted seaman from the *Warwick Castle*. The liner's chief officer, who with Captain Shaw had been clinging to a raft for several hours, was swept from the raft as the destroyer approached, while Captain Shaw died aboard the warship shortly after being picked up.

At the time of her sinking, the *Warwick Castle* had been carrying a number of small landing craft, one of which was found by a Canadian corvette nearly a week later with five crewmen and six naval ratings aboard. They had been without food and water. Suffering from exhaustion and exposure, the men were in an exceptionally weak state.

One of them was George Charles Vetcher, who had taken his first steps to sea in 1895 as a saloon boy in the Union liner *Greek* for a monthly wage of twelve shillings and sixpence. As a 'bedroom' steward, he served in the *Scot*, *Dunottar Castle*, the two-funnelled *Edinburgh Castle* and several other ships before his appointment to the *Warwick Castle*. His courage and determination during those six dreadful days in the landing craft won him the British Empire Medal. George Vetcher BEM retired from Union-Castle in the early fifties.

Another 'old hand' of the company who spent a harrowing time in one of the lifeboats was Chief Steward Leonard Pyne who, in the words of First Officer (later Captain) A.M. Black in a letter to the company, 'showed a very fine example both before and after being rescued by the *Achates*. Despite his age, he pulled steadily upon an oar for about two hours under very unfavourable weather conditions, remained calm and cheerful throughout, and helped other survivors as they themselves were rescued.' For that he received a Commendation. Prior to his joining the *Warwick Castle*, Chief Steward Pyne had been on the *Llangibby Castle* when it was torpedoed in January 1942. With serious damage to its stern and rudder, the intermediate liner reached the Azores where temporary repairs were carried out. Pyne rejoined the *Llangibby Castle* in time for the D-Day landings and thereafter was ashore, assisting in the preparation of meals for the thousands of troops passing through Britain to France. In 1946, his was among the names on the King's New Year Honours List for the award of the MBE. He retired from the company after fifty years of service, which had begun in 1906 as a saloon boy in the *Carisbrooke Castle*.

For his own actions, First Officer Black was awarded the OBE (CD) for bravery at sea.

2 

1 *The* Stirling Castle *in Cape Town on 23 September 1939, discharging her cargo from England. Her superstructure has been painted grey but her hull is still lavender.*

2 *Troopships* Stirling Castle *and* Athlone Castle *on the Clyde in 1944.*

1

THE WINCHESTER CASTLE

Of all the mailships, the *Winchester Castle* probably had the most varied wartime service. The following record is adapted from a pen-sketch contained in a pamphlet issued by Union-Castle when the ship was withdrawn from the mail run in 1960.

15 DECEMBER 1939 Taken over by the Liner Division of the Ministry of Transport. [She was later fitted out as a personnel ship.]

1940/1941 Trooping to Bombay, then to the Clyde to assist in the training of commandos in Loch Fyne and the Western Isles. It was here that Lord Mountbatten visited the ship. During the training exercises, the darkened ship would approach one of the beaches for the commandos aboard to lower their landing craft for a mock assault on the beach.

25 MARCH 1942 Escorted by the battleship HMS *Ramilles* and her flotilla, the *Winchester Castle* and several other transports sailed from the Clyde for 'Operation Ironclad' – the Madagascan Campaign. On board the mailship were commando units and the East Lancashire Regiment. During the campaign, she served as the operational headquarters, and one of her cabins was converted into a radio station, Radio Diego Suarez, for propaganda broadcasts, mainly in French, to the population of the island. The ship was awarded Battle Honours for her role in the Madagascan landings; and her master, Captain S.B. Newdigate, was awarded the DSC, Bosun G.F. McCawbrey received the DSM for gallantry, while three other members of the ship's company – Chief Officer J.W. Brooks, Second Officer R.H. Pape, and AB H. J. Whitford – were Mentioned in Despatches.

JUNE 1942 Fetched troops of the King's African Rifles from Kilindini to take them to Bombay, whence they would travel to Burma. Before returning to the Western Isles, she took American troops to Britain.

OCTOBER 1942 In convoy with other ships, including the *Warwick Castle* and *Durban Castle* (and the *Llangibby Castle* from Gibraltar), she sailed for the Mediterranean, where they landed troops at Sidi Ferruch Bay, near Algiers, at the start of the North African landings.

1943 For the landings at Sicily she brought part of the Eighth Army from Egypt, and after participating in the Salerno and Anzio landings, she rounded the Cape to move troops from Mombasa to Bombay.

1944 During the D-Day operations, the Cape liner was lying off the Côte d'Azur to land troops near Cannes.

2

1945 Trooping duties took her to the Indian Ocean once more, initially to ferry troops from Britain to the Far East and thereafter, for nearly eighteen months, she moved troops between Mombasa and Britain.

10 APRIL 1947 Released by the British Government to resume service for the Union-Castle Line. [Although she was one of the last to rejoin her company, she was the first mailship to have her hull restored to its lavender colour, a task accomplished while still repatriating troops.]

THE WINDSOR CASTLE

When war had seemed to be threatening in 1938, the September sailing from Southampton of the recently re-engined *Windsor Castle* was cancelled, with the intention of her being refitted as a troopship, but as tensions between Britain and Germany eased somewhat, the threat of war appeared to recede and shipping continued as usual. A year later, however, with the *Windsor Castle* in South African waters, the feared declaration of war came to pass, and within a few months the *Windsor Castle* underwent her conversion to a troopship.

On 23 March 1943, the day her sister ship, the *Arundel Castle*, arrived in Liverpool with hundreds of injured Allied prisoners of war from Germany via Sweden, the *Windsor Castle*, with some 2 000 troops on board, was in the Mediterranean Sea. It was the early

3

1 *The* Warwick Castle *leaving Cape Town on 11 December 1939.*
2 *The* Winchester Castle *at B Berth in Cape Town on 28 September 1939, loading for England.*
3 *Bosun George MacCawbrey, who was awarded the DSM for bravery while serving on the* Winchester Castle *during the Madagascan campaign.*

1

2

WINDSOR CASTLE BOMBED

VESSEL NOW SAFE: NO CASUALTIES

ATTACKED SEVERAL HUNDRED MILES OFF IRISH COAST

GERMANS SAY SHE RECEIVED A DIRECT HIT

London, Tuesday.

THE Windsor Castle, the well-known 19,000-ton Union-Castle liner, was attacked by a German aeroplane when she was several hundred miles west of the Irish coast.

hours of the morning when the ship, conspicuous in the bright moonlight, was sighted by the pilot of a lone German bomber. Swooping low over the troopship, it dropped a torpedo. Within seconds of hitting the water it crashed into the after end of the ship's engine room.

In his report on the events that followed, Third Officer A. Landless wrote:

At about 0230 I was awakened by the sound of an explosion that appeared to be at the after end of the vessel. Almost immediately the emergency alarm bells were ringing and I heard what I took to be distress rockets being fired. In trying to switch on the electric light, I discovered that the lighting system had failed, which led me to believe that the vessel had been struck in the engine room. I went to the Bridge and there I found the Captain and other officers . . . On arriving at my boatstation, which was on the port side of the vessel, I found people lined up ready to leave. The boat was already swung out, about 20 people got into it and were lowered to the water safely, the boat was then filled up, the two lifeboats next astern were also lowered into the water and filled up with personnel.

It was a clear night and when the moon was not obscured by clouds, it was fairly light. There was a moderate swell running but no great difficulty was experienced in getting the boats clear of the falls. Davits and all lowering gear worked satisfactorily . . . When I finally got into a lifeboat and was clear of the vessel, I saw men in the water, supported by lifejackets, and others clinging to rafts, and so proceeded to pick up survivors . . . Two destroyers were standing by near the vessel and one of them commenced to go alongside to take Military Personnel off. On attempting to put the lifeboat alongside the destroyer, I was told to keep clear of the torpedoed vessel.

By this time, we had 82 people in the boat, which was certified to carry 65 people . . . I saw a second destroyer go alongside the vessel. Shortly after this, I saw a raft with six men clinging to it; so, making a rope fast we proceeded to tow them alongside the first destroyer which was now clear of the vessel. On approaching, we were told that the destroyer could not take any more survivors aboard, that they were standing by the vessel, and that another destroyer would be out at daybreak in about three hours' time to pick up further survivors.

The men on the raft which we were towing were being repeatedly washed off it and one man was suffering from cramp. McNeish, Assistant Bath Steward, who behaved splendidly in the boat, volunteered to go into the sea, lash the men onto the raft and bring back to the boat the man suffering from cramp. This operation was carried out successfully.

Great difficulty was being experienced in rowing the boat owing to the number of people in it. After about half an hour of pulling and manoeuvring, we managed to get alongside an empty lifeboat floating near us. All the men on the raft were put into this empty boat, their bodies rubbed to restore circulation and wrapped in blankets. A few people from my boat were put into the other boat, and the two boats tied together. Finally, we succeeded in rounding up three more lifeboats . . .

The destroyer [HMS] Whaddon signalled us to go alongside; within half an hour, over 200 survivors from the lifeboats were safely aboard the destroyer. The time was then about 0830.

Her master, Captain J.C. Brown, and a small band of volunteers reboarded the stricken ship in a vain salvage attempt; gradually as the ship settled by the stern, Captain Brown ordered the men to abandon ship. A destroyer edged alongside the bow to take the men off, and no sooner had the last man – Captain Brown himself – slid down a rope on to the foredeck of the destroyer, than the liner tilted her bow to the sky and sank shortly before 17:30 that afternoon, nearly fifteen hours after being hit. Third Officer Landless continues:

At about 1130, the destroyers [HMS] Egglesford and Whaddon, full of survivors, proceeded to Algiers, arriving about 1730. Military personnel were then disembarked; very few were missing. Members of the crew, 180 persons, were sent aboard the *Orion* where accommodation and meals were provided . . .

Survivors left for England (aboard the *Cuba*) and arrived at Gourock on 5 April 1943.

❖

The significance of the role played by Union-Castle during World War II can be gauged by the fact that almost 1,3 million troops and government passengers were carried by the company's ships, which covered nearly seven million nautical miles.

One hundred and seventy-six sea-going members of the Union-Castle staff were decorated, among them Commodore Ernest Thornton, the senior master of the company, who was knighted for meritorious service. Probably the most famous among those to whom decorations were awarded was Captain Richard Wren, who received a DSO for commanding the *Rochester Castle*, one of the vessels to reach the beleaguered island of Malta in Operation Pedestal. Nineteen shore personnel were decorated, including Sir Vernon Thomson for his services as the shipping advisor to the Ministry of War Transport. Among others to receive awards were Mr A. M. Campbell, the chief agent for and a director of Union-Castle in South Africa (CMG), and Mr James Gray, the engineering superintendent (CBE).

The following figures indicate the price Union-Castle personnel paid in service to their country during World War II:

CASUALTIES (KILLED, MISSING OR WOUNDED):

Sea staff	283
Shore staff	23

PRISONERS OF WAR:

Sea staff	51
Shore staff	11

3

4

5

1 *The* Windsor Castle *at anchor in Table Bay on 21 April 1941.*

2 *An undated newspaper clipping. The official history of the Union-Castle Line makes no mention of this incident.*

3 *The* Athlone Castle *docks at A Berth in Cape Town harbour in July 1945, bringing home the first group of South African prisoners of war to be repatriated after World War II.*

4 *One of the most famous of the Union-Castle masters, Captain Richard Wren, was awarded the DSO for his command of the* Rochester Castle *during Operation Pedestal, the objective of which was the relief of the besieged island of Malta in August 1942. Although his vessel came under heavy attack and was severely damaged, Wren succeeded in bringing her into Valetta harbour. Not known for his diplomacy, Captain Wren nevertheless later commanded several of the passenger ships, including the* Capetown Castle, *but the rank of commodore eluded him.*

5 *Master of the* Windsor Castle *when that vessel met her end in March 1943, Captain J. C. Brown, CBE, RD, RNR, rose to the rank of commodore of the Union-Castle fleet, a position he held from 1947 to 1950. In his youth he had served in sail and in the Royal Naval Reserve before joining Union-Castle in 1908. At the outbreak of World War I, he transferred to the Royal Navy, serving first on HMS* Goliath *(sunk in the Dardenelles) and later, after recovering from wounds received at the landings at Anzac Beach, as a gunnery officer on HMAMC* City of London. *One of this ship's tasks had been to locate the German raider* Wolf, *but she evaded them on several occasions. In 1940, while in command of the* Athlone Castle, *Brown discovered among a group of German prisoners of war on board his ship a German shipmaster who, as a young officer, had been on the* Wolf *at the time the* City of London *was searching for her. Despite their countries being at war again, Brown and the German had much to talk and reminisce about.*

After the sinking of the Windsor Castle, *Captain Brown transferred to the* Arundel Castle. *His promotion to the rank of commodore and command of the* Pretoria Castle *on her maiden voyage represented the pinnacle of his career and, in the eyes of those who knew him, was the deserved reward for a remarkable man whose zeal as a shipmaster was superseded only by his zeal as a devout Christian, a commitment that earned him the nickname 'Eternity' Brown.*

1

6

The new order

1945-1955

2

In the immediate postwar period, ideal circumstances prevailed for the resumption of lucrative shipping links between South Africa and Britain, which, before the war, had been the Union's major trading partner.

Among the factors that favoured the shipping companies were:

* The ability of South Africa to provide Europe with urgently required food, and cement for the reconstruction of devastated cities and towns.
* South Africa's need for imported consumer goods, which she had largely had to forgo since the outbreak of war;
* South Africa's industrial sector, which had been forced to operate a programme of self-development during the war years, was now ripe for expansion into large-scale schemes requiring the importation of sophisticated electrical plant and machinery.
* Thousands of people were wanting to relocate from bleak, war-ravaged Britain and Europe to southern Africa, where they perceived there to be greater opportunities for a prosperous future.
* South African wartime brides were longing to join their husbands in Britain.
* There were hundreds of child-refugees who had been sent to South Africa for safety during the war and who now needed to be repatriated.
* Many hundreds of southern African residents were wanting to visit friends or family in Europe, or simply resume holiday plans that they had had to postpone at the outbreak of war.
* A huge backlog in shipments of mail needed to be cleared.

But despite the potentially lucrative two-way demand for passages and cargo space between South Africa and Britain, the shipping industry was inhibited by a scarcity of ships. Some of the mailships were still employed in the repatriation of troops, prisoners of war and displaced persons, while others were in shipyards being transformed from their wartime troop-carrying roles to their prewar standards of luxury. It took months to

3

restore the mail service to South Africa, and in the absence of a mail contract, the mail was carried by the first available ship.

Union-Castle chairman Sir Vernon Thomson, who had taken charge of the company in 1939, was a far-sighted man, mindful that in the relatively short duration of the war, rapid technological and sociological developments had occurred and that Union-Castle should be alert to the needs of the changing world. In fact, as early as 1943 he had circularized all Union-Castle offices in Britain and southern Africa requesting senior employees to furnish him with their comments and recommendations regarding trends that would affect the future of the company.

An accelerated mail service involving either a ten-day schedule using six ships or a twelve-day schedule with a fleet of seven ships was among the recommendations, in support of which it was cited that the *Stirling Castle*, *Athlone Castle* and *Capetown Castle* had shown during the war that they were capable of much higher speeds than had been necessary on the more leisurely prewar mail service. Another recommendation along these lines was that the hull of the *Winchester Castle* should be remoulded as that of the *Carnarvon Castle* had been in 1937, thereby enabling the ageing vessel to achieve higher speeds. Yet another respondent suggested that the mailships be re-engined and that two intermediate vessels be given the engines removed from the *Athlone Castle* and the *Stirling Castle*. Gas turbine propulsion was also proposed as a possible means of increasing speeds to meet the requirements of a faster service. Despite these comments, however, the thirteen-and-a-half-day schedule continued until the mid-sixties.

Aggressive marketing had been the subject of a memorandum written as early as 1939, but it was given wider circulation after the war because of its pertinence to the postwar scene. In it the writer suggested that Union-Castle agents were too complacent in their quest for passenger bookings and quoted an example:

> I think of one instance at Murraysburg in the heart of the Karoo where the agent had not done a booking in five years. I asked him if he had anyone in the district who had thought of taking a holiday and he referred me to a local Afrikaans gentleman. Before I left the town the following day, I had booked this gentleman and twelve other Afrikaans-speaking people from Port Elizabeth to Beira and back, all of whom had never been on a vessel before.

Another agent warned that Union-Castle would experience severe competition from the Blue Funnel Line which, prior to the war, had offered passages between Britain and South Africa on their Britain-South Africa-Australia service. 'And they cater for the family man,' he wrote, implying that Union-Castle neglected this aspect.

Among the memoranda that reached the desk of the chairman shortly after the war were several forecasting that the greatest competitor for Union-Castle would be the aeroplane, particularly as wartime exigencies had seen the development of the jet engine and demonstrated that large aircraft could be adapted for transporting passengers over long distances. One respondent forecast that while there was the hope that people would

1 The Winchester Castle *in a severe gale in the Bay of Biscay.*
2 Sir Vernon Thomson, chairman of Union-Castle from 1939 to 1953.
3 The Stirling Castle *off the Atlantic coast of the Cape Peninsula.*

1

2

continue to patronize the ships for vacational purposes, 'with aeroplanes capable of carrying up to four hundred passengers, the position [for Union-Castle's passenger ships] would be serious, provided that [air] fares are within the reach of the average person . . .' Other memoranda were in similar vein:

> The community will become progressively air-minded and air competition will increasingly be felt. The development of world-wide air services . . . will undoubtedly create new traffic but much of the business they will attract will not be new. A proportion will be secured at the expense of existing means of transport, both rail and sea, and it is unfortunately probable that much of this diverted traffic will be of the most remunerative order – first class passengers and high-rated freight . . . [Therefore] it must be regarded as a cardinal necessity that every attention be directed to the making of our services as attractive as possible to new business created by a travel desire arising from war experiences and particularly to existing classes of business not certain to be attracted to the air.
>
> Interchangeability with air services of returning orders would appear desirable as helping to retain part of our business . . . Special attention to family facilities will be desirable.
>
> Wartime development in aeronautical science and design covering gas turbine engines, jet propulsion, rocket boost on take-off, admitting increased payloads, stratosphere flying . . . have so widened the scope, elasticity and efficiency of air transport, that today, and in the future, the air will unquestionably command certain classes of traffic.

Outlined in this memorandum were the types of passengers likely to travel by air in the future: business executives, government employees, sports teams, visiting musicians and leading theatrical artists, teachers travelling during the annual long holiday, students proceeding overseas for examinations, 'persons for whom a sea voyage is no longer attractive, travellers from mid-continental areas such as Johannesburg northwards who presently incur the loss of time and considerable expense en route to an embarkation port'.

Central and East African travellers, for whom aircraft would provide a far more convenient mode of travel, were also singled out, as was that segment of the population for whom the anticipated postwar boom was expected to create greater affluence.

One aspect suggested by Mr G. T. Hankinson of the Johannesburg office was 'the possibility that the Company may find it advisable (if permitted by the British and South African governments) to operate an Airways Service as an adjunct to our Sea service'. He also thought that aircraft accidents and baggage restrictions versus the leisurely lifestyle offered by the ocean liner would continue to influence many travellers in favour of a sea voyage.

Sir Vernon Thomson himself fell prey to the lure of air travel when, in 1945, he flew to South Africa (a thirty-six-hour trip in those days) to negotiate a new ten-year mail contract to take effect in January 1947.

Inter alia, the new contract made provision for:

* voyages of thirteen and a half days in each direction between Southampton and Cape Town;
* the purchase by Union-Castle of more products of the Union, particularly in respect of stores for the ships;
* the use, as far as was practicable, of the ship repair facilities of the Union's ports; and
* the employment of 'Union nationals to an extent of not less than twenty-five percent of the personnel [officers and ratings], provided that
  a) a sufficient number of suitable, qualified applicants are available, and
  b) the terms and conditions of their employment shall be those respectively applicable to other personnel . . . employed by the contractor'.

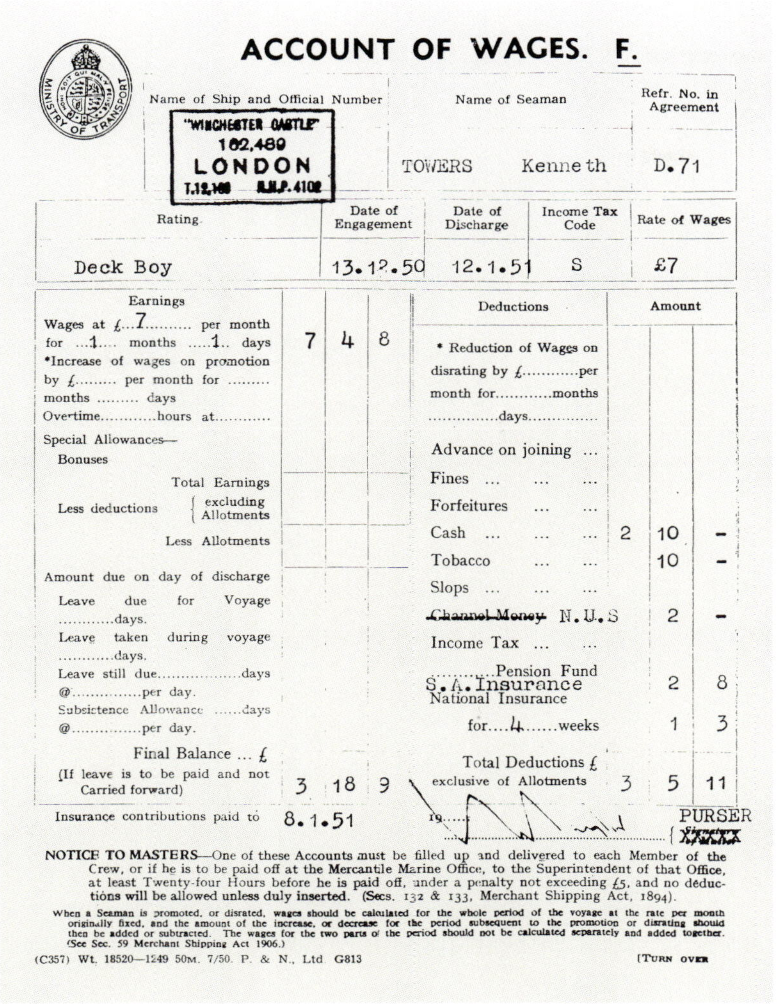

ACCOUNT OF WAGES. F.

MINISTRY OF TRANSPORT

Name of Ship and Official Number	Name of Seaman	Refr. No. in Agreement
"WINCHESTER CASTLE" 182,480 LONDON T.12,169 [illegible].4102	TOWERS Kenneth	D.71

Rating	Date of Engagement	Date of Discharge	Income Tax Code	Rate of Wages
Deck Boy	13.12.50	12.1.51	S	£7

Earnings	£	s.	d.	Deductions	£	s.	d.
Wages at £...7......... per month for ...1.... months .....1.. days *Increase of wages on promotion by £......... per month for .... months .... days Overtime...........hours at........... Special Allowances— Bonuses	7	4	8	* Reduction of Wages on disrating by £...........per month for...........months ....days..............			
				Advance on joining ...			
Total Earnings				Fines			
Less deductions { excluding Allotments				Forfeitures			
Less Allotments				Cash	2	10	-
				Tobacco		10	-
Amount due on day of discharge				Slops			
Leave due for Voyage ....days.				~~Channel Money~~ N.U.S		2	-
Leave taken during voyage ....days.				Income Tax			
Leave still due..................days @..............per day.				..........Pension Fund S.A. Insurance		2	8
Subsistence Allowance ......days @..............per day.				National Insurance for....4......weeks		1	3
Final Balance ... £ (If leave is to be paid and not Carried forward)	3	18	9	Total Deductions £ exclusive of Allotments	3	5	11

Insurance contributions paid to 8.1.51

19...... PURSER { Signature of Master

NOTICE TO MASTERS—One of these Accounts must be filled up and delivered to each Member of the Crew, or if he is to be paid off at the Mercantile Marine Office, to the Superintendent of that Office, at least Twenty-four Hours before he is paid off, under a penalty not exceeding £5, and no deductions will be allowed unless duly inserted. (Secs. 132 & 133, Merchant Shipping Act, 1894).

When a Seaman is promoted, or disrated, wages should be calculated for the whole period of the voyage at the rate per month originally fixed, and the amount of the increase, or decrease for the period subsequent to the promotion or disrating should then be added or subtracted. The wages for the two parts of the period should not be calculated separately and added together. (See Sec. 59 Merchant Shipping Act 1906.)

(C357) Wt. 18520—1249 50M. 7/50. P. & N., Ltd G813 [TURN OVER

3

A MAILSHIP CHRISTMAS

Christmas at sea on board a mailship was always very special. At the top of the foremast a great Christmas tree was fixed, and special programmes heralded the festivities aboard. The Cape Argus *of 23 December 1955 carried the following article:*

> *The most important man aboard the* Stirling Castle *on Christmas Day will not be the Captain, but a saloon steward . . . After the Church Service, 25-year-old Mr James Lindburg of Southampton will be the centre of attraction. At the strike of a gong and heralded by trumpets, he will enter the big dining saloon as Father Christmas and distribute presents to more than one hundred children aboard the liner . . . Mr Lindburg looks the part too, for he is over six feet, thick set, and has a round jolly face . . .*
>
> *Today, the catering staff were busy putting up last-minute decorations throughout the ship. The holly and the mistletoe will be put up tomorrow night.*
>
> *A party of young stewards spent the morning blowing up balloons.*

Included as a sop to the South African Government, which sometimes drove a hard bargain with the mailship company (which, in turn, was always anxious to protect its precious contract), the latter clause hardly altered employment opportunities for South Africans in the Union-Castle fleet. In reality, there were few South Africans wishing to embark on a sea career; rather, that clause enabled hundreds of South Africans to work their passage to Britain by signing on for a one-way voyage during which they would perform only menial tasks. Few South African-born men reached senior sea-going positions in Union-Castle; Captain Norman Lloyd was the first to command a Union-Castle vessel (one of the cargo-ships), and he later went on to become commodore aboard the *S.A. Vaal*, but in all, only three South African-born officers were ever given permanent command of a mailship.

Another concession to the South African authorities was the clause in which Union-Castle agreed to register certain of its ships at Union ports. Initial excitement at the prospect changed to considerable dismay in some shipping circles when the identity of the vessels to be transferred to the South African register became known. The ships concerned (the *Drakensberg Castle* and *Good Hope Castle* – freighters employed on the southern Africa-America trade) were a far cry from the mailships that many had envisaged would fly the South African flag. Twenty years would elapse before that happened.

Nevertheless, Sir Vernon Thomson gained for Union-Castle considerable favour from his visit to South Africa when he announced that a contract had been awarded to the Harland & Wolff yard in Belfast for the construction of two 28 000-ton mailships to replace the *Warwick Castle* and the *Windsor Castle* – both lost during the war. Because the new ships were the largest ordered up to that time for the South African trade, the announcement generated considerable interest in both Britain and South Africa.

As none of the prewar passenger mailships was quite ready to take the first sailing on the mail schedule in 1947, it fell to a fruitship, the *Roxburgh Castle*, to inaugurate the postwar mail service. Built in 1945 to replace an earlier vessel of the same name that had been lost in 1943, she left Southampton for the Cape on 2 January 1947. Four days later the fruitship *Riebeeck Castle* sailed from Cape Town to start the northbound schedule. As both ships could maintain the relatively high speed of about 18 knots with a capacity load of over 8 000 tons of cargo, they were perfectly adequate short-term substitutes for the passenger liners. It was only days later, however, that, with a maximum passenger complement and holds full to the hatch-coamings, the *Capetown Castle* made her way down Southampton Water to be the first of the passenger mailships to re-enter service.

Following her was the newly named intermediate liner, *Warwick Castle*. As the *Pretoria Castle*, she had been completed in Belfast for the round-Africa service in 1939, and it was under that name that she had served in World War II. At the end of the war, Union-Castle repurchased her from the Government, and after a refit that restored her to her former gracious lines, she joined the mail service until the other ships returned. Her eight-cylinder engines enabled her to reach 19 knots, which meant that she could cover the distance between Southampton and Cape Town in almost the same time as the mailships. Her sister ship, the *Durban Castle* (which, in 1938, had been the second ship in a new trend of naming some Union-Castle ships after imaginary South African castles), was also drafted into the mail service from 1947.

On 15 May 1947, it was the turn of the *Athlone Castle* to re-enter the mail service. In

1 *This advertisement appeared in the July 1947 issue of* The South African Shipping News and Fishing Industry Review.

2 *A poster promoting the adventurous aspect of sea travel.*

3 *An account of wages for deck boy Kenneth Towers, one of the many South Africans who worked a passage on the mailships.*

1

2

3

POSTCARD MESSAGE

Written on board the Arundel Castle *in May 1951, and posted in East London to an address in Pinelands, Cape Town:*

> *Just a few lines before we go ashore for the day. The three days in P.E. were very enjoyable and the weather was perfect; not a scrap of wind or rain the whole time. This ship is far steadier than the Stirling; in fact the vibration isn't noticeable at all. Even Rob didn't feel a thing. We have a 3-berth cabin to ourselves.*
>
> *Love*
>
> (SIGNATURE INDISTINCT)

MURDER ON THE DURBAN CASTLE

During the postwar period, while the mailships were being refitted and others were employed as immigrant liners, the Durban Castle *made several voyages on the mail schedule. Among her passengers on a voyage from Cape Town to Southampton in October 1947 was the young British actress Gay Gibson, who had come to South Africa to visit her father and had subsequently appeared in a play in Johannesburg.*

When the vessel was eight days out of Cape Town, the nightwatchmen responded to an alarm bell from her cabin. There they found a steward, James Camb, who assured them that all was in order. They reported the incident to the officer of the watch who shrugged it off. Only when the stewardess arrived with the morning tea and found Miss Gibson missing was the alarm raised. Captain A.G.V. Patey, later commodore of the line, turned the vessel to search for the actress, but to no avail. A shipboard search also revealed no trace of her.

The nightwatchmen's report was followed up and Camb was interviewed by the master who ordered the ship's surgeon to examine him. Although fresh scratches, consistent with a clawing action, were found on his face, Camb vehemently denied involvement in the mysterious disappearance of the actress. He was kept in custody until British police removed him from the vessel off the Isle of Wight and formally charged him with the murder of Gay Gibson. Camb made a statement to the police that he had gone to the cabin to have a drink with her, that she had succumbed to a fit and had apparently died. In a panic, he had pushed the body through the porthole.

The trial caused a sensation and was front page news for weeks. A murder charge without the body having been recovered made for a most unusual – and difficult – case, but despite Camb's insistence on the truthfulness of his statement, the jury returned a verdict of guilty.

Camb's sentence of death was upheld by the Court of Appeal but it was later commuted to life imprisonment. Released on parole in 1959, he was later found guilty on four different counts of indecent assault and returned to prison for an indefinite period.

4

the postwar refit of the vessel, indirect illumination had been provided in her first class public rooms, making her the first British passenger liner so fitted. In a brochure to mark the return of the *Athlone Castle* to the mail service, the public relations department of the company enthused:

> Her handsome and lofty Lounge, Drawing Room, Long Gallery (with an up-to-date Library), the Smoking Room and the Dining Saloon with sycamore chairs and ivory-coloured walls, have all assumed their prewar character, whilst in Cabin Class, a high standard of refinement and comfort has also been attained.

The *Stirling Castle* only arrived in South Africa later that year on her first postwar voyage as a mailship. The other three mailships – *Carnarvon Castle*, *Winchester Castle* and *Arundel Castle* – were required for a different service. Initially they were used to repatriate the wives and children of British servicemen (mostly RAF personnel or Royal Naval men) who had been deployed at southern African bases at some stage of the war. Their second commission was the transporting of immigrants.

During the war, thousands of British servicemen had passed through South African ports en route to or from various theatres of war. Attracted by its climate, many decided that once the war was over they would settle in South Africa, where they also perceived there to be greater employment opportunities. Welcoming the interest in immigration to the country, which was in need of skilled workers for the rapidly expanding mining and industrial sectors, the South African Government approached Union-Castle to provide ships to convey the new settlers from Britain – a scheme that complemented the British repatriation of women and children.

For these new roles the troopdecks were modified and a number of smaller cabins were provided, but the accommodation remained rather austere. And whereas their peacetime passenger complement had been close to 600, the *Winchester Castle* and the *Carnarvon Castle* now had capacity for more than a thousand passengers, while the *Arundel Castle* carried nearly 900.

1 *The customs shed, Cape Town. With immigration to South Africa at its height in the immediate postwar period, port officials worked under considerable pressure to clear the large numbers of immigrants arriving not only in the mailships but also in liners belonging to Ellerman & Bucknall, Shaw-Savill and Holland-Afrika, as well as the Union-Castle intermediates and the Dutch immigrant ships.*

2 *The first class dining saloon on the* Capetown Castle *in 1948. Judging from the ladies' attire, it is probable that this photograph was taken on sailing day when passengers could invite guests for luncheon on board the liner.*

3 *One of four postcards of the* Arundel Castle *issued after 1937.*

4 *The* Athlone Castle.

1

On the southbound voyage, the ships were full, but northbound, after the initial repatriation of servicemen and their families had been completed, the ships were travelling nearly empty. This provided an opportunity for cheap travel for South African residents – an opportunity seized by many who desired to visit relatives or friends in Britain.

One voyage of the *Winchester Castle* in 1948 was particularly noteworthy. Once the ship had landed her 900 British immigrants in Cape Town and refuelled, she was directed to Mombasa to embark a similar number of Polish women and children who had been in Kenya during the war. The master of the *Winchester Castle* was due to retire, and as neither he nor his ship had ever had an opportunity to break a record, he found the chance to achieve fame – he would break the Cape Town-Durban record.

Keeping well inshore to avoid the Mozambique Current sweeping southwards along the east coast of South Africa, the ship was abeam the Bluff at Durban after a passage from Cape Town of only forty-eight hours. There was much cheering and cap-waving to celebrate the record. The *Winchester Castle* then continued to Mombasa, embarked the Polish refugees and returned to Britain. It was not a pleasant voyage, for there was considerable conflict between the passengers and members of the ship's company, usually over indiscipline among the children – a problem more often than not exacerbated by the language barrier and differing cultures.

Not only were the captain's memories of his final command soured by the frustrations of the last leg of his voyage, but also the euphoria of his earlier Cape Town-Durban run quickly evaporated when he learned that the record had already been set by another Union-Castle vessel back in 1937. That record-breaking vessel had been none other than the smallest deepsea unit of the fleet – the fruitship *Roslin Castle*!

Back in Belfast, work had begun on the first of the 28 000-ton liners. The keel had been laid shortly before Christmas 1945, and steadily the vessel took shape according to plan. Names had been chosen for both ships: the first to be launched would bear the name *Pretoria Castle*. This choice had clearly been a political move, influenced by the rising tide of Afrikaner nationalism as well as by the swiftly expanding Afrikaner involvement in commerce and industry. (Doubtless the 1939 intermediate liner, *Pretoria Castle*, had been renamed *Warwick Castle* in 1946 in order to release 'Pretoria' for the new flagship.) The second of the two ships was to be called the *Edinburgh Castle*, a name borne by two earlier liners and one that reflected the Scottish bond which the company always cherished. After all, Sir Donald Currie had been a Scot, as was the current chairman.

Sir Vernon Thomson already had in mind the person he wished to launch the *Pretoria Castle* – Mrs Issie Smuts, wife of the wartime hero and now prime minister of South Africa, Field Marshal ('General') Jan Smuts. However, as she refused to travel to Belfast for the ceremony, all the appropriate technology of the time had to be enlisted to ensure that 'Ouma' Smuts could nevertheless launch the largest liner yet built for the South African trade. And so it was arranged that she should press a button in the sitting room of her home in Irene, Transvaal, thereby triggering an electric impulse that would be transmitted by landline to Cape Town, whence it would be sent by radio to London and there retransmitted by landline to Belfast. There the impulse would release a bottle of South

2

3

THE DECK BRANCH

Dating from the age of sail, and thus pre-dating the Engineering Branch, the Deck Branch (or Seaman Branch) is the oldest and therefore the most senior of the lower deck hierarchy. The duties of the Deck Branch range from the maintenance of the paintwork, decks and cargo gear of the ship, to serving as lookouts while the ship is in busy shipping lanes or at times of poor visibility. They also assist with the handling of mooring lines when the ship is docking or undocking.

Like the other branches on board ship, the Deck Branch has its own hierarchy, commencing at the bottom with the deck boys and rising to boatswain (or bosun) – a man with vast experience of practical seamanship as well as possessing ability to control his subordinates. He is the link between the Deck Branch and the chief officer, on whose shoulders rests the responsibility for the proper maintenance of the ship. Thus a good bosun is vital to the smooth operation of a ship. On the old passenger liners with a complement of some fifty seamen and the need for ongoing maintenance work, the role of the bosun was of even greater importance.

The bosun, carpenter (a skilled shipwright) and the master-at-arms (the ship's policeman, who probably had been recruited from the police force of one of the larger British cities) were the aristocracy of the lower deck. Although they shared the petty officers' mess, each had his own cabin and enjoyed special respect from the rest of the seamen.

On the passenger liners, the Deck Branch was divided into three watches, each of which lasted four hours and comprised a bosun's mate, who was in charge, seven seamen and a few deck boys. Also attached to each watch were three quartermasters, who steered the ship on orders from the officer of the watch. Even in the latter years of the mail service, and despite the fact that every ship was equipped with an autopilot, steering was invariably done manually.

In addition to the watches, there were small teams of seamen who did 'daywork'. At sea these men would be assigned to maintenance work: usually cleaning paintwork, chipping rust, or washing decks – important functions for keeping passenger ships in good condition. No effort was spared in the maintenance of the hundreds of square metres of teak decks in the mailships, and although the daymen would do some of the deck-cleaning, the bulk of that work was done by the seamen in the middle watch (the 'graveyard watch') from midnight to 04:00 when the promenade decks were largely deserted. Using hoses, brooms, caustic soda, soft-soap and holystones, the seamen would ensure that the decks were spotlessly clean well before the first early-risers among the passengers came on deck. These well-maintained teak decks were an attractive feature of all passengers liners until the early sixties when it was found to be quicker and more economical to use a composition in the construction of ships' passenger decks.

While the ship was in port, the daymen would be allocated to the ship's cargo holds to assist with the correct loading, stowing and discharging of cargo. Their presence in the holds also served as a deterrent against the broaching of the cargo by dockers.

African wine to smash against the bow of the new liner and also set in motion the launching mechanism.

Thus, shortly after 14:25 on 19 August 1947, and preceded by the playing of several Afrikaans folksongs, Mrs Smuts's voice, relayed by radio from South Africa, came clearly over the public address system at the shipyard: 'I name this ship *Pretoria Castle*. May God protect the good ship *Pretoria Castle*, and all who sail in her.' Mrs Smuts then made the same pronouncement in Afrikaans and pressed the button. The bottle of wine christened the ship, which had a large South African flag flying at the bow. To the cheers of thousands who had assembled to watch the launch, the *Pretoria Castle* immediately began to glide down the slipway.

The next morning, the *Rand Daily Mail* of Johannesburg gave its readers the following description of what had transpired in the sitting room of the Smuts home:

> Mrs Smuts sat back and, with a sigh of relief, turned to Mr A. London, the Johannesburg Manager of the Union-Castle Company, and said: 'I am very glad it passed off so well. I was very nervous about it. I am very proud to have launched the *Pretoria Castle*. Of course, there is no place in the world like Pretoria and I am very glad they have named the ship after Pretoria. One day, I hope to see my ship when she visits a South African port.'

While the overall design of the *Pretoria Castle* was similar to that of the *Capetown Castle*, there were also significant differences, the most apparent being her additional 2 000 tons of cargo space and her steam turbines – a departure from the type of machinery in the motorships that had been built since 1926.

Two months later, the Union-Castle publicity team swung into action again – this time for the launching of the *Edinburgh Castle*. Sir Vernon scored a public relations triumph when Princess Margaret agreed to officiate at the launching and, as with the *Pretoria Castle*, the event attracted wide media coverage, particularly as it was to be the princess's first solo public engagement. The launch took place on 16 October 1947. Unfortunately, the BBC could relay only the last ten minutes of the ceremony on their shortwave transmission because the event coincided with the one o'clock news bulletin.

For table decorations at the luncheon, and for the huge massed flower arrangements adorning the venue, fresh spring flowers from the Western Cape had been shipped to

1 *The* Carnarvon Castle *as an immigrant liner in the immediate postwar period. She still has her wartime signal mast atop the bridge.*

2 *On board the* Windsor Castle, *approaching the entrance to Durban harbour. The foredeck and the fo'c'sle area were home to the lower deck ratings.*

3 *Early risers would have seen the crew washing and scrubbing the teak decks which, with the exception of the* Transvaal Castle, *were a feature of all the mailships. The compound decks of the* Transvaal Castle *drew criticism from the traditionalists, who preferred the bleached teak of the older vessels.*

1

2

Britain under refrigeration. Against a backdrop of proteas, silverleaf, ericas and pin cushions, Sir Vernon Thomson paid tribute to the princess:

> We felt greatly honoured by the presence of Her Royal Highness, the Princess Margaret, to perform today's ceremony. We rejoice that this, her first individual public function, has passed off so successfully, so admirably . . .
>
> I hope you all observed when the vessel left the slips and became waterborne, how nicely she curtsied to the Royal lady who had just named her. [He had used a similar metaphor when speaking of Mrs Smuts at the launch of the *Pretoria Castle*.] . . . I am sure that it will be a real source of satisfaction to South Africans that Her Royal Highness, who left such happy memories behind her there earlier this year, has now named a ship which will ply regularly between South Africa and the United Kingdom . . .

Perhaps because of Donald Currie's gift of £5 to a young student called Smuts in 1891 and a rebate on his passage money at the time, Union-Castle had enjoyed considerable support from the Smuts government. In the wake of the South African general election of 1948 – a watershed for the country – Union-Castle's British control threatened the company's privileged position.

The election victory of the Afrikaner-based Nationalist Party over the Smuts government introduced a range of different policies and attitudes in the country. The new government soon indicated its intentions to give preference to South African interests and particularly to those in which Afrikanerdom was well represented. Immigration from

AERIAL VIEW OF CAPETOWN

Union-Castle Line Tourist Class

MENU

R.M.M.V. "Stirling Castle"

DINNER

Cream of Tomato

Tronçons of Agulhas Sole au Citron

Pale Ham and Spinach

Roast Chicken with Stuffing

Fresh Garden Peas au Sucre

Potatoes : Château Vapeur

SWEETS :

Plum Pudding Sweet Sauce

Fruit Salad with Cream

Dessert Coffee

B23. 48. DECEMBER 14, 1950.

3

THE UNION-CASTLE MAIL STEAMSHIP COMPANY, LIMITED.

(REGISTERED IN ENGLAND.)

Head Offices :—3, Fenchurch Street, London, E.C.3.

Royal Mail Service.

TOURIST CLASS PASSENGER'S TICKET.

4

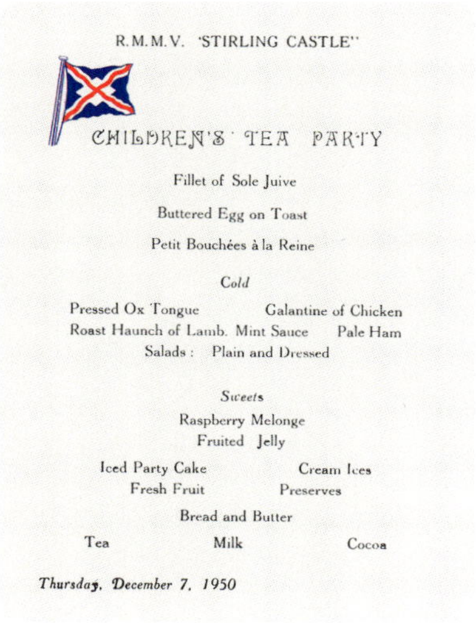
R.M.M.V. "STIRLING CASTLE"

CHILDREN'S TEA PARTY

Fillet of Sole Juive

Buttered Egg on Toast

Petit Bouchées à la Reine

Cold

Pressed Ox Tongue Galantine of Chicken

Roast Haunch of Lamb. Mint Sauce Pale Ham

Salads : Plain and Dressed

Sweets

Raspberry Melonge

Fruited Jelly

Iced Party Cake Cream Ices

Fresh Fruit Preserves

Bread and Butter

Tea Milk Cocoa

Thursday, December 7, 1950

5

Britain was not encouraged as it had been during the time of Smuts; rather, immigration schemes aimed at inducing Dutch and German citizens to settle in South Africa received a higher profile.

Soon after the new government had assumed office, there were calls for a South African shipping company to be established to carry the mail, not only to Britain but also to countries on the European mainland. Local shipping expertise in South Africa was not plentiful, however, and certainly at the time there was no capital available to begin a rival operation to Union-Castle, but the company could no longer be assured of retaining the mail contract indefinitely.

As the arrival date of the *Pretoria Castle* in Cape Town drew near, the Mother City shipping began to buzz with excitement, and the rise of nationalism and all that it foreshadowed was temporarily forgotten. On Thursday, 22 July 1948, the SABC had relayed the BBC commentary of the departure of the Union-Castle flagship from Southampton; five days later, another BBC report – this time from the ship itself – had described, among other things, the Crossing the Line ceremony. When the ship arrived off the port limits at daybreak on Thursday, 5 August 1948, Capetonians were not disappointed. The *Cape Argus* of the following day commented at length on the new vessel and the significance of its arrival:

> For residents of Cape Town of many years' standing, and perhaps specially for children, the conspicuously-coloured liners of the Union-Castle Company are features of the local scene, as familiar, and almost as indispensable, as Table Mountain itself. Every mailship comes to be regarded as in some sense a friend, and each of them acquires a personality of her own, so that people come to think of the old *Balmoral Castle* or even the old *Saxon* with a certain reminiscent affection.
>
> Today, it is a special pleasure to welcome the newest addition to this Company of friends in the person of the *Pretoria Castle*. This vessel, whose massive yet graceful lines are so characteristic of the Company's ships, is as fine an example of a modern liner as each of her predecessors was in its day. Her very existence is a sign of the return to those peaceful times which were punctuated by the regular appearance of some larger, newer, finer mailship and also, a symbol of the steadily growing volume of the Union's trade.
>
> It might be added that the Company deserves a word of appreciation for its decision to make possible an even faster mail service than the present one by equipping the vessel and her successor for speeds which will enable them to operate the service in one day less than at present. The whole conception of this great vessel is a mark of the Company's confidence in the future of South Africa and South Africans appreciate it.

The liner's arrival in Cape Town was described live to SABC radio audiences throughout the country, and her master, Commodore J.C. Brown, was interviewed by both the SABC and the press.

At every South African port there were welcoming functions. On hand to greet the liner at Durban were 470 Pretoria schoolchildren, their thirty teachers, two representatives of the Transvaal Education Department, two supervisors and four nurses, all of whom had been brought to the port by train at Union-Castle's expense. Sir Vernon Thomson, who had sailed from Southampton to Cape Town in the liner, intended to be in Durban to welcome the children and their chaperones, but because he was delayed by a lengthy meeting in Cape Town, he missed the flight to Durban. Immediately, a military plane was placed at his disposal and he fortunately arrived in time to greet the children. After lunch on the ship, the young visitors spent the afternoon on the beach before boarding their trains for the overnight journey back to Pretoria.

At a luncheon on board the Union-Castle flagship two days before she sailed from

1 *The* Pretoria Castle*, the first post-World War II mailship. Until 1956, she had brown masts and derricks.*

2 *Part of the engines of the* Pretoria Castle *at the Harland & Wolff engine works in Belfast, November 1947.*

3 *Tourist class passengers ate well but the fare in first class was said to compare with cuisine prepared in even the best hotels ashore.*

4 *Thousands of excited travellers would have collected their tickets (in a folder such as this one of 1951) from the Union-Castle offices.*

5 *For children, one of the highlights of the voyage was the special tea party.*

1

2

3

THE CATERING BRANCH

A complement of hundreds of passengers and four or five hundred crewmembers demanded extensive and complex catering arrangements, especially since culinary excellence and variety were Union-Castle trademarks. To meet passenger expectations, therefore, Union-Castle only signed on those highly qualified chefs who were not only prepared to tolerate the relatively spartan equipment and conditions but also enjoyed the challenge of doing so.

Apart from table service, stewards' duties included setting tables, cleaning the deck of the dining saloon and restowing tableware. For these duties there was a working rig (a jacket with pale blue stripes, and dark trousers) but the uniform that will be more familiar to former mailship passengers was the starched white jacket with a step collar, a plaited purple braid on the shoulders denoting senior stewards.

Carrying several plates or food platters at a time, the stewards would sweep through the 'out' swing doors of the galley into the dining saloon, hurry to the table and serve. With perhaps 200 people to feed in an hour before the second sitting, and considering that passengers had to be served almost irrespective of sea conditions, it is not surprising that, in their haste, stewards dropped dozens of plates. In rough seas, the table cloths were dampened and sides, known as 'fiddles', put along the tables to prevent plates sliding to the deck. There were exceptional times when the ship was rolling too severely for the stewards to be able to carry the plates, and meals were either suspended, or simpler fare, such as sandwiches, was served to those passengers whose constitution permitted them to eat. Food preparation under such conditions was a nightmare. Special clamps were used to secure pots to the stoves in the galley as stocks and sauces slopped about with each roll of the ship, and fat and oil became extremely hazardous to work with.

An interesting departure from the male-dominated traditions was the introduction in 1961 of 'stewardettes' in the one-class dining saloon of the Transvaal Castle. *This step can be attributed largely to economics, the belief being that women could be paid less than their male counterparts and therefore result in a considerable saving on the portage bill for the mailship. But once the women's liberation movement had gained ground this discrimination did not last long and, for practical reasons, many of the women were replaced by men.*

A reminder of days when it was deemed essential to supplement diets at sea was the serving of beef tea mid-morning and mid-afternoon by stewards, who would make their way around the promenade decks and into the public rooms with trolleys laden with large pots of the beverage. This custom lingered well into the latter days of the mail service when, as one of the measures taken to cut costs, it was abandoned.

Sceptics have often remarked that the route between Cape Town and Southampton is clearly marked on the seabed by the crockery and cutlery thrown overboard by scullery hands who grew weary of the monotony of washing the dishes almost continually from early morning to late at night. Finds of crockery during recent dredging in Table Bay harbour suggest that the practice of ditching dirty crockery was not confined to periods at sea. Dishwashers later replaced the scullery boys.

The nomination as Captain's Tiger (or personal steward) was sought after by many stewards. Attached to the position were numerous privileges, including less mundane work and perhaps a more leisurely existence. But such perks mattered little when a captain was known for his volatile temperament. Few stewards wanted an assignment to such men, and most would have preferred the duties of their fellow-stewards.

The responsibilities of the Catering Branch extended well beyond culinary matters to the general welfare of the passengers. Cabin stewards and stewardesses cleaned the cabins, changed the linen and brought early morning tea or coffee to the passengers. In first class, considerably more individual attention was paid to passengers, particularly in the preparation of the wardrobe for the day, and in the provision of meals, drinks and snacks in the cabin.

The children's hostesses, often recruited from the ranks of nurses or pre-school teachers, were based in the playroom to relieve parents of the entertainment of their children. In the playroom, South African children were particularly pleased to find numerous British toys that were not easily obtained in South Africa and which helped to pass the time on the long passage to or from Britain.

Those stewards – and others in the Catering Branch – who had direct contact with the passengers benefited greatly from gratuities. Excluding the generous overtime paid by Union-Castle – and an energetic steward would volunteer for extra duties with that in mind – a basic wage could be trebled or even quadrupled if the steward provided good service to those passengers in his care.

SIR FRANCIS VERNON THOMSON

Sir Donald Currie, that energetic and farsighted Scot, would have found a kindred spirit in the man who in later years took over as chairman of Union-Castle. It was Vernon Thomson's tireless work, from the early 1930s until his death in harness in 1953, that raised Union-Castle to rank second only to P&O among British passenger fleets.

Like Currie, Thomson's family was from Scotland and, like Currie too, Thomson began his shipping career at an early age. He had just turned sixteen when, in 1897, he joined the shipping firm of Philipps, Philipps & Company, whose chairman, Sir Owen Philipps (later Lord Kylsant), was to play a significant role in Union-Castle's history. (Philipps's company also managed the affairs of King Line, one of the better-known British tramp companies.)

On behalf of Philipps, Philipps & Company, Thomson spent twenty years at the hub of the ship chartering business – the Baltic Exchange – where he gleaned the finer details of ship management and of which he was elected president in 1931. As early as 1914, his considerable ability was abundantly apparent and for the duration of World War I he served the Ministry of War Shipping as the assistant director of its ship management section. For this and other services to the State he received the KBE. (By that time he had already been appointed to the board of Philipps, Philipps & Company [in 1911] and was soon [in 1921] to join the board of the King Line.)

On the resignation of Sir Owen Philipps from the chairmanship of both King Line and Philipps, Philipps & Company in 1931, Sir Vernon, then fifty years old, took over the reins. An energetic man, he was elected to the board of Union-Castle in 1932, and within seven years had succeeded Sir Robertson Gibb as its chairman, holding the dual chairmanship of both King Line and Union-Castle.

As in World War I, he was called to assist the Ministry of War Shipping from 1939 to 1945, this time as principal shipping adviser and controller of commercial shipping. Back in the thick of things at Union-Castle from late 1945, Sir Vernon immediately succeeded in negotiating a new mail contract with the South African Government and proceeded to re-establish Union-Castle's prewar superiority on the South African trade. It was he who also engineered Union-Castle's acquisition of King Line in 1948 – a logical step since he was chairman of both.

A man of strong religious convictions, Sir Vernon Thomson neither smoked nor touched alcohol and he never married, choosing to live first with his aged mother – whom he supported from the day he received his first pay-packet – and then with one of his brothers.

His keen eye for detail was evidenced by his meticulous scrutiny of every contract, every ship's plan and every other document that crossed his desk. James Gray, the chief marine director of Union-Castle, recalled:

> *When on those ceremonial occasions in Belfast [the launching of ships], everything went like clockwork, so smoothly that we took it all for granted . . . He invariably travelled a day ahead of his guests with no other purpose than to rehearse every item of the programme until he was satisfied as to its execution and timing. And at daybreak the next morning, he would be at the docks to greet us individually.*

To many shareholders and the financial press Sir Vernon was a tight-fisted Scot who prevented the payment of decent dividends, but beneath the rather stern, and at times dour, façade, there lay a kindness and concern for people best illustrated by the celebrations to mark his seventieth birthday. Knowing the chairman's love of roses (he invariably wore one in his buttonhole), his office staff had presented him with a glass rose bowl. He was not only delighted with the gift, but so moved by the gesture that, from his own bank account, he wrote a cheque to the value of twenty-five guineas to each member of staff, messenger or manager. Then he invited all to see the bowl in place on his desk. But a further treat was in store for the London and Southampton employees. They were entertained to tea on the Rhodesia Castle, *which was in London at the time. And Sir Vernon greeted each one individually by name.*

His ships and the men who sailed them were closest to his heart. The masters had direct access to him, and he enjoyed meeting them; indeed, he made it his business to chat with the master of every ship, mailship or freighter, before it sailed from England – and on its return. Many employees of Union-Castle, junior or senior, related that, having met them once, Sir Vernon would call them by name whenever their paths crossed again, though many months, even years, might have elapsed between encounters.

He died as he probably would have wished – wearing out, rather than rusting away. Sitting at his desk in the Fenchurch Street head office of Union-Castle on 29 January 1953, he suffered a mild heart attack. While recovering in the Middlesex Hospital his preoccupation with work continued as he attempted to run the company from his bed. It was that which probably killed him, for he suffered a second – and this time fatal – heart attack on 8 February.

Sir Vernon's death left the company in some confusion. His rather dictatorial approach to his job had neither allowed for the delegation of responsibility nor for the training of a corps of successors. It nevertheless was written of him in the journal South Africa:

> *So passes one of the most distinguished figures in the British shipping world, and a man of individuality whose service to that country and Southern Africa was outstanding . . . The transformation which the Union-Castle fleet has undergone . . . may be looked upon as, in a special sense, his memorial for, such being the nature of the man, there was hardly a detail of this gigantic operation which did not bear the stamp of his individuality and taste . . . He had his hand firmly and constantly on every detail.*

4

5

Cape Town to Southampton, the company entertained some 200 prominent people, including politicians of various persuasions. At his table, Sir Vernon had on his right the recently elected Nationalist prime minister of South Africa, Dr D.F. Malan, and on his left Field Marshal Smuts. No doubt he took it all in his stride.

Only a few months after the maiden voyage of the *Pretoria Castle*, the arrival of the *Edinburgh Castle* on 23 December 1948 further stimulated a fascination for sea travel in South Africa, although it was six years later that she completed a run which was to secure her a place of distinction in the Union-Castle annals.

Commanding the *Edinburgh Castle* on her maiden voyage was Captain T.W. McAllen, whose sea career had started at the age of twelve when he entered the merchant navy as an apprentice. Like other masters of the mailships, all of whom were held in the highest esteem and frequently accorded celebrity status in the various ports at which they called, he was requested to perform special duties from time to time, such as the occasion on 1 March 1949 when he travelled to the windswept point of Cape Agulhas as the guest of

1 *A buffet lunch at sea on board the* Windsor Castle, *circa 1963.*
2 *Stewardettes in the galley on board the* Transvaal Castle, *1962.*
3 *Chefs on board the* Edinburgh Castle *enjoy a special drink with Captain Dylan Cambridge, DSO, RD, RNR.*
4 *The tourist class lounge on the* Stirling Castle.
5 *The tourist class dining saloon on the* Stirling Castle.

1

2

DIALOGUE BETWEEN MAILSHIPS AT SEA

To most passengers, the passing of the mailships at sea in close proximity and at full speed seemed a remarkable product of the liners sticking rigidly to their courses. It was, however, a carefully orchestrated event which made a pleasant interlude on the long voyage for both passengers and the ship's company.

Radio contact between the two ships was established well before the intended passing, and the ships adjusted speed to ensure that it occurred during daylight hours. With each ship plotting the movements of the other by radio direction finder, courses were altered to bring the vessels within a mile of each other. Once all the calculations had been made, the time of the passing would be announced earlier in the day.

Passengers thronged the railings to watch for the other liner. Excited cries and frantic pointing would indicate the smudge on the horizon which gradually emerged as the ship for which all had been waiting. Cameras were at the ready to record what was indeed a dramatic event as the two liners swept past each other at a combined 42 knots.

While the crews yelled across the gap and passengers waved, the two masters exchanged the traditional courtesies of dipping ensigns flying from the gaff on the mainmast. First to dip the ensign was the junior of the two masters. The ensign remained at the dip until the senior master had dipped and run up his ensign.

This practice occurred whenever Union-Castle ships passed, and not only those on the mail service. Occasionally this tradition led to difficulties in protocol, particularly when one of the larger mailships passed an intermediate whose master, although perhaps senior in years' service, was on a less prestigious unit of the fleet. In port it was a simpler matter; the moving ship dipped the ensign first, irrespective of the seniority of the master.

A practice behind the scenes during the passing of the mailships was that the southbound vessel would radio to the other the 'Skidlist' – the names of those of the ship's company who would sign off at Southampton for protracted leave, or to transfer to another ship.

As the two ships drew astern of each other, the camera lens caps were replaced and the passengers settled back into their shipboard routine.

STORMS AT SEA

On numerous occasions, the notoriously bad weather in the Bay of Biscay filled passengers with alarm as their ship was battered by heavy seas. On one voyage, the Carnarvon Castle *arrived in Cape Town having experienced the worst that the dreaded Bay could offer. The headline of the* Cape Argus *on 10 December 1954 read:*

THREE HURT IN MAILSHIP STORM ORDEAL

60 FT. WAVES, 70 M.P.H. GALE HIT CARNARVON CASTLE

The Carnarvon Castle *entered Cape Town harbour at 8.05 p.m. yesterday, fourteen hours late and with three passengers injured after the vessel had received a severe battering in a 70 m.p.h. gale in the Bay of Biscay on November 26.*

The following account by a passenger was related in the article:

We went to bed that night fully clothed and just clinging for dear life onto our bunks as the great ship heaved and rolled. Hardly any passengers went to the dining saloon and tea and sandwiches were served in the cabins.

Because of the ship's late arrival, the post office employees had to work through the night to ensure that the mail was delivered the following day.

Many believe that the sea off the South African coast surpasses the Bay of Biscay for its ferocity. On one voyage from Durban to East London in November 1962, passengers aboard the Edinburgh Castle *had begun to watch a film in the ship's lounge when suddenly the ship's bow plunged rapidly. Then there was a crash and the whole ship shuddered as a giant wave swept across the foredeck, smashing an empty horsebox and deck equipment as well as three large windows at the forward end of the promenade deck. Cabins forward of the ship's shop on the starboard side had to be evacuated as the surge of water had breached a door, resulting in considerable flooding.*

In strong winds, the high-sided mailships were particularly difficult to manoeuvre in port. Wind often caused delays in Cape Town and Port Elizabeth, while the narrow confines of East London harbour left little room for error when turning the ships, and frequently gales forced the liners to continue their voyage to the next port without entering the Buffalo River.

THE MAILSHIP WEEKEND IN PORT ELIZABETH

During their coastal schedule, the upcoast mailships used to spend the entire weekend in Port Elizabeth, arriving on a Saturday morning and sailing on the Sunday afternoon. The downcoast mailship would berth at daybreak on Saturday and leave that afternoon. During the wool or fruit seasons, however, when hundreds of bales of wool or cases of fruit had to be loaded, the ship would only sail on the Sunday afternoon.

Organized commerce in Port Elizabeth frequently agitated to alter the schedule so that two ships would not be in port together over a weekend. It was felt that, owing to the priority accorded the mailships, other vessels did not enjoy a satisfactory service, while the port services themselves were placed under severe pressure every weekend. Understandably, many people connected with the Union-Castle office and associated firms resented the loss of their weekend leisure time. Furthermore, there was little hope that goods discharged from a mailship on a Saturday or Sunday, would reach their consignees before Monday, thus negating the usual benefits. Local business too would have preferred the ships to call on weekdays, so that the 700-odd passengers could provide shops with additional revenue. (Strict trading hours regulations forced shops to close at midday on Saturdays.)

Union-Castle, however, was quick to point out that, since the wool sales were held on Tuesdays and Fridays, the mailships were in a good position to accept substantial cargoes of wool on the Saturday.

Occasionally, there were benefits to be derived from the mailships' simultaneous sojourn in Port Elizabeth and these were then fully exploited, as the Cape Argus *of 21 September 1955 reported:*

OPERATION SWOP FOR TEST MATCH MAILSHIPS

The Union-Castle Company will carry out 'Operation Swop' in harbour at Port Elizabeth on Saturday morning when the Edinburgh Castle *from Cape Town and the* Carnarvon Castle *from East London and Durban are due to dock.*

Each mailship will bring about 400 passengers to see the rugby test. [South Africa versus the British Lions.] Passengers from the Edinburgh Castle *will be transferred to the* Carnarvon Castle*, and vice-versa for the return passage . . . Both ships will sail on Sunday.*

honour of the South African Railways and Harbours Administration. There he ceremonially re-lit the 12-million-candle-power lighthouse lamp for its second century of operation.

In 1950, still in command of the *Edinburgh Castle*, McAllan was made commodore of the Union-Castle fleet, a position he held until his retirement in 1953. One year later a great honour went to his former command. Under the heading 'Record Run by Mailship in Gale', the *Cape Times* of 18 January 1954 reported:

> Thousands of people went to the docks or stood on the promenade at Green Point yesterday to see the 28,705-ton liner *Edinburgh Castle* come up Table Bay in a south-easter to end the fastest passage ever made between Britain and the Cape . . . The actual running time was 11 days 13 hours and 11 minutes which is a day less than the previous record set up by the *Carnarvon Castle* in 1938 over a slightly longer passage from Southampton. The times for the *Edinburgh Castle* are from Plymouth.
>
> The south-east trades worked up to a full gale in the last forty-eight hours of the record-breaking passage, but the liner fell only two hours behind the schedule she had set for herself after being delayed at Plymouth for five days by boiler trouble.
>
> On arrival at Cape Town, she had recouped nearly two days. At lunchtime yesterday, the *Edinburgh Castle* was sighted to the north-west. Pilot C.A.E. Deacon, accompanied by immigration and customs officers, set out from the port to meet the liner when she was still some distance off, but by the time the tug rounded the breakwater, the ship was bearing down on her fast . . . The immigration officers had interviewed the 500 passengers within an hour and a half, and within two hours of the liner docking, passengers for the coast started to embark.

Despite the enormous cost of bringing the ship out from England at such high speed – her average speed of 22,2 knots enforced an additional fuel consumption of 600 tons on the run – the record-breaking voyage generated much goodwill for the company. Ironically, the liner was unable to leave for the coast when ready because a south-east gale, gusting up to 100 kilometres an hour, represented a grave danger to the lightened ship and departure was delayed several hours.

Following the death of Sir Vernon Thomson in 1953, Union-Castle found itself in circumstances similar to those prevailing after the demise of Sir Donald Currie and the later ignominious fall of Lord Kylsant. Like Currie and Kylsant, Thomson had possessed dictatorial ways and had made virtually every policy decision affecting the company since 1939. Now, in the vacuum left by his death, there was a distinct lack of direction, and although the mantle of chairman fell to Sir George Christopher – a most able man, steeped in the operation of freighters, though not fully conversant with the operation of passenger liners – there was a management crisis.

In addition to the problematic internal politics of the company, air travel was posing a far greater threat to passenger liner operators than had been imagined. This was particularly true of the South African trade, for the Springbok Service of South African Airways and the British Overseas Aircraft Corporation had introduced jet aircraft on the London-Johannesburg route in 1952.

Amid the financial difficulties being experienced by Union-Castle, in 1955 came rumours of a takeover. P&O, and even Cunard, were whispered as possible buyers. Another contender, it was said, was the trampship operator, Jack Billmeir, who was buying considerable numbers of Union-Castle shares.

After a wrangle – at times acrimonious – between the eventual buyer and some of the more senior Union-Castle shareholders who opposed the takeover, it was announced that a party who twice before had offered to purchase Union-Castle was to take control.

---

1 *The arrival of the* Edinburgh Castle *after her record-breaking voyage to Cape Town from England in January 1954.*

2 *The* Athlone Castle *passing the* Carnarvon Castle *at sea.*

1

7

A change of flags

1955-1973

2

Because the Fenchurch Street offices of Union-Castle had been visited on several occasions by Clan Line officials, speculation was rife that the cargoship owners would be making a bid for Union-Castle. It was not surprising, therefore, that the newspapers of 4 October 1955 carried the story of a proposed merger between Union-Castle and Clan Line. Hectic lobbying brought an announcement the following day that a group of influential shareholders, including the trampship owner, Jack Billmeir, and the financier, Harold Drayton, intended to oppose the merger. Commented Billmeir, 'Union-Castle is a grand name in shipping, and should be able to hold its own. It would have, if I had been in charge . . . If Clan Line can do better, why not Union-Castle?'

A court bid in December of that year to halt the merger was dismissed, paving the way for further negotiations, which culminated in a profitable deal for Union-Castle shareholders and the withdrawal of formal opposition.

A merger it was not! When the legal complexities had been settled and a new company – the British & Commonwealth Shipping Company – formed, it was clear that Clan Line was in the driving seat, for it had contributed nearly sixty per cent to Union-Castle's forty per cent of the assets of the combined operation. Taking advantage of the restructuring, the chairman of Union-Castle, Sir George Christopher, retired, whereupon Lord Rotherwick (born Herbert Robin Cayzer) added Union-Castle's chief executive responsibilities to his own already bulging portfolio, appointing his nephew, Sir Nicholas Cayzer, as deputy chairman.

Each of the major companies in the British & Commonwealth Group (B&C) brought associated companies with them. Clan Line had the Scottish Shire Line and Houston Line, while Union-Castle had the trampship company King Line as well as Bullard King, whose ships had traded to South Africa for a century. B&C immediately rationalized their sailings on the respective routes and disposed of redundant vessels.

3

4

Each of the shipping lines within the B&C group retained its separate colours, and although the brown paint on the masts of Union-Castle ships was replaced with white, the familiar lavender hull as well as the red and black funnel colours remained. They were, however, required to fly the B&C pennant. Naturally, there was anxiety among Union-Castle personnel, both ashore and afloat, concerning their future within the new organization. To allay disquiet, Sir Nicholas Cayzer had written to all staff members, assuring them of the security of their jobs and promising that there would be no pooling of sea-going personnel. Vain words, for within a short period several former Clan Line men were aboard the mailships, and a few Union-Castle chief officers were learning the ways of command aboard Clan ships. As time passed increasing numbers of Clan Line men moved to the mailships – a development that fostered resentment among some Union-Castle officers who remained in the cargo fleet and for whom an appointment to a passenger ship would have been both a compliment and the realization of a lifelong ambition. Rationalization was the next step, and this resulted in several retrenchments. Understandably, many Union-Castle stalwarts felt that the 'club' atmosphere of the company had gone.

When the new mail contract was debated in the South African parliament in 1956, the member for Simon's Town, Mr L. Gay, conveyed to the House his dissatisfaction with the service that Union-Castle had offered prior to the merger. He alleged that the company had lagged behind many of the other big passenger ship operators in the general treatment of passengers, and he complained that in the new mail contract no provision had been made for the upgrading of passenger comfort. Many of the stewards, he maintained, were simply dodging National Service in Britain, and the company was accepting people who were unfit for the job. He noted too that there was a significant difference between the younger and the older section of the company's personnel, the latter group having grown up in the tradition of the company. 'It may be,' he went on, 'that, with the changeover of ownership and control of the line, we shall see an improvement.'

While there were several measures aimed at reducing costs – including the abolition of the long-standing custom of serving beef tea at 10:00 each morning – the Cayzers did improve the situation considerably. Many of the changes – some said they were reminiscent of the days of Sir Vernon Thomson – were masterminded by Sir Nicholas Cayzer's brother, Bernard, who later, upon the death of Lord Rotherwick in 1959, became deputy chairman when Sir Nicholas was appointed chairman. Bernard Cayzer took a special interest in the shipping portfolio of B&C, and overall passengers did get a better deal, often manifested in small, yet meaningful, ways. For instance, Bernard Cayzer was appalled to learn that the deckchairs were stowed two days before arrival in Southampton and immediately ordered that they be available to passengers even as the ship entered Southampton Water. The pianists, who had been accustomed to dashing for their cabins shortly after ten each evening, were instructed to continue playing until the last passenger had left the lounge. And the standard of catering – in earlier days the boast of the mailships – also improved.

At this time, B&C began to diversify into property, air travel, hotels and insurance but its activities nevertheless continued to be dominated by shipping.

Shortly before their merger with Clan Line, Union-Castle had placed an order with Harland & Wolff for another 28 000-ton mailship, similar in many respects to the *Edinburgh Castle*. Immediately upon taking over, however, the Cayzers stopped construction work on the new liner until they had signed a revised contract in terms of which the new ship would be substantially different from that of the original order. She was to be nearly 5 metres longer than the *Edinburgh Castle*, while the main feature of the revised contract – her 46 000 shaft horse power – was to make her second only to the 1960 *Windsor Castle* in terms of power among the Cape mailships.

The tenth of December 1957 arrived – the day appointed for the launching of the vessel as *Pendennis Castle*. As scheduled, Lord and Lady Rotherwick and the rest of the VIP contingent mounted the rostrum above the Belfast slipway for Lady Rotherwick to perform the ceremony. But this time it was to be just the naming. A labour dispute that had been brewing for weeks had come to a head. It therefore fell to a distressed Sir Frederick Rebbeck, chairman of Harland & Wolff, to explain to the waiting guests that there would be no launch that day as the shipwrights had gone on strike.

The Union-Castle public relations team sprang into action to amend the already distributed publicity material. The hastily revised press release read:

> Referring to Union-Castle Line News Bulletins Nos. 7/57 and 7(a)/57 of the 10th December, please note that the first paragraphs of these notices should now read :
>
> > 'The new Union-Castle liner *Pendennis Castle* was named at Belfast to-day (10/12/57) by the Lady Rotherwick, wife of the chairman of The British & Commonwealth Shipping Company Limited.'

The ship eventually slid into the water, unheralded, on Christmas Eve, 1957.

---

1 *The* S.A.Vaal, *ex* Transvaal Castle, *was the first South African-flagged mailship.*
2 *Joining Union-Castle in 1917, George Mayhew, OBE, was the only person who rose through the ranks from cadet to master, and ultimately, after seven years as commodore of the fleet, to membership of the board of directors.*
3 *Lord Rotherwick, chairman of Clan Line Steamers, became chairman of British & Commonwealth and, after the merger, of Union-Castle until his death in 1958.*
4 *Bernard Cayzer, nephew of Lord Rotherwick, took great interest in the mailships.*

1

2

3

4

1 *Conscious of the probability that the mail schedule would have to be accelerated in the future, the Cayzers halted the construction of the* Pendennis Castle *in mid-1956 to allow for a better engine design and for her lengthening. Here the midships section has been separated to make way for the additional section. The ribs of the forward section are at an advanced stage of construction. The decision to improve the design of the liner was an example of the prudent management exercized by the Cayzers. Given her size, the* Pendennis Castle *was an extremely powerful vessel. As proof, she held the final record for an ocean passage by a mailship when she covered the Southampton-Cape Town distance in ten and a half days.*

2 *The naming of the* Pendennis Castle *by Lady Rotherwick. Due to strike action by the Harland & Wolff shipwrights, the liner was not launched at the time.*

3 *Without the usual launching ceremony, the* Pendennis Castle *finally slides down the ways at Harland & Wolff's yard on Christmas Eve, 1957.*

4 Pendennis Castle, *the 'funship' of the fleet.*

1
2

3
4
5

6
7
8

9

There was considerable embarrassment among the top echelon of Harland & Wolff and undisguised anger on the part of Lord Rotherwick who, reputedly, told Sir Frederick that the *Pendennis Castle* would be the last vessel ordered by his company from the Belfast yard. He stuck to his word. All subsequent orders for ships, including two large passenger mailships, two cargo mailships, two fruitships and twenty-one Clan Line ships after 1959 went to Scottish or English yards. Because Harland & Wolff were not in contention for these contracts worth millions of pounds, and because of the adverse publicity generated by the non-launch, the yard hit hard times during which scores of workers were laid off.

Referring to the incident and to the attempts by Harland & Wolff to woo Clan Line into building their ships in Belfast rather than in Scotland, *Lloyd's List* commented: 'The dispute comes at an unfortunate time for Harland & Wolff. The Union-Castle Company has been associated with the Queen's Island for more than half a century and during the past thirty years has taken delivery of twenty-seven Belfast-built ships.'

Despite the inauspicious start to her career, the new vessel was arguably the best mailship ever built. Her power and increased cargo capacity made her highly profitable for the South African trade, but it was to her image among potential passengers that the public relations experts turned their attention, particularly as aircraft were making increasing inroads into the travel industry.

Eager to dispel the perception gained during its earlier years that Union-Castle was a rather conservative company that frowned on extravagant displays, the new management centred its marketing strategy around the concept of 'It's Fun Getting There'. Among the guests invited to join the ship for its shake-down cruise from the Firth of Clyde (she had steamed across from Belfast in mid-November 1958) to Southampton, were many influential shipping and travel journalists as well as several columnists, all of whom

10

must have been given the time of their lives, for there was no jarring note in any of the subsequent media reports. The concept of the *Pendennis Castle* as the 'funship' was gathering momentum, and visits to the ship by show-business personalities gave further impetus to the shrewdly managed campaign. A climax to the excitement came on New Year's Day 1959, shortly before the ship was due to leave Southampton on her maiden voyage. The New Year's Honours List announced that the ship's master, Commodore George Mayhew, had been awarded the CBE.

The entry of the *Pendennis Castle* into the service meant that the old *Arundel Castle* could be withdrawn after a thirty-seven-year career with Union-Castle, the longest of any mailship in the fleet and second only to the intermediate steamer *Llanstephan Castle* which went to British shipbreakers thirty-eight years after entering the service.

Although the *Arundel Castle* was in such poor condition that she should perhaps have been withdrawn earlier, her final sailing from Cape Town in 1958 was filled with nostalgia as she was the first mailship to be withdrawn from service since the war. Besides those bidding farewell to friends on board the old mailship, thousands of Capetonians turned out to see her leave and ships' foghorns blared as the tugs pulled her away from A Berth. Once out in the roadstead, she was followed for some miles along the Green Point/Sea Point stretch of coastline by all the tugs in line astern and dressed overall for the occasion. Then, as the tugs turned and headed back to port, the liner's master, Captain Donald MacKenzie, ordered the helm several points to starboard, the ship turned seawards and, with her speed approaching 19 knots, she headed for Southampton for the last time. A month or two later, Captain MacKenzie and a skeleton crew took her to Hong Kong where, in Gin Drinkers' Bay, she was beached and systematically cut up.

It is generally agreed that the most magnificent vessel to sail the Sunshine Route – as the run between Britain and South Africa was frequently referred to – was the 37 647-ton *Windsor Castle* (built by Cammell, Laird & Co. of Birkenhead), and for a while renewed interest in sea travel was stimulated at a time when aircraft were jetting more and more people to and from Europe.

As was the case with her four-funnelled namesake, which had been launched in 1921 by the Prince of Wales (who was later, coincidentally, to become Duke of Windsor), the launch of the Cayzers' new flagship was to be a royal event, Queen Elizabeth, the Queen Mother, having graciously consented to perform the ceremony. So great was the interest in the occasion that the BBC's television network provided live coverage of the launch.

In his book *Every Thursday at Four o'Clock*, Henry Damant, the former Union-Castle public relations manager, described a behind-the-scenes incident at the launching:

> The Queen Mother was scheduled to name and launch the vessel at 1.30 p.m. At 1.25 p.m. she suffered a severe nose-bleed and consternation reigned. The majority of those present were completely oblivious of what was happening . . . [but] . . . the calmest person was the Queen Mother. Happily, she was able to emerge only a minute or so late, looking as though nothing had happened, though the more observant might have detected the odd splatter on her dress. A great roar of applause greeted

1 *The library on board the* Pendennis Castle.
2-8 *Views on board the* Pendennis Castle.
9 *On board the* Arundel Castle *on her last voyage.*
10 *The* Arundel Castle *sails from Cape Town for the last time.*

1

2

her as she came onto the platform, where she successfully performed the launching ceremony in magnificent style.

The Cayzers must have sighed with relief to see the 238-metre-long hull slide into the water on 23 June 1959, as only a few weeks earlier a month-long strike had threatened the *Windsor Castle* with a fate similar to that of the *Pendennis Castle*.

Publicity material issued at the time of launching the *Windsor Castle* described the new liner as the 'Great New Mailship of the Sunshine Fleet' and pointed out that she was the largest passenger liner to be launched in Britain since the Cunarder, *Queen Elizabeth*, in 1938. A later brochure read:

> The sun shines from a cloudless sky over most of her route. She travels over smooth seas, but she is fitted with stabilisers for extra mill-pond steadiness. Every one of her cabins, for passengers and crew, is air conditioned. So are the dining saloons, her big [238-seat] cinemascope cinema and the hairdressing saloons.
>
> First Class and Tourist Class – each has a complete deck for its public rooms. Each has a swimming pool, complete with veranda lido, on deck.
>
> There is a special health spa, consisting of a medical diagnostic unit and treatment centre, including hydrotherapy with sauna bath, Vichy Douche, aerated and needle baths; also facilities for physiotherapy with massage, electrical treatment, diathermy and wax bath. This will be under the guidance of a specially trained doctor, nursing sister and physiotherapist, and the aim will be to give passengers expert advice and treatment with regard to the improvement of health and keeping fit. There is also a well-equipped gymnasium.
>
> The kitchens, under a master Chef, are designed to make every meal a banquet. Games decks, sunshine decks, dance floors, nurseries, ship-to-shore telephones, two good shops . . . even a garage for passengers' cars.
>
> The luxury of the *Windsor Castle's* furnishings . . . from chandeliers to cutlery, from curtains to chairs . . . the efficiency of her service, the courtesy of her officers and crew – well, you must take a trip in her, and soon.

The descriptions of the public rooms were almost as ornate as the rooms themselves.

> *FIRST CLASS LOUNGE*
> Very big, modern in feeling, it faces forward as an observation lounge during the day, with windows overlooking the ship's bows . . . Behind the orchestra is a glass aviary designed by Lin Tissot and made in Venice. The chairs, high-backed and tub-shaped, are specially comfortable . . .
> *TOURIST CLASS DINING SALOON*
> Down the wide staircase and through an entrance lobby. A wall of mirrors faces fine classical Greek murals by Sidney Smith. Tables round three sides have banquette seating. The lighting suggests warm sunshine. The colour scheme is in black, the new sand colour, terra-cotta and cerulean blue. A dance floor can be cleared for gala nights.

Descriptions of several other public rooms were similarly detailed.

The enthusiastic public relations staff of Union-Castle's Cape Town office put their heads together to devise an attention-arousing programme worthy of the company's new flagship. Their proposal submitted that the new liner should complete the voyage in record time to anchor in Table Bay a day earlier than the usual schedule prescribed. A record passage, it was argued, would immediately catch the public's interest. Having embarked dignitaries via the accommodation ladder, the ship would then do a 'show-the-flag' cruise by steaming along the Atlantic seaboard of the Cape Peninsula and into False Bay, where she would pass as close as possible to Simon's Town, Fish Hoek, Muizenberg and Gordon's Bay before returning to dock in Cape Town harbour early the following morning. Undoubtedly, there would have been considerable public support for such a memorable welcome, particularly as no Union-Castle liner had entered False Bay since the war. Union-Castle itself would have benefited too, not only from the goodwill generated by such a bold programme but also by further stimulating an interest in sea travel.

Great was the disappointment when head office in London politely, yet firmly, declined the suggested programme, opting instead to focus media attention on the vessel's health spa. The selected groups of visitors to be shown around the ship in Southampton and Cape Town on that maiden voyage were all to be carefully steered in the direction of the health spa.

3

In response to the prospect of the bigger ships, the South African Harbour Services had set about providing larger wharfside cranes at the main ports, and in East London the turning basin, which had already been enlarged in 1947, underwent further enlargement. Indeed, such was the extent of planning for manoeuvring the ship in the narrow confines of the Buffalo River, that the senior pilot at East London was sent to board the *Windsor Castle* in Port Elizabeth on the upcoast voyage so that he could become fully acquainted with the intricacies of the new mailship before her arrival off the Buffalo River. One contemporary newspaper report summed up the feeling after the ship's downcoast call at the port:

WHEW!

> When the *Windsor Castle* sailed safely out of Buffalo Harbour yesterday afternoon, there were sighs of relief from various quarters of the port. The biggest ship on the South African run had been in and out of the harbour twice without a hitch, thus setting the seal of success on the years of work and planning that had gone into the harbour extensions . . . Work on the widening [of the C.W. Malan turning basin] started more than two years ago . . . and the *Windsor Castle* turns with 400 ft. to spare.

When the *Windsor Castle* made her first call at Port Elizabeth, the downcoast mailship was the *Winchester Castle* on her farewell visit to the port. Days later, she would leave Cape Town for the last time after a career spanning thirty years.

While the *Windsor Castle* was in Las Palmas on her second voyage to South Africa, the northbound *Capetown Castle* arrived off the port early in the morning and stopped to pick up the pilot. Once the pilot had boarded, Captain Bill Byles passed the order for slow ahead to get the ship under way. In the engine room, immediately after Chief Engineer Stanley Logan and his staff had responded to the command from the bridge, a blast and flash of flame swept the starting platform. A greaser and two engineers suffered extensive burns and died on board. Sixteen others, including Chief Engineer Logan, were also caught by the flash. Although severely burnt and his strength failing quickly, Logan stayed in the engine room to try to prevent further damage and even assisted in the rescue of others. He and four of his shipmates later died in hospital.

The blast had been heard ashore, bringing harbour craft hastening to render assistance. Boats from the *Windsor Castle*, already in port, carried medical personnel and fire-fighting teams from the line's flagship to the *Capetown Castle*. Immediately the alarm had been raised on board, the passengers, most of whom had been on deck at the time to watch the arrival at Las Palmas, calmly mustered at their boatstations; the boats were lowered and all were evacuated from the ship. The fire was extinguished late that afternoon but not before extensive damage had been done to the engine room.

Afterwards, several tales of good fortune were related, none more dramatic than that of the engineer who was emerging from an engine room store when the blast occurred, searing the tip of his nose. Another second or two, and he would have suffered the same fate as some of his shipmates.

Captain John Oakley, master of the *Windsor Castle*, sent a cable to London in which he commended the great gallantry shown by the engine room and deck staff of the *Capetown Castle*.

The Southampton-bound passengers completed their journey by air. Temporary repairs to the liner were made in Las Palmas, and under escort from the German salvage tug *Atlantic*, the *Capetown Castle* made her way to Southampton, where a complete engine refit was carried out. To fill the breach in the mail schedule left by the withdrawal of the liner, the intermediate steamer, *Braemar Castle*, brought passengers and some cargo to South Africa, while the fast refrigerated cargo liner, *Rowallan Castle*, was drafted to the role of mailship for a voyage to South Africa.

First class accommodation on the mailships, as well as food and service, were distinctly superior to the food and amenities provided in cabin class, and continued to reflect all the connotations of social stratification that had once been so prominent in the now fast-vanishing era of Empire. South Africans, it was argued (somewhat ironically) in some

1 Special rates were offered over the Christmas period to boost passenger bookings for northbound voyages during the northern hemisphere's winter.
2 A poster advertising both the mail service and the intermediate service.
3 Part of the engine room on board the Capetown Castle.

1

HARLAND & WOLFF

In 1858, a small shipyard on Queen's Island, Belfast, was bought by the yard's manager, E.J. Harland, who invited a German designer, Gustav Wilhelm Wolff, to head up the design team. Soon Wolff became a full partner in the new firm of Harland & Wolff, which was formally established in 1861. Well-known shipping companies, such as the White Star Line and Bibby Lines, ordered their ships exclusively from Harland & Wolff, whose reputation grew with each ship that was launched from their slipway.

Between 1891 and 1892, having singled out the Union Steamship Company as an important shipping line whose custom they wished to secure, Harland & Wolff built three intermediate steamers for the line – at cost. Other ships for Union followed, all at substantially reduced contract prices. Meanwhile, Gustav Wolff bought a considerable number of Union Line shares to give him a sound footing when negotiating further contracts with the company.

Ten G-Class intermediate liners and the mailships Norman, Briton, Saxon *and* Celt *(launched as the* Walmer Castle*) established the Belfast yard as the Union Line's, and after amalgamation Union-Castle's, premier shipyard. Great liners for the North Atlantic trade also came from Harland & Wolff's yards, notably the* Oceanic, Titanic *and* Olympic.

When Union-Castle was taken over by the Royal Mail Group in 1912, it became, in effect, married to Harland & Wolff, for one of the duumvirate then controlling the huge group was Lord Pirrie, chairman of Harland & Wolff. Lord Pirrie's business ally in the takeover was Sir Owen Philipps, later Lord Kylsant, who was chairman of the Royal Mail, Elder Dempster and King Lines. Together, Pirrie and Philipps took advantage of the Trade Facilities Act, in terms of which government subsidies were available to shipowners wishing to enlarge their fleets, but, with the repeal of this concession in the late twenties, several shipowners cancelled orders, catapulting Harland & Wolff to the brink of bankruptcy. To make matters worse, in 1930 Union-Castle ended its repair contracts with Harland & Wolff in order to widen the field of tenderers and encourage more competitive charges.

Its woes compounded by the effects of the Great Depression, the entire Kylsant group collapsed. To prevent almost certain closure of the yard and, in consequence, widespread unemployment, Harland & Wolff was rescued by the government of Northern Ireland. As a result of negotiations with the Midland Bank, a financial package was devised to enable the shipyard to tender successfully for the construction of the mailships Stirling Castle *and* Athlone Castle, *as well as for the fruitships* Roslin Castle *and* Rothesay Castle. *The hand-over of the two mailships drew great publicity for the yard, yielding further orders from other shipping companies. During World War II the Harland & Wolff yards worked feverishly building, repairing or converting ships for wartime duties.*

It was the unfortunate launching debacle of the Pendennis Castle *in 1957 that ended the long and happy relationship between the shipyard and Union-Castle, and indeed, together with increasing competition from Japanese yards, may have been a major contribution to its decline. However, as a nationalized company today it still builds ships – mainly smaller vessels than those for which it achieved fame – and it is also a competitive ship repair company.*

SHIPS BUILT BY HARLAND & WOLFF

UNION LINE

INTERMEDIATES (FROM 1893 TO 1900)

GAUL	*GREEK*
GOTH	*GUELPH*
GASCON	*GAIKA*
GOORKHA	*GERMAN*
GALEKA	*GALICIAN*

MAILSHIPS

NORMAN	1894
BRITON	1897
SAXON	1900

UNION-CASTLE LINE

MAILSHIPS

WALMER CASTLE (ORDERED BY THE UNION LINE AS THE *CELT*)	1902	*WARWICK CASTLE*	1931
		ATHLONE CASTLE	1936
KENILWORTH CASTLE	1904	*STIRLING CASTLE*	1936
EDINBURGH CASTLE	1910	*CAPETOWN CASTLE*	1938
ARUNDEL CASTLE	1921	*PRETORIA CASTLE*	1948
CARNARVON CASTLE	1926	*EDINBURGH CASTLE*	1948
WINCHESTER CASTLE	1930	*PENDENNIS CASTLE*	1958

INTERMEDIATES		CARGOSHIPS	
DUNLUCE CASTLE	1904	*DROMORE CASTLE*	1919
GALWAY CASTLE	1911	*DUNDRUM CASTLE*	1919
LLANGIBBY CASTLE	1929	*ROSLIN CASTLE*	* 1935
DUNBAR CASTLE	1930	*ROTHESAY CASTLE*	* 1935
DUNNOTTAR CASTLE	1936	*WALMER CASTLE*	1936
DUNVEGAN CASTLE	1936	*ROCHESTER CASTLE*	* 1937
DURBAN CASTLE	1938	*ROXBURGH CASTLE*	* 1937
PRETORIA CASTLE	1939	*RICHMOND CASTLE*	* 1939
(POSTWAR *WARWICK CASTLE*)		*ROWALLAN CASTLE*	* 1939
BLOEMFONTEIN CASTLE	1950	*ROWALLAN CASTLE*	* 1943
RHODESIA CASTLE	1951	*RICHMOND CASTLE*	* 1944
KENYA CASTLE	1952	*ROXBURGH CASTLE*	* 1945
BRAEMAR CASTLE	1952	*RIEBEECK CASTLE*	* 1946
		RUSTENBURG CASTLE	* 1946
		TANTALLON CASTLE	1954
		TINTAGEL CASTLE	1954

* REFRIGERATED VESSELS

UNION-CASTLE SHIPS REFITTED BY HARLAND & WOLFF

SCOT (UNION LINER)
ARUNDEL CASTLE
WINDSOR CASTLE
CARNARVON CASTLE
WINCHESTER CASTLE
WARWICK CASTLE

Several ships during and immediately after World War II, as well as

PRETORIA CASTLE 1965 IN SOUTHAMPTON
EDINBURGH CASTLE 1965 IN SOUTHAMPTON

2

3

4

quarters, found the British adherence to the separation of classes an anathema, and long before the last passenger mailship for the South African trade was on the drawingboards of the John Brown yard on the Clyde, a plea had been made to abolish the first and cabin class structures on the mailships. In Britain, there were already moves towards a 'classless' society, and in response to these sentiments the Cayzers determined that on the new ship all passengers should be able to enjoy the full deckspace, all activities offered, all public amenities and the same cuisine. So when the *Transvaal Castle* entered the mail service in 1962, it did so as a 'one-class' mailship – the only one to be built for the Cape run.

The ship's public rooms were attractively decorated. Murals by Felix Kelly depicted scenes from the Western Cape, and the incorporation of slender arches and trelliswork gave the dining saloon a cosy atmosphere. Off the promenade deck was the Assembly Room – a large open lounge, decorated in pastel shades with a huge Venetian mural and candelabra adorning the bulkhead. Forward of the Assembly Room was the very popular, yet intimate, Orangery – a low-domed lounge with a service bar – while several other smaller venues provided a more cosy atmosphere for a quiet drink or chat before dinner. From the Verandah Café, also known as the Golden Room, passengers could relax in comfortable chairs to watch activities on the games deck and around the swimming pool. Up forward was an extensive recreation deck, protected from the wind. The suites, the tariff for which in 1962 was R1 400 (or £700) for two people travelling between Southampton and Cape Town, were spacious, tastefully appointed and featured many modern luxury facilities. Most of the cabins were decorated in pastel green with counterpanes and curtains in autumnal shades. At the time of the liner's maiden voyage, a single fare to Britain in a four-berth cabin was R240 (or £120).

The response from the South African media to the new liner was most positive, and since everyone had the run of the ship, the *Transvaal Castle* became extremely popular with the travelling general public.

The sixties saw many changes in Africa, not the least being the demise of colonial rule. In 1957, the Gold Coast had become the first sub-Saharan British colony to gain autonomy, from which time there was a rush towards independence among other British-ruled

---

1 *In the middle of the Depression years and towards the end of the Kylsant era, the* Winchester Castle *(the second motorship on the Cape mail service) was built as part of a bold programme to modernize the mailship fleet. She was launched in Belfast on 19 November 1929.*

2 *Apart from the traditional use of the ship's bell to signal the end of the watch, the bell was rung before sailing to alert visitors to the fact that they should proceed ashore. There were three announcements to that effect and three tollings of the bell.*

3 *'Billy Bunter' wins the fancy dress competition held on board the* Pendennis Castle.

4 *For the annual boat race in Cape Town, teams were drawn from various sections of the local maritime fraternity and always included one from whichever Union-Castle mailship was in port at the time. In 1958, the officers' team from the* Carnarvon Castle *won. In the centre of the front row is Captain Bill Byles (later commodore of the fleet). On his right is First Officer N. E. Upham (later captain) and on Captain Byles's right is Chief Officer F. J. Pye, MBE, who also became a master in the fleet. He had been second officer on the cargoship* Richmond Castle *when it was torpedoed in the North Atlantic on 4 August 1942. For six days, and in dreadful weather conditions, he was in command of one of the lifeboats. During the ordeal, nine men succumbed to the elements. Late on the afternoon of 10 August, the lifeboat was sighted by a ship which altered course to rescue the men. For his service to others, Pye was awarded the MBE.*

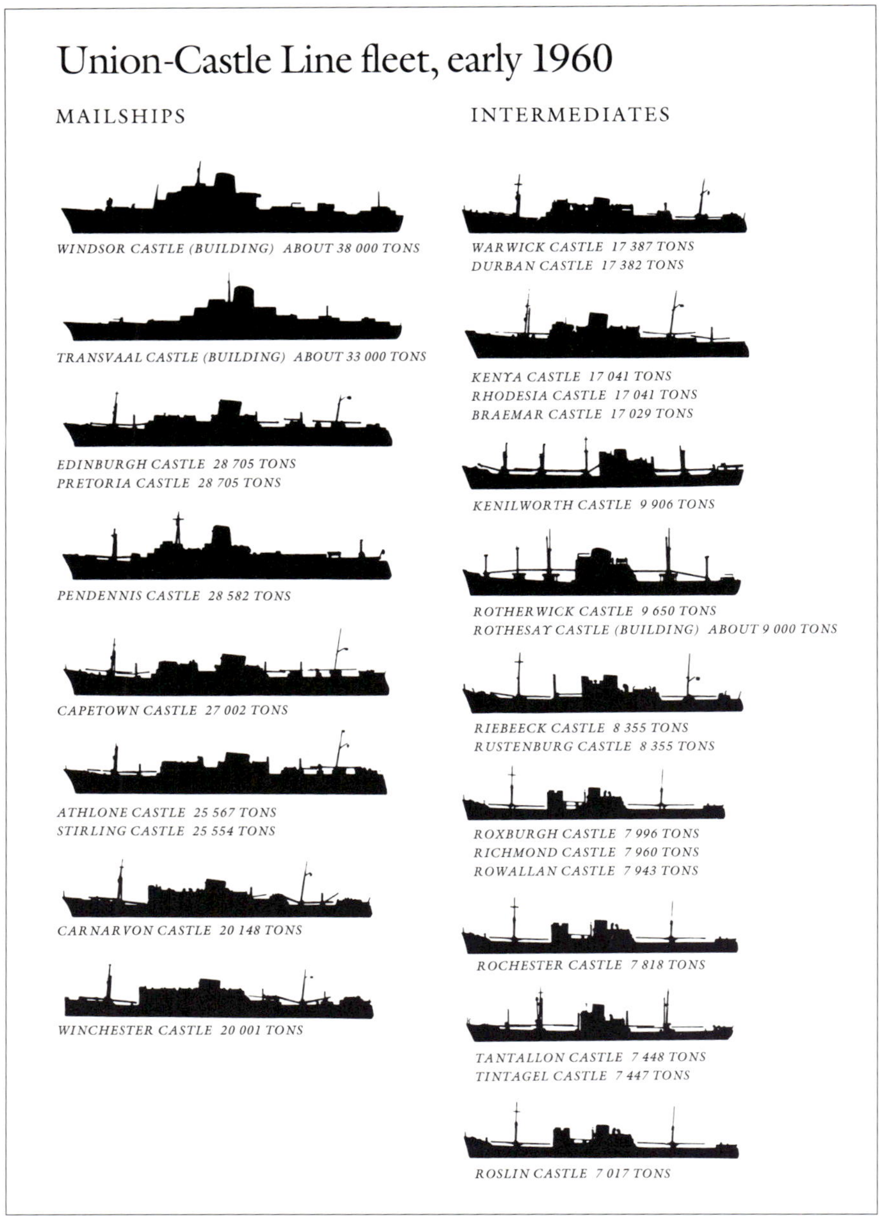

1

3

2

territories. One of the results was the withdrawal of British civil servants from the colonies and the return to Britain of hundreds of expatriates. For a year or two this led to a major increase in the number of northbound passengers, both on the Union-Castle intermediate ships serving East Africa, which sailed full to Britain, and on the mailships, which carried many of those leaving former Bechuanaland, Basutoland, the federation of the Rhodesias and Nyasaland. The rush was short-lived, though, and the subsequent decline in the number of passengers sailing to and from East Africa soon rendered the round-Africa intermediate service uneconomic, and by the end of 1967 all ships had been withdrawn. The main service also suffered from the decline in the complement of passengers travelling to and from the former protectorates and colonies in southern Africa.

Further setbacks to the passenger ships were the Sharpeville shootings and other signs of unrest in South Africa in the early part of 1960. These resulted in a marked drop in the rate of immigration to the country as well as in the general tourist demand for passages.

But a still more threatening adversary of the seaborne passenger trade was gathering strength. From the mid-fifties South African Airways, working closely with the British Overseas Airways Corporation (BOAC), had steadily introduced larger and more efficient aircraft on the Johannesburg-London route, culminating in October 1960 with the entry of the Boeing 707. This aircraft had a profound effect on passenger traffic, the greatly reduced travelling time to London being so attractive that in the first five years of operation there was almost a sixty per cent swing from sea to air travel. Also significant

4

5

was the tendency for highly rated freight and mail to be despatched by air, rather than via the mailships. It therefore followed that the entry to the mail service of the *Transvaal Castle*, the last passenger liner built for the South African trade, meant that yet another older ship would be withdrawn.

In May 1962, there were nostalgic scenes at all the major South African ports as two Union-Castle liners made their last calls. After thirty-six years of colourful service, the *Carnarvon Castle* left for Southampton for the last time on the mail run. Also on her last voyage, and scheduled to leave Durban on the same afternoon as the *Carnarvon Castle*, was the intermediate vessel *Warwick Castle*, which had arrived from Britain via Suez.

1 *The 1960 fleet list, adapted from publicity material used by the B&C Group.*
2 *Normally the bridge was strictly off limits to passengers; organized visits to the bridge were therefore extremely popular.*
3 *A variety of labels were provided for passengers' luggage, and for most people, sticking them on to items of baggage usually constituted the high point in the often frenetic build-up to boarding the ship.*
4 *An early morning arrival of the* Windsor Castle *at Cape Town. The ladder is down in anticipation of the arrival of the pilot tender.*
5 *The bridge party on board the* Windsor Castle *as the vessel prepares to sail. Uniform regulations were strictly applied at all times.*

1

C DECK
B DECK
KEY TO SECTIONAL-ELEVATION
TOURIST CLASS
UNION-CASTLE
R.M.S.
PENDENNIS
CASTLE
TOURIST
Class
UNION-CASTLE
R.M.S.
EDINBURGH
CASTLE
MAIL SERVICE
Coastwise
Fares
AND SAILINGS
UNION-CASTLE
PASSENGER
ACCOMMODATION

2

3

Eased off her berth at the T Jetty shortly after 16:30, the *Warwick Castle* steamed slowly up the channel towards the harbour entrance to await the departure of the *Carnarvon Castle* at the usual sailing time of 17:00. The tugs turned the mailship, which was to lead the *Warwick Castle* out of port, in line ahead. A journalist, sent by Durban's *Daily News* on the coastal voyage of the *Carnarvon Castle*, despatched the following report:

DURBAN'S STIRRING FAREWELL TO TWO GALLANT VESSELS

Durban yesterday afternoon saluted two ships she will not see again – and sent them on their final voyages with an unforgettable farewell. Few among the hundreds who crowded the Point Docks or lined the decks of the *Carnarvon Castle* and the *Warwick Castle* . . . could have been unmoved by the port's stirring send-off as the old vessels began a voyage that will take them to the breakers' yards and into history.

Vessels lying in port raised a noisy lament as the two veterans – the *Carnarvon Castle*, brave with gay bunting, and the *Warwick Castle* flying a simple goodbye message to Durban – moved from their berths in the fast-fading light of the winter's afternoon.

Plumes of steam floated away from blaring sirens – noisy, crotchety and plaintive – in all parts of the harbour.

The accolade came from tugs, ocean-going liners and freighters . . . It came too from fussy shunting engines in the dockland marshalling yards, and from grimy locomotives over at the coaling appliances at the Bluff.

The *Carnarvon Castle*'s reply was sonorous and vibrant, as was the *Warwick Castle*'s as she moved to her station astern, attended by harbour craft and a circling aircraft. There were moist eyes among those on deck. Moved as well were many who ribboned the quayside from drab B shed to the end of the Point – and from the base of the North Pier along its entire length.

Some among them had sailed in the *Carnarvon Castle* on her maiden voyage in 1926; some served in her when, as an armed merchant cruiser, she engaged . . . an enemy raider. Others knew her as a trooper that carried them back from the war, and some remembered her as an immigrant ship that brought them to a new life in Southern Africa.

From the hooters of hundreds of cars parked on the North Pier came a last sustained

1 *The last sailing of the* Winchester Castle *from Cape Town.*

2 *Union-Castle offices provided numerous brochures relating to schedules, fares and special excursions. Also available were accommodation plans of the ships to enable passengers to select their cabins when booking a passage.*

3 *The* Transvaal Castle *dressed overall for her maiden voyage departure from Southampton. Astern, the crack North Atlantic Blue Riband holder,* United States, *prepares to sail. On the extreme left is the Cunarder,* Queen Mary.

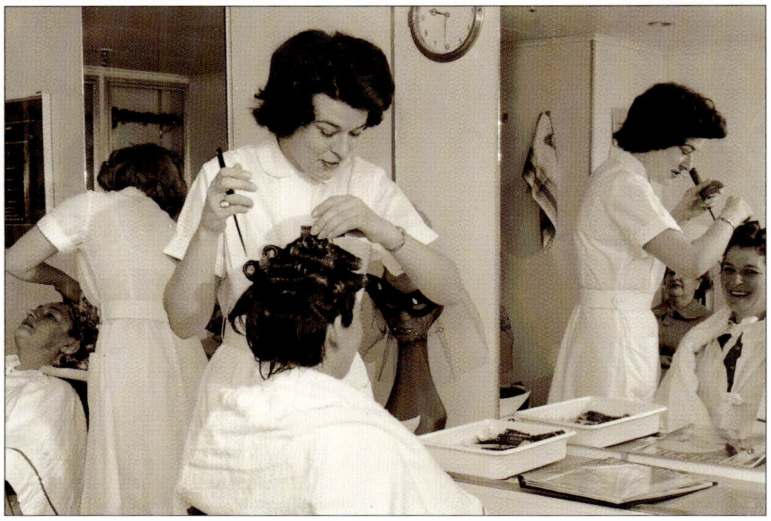

1 3
2 4

5 6

farewell as the *Carnarvon Castle* . . . dipped grandly to meet the oncoming swells at the harbour entrance.

As she swung away to the south-west, the flags were lowered. The ceremony was over. The *Carnarvon Castle* moved on into the night and into her own niche in the seafaring history of South Africa.

At East London, the *Warwick Castle* preceded the mailship out of port, and at Port Elizabeth the *Carnarvon Castle* left several hours ahead of the intermediate ship which had been delayed in docking because of congestion in the port.

Farewell ceremonies for the two ships at Cape Town were days apart, again because the *Warwick Castle* had to await a berth.

Gold bullion worth millions of rands was loaded on the weekly mailship in Durban for shipment to Britain. Once the quay had been cleared of all people, a steam locomotive pulled armoured railway coaches carrying the gold on to the quay. South African Reserve Bank officials and a special unit of the South African Railway police guarded the consignment which usually consisted of about 500 boxes, each with two ingots. The chief officer was responsible for loading the gold into the ship's bullion room, a large specially fortified strongroom off number three hold. Besides the chief officer, in attendance were the purser and extra second officer who, with the Reserve Bank men, did the tallying of the gold, while the fourth officer was in the bullion room. Immediately the gold had been stowed, the bullion room was sealed in the presence of the master, chief officer, purser, extra second officer and the bank officials, and a police guard was mounted during the ship's stay in South African ports. The master and purser each kept one of the keys to the

7

room, and on arrival in Southampton had to unlock the bullion room in the presence of officials from the Bank of England. A senior Union-Castle representative and specially chosen underlings, for whom the selection was both an honour and an opportunity to escape the office for two days, were also present when the gold was offloaded under strict security before anyone went ashore. Special cargo slings were used for the operation. As in Durban, the wharf was cleared of people before the precious consignment was put into two armoured railway trucks which were attached to the back of a London-bound train. Once the gold had been delivered to the Bank of England later that day, Union-Castle's responsibility ended, leaving the two young clerks to experience the delights of London before returning to Southampton on the morning train.

It is said that on one occasion, the two bullion trucks were uncoupled erroneously from the London-bound train at Basingstoke by a shunter, ignorant of their contents. Naturally, there was dire consternation when the train reached London without the gold; an immediate search located the two trucks in a siding, with the gold still on board. On another occasion the disappearance of twenty gold bars led to an international hunt involving British and South African police and Interpol.

With the usual security measures in force, gold worth R16 million in 893 boxes had been put on board the *Capetown Castle* in Durban in January 1965. Because this was an abnormally large shipment – a result of South Africa wishing to take advantage of a rising gold price – some of the gold could not be accommodated in the usual bullion room and had to be placed in an adjacent compartment, normally used to carry special items of mail or other high-tariffed freight, such as export clothing. For this valuable cargo of gold, the compartment had been specially reinforced and the door had been welded closed.

1 *The Cellar Bar,* Transvaal Castle.
2 *Evening entertainment on the mailships was carefully planned. Apart from dances, film shows and talent concerts, there were bingo evenings, fancy dress competitions and – seen here on the* Transvaal Castle *– 'horse-racing'. Using curved nail scissors, ladies are cutting up the middle of a strip of tape, while bets are placed on the winner. Note the top-hats and other dress associated with horse-racing. There was also 'frog-racing', whereby wooden frogs on strings were coaxed to the winning line by volunteer 'jockeys'. Gullible passengers were told beforehand that the 'frogs' were bred specially in the depths of the engine room.*
3 *The dining saloon,* Transvaal Castle.
4 *The hairdressing salon,* Transvaal Castle.
5 *Detectives searching for gold stolen from the* Capetown Castle*'s temporary bullion room. This photograph was taken in Durban on the vessel's return to South Africa in March 1965 after the discovery of the theft.*
6 *The small locker in which some of the gold was discovered while the* Capetown Castle *was in Durban.*
7 *With a truncated mainmast, the* Carnarvon Castle *makes her final departure on the mail service. Cape Town's famous tug,* T. S. McEwen *(to the right but off the photograph) emitted huge palls of smoke, often impeding the pilot's view at crucial times. Shortly after this photograph was taken, one of those palls of smoke drifted across the departing mailship, much to the annoyance of the press and maritime photographers at the harbour entrance.*

1

FROM MARISCHAL MURRAY TO MARTIN LEENDERTZ

AN EXTRACT FROM A LETTER DATED 16 APRIL 1962

. . . As for ships and Union-Castle in particular, they're going down and down. I can't describe the horrors of the Union-Castle of the new regime. Noise everywhere. The barmen and stewards play their own radios etc. in the public rooms; on deck the hooligans have their transistor radios . . . A pity you can't see the horror that is the Transvaal Castle. *Public rooms not bad – but decks!! There aren't any except where lunatics fling things about. Both 'Promenade' decks are about 12 ft. wide, if that. Just enough space to walk past an extended deck chair. The lower promenade has a surface (composition of some sort) like asphalt.*

29/12/1966. AIR MAIL.

Dear Aunty Joyce & Uncle Bud & Pat
Just a short pc. to thank you ever so much for your Christmas present. Had a wonderful time opening presents on Christmas morning at 6 AM which was when the dance ended so guess who didn't sleep at all Christmas Eve!! We had a wonderful trip, & it was very exciting arriving in England (& ALSO cold & wet ---!!) Survived the chaos of Immigration officers & Customs fairly well, got myself on the boat train & the next thing we were in Waterloo. Friends met me (great excitement & noise!!) & then I came to Charlotte's to drop my luggage & ask for a room as I had nowhere to stay — they had one for me so I'm all settled in. Will be writing to N & R soon as get news from them. Love to all

Mr & Mrs A. D. Townshend & Pat,
Dunlewy,
9 Clifton Road,
Mowbray.
Cape.
South Africa.

NATURAL COLOUR
J. Arthur Dixon
PHOTOGRAVURE
POST CARD
Windsor Castle
(Tonnage 37,640)
Union-Castle Line to South and East Africa
Printed and Published by J. Arthur Dixon Ltd., Newport, I.W. England

2

22.4.70.

Dear Ingpens,
Thanks so much for your Bon Voyage card. It was much appreciated. Our trip has been very pleasant so far, with smooth going all the way. The heat is our chief complaint. It has been almost unbearable the last 4 days, as we crossed the Equator. We loved the King Neptune ceremony. It was quite priceless. Haven't found either of your officer friends, Brian, due to a distinct shortage of males. Have been up on the Bridge & seen how everything is supposed to work. Arrive Las Palmas tomorrow. Enjoying ourselves. Love Lesley

Mr & Mrs R. Ingpen,
12 Muswell Hill Rd,
Mowbray.
Cape
South Africa.

NATURAL COLOUR
J. Arthur D
PHOTOGRAVURE
POST CARD
S.A. ORANJE
(Tonnage 28,625)
SS. 630
Printed and Published by J. Arthur Dixon Ltd., Newport, I.W. England
CORREOS
ESPAÑA

3

The ship called at all the South African ports, including Mossel Bay, and early in February, arrived at Southampton via Las Palmas. When the strongrooms were opened, twenty gold bars, packed two to a box and worth R200 000, were found to have been stolen. Southampton police requested the aid of their South African colleagues, who launched extensive inquiries at each port where the vessel had called.

Even Las Palmas was considered a likely place for the gold to have been smuggled off the ship. Passengers and crew on the southbound *Windsor Castle*, which had been in the island port at the same time as the northbound *Capetown Castle*, were quizzed by Cape Town police. They were particularly interested in the reported presence of a grey Rolls Royce that had been parked near the berth occupied by the *Capetown Castle* during her short stay to take on bunkers.

In Southampton, police interviewed hundreds of passengers, crew members and dockers; they inspected every possible place on board the liner where the gold could have been secreted, and even opened hundreds of crates of South African fruit which the liner had brought to Britain. Meanwhile, the press were making a meal of the theft. International syndicates, shady masterminds and references to previously planned heists featured in speculative newspaper reports.

When the *Capetown Castle* was due to leave on her next southbound voyage, the police set up an office on board to continue their shipboard enquiries, particularly their interviewing of those crew members who had served in the ship on her previous voyage.

The painstaking police work finally paid off. Two crew members who had not returned to the ship broke under police interrogation in Britain. Their *modus operandi* was as simple as it was hard to believe. They had crawled through a ventilation shaft, removed a grille to gain access to the mailroom, and then cut a hole in the deckhead of the temporary bullion room. Ten boxes, each containing two gold ingots, had been manhandled back along the ventilation duct. Six ingots had been hidden in a winch housing on the promenade deck and the rest amid the frames comprising the inner strengthening of the forward part of the ship.

Boarding the ship immediately she docked in Durban in March, more than a month after the theft had been discovered, two Southampton detectives and members of the South African Police found the gold in the places described by the two thieves.

A later supposition indicated that, intending to steal part of a consignment of men's suits frequently carried in the makeshift strongroom, the thieves had broken into the compartment and in the initial euphoria of their discovery, removed the gold. Not knowing what to do with this unexpected bonanza, they hid it. Whatever the motive, they each received a ten-year prison sentence.

4

UNION-CASTLE OFFICERS

'. . . I arrived in Glasgow early the next morning where, in accordance with my instructions, I joined the Good Hope Castle *at Number Two Ballasting Crane, Queens Dock,' wrote Captain Reg Kelso of his experience when, fresh from the trainingship HMS* Conway, *he reported to his first ship as a cadet. 'As I reached the top of the gangway, a young man in a white jacket appeared from a doorway and said the never-to-be-forgotten phrase, "Good morning, Sir. Have you had breakfast?" Immediately I was aware of a feeling of welcome, of warmth and of friendship – a feeling which never left me, ashore or afloat during the next forty-two years.'*

Once cadets had obtained their second mate's certificate, they had to re-apply to the company if they wished to continue in the Union-Castle fleet. Reg Kelso did.

'My first mailship,' he continued, 'was the Capetown Castle, *which I joined with a brand new Second Mate's Certificate. This in itself was an innovation because hitherto, Junior Fourth Officers were all holders of a First Mate's Certificate, at least, and most had a Master's Certificate, but in that post-war period, more tonnage was being manned and such luxuries had to be trimmed.*

'As Junior Officer of the watch, one had a well established routine, and woe betide the upstart who tried to exceed his authority. After "steadying on" the steering compass as well as the standard compass, and checking the compass error by celestial bearing, one retired to the wing of the bridge, unless invited into the wheelhouse by the Senior . . . Talking to the quartermaster or Bridge Boy was frowned upon unless absolutely necessary . . . Rounds of the exterior passenger decks had to be completed quickly and discreetly, with anything of a contentious nature avoided, lest the Senior Officer be called upon to write a report . . .

'By day, passengers had to be shown around the Bridge and during this time, the Senior invariably stalked the Bridge wing mouthing "Get rid of them" . . . The social life was everything we had heard about during our cadetship. Meals were taken in the First Class Dining Saloon, complete with orchestra and frock-coated Head Waiter. We dressed in mess kit with stiff starched shirt and wing collar, but after a week, the two-paged menu became almost boring, and the fillet mignon ceased to be a novelty . . . We were not encouraged to mix with the passengers – Be polite and do not seek to prolong the conversation, was the instruction. . .

'In port, we worked watches, supervising the cargo work, and in our off duty periods, we enjoyed South African hospitality to the full, playing golf, cricket and rugby, climbing Table Mountain, and awaiting with dread, the arrival of a letter promoting us to Third Officer of a cargoship. The radio room kept us fully informed of the movements of our contemporaries, and every chartroom had an updated Staff List of every ship in the fleet. This was scrutinised anxiously to see who might be next to move.'

Those wishing to embark on an engineering career joined Union-Castle from one of the shipyards, especially Harland & Wolff, with which Union-Castle had close ties, or from other heavy engineering works. Their first appointment would be as a junior engineer aboard a cargoship, and depending on ability, promotion could follow. The third, second and chief engineers aboard the mailships were fully certificated men of proven record and with extensive experience.

The master always distanced himself from the rest of the officers, although there was usually good rapport between him, the chief engineer, the staff commander and the chief purser. In the earlier days, there was strict separation between the navigating officers and the engineers, a practice which disappeared slowly throughout the British Merchant Navy. No social contact with the crew was allowed; cadets were trained not to speak to the crew, thus sustaining the clear division between upper and lower deck.

Accommodation for most of the officers was on the boat deck. The master had a suite comprising a cabin, a dayroom and bathroom. Similar, but smaller, facilities were provided for the chief engineer. The chief purser's accommodation was near to the Bureau. Generally, the officers' accommodation was comfortable, although in all the prewar vessels there were only two showers and four toilets among the officers. Facilities in the newer ships were vastly improved with most officers having their own bathroom.

Until 1939, ships of the Deutsche Ost-Afrika Linien had called at the small port of Walvis Bay on the arid west coast, and in the postwar years the Union-Castle intermediates also steamed along the desert coast to Walvis Bay, which served South West Africa. Following the withdrawal of several intermediate liners, the mailships called there on a monthly basis from May 1962 until July 1965. The locals were delighted in that the calls at the port not only provided a reliable passenger and cargo link, but also benefited the economy of the town. The general enthusiasm, however, was not shared by the mailships' engineers who, despite the port call, were still expected to maintain the usual schedule.

In the face of the decline in sea travel, B&C announced innovations to the mail service that would take effect in 1965. Two new cargo mailships would replace the ageing *Athlone Castle* and *Stirling Castle* on an accelerated eleven-and-a-half-day service, for which the *Pretoria Castle* and *Edinburgh Castle* would be refitted, their hulls skimmed and machinery adjusted to give them an extra turn of speed. Too slow to maintain the new service, the *Capetown Castle* would become an intermediate liner on a fifteen-day service to Cape Town, with occasional calls at Walvis Bay.

On the launching in October 1965 of the *Southampton Castle* – the first of the two cargo mailships – a newspaper report commented:

1 *Senior executives of the British & Commonwealth Group with Captain A.G. Patey on board the* Transvaal Castle. *From left to right: Captain Patey, Sir Nicholas Cayzer (chairman, B&C), Mr Clive Corder (chairman, Cayzer Irvine, South Africa), Mr John Bevan (director, B&C), Mr J. Thomson (financial director, B&C), Mr Rex Austin (managing director, Union-Castle South Africa) and Mr Ted Lemon.*

2 *Written on a postcard of the* Windsor Castle, *December 1966.*

3 *Written on board the* S.A. Oranje, *April 1970.*

4 *Commodore Alec Hort and his senior officers on rounds aboard the* Windsor Castle. *Commodore Hort's first command was the* Durban Castle *in 1946, ten years after joining Union-Castle as a fourth officer out of Hogarth trampships. He was appointed commodore in 1969 and retired the following year.*

1

2

> The new cargo mailship which was launched by Princess Alexandra yesterday, is likely to set new standards of efficiency in cargo handling.
>
> Her designers have made impressive provision for the variety of cargo she and her sistership, the *Good Hope Castle*, will be required to carry between Southampton and South African ports.
>
> She has . . . 13 tanks with a total capacity of 60,000 gallons for the bulk carriage of Cape wines, or other liquids.
>
> Container stowage, today's time saver in shipping, will be a feature. Although they are primarily designed for the carriage of South African fruit, the insulated spaces throughout the ship have been arranged and designed to give flexibility in the handling of many other products which require frozen or chilled carriage.
>
> For the non-passenger cargo liners which will be the most powerful afloat with a service speed of 22,5 knots, the design of the hull was of special importance. Its form is the result of extensive model tests, incorporating a cruiser stern and curved stem. A bulbous bow has been fitted to reduce resistance and save power . . .

When she arrived at Cape Town on her maiden voyage, the *Southampton Castle* received relatively little notice compared to the fanfare treatment usually accorded mailships on their first call, though one aspect on which the media focused was the degree of automation introduced into the ship's machinery and cargo equipment.

With the customary poignant ceremonies, the *Athlone Castle* and *Stirling Castle* left the mail service in the latter half of 1965, the *Athlone Castle* sailing to breakers' yards at Kaohsiung and her sister ship to Japanese scrappers at Mihara in March 1966.

3

4

5

Apart from the unusual need to enter drydock in Durban for repairs to her starboard propeller, the *Stirling Castle's* final voyage was notable for it being the last time a mailship anchored off Mossel Bay to land and embark passengers by basket – a method used previously at Port Elizabeth and East London until harbour improvements at those ports allowed the mailships to come alongside. Mossel Bay, the Cinderella port since the slump in the ostrich feather trade shortly after the turn of the century, did not warrant a call by the mailships on their accelerated schedule, which the *Windsor Castle* had inaugurated late in July 1965. The ochre, wool and timber from its hinterland could be moved to either Port Elizabeth or Cape Town by coaster or lorry for export.

The British shipbuilding industry continued to be bedevilled by labour disputes. This

1 *The* Southampton Castle, *the first cargo-only mailship built for the mail service and the last mailship on the run. Referring to the unusually large space abaft the stern deckhouse on the ship, a bold maritime personality commented that she would make a fine armed merchant cruiser.*

2 *On board the* Pretoria Castle, *1960. Although this is a posed publicity photograph, it indicates the standard of service provided for first class passengers who had at their bidding a cabin steward and stewardess.*

3 *The* Carnarvon Castle *anchored off Mossel Bay, circa 1959. The* Stirling Castle *made the last official mailship call at the port in 1965.*

4 *A children's hostess in the ship's playroom, which was well equipped with toys.*

5 *The Long Gallery,* Pretoria Castle.

1

2

time they affected the delivery of the second cargo mailship, the *Good Hope Castle*, which was delayed for nearly five months. The *Capetown Castle* was therefore required to make two additional voyages on the mailship schedule, although allowance had to be made for her slower speed.

On one of her southbound voyages, which included a call at Flushing at the mouth of the River Scheldt, she quietly took to the mud. Anxiously watched by many of her 250 passengers, six tugs tried to pull her off at the following high tide, but in vain. Later in the day, however, a second attempt met with success, and after an underwater survey to assess the damage, followed by a team of divers disentangling a towing hawser from around her propellers, the liner continued her voyage.

Withdrawn from service in 1967, the *Capetown Castle* went to the scrapyards in La Spezia. When, however, her master was given the order to beach her, he is said to have retorted: 'I have spent my life being paid to keep ships off the beach. If you want her there, you'll have to do it yourselves.'

The new schedule caused a break with traditions that had been an integral part of Union-Castle's operation since 1938. Departure day from Southampton was changed from Thursday at 16:00 to Friday at 13:00 so that ships would arrive in Cape Town at daybreak on Wednesday, rather than the customary Thursday. Similarly, there were changes to the coastal schedule. Needless to say, Port Elizabeth traders greeted them with great enthusiasm, for instead of the ships spending the weekend in port, they would now arrive on a Friday morning and leave for East London on the Saturday, while the downcoast vessels would also call on a Friday. These changes substantially benefited commerce in the city.

3

4

It followed that Cape Town's traditional Friday mailship sailing would also be brought forward. The new departure time was scheduled for Wednesdays at 13:00 and docking time in Southampton, after eleven days at sea, was to be early on Mondays.

Seven ships were now operating the new schedule:

PASSENGER MAILSHIPS	CARGO MAILSHIPS
Windsor Castle	*Southampton Castle*
Pendennis Castle	*Good Hope Castle*
Edinburgh Castle	
Transvaal Castle	
Pretoria Castle	

In 1964, the South African Marine Corporation (Safmarine) had tendered for the mail contract, but since the corporation had lacked sufficient fast ships at that stage to operate according to the required schedule, the South African Government re-awarded the contract to Union-Castle. However, in October 1965, B&C announced that a deal in

1 *The last voyage of the* Stirling Castle.
2 *After dinner drinks with Captain Dylan Cambridge, DSO, on the* Edinburgh Castle. *Desmond Lawrence, the last managing director of Union-Castle South Africa, and Mrs Lawrence are on the left.*
3 *The* Pendennis Castle.
4 *The* Athlone Castle *sailing for the last time from Cape Town.*

1

THE MAIL

The hub of the Union-Castle mailship service was the Ocean Mail Contract. It determined the mailships' schedule and gave them priority attention in all four South African ports of call. Even in the midst of severe port congestion, as experienced during the Suez Crisis of 1956/57 and the Suez closure from 1967 to 1975, the mailships berthed and sailed according to schedule. Such regularity and reliability assured shippers of specific delivery dates and attracted thousands of tons of highly tariffed cargo to the line.

From the days when the early mailships brought only a few bags of mail to more recent times, the mail was eagerly awaited. It consisted not only of letters, but also of thousands of parcels, magazines and newspapers.

The mailbags were handled only in Southampton and Cape Town. On the days prior to sailing, post office vans brought the mail on to the wharf where, with the second officer supervising operations, each bag was tallied as it was put into the cargo sling for hoisting aboard and stowage in number one hold. The volume of mail increased greatly on sailing day when sling after sling was loaded. Stowed in a special mail room off number three hold were registered items and diplomatic mail, known as 'Red Mail', the tallying of which was carried out exceptionally carefully.

The landing of mail was always accorded priority in port. In the early years, the mail was taken from the mail room and sorted on deck the day before arrival so that it would be ready for discharge and rapid delivery. In latter years cranes would work number one hold even as the immigration and customs formalities were being conducted on board.

Once, when a bag of mail fell between the Pendennis Castle *and the quay, a seaman and a docker jumped into the water to retrieve it, an incident which made the newspapers.*

In Southampton, the second officer was always the last to leave the ship as it was his responsibility to check that the mail had been landed correctly. During the Christmas rush he would not get away for hours.

MAIL LANDED AT CAPE TOWN IN A SINGLE VOYAGE

1857	*CELT*	10 567	LETTERS AND 3 671 NEWSPAPERS
1862	*CELT*	200	BAGS OF MAIL
1949	*PRETORIA CASTLE*	25 495	BAGS OF MAIL
1962	*CARNARVON CASTLE*	2 145	BAGS OF MAIL

By the early sixties, a large proportion of the mail was being sent by air.

excess of £10 million had been concluded whereby the *Pretoria Castle* and *Transvaal Castle* would be sold to Safmarine and paid for over ten years. This gave Safmarine a two-sevenths share in the mail service and, more particularly, placed part of the mail contract – hitherto operated by a foreign shipping company – under South African control. It also meant that passage monies for at least two-sevenths of the mailship fleet would remain in South Africa, thus blocking a substantial drain of finance from the country.

The news was received with euphoria in South Africa, as the pair were the first passenger liners to be owned by a local concern. It was also seen as a development that represented a shift from dominance by Union-Castle – and more latterly B&C – over the South African Conference. But in some British shipping circles the move was regarded as simply a sop to the Nationalist Government, which was becoming increasingly isolated by the British Labour Government. B&C, it was pointed out, had a substantial shareholding in Safmarine; thus it would gain from the profits of the two ships without incurring operating expenses. The liners were to be retained initially on the British register, mainly because there was no hope of Safmarine finding sufficient numbers of qualified and experienced personnel to operate them.

Renaming ceremonies were held in Cape Town for each of the vessels. The *Transvaal Castle*, painted in her Safmarine colours (white hull and superstructure, with a grey funnel bearing a band each of blue, white and orange), made a particularly fast passage from Las Palmas to arrive well before the usual time on 12 January 1966. In fact, the pilot and tug crews had been on standby throughout the night to ensure immediate docking on arrival and an early start on her cargo work, which would have to be interrupted for several hours later in the day while the ceremony took place. An unforeseen problem was evident when the ship arrived. The buffeting she had received from a force nine gale between the English Channel and Las Palmas had stripped the new white paint from sections of the hull. Globe Engineering promptly set to work and had restored the hull's paintwork well before the commencement of the ceremony. At the same time, signwriters busily set about painting in the ship's new name on both quarters, on the lifebelts and on the inboard sides of the lifeboats. (Although she had made the voyage from Southampton officially as the *Transvaal Castle*, her name had been painted out in readiness for the changes that would need to be hastily effected upon her arrival in Cape Town.)

By 15:15 a huge crowd had assembled on the quayside, while important guests and political dignitaries were seated on the balcony of the Customs Hall at F Berth. The band of the South African Navy thumped out a miscellany of appropriate maritime tunes, and the ship's officers, dazzlingly smart in their number ones, stood briskly to attention, saluting in perfect unison at the appointed moments, just as they had been drilled on the outward voyage. It was a stirring occasion.

After speeches by Sir Nicholas Cayzer and Dr H.J. van Eck, chairman of the Industrial Development Corporation, the unveiling of the new name was performed by the wife of the state president, Mrs C.R. Swart, who drew aside a green curtain at the base of the funnel to proudly reveal the name *S.A. Vaal.* (Suggestions that the Union Jack and the South African flag be used as the curtain had been regarded as politically unwise, hence the green curtain.)

In his address, Sir Nicholas said:

> The official handing over of the *Transvaal Castle* to her new owners, the South African Marine Corporation, represents as it does the first participation of a South African company in this important link in the trade between our countries.

2

3

1 *Hoisting the mail from the forward hold of the* Saxon *off Port Elizabeth, circa 1907. The hatchcovers and method of battening them down changed little over the years; the system used on the* Pretoria Castle *of 1948 was not much different to that depicted in this photograph.*

2 *In September 1972, the* Windsor Castle *landed more than 13 000 mailbags – the first seaborne mail shipment to South Africa since the British dockers' strike in July and August. In addition, there was also a huge consignment of backlogged periodicals. The ship was late because of the vast amount of cargo to load at the end of the strike. The rest of the cargo was brought by subsequent ships.*

3 *On the day before arrival at Southampton or Cape Town, the mailbags were brought out from the hold, sorted and stacked along the first class promenade deck so that no time would be wasted in despatching them the following morning. As both discharging techniques and postal distribution services improved, this practice was abandoned in the early years of the twentieth century.*

SOUTHAMPTON

The home port of the mailships since the days of the Union Line, Southampton depended on the passenger trade for its livelihood.

Although 'mailship days' were exceedingly hectic, there was little ceremony to mark the arrival or departure of the weekly mailship, for a dozen or more passenger liners of several companies passed through the port each week. Nor were there the crowds that greeted the mailships at all their South African ports of call, for many of the passengers caught the 'boat train' which, within two hours, would take them to Waterloo Station in the heart of London, from where they would travel to their various destinations. Nevertheless, there was no denying the excitement among the 700-odd passengers, eager to meet relatives or friends, or to discover the delights of Britain or Europe, perhaps for the first time.

Most of the crew were resident in the Southampton area, but before they could return home after the six-week voyage, they would have to sign off the ship's articles, often queueing for a while, but in good spirits. The stewards and galley staff could only leave once everything had been cleaned up after breakfast and once the last passenger had disembarked, a requirement that few begrudged since they were usually the recipients of generous gratuities from the passengers.

While breakfast was in progress on arrival day the 'Hello Gang' came on board – a group of relief officers whose job it was to caretake the ship and supervise the multitude of tasks to be carried out during the two weeks in port while the regular men enjoyed a spell of leave. The nickname for these officers stemmed from the rush with which essential information was conveyed to them. The more senior officers had to report on the voyage to a superintendent either on board or in the Southampton office. Usually these were brief meetings, held more out of courtesy than need, but there were occasions when explanations or information pertaining to an abnormal occurrence during the voyage was required.

The catering superintendent and his staff would arrive shortly after docking to take stock of some 18 000 pieces of silver cutlery, 45 000 items of glassware and crockery, about 80 000 items of linen, and thousands of other items, including the ship's liquor supplies. Even the number of tots served during the voyage had to balance. The catering men from the shore also checked carpets, chairs and curtains for repairs or cleaning. A thousand mattresses, some 3 000 pillows and approximately 400 bags of linen went ashore for specialized laundering, while teams of workers began the massive task of cleaning the ship thoroughly.

Having discharged her South African cargo, the ship moved to another berth (in later years to Berth 104) to load for her outward voyage. A few days before sailing, the lorries of Southampton chandlers would convey to the ship vast quantities of stores, sufficient to feed 1 000 people for several weeks. To cater for 130 000 individual meals as well as morning and afternoon teas during one round voyage of the Windsor Castle, *the volume of stores consumed included an impressive*

38	*tons potatoes*	*1 500*	*litres milk*
20	*tons meat*	*15*	*tons fresh vegetables*
7	*tons poultry and gamebirds*	*11*	*tons flour*
8	*tons fish*	*6 000*	*litres beer*
3	*tons bacon*	*50 000*	*minerals*
3 600	*litres ice cream*	*3 500*	*bottles spirits*
80 000	*eggs*	*1*	*ton tea and coffee*
3	*tons butter, cheese and cream*	*1*	*million cigarettes*
4	*tons sugar*		

Besides the crates of toiletries and other non-edible stores, detergents to clean the ship as well as to wash 120 000 items of linen and 5 000 articles of uniform also had to be carried. In addition, 4 000 tons of fuel and 3 000 tons of fresh water were pumped aboard. (Once the accelerated service had been introduced, the volume of bunkers and stores required was reduced, but there was always an adequate surplus to allow for delays or breakdowns at sea.)

Two days before sailing, the hotels in Southampton began to fill up with passengers waiting to board. The officers and crew began arriving and the staff from the Harland & Wolff workshop worked at often feverish pace to finish routine maintenance or special repairs.

On the day before sailing, the old faithfuls among the crew would return to the ship, having signed the articles at the office of the shipping master. New hands recruited to fill vacancies were sent to the ship, where they were interviewed by the departmental head who paged through each man's discharge book to check his past record. If accepted, he went to the shipping office to sign on.

Board of Trade officials inspected the life-saving equipment and watched the mandatory lifeboat and fire-fighting drill before joining port officials at lunch on board. Apart from humouring officialdom, this lunch gave the chief steward an opportunity to assess the competence of new hands to the ship.

On sailing day, journalists came on board the mailship to interview any interesting personalities among the passengers. Generally, Union-Castle enjoyed the publicity generated by the pressmen for whom the lunch was a highlight of the week. Sir Vernon Thomson usually took lunch on board as well, a practice continued by Bernard Cayzer, who on one such occasion noticed a man seated on his own at a table. No one knew who the visitor was, save that he was a regular diner on all the mailships when in Southampton. Cayzer introduced himself and diplomatically enquired as to the other's business. To the astonishment of all, the man explained that some time previously he had been entertained on board by a passenger, and having enjoyed the meal so much, he had returned the following week. Unchallenged, he had dined at the expense of the company each week thereafter. Amused by the man's opportunism, Cayzer immediately arranged for the stranger to continue taking his Thursday luncheon on board the mailships.

After lunch, excitement mounted until the stroke of four o'clock when the mailship would move slowly from the quay, and the voyage on the Sunshine Route began.

1

2

The *Transvaal Castle* and the *Pretoria Castle* have been acquired by Safmarine, and in due course, when the *Edinburgh Castle* comes to the end of her useful life, she will be replaced by a Safmarine ship . . .

A moment of sadness, that would be only natural, for who among us would wish to part with this great ship. But the time has come for South Africa to play her part in this important service and that it should be achieved in this manner is a development with which I am proud and happy to be associated . . .

Three weeks later, the *Pretoria Castle* was renamed the *S.A. Oranje* by Mrs Betsy Verwoerd, wife of the South African prime minister. This time Sir Nicholas referred to the two 'happy coincidences' in the career of the ship: she had been launched and named by Mrs Issie Smuts, wife of the then prime minister of South Africa; now the liner was to be renamed by the wife of the current prime minister. In addition, 'the contract for the building of the ship was signed in the year that Safmarine was born'.

The chairman of Safmarine, Mr Fred Bamford, spoke of the future of shipping, and enlarged on some of the remarks made by Sir Nicholas at the previous renaming ceremony:

. . . I am inclined to think of that new ship [a replacement mailship], its shape and speed and the conditions that will await her arrival. There is a new pattern emerging of both ships and conditions that must be followed very carefully before committing companies to expensive replacements. While this ship, the *S.A. Oranje*, and the other six that form the team to carry out the mail contract, are already speedy, necessarily, to accomplish their regular delivery commitment within the given time, other so-called ordinary dry-cargo ships are also being built for greater speed and are being equipped with gear designed for rapid cargo handling. There is at this moment, too, a study being made on containerisation . . . In fact, there is a world-wide development towards building faster ships, flexible in world trades, automated . . . all in the interests of cutting time in ports, which is costly . . .

Bamford's words were ironically prophetic. Within eleven years, the trends of which he spoke would have wiped the mailships from the face of the sea.

For a few years, through force of circumstance, the Safmarine mailships continued to sail under the British flag. But finally, after considerable negotiations with officialdom in both South Africa and Britain, transfer to the South African flag took place on 12 February 1969 and 17 March 1969. Again impressive ceremonies were held in Cape Town. On these occasions State President Jim Fouché and Prime Minister B. J. Vorster officiated respectively aboard the *S.A. Vaal* and *S.A. Oranje*.

A few Safmarine officers were transferred to the mailships, one of whom was Captain Robin McA. Thomson. Having learnt his seamanship on the training ship *General Botha*, and after a spell in the Blue Funnel Line, he had joined Safmarine as a third officer in 1947, gaining command in the early fifties. His experience and his polished demeanour made him an obvious choice for transfer to the mailships, initially as staff commander on the *S.A. Vaal*, before being appointed to command the *S.A. Oranje*. When Commodore Norman Lloyd on the *S.A. Vaal* retired, Captain Thomson succeeded him as commodore, an appropriate climax to a fine career.

After the withdrawal of all the intermediate vessels and the *Capetown Castle*, the British possessions of St Helena and Ascension islands were not regularly served by ship. This presented serious problems, for although a modest airport on Ascension afforded the island air links with the outside world, heavy cargo still had to be brought by sea. St Helena was even more isolated, since the mountainous terrain precluded the building of any form of landing strip. Continued sea links with both islands were therefore essential. For a while the mailships were diverted to the islands, but as the older vessels were already struggling to maintain the tight schedule it was decided that the fast cargoships *Southampton Castle* and *Good Hope Castle* should make the call. The pair were sent to the Cammell Laird Yard at Birkenhead where accommodation for twelve passengers was added to each vessel, and thus equipped, the ships provided a six-weekly service to the islands.

Not since the wreck of the *Tantallon Castle* in 1901 had a mailship been lost during peacetime, and apart from the explosion in the *Capetown Castle* in 1960 and a few minor incidents, Union-Castle's safety record had been exemplary.

Then in June 1973, news broke that the *Good Hope Castle* was missing somewhere between the islands of Ascension and St Helena. She had left Ascension Island on Friday, 29 June 1973, at 16:00, bound for St Helena – a thirty-hour voyage away – and thereafter for Cape Town. It was reported that neither the northbound *Southampton Castle*

3

nor St Helena Radio had been able to make contact with the *Good Hope Castle*, and when the ship failed to arrive at St Helena an all-ships alert was broadcast.

As dinner was being served on the *Good Hope Castle* on that Friday evening, down in the engine room a pipe carrying lubricating oil to the starboard main engine fractured, spraying oil on to an exhaust uptake. Although an initial outbreak of fire was brought quickly under control, a flare-up caused it to spread to the accommodation. While the crew fought the fire throughout the night, the master, Captain R.J. Miller, ordered that the passengers – the wife of one of the officers, twelve cabin passengers and seven deck passengers – be accommodated in the lifeboats which were readied for launching. Shortly after daybreak the following morning, the ship developed an alarming list from the tons of water that had been pumped on board in an attempt to extinguish the fire. In view of the danger to life, Captain Miller decided to send two boats away with passengers and some of the crew, while he remained on board with fifteen others to continue the battle against the fire. Eventually, with the fire progressively gaining hold, he gave the order to abandon ship. All the boats remained in the vicinity of the burning vessel, so that when the tanker *George F. Getty* came on the scene it picked up everyone, landing them at Ascension the following day (Sunday). Meanwhile, the *Southampton Castle* had been diverted to search for her sister ship, which she sighted on the Monday morning. Reporting no sign of smoke from the fire-ravaged vessel, she was ordered to Ascension where she embarked the master and several officers and men of the *Good Hope Castle* and took them back to the ship, but the heat still emanating from the hull prevented anyone from boarding. Since the *Southampton Castle* had to resume her voyage, another of the B&C

1 *Evening in Southampton.*

2 *The pilot launch closing with the* Pendennis Castle *off the Nab Tower. Depending on weather conditions, the outward mailships occasionally rounded the Isle of Wight to westward, dropping the pilot off the Needles, at the same time allowing passengers a good view of the white cliffs of Allum Bay as well as the Needles themselves.*

3 *Commodore Norman Lloyd, master of the* S.A.Vaal, *was an officer in the Royal Naval Reserve, and so flew the Blue Ensign. When the port of registry of the liner was changed from London to Cape Town in an impressive ceremony, the ensign was struck in favour of the South African flag.*

1

vessels – the *Clan Malcolm*, bound for Cape Town from Birkenhead – was directed to Ascension to pick up sufficient members of the mailship's crew as were necessary to reboard her. The remaining twenty-seven crew members and the officer's wife returned to Britain on the *Southampton Castle*.

An aircraft was chartered by head office to fly out members of the Union-Castle technical staff to inspect the damage. En route to Ascension it circled the *Good Hope Castle*. The listing ship was a sorry sight, and it could be seen too that the fire had flared up once again. A further attempt was made to reboard her from the *Clan Malcolm* but without success. The freighter finally returned the ship's men to Ascension, from where they and six passengers were flown to Britain; the rest of the passengers were taken to St Helena to await the next ship to Cape Town.

When the German salvage tug *Albatross* arrived to tow the stricken vessel, inclement weather made it impossible to connect a hawser, and it was not until 11 July that the *Good Hope Castle* could at last be towed to Antwerp for extensive repairs.

In view of the delay in the *Southampton Castle* reaching Britain (well outside the voyage duration allowed for in the mail contract), Union-Castle was anxious that the South African postmaster-general should be kept informed of events. The Cape Town office was therefore instructed to

> . . . advise the Postmaster-General of the foregoing [the delay to the vessel] and crave his indulgence for this deviation without prior consultation with him but feel sure in the circumstances of the situation he will approve of the action we took STOP Southampton Castle because of the foregoing deviation and of delay on passage from Cape Town to St Helena caused by engine trouble will be approximately 24 hours late arriving Southampton.

Once the immediate danger to the vessel had passed, the Cape Town office of Union-Castle voiced their displeasure at the apparent lack of information forthcoming from London, and the initial delay in notifying them of the incident, about which most Capetonians had heard via the media. They felt particularly vulnerable to press speculation, since allegations had been published locally that the engines and radios in two of the lifeboats were not working. The silence from Union-Castle itself had been interpreted as something being amiss.

The company had not wanted exact details of the incident to leak out, explained the reply from London, because it feared that with the abandonment of the ship – worth millions of pounds and carrying a cargo worth almost as much – she might have fallen prey to salvage hunters who could have claimed her as prize. Neither did London wish to have photographs of the ship published before she arrived safely off the European coast because of the adverse publicity which could have ensued from photographs of the derelict mailship on the high seas.

Following the vessel's arrival in Antwerp, surveyors and underwriters established that although, miraculously, eighty-five per cent of the mailship's cargo had not been affected by the fire (it had been restricted to two holds and had not spread), repairs to the ship

2

would still cost £2 million as the fire had affected the ship's accommodation, the two holds forward and the engine room.

On 25 July 1973, British & Commonwealth chairman Sir Nicholas Cayzer prefaced his address to the eighteenth annual general meeting of the group's shareholders with this reference to the *Good Hope Castle*:

> She was a vital unit, for in the event that she had been lost, it would have been virtually impossible at short notice to acquire a replacement with the necessary speed and cargo carrying capacity . . .
>
> It was a great relief to all of us to know that there was no loss of life or serious injury. I would like to say how much I admired the calmness and fortitude of the passengers in what must have been for them frightening and trying circumstances. Our best thanks are due to the Master and ship's company of the *Good Hope Castle* for ensuring the safety of those entrusted to their care. I should also like to place on record our sincere thanks to the Master and crew of the *George F. Getty* and also those on Ascension Island who did so much for everyone involved in the disaster.

Until the *Good Hope Castle* returned to the mail service in June 1974, the *Rotherwick Castle*, one of a pair of refrigerated vessels built in 1959, took her place, although allowance had to be made for her service speed of 18 knots compared to the 22 knots of the *Good Hope Castle*. The *Pendennis Castle*, the fastest unit of the fleet, made the calls to St Helena and Ascension.

1 The S.A. Vaal. *Her one-class arrangement for passengers was welcomed by most who travelled in her. Even those accommodated in the inner four-berth cabins had access to all the facilities on the ship and enjoyed the same menu as those occupying the suites. For that reason, fares for passengers in the* S.A. Vaal *were higher than those applicable to similar accommodation on board other mailships. In 1967, the cheaper single seasonal fare between Cape Town and Southampton on the* S.A. Vaal *was R256 compared to R242 on the* Windsor Castle. *At the other end of the scale, her suite fare of R1 550 for two people was R500 less than the equivalent in the* Windsor Castle.

2 The Good Hope Castle, *nearly lost in a serious fire in June 1973.*

THOSE IN COMMAND

Armed with recommendations from various officials, the Union-Castle board made the final decision as to who would command a mailship, an appointment that came only after a proven record of excellent service, including time as a mailship staff commander, a spell of command first on board one of the cargoships and then on one of the intermediates.

Reflecting the sequence of promotion were the appointments made when Commodore Mayhew was hospitalized suddenly in Cape Town in March 1957. His place on the Pretoria Castle was taken by Captain Jackie Fisher, then on the intermediate Warwick Castle which was also in Cape Town at the time. Captain W. Anson, master of the Roslin Castle loading fruit for Britain, replaced Fisher on the Warwick Castle, while Chief Officer D.A. Rees on the Pretoria Castle was promoted to acting master of the fruitship.

Most appointments to master of a mailship were entirely successful; others, including one or two appointments to the top position of fleet commodore, were not.

The successful master of any passenger ship requires many attributes, of which superb seamanship is but one. Of equal importance are the qualities of decisive leadership, resilience and great wisdom. Human relations skills will doubtless earn immense popularity among the passengers but it is the ability to exercise cool, calm, astute judgement under conditions of extreme stress or danger that saves lives, ships and cargo.

The weight of such responsibility, plus the constant demands on the time and energies of the mailship master created stress in itself, without having to cope with emergencies. As a result some sought solace in alcohol and a few retired early, but the great majority of those who commanded the Cape mailships revelled in the job and were superb seamen.

Mailship masters had direct access to the Union-Castle board and the ear of the chairman at virtually any time, particularly in the Thomson era. Bernard Cayzer continued this tradition, journeying to Southampton almost every week to chat to both the incoming master and the one whose ship was about to sail. This gesture meant a great deal to the masters and helped ease the strain and pressure generated by the loneliness of command of a ship worth millions of pounds, the ultimate responsibility for the safety of over a thousand people and being answerable for damage to thousands of tons of valuable cargo.

There were occasions when individuals were carpeted before the chairman and, when warranted, before the board of directors to explain an indiscretion or an accident. Captain Bill Byles had to account for the collision between the Carnarvon Castle and a German freighter while the latter was at anchor in Algoa Bay. The master of the Stirling Castle found himself interrogated about damage sustained when the vessel hit an outcrop while rounding Cape Verde. And there were others.

One of the most successful masters on the mail run was George Mayhew, a stalwart of the company from 1917, when he joined as a cadet, until his retirement as a director some fifty years later. He knew stress in its fullness. He had been in command of the refrigerated cargoship Roxburgh Castle in 1943 when she was torpedoed off the Azores and he had one of the most harrowing encounters with bad weather off the South African coast ever recorded by a mailship master.

On her third southbound voyage, the Pendennis Castle, with Commodore Mayhew in command, experienced not only a dreadful crossing of the Bay of Biscay, but also adverse weather all the way to Cape Town. Worse was to come. Gales lashed the ship for the entire South African coastal passage. In Port Elizabeth, the wind prevented the tugs from towing the vessel off the quay at sailing time. She eventually left several hours later than the tight schedule prescribed. The same gale whipped the East London roadstead into such a cauldron that docking became too dangerous and, unable to land her passengers, the ship continued to Durban. Downcoast, further delays were experienced due to the continued heavy weather.

Cape Town was no better. On departure day the pilot boarded but refused to sail the ship as he considered the wind too strong. Near to 17:00 Mayhew and the pilot decided to attempt to sail the liner. An additional tug was called for and the vessel was towed down the Duncan Dock into the teeth of the gale. The pilot ordered full ahead and, once she was under way, for the tugs to slip their hawsers. At that crucial moment when the ship began to gather speed for her dash through the harbour entrance, Mayhew got cold feet. He slapped the engine room telegraph to STOP. The ship now began to drift before the gale. The pilot was appalled. He yelled for full power and after much hesitation Mayhew responded. Such was the power of the Pendennis Castle that she picked up speed so quickly that the pilot tender could not keep up with her. It is said that the ship was doing 116 revolutions when she sped through the harbour entrance. That day the pilot disembarked off the breakwater, once the mailship had reduced speed. An obviously shaken Mayhew went below for a well-earned rest. Such was the toll that command of those magnificent ships took on even the most experienced and sanguine of masters.

Mayhew had been promoted to commodore of the fleet in 1953, flying his flag in the Pretoria Castle. In 1958 he was transferred to the fleet's new flagship, the Pendennis Castle, and in 1960 he commanded the Windsor Castle for her maiden voyage. Thereafter the Cayzers appointed Mayhew as group marine superintendent, and shortly afterwards he joined the B&C board of directors – the only Union-Castle master to do so.

1

2

3

4

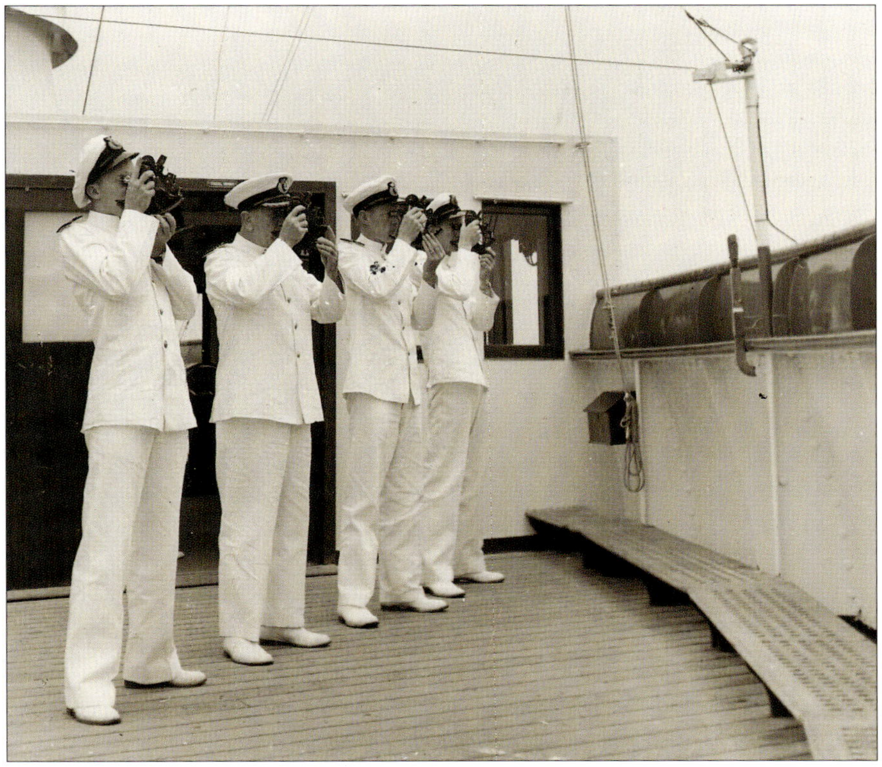

1 *With a distinguished war service, in which he commanded* inter alia *the* Llangibby Castle *during the D-Day operations, Captain T.W. McAllen became commodore of the Union-Castle fleet in 1950.*

2 *Commodore Harold Charnley on the bridge of the* Windsor Castle *with Commodore George Mayhew, the retired director of British & Commonwealth and former commodore of the fleet. (On this voyage he was travelling as a passenger.)*

Apprenticed to Messrs Stephen Sutton of Newcastle-upon-Tyne, Harold Charnley went to sea at the age of fifteen. Typical of the British trampships of the time, the Sutton ships were not always comfortable, but life in the trampships schooled the young Charnley in every aspect of seamanship and navigation, so that he easily obtained his master's ticket in 1939. The following year he moved to Shaw Savill and joined the refrigerated vessel, Waiotera, *which was sunk.*

His first encounter with Union-Castle was when he joined the Capetown Castle *as fourth officer in 1942. He then rose through the ranks to gain his first command in 1965 on the* Margaret Bowater, *a unit of the British & Commonwealth group, taking woodpulp from Scandinavia to Merseyside. After several years in command of various cargoships, including the mailship* Good Hope Castle, *he commanded first the* Pendennis Castle, *and three years later, in March 1973, the* Windsor Castle *where he became commodore of the fleet until his retirement in 1975.*

3 *After a rough passage during which paint had flaked off the bow, the* Pretoria Castle, *in Safmarine colours, berths in Cape Town on the morning of the name-changing ceremony, at which she was renamed the* S.A. Oranje.

4 *Resplendent in their tropical number tens, officers on watch on the* Pretoria Castle *take a sunsight to ascertain the ship's latitudinal position.*

1

8

Farewell to the Sunshine Route

1973-1977

2

As the sixties had celebrated the 'coming of age' of air travel and witnessed dramatic advances in space aviation, so the seventies quietly – and for many, regretfully – bade farewell to the great age of passenger liners and a mode of transport that for centuries had been the only means of traversing the oceans of the world.

Although not solely responsible for the change in travel habits, it was probably the Boeing 747B (the 'jumbo' jet) that sounded the final warning bell for the mailships. On 10 December 1971, the first service flight of South African Airways' newly acquired 'jumbo' left from Jan Smuts Airport in Johannesburg. In only two flights, as many passengers had been conveyed to London as in one of the mailships. By 1974 a ninety-day return air fare of R722 was being advertised for a flight from Cape Town to London (including five stopovers in Europe). This was hardly more expensive than the cost of the cheapest four-berth cabins on the *Edinburgh Castle* and *S.A. Oranje* when, during the low season, passengers paid R289 for a one-way ticket. Because of the seasonal nature of passenger traffic, however, the return voyage would have had to be taken during peak season when higher rates (R362) applied, making the total sea fare R651. On top of that, twenty-two days at sea required additional pocket money.

The air traveller was also able to benefit from the exceptionally low rates of the so-called excursion (APEX) airfares which, in the off-peak season, could be as little as R490 for a return flight to London from Cape Town. This was a dream come true for students, not to mention the average salaried employee with limited annual leave who had neither the time nor the money to spend on what amounted to a three-and-a-half-week leisure cruise. And even people for whom time and money were not criteria began to take to the air, preferring to spend longer at their final destination than in travelling. Businessmen and sportsmen too welcomed the advantages of air travel, which included daily flights between South Africa and London.

3

4

Of course, South African Airways and British Airways were not alone in providing competition for the mailships; eight other airlines were also operating regular flights to Europe, most of them using jumbo jets. Steadily, the mailships' clientele was being eroded.

Additional to the pressures brought about by competition from the airways, Union-Castle had other setbacks to cope with, all of which contributed to greatly increased operating costs. One such setback was the seamen's strike of 1966, which severely disrupted the mail service and forced shipowners to increase substantially the wages of their crews. This, in turn, had necessitated a rise in passenger fares. Then, when the Organization of Petroleum Exporting Companies (OPEC) suddenly increased the oil price in 1973, bunker prices soared, further escalating passenger fares. A sticker on the October 1973 Union-Castle/Safmarine fares and sailings brochure drew the attention of would-be passengers to the problem.

OIL SURCHARGE

> Due to the increased cost of bunker fuel, our Principals are obliged to apply a ten percent oil surcharge on all passage fares shown in this brochure.
> Due to the current World fuel shortage, mail vessels will, until further notice, operate at reduced speed.
> Departure dates from U.K. remain unchanged, but arrival at Cape Town is one day later. Departure from Cape Town for England is now one day earlier than shown.

Naturally, the cost of aviation fuel also increased, but the increase applicable to bunkers was proportionally higher, particularly since the mailships each consumed over 200 tons of fuel per day, even with a revised twelve-day passage.

Between 1965 and 1974, the costs of an ocean passage more than doubled, whereas the excursion rate air fares had decreased. Preferring the comfort of first class travel aboard an aircraft, the more affluent passengers rapidly abandoned the mailships. The only ones who continued to travel by sea were those with whom old habits died hard, or who thoroughly enjoyed the leisurely and sociable lifestyle afforded by the ocean liner. There were others too who had a genuine love of the sea itself, and then there were those who remained sceptical of the safety of the aeroplane. On some voyages, fewer than fifty passengers occupied the first class accommodation, while during the low season, many tourist class berths were empty.

Over the years Union-Castle had tried air-sea holiday packages which, it was hoped, would encourage travellers to fly in one direction between Britain and South Africa and to enjoy a sea voyage in the other direction. The scheme certainly attracted some business. However, a subsidy of R800 000 per annum from the South African Government for the maintenance of the mail contract notwithstanding, the high operating costs of the ships signalled the imminent end to the mailship service in its traditional form.

At the annual general meeting of B&C in 1973, Sir Nicholas Cayzer alluded to the negative trend in the passenger shipping portfolio of the group: 'I did inform you that bookings were below expectations and, although it would appear that there has been a lengthening of the booking season, it would be wrong to assume that there will be any improvement on the 1972 figures.' He also referred to the group's diversification of interests:

> Every strike of gas or oil in the North or Celtic seas means potentially more business for the Bristow Helicopter fleet; expansion of the economy encourages the acquisition of machine tools; the maintenance of high charter rates improves the prospect of the profitable employment of our bulk carriers, and generally, our liner shipping earnings

1 *The* Edinburgh Castle.

2 *A product of Eton College and Corpus Christi College, Cambridge, Sir Nicholas Cayzer, later Lord Cayzer, was appointed to the boards of Clan Line Steamers and Cayzer Irvine & Co. only months before World War II. When Clan Line and Union-Castle interests merged in late 1955, he became vice-chairman of British & Commonwealth and in 1958, on the death of his uncle, Lord Rotherwick, he took over the entire group as chairman. An affable, unassuming yet astute man, Sir Nicholas became extremely popular with the maritime fraternity in both Britain and South Africa. Under his chairmanship, B&C diversified its interests to include portfolios that strengthened their financial position against the fluctuations of maritime investments.*

3 *One of the last attempts to stimulate interest in mailship travel.*

4 *A four-berth cabin,* S.A. Oranje.

1

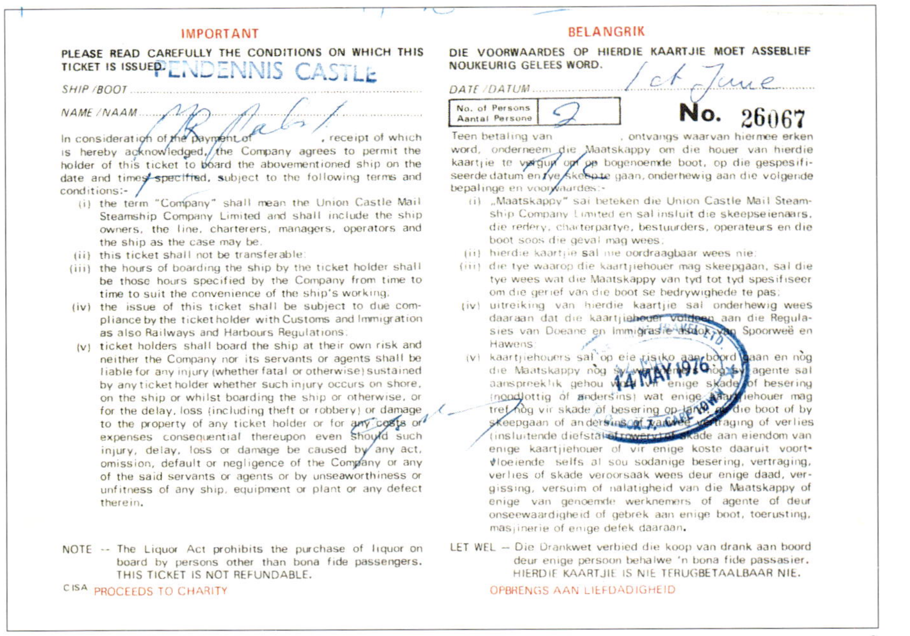

IMPORTANT

PLEASE READ CAREFULLY THE CONDITIONS ON WHICH THIS TICKET IS ISSUED. PENDENNIS CASTLE

SHIP/BOOT ....

NAME/NAAM ....

In consideration of the payment of , receipt of which is hereby acknowledged, the Company agrees to permit the holder of this ticket to board the abovementioned ship on the date and times specified, subject to the following terms and conditions:-

(i) the term "Company" shall mean the Union Castle Mail Steamship Company Limited and shall include the ship owners, the line, charterers, managers, operators and the ship as the case may be.

(ii) this ticket shall not be transferable:

(iii) the hours of boarding the ship by the ticket holder shall be those hours specified by the Company from time to time to suit the convenience of the ship's working.

(iv) the issue of this ticket shall be subject to due compliance by the ticket holder with Customs and Immigration as also Railways and Harbours Regulations.

(v) ticket holders shall board the ship at their own risk and neither the Company nor its servants or agents shall be liable for any injury (whether fatal or otherwise) sustained by any ticket holder whether such injury occurs on shore, on the ship or whilst boarding the ship or otherwise, or for the delay, loss (including theft or robbery) or damage to the property of any ticket holder or for any costs or expenses consequential thereupon even should such injury, delay, loss or damage be caused by any act, omission, default or negligence of the Company or any of the said servants or agents or by unseaworthiness or unfitness of any ship, equipment or plant or any defect therein.

NOTE -- The Liquor Act prohibits the purchase of liquor on board by persons other than bona fide passengers. THIS TICKET IS NOT REFUNDABLE.

CISA PROCEEDS TO CHARITY

BELANGRIK

DIE VOORWAARDES OP HIERDIE KAARTJIE MOET ASSEBLIEF NOUKEURIG GELEES WORD.

DATE/DATUM 1st June

No. of Persons Aantal Persone	2

No. 26067

Teen betaling van , ontvangs waarvan hiermee erken word, onderneem die Maatskappy om die houer van hierdie kaartjie te vergun om op bogenoemde boot, op die gespesifiseerde datum en tye skeep te gaan, onderhewig aan die volgende bepalinge en voorwaardes:-

(i) „Maatskappy" sal beteken die Union Castle Mail Steamship Company Limited en sal insluit die skeepseienaars, die redery, charterpartye, bestuurders, operateurs en die boot soos die geval mag wees;

(ii) hierdie kaartjie sal nie oordraagbaar wees nie;

(iii) die tye waarop die kaartjiehouer mag skeepgaan, sal die tye wees wat die Maatskappy van tyd tot tyd spesifiseer om die gerief van die boot se bedrywighede te pas;

(iv) uitreiking van hierdie kaartjie sal onderhewig wees daaraan dat die kaartjiehouer voldoen aan die Regulasies van Doeane en Immigrasie asook van Spoorweë en Hawens;

(v) kaartjiehouers sal op eie risiko aan boord gaan en nòg die Maatskappy nòg sy werknemers nòg sy agente sal aanspreeklik gehou word vir enige skade of besering (noodlottig of andersins) wat enige kaartjiehouer mag tref nòg vir skade of besering op land, op die boot of by skeepgaan of andersins of vir enige vertraging of verlies (insluitende diefstal of rowery) of skade aan eiendom van enige kaartjiehouer of vir enige koste daaruit voortvloeiende selfs al sou sodanige besering, vertraging, verlies of skade veroorsaak wees deur enige daad, vergissing, versuim of nalatigheid van die Maatskappy of enige van genoemde werknemers of agente of deur onseewaardigheid of gebrek aan enige boot, toerusting, masjinerie of enige defek daaraan.

LET WEL -- Die Drankwet verbied die koop van drank aan boord deur enige persoon behalwe 'n bona fide passasier. HIERDIE KAARTJIE IS NIE TERUGBETAALBAAR NIE.

OPBRENGS AAN LIEFDADIGHEID

14 MAY 1976 CAPE TOWN

2

STOWAWAYS

Because of the high profile enjoyed by the company in South Africa, Union-Castle made a point of encouraging the public to visit their ships when they were in port. Parties of school children, members of farmers' associations, women's groups, and many others were regularly welcomed on board the liners. Similarly, friends of passengers only needed to ask at the company's office for permission to board on sailing day and the necessary permit was issued. Inevitably, this system was abused over the years.

Of all the mailships, the Pendennis Castle *seems to have been the most appealing to persons wishing to abuse Union-Castle's open-house policy. On her northbound voyage in December 1972, eight stowaways were discovered during the voyage. Of these, four were members of a family – father, mother and two young sons – that had fallen on hard times in South Africa and had decided to return to Britain. Although it could not be proved conclusively, there was strong evidence to suggest that a member of the crew had assisted the family in stowing away, for the seaman had been observed with one of the children a day or two before the family's presence was detected. An American woman and her six-year-old son were also among the stowaways on that voyage, as was an ex-steward of the P&O liner* Chusan. *That unhappy man had deserted while his ship was in Durban on her way to Australia and, wishing to return to Britain, had hidden himself in the* Pendennis Castle.

In a number of instances, crew members actually hid stowaways in their cabins, although they had to be sure that their cabin mates would turn a blind eye. Captain Charnley of the Pendennis Castle *had to deal with a French woman who had been smuggled on board at Cape Town and had been hidden in a cabin housing three seamen. It seems discretion was not her strong point as the master-at-arms overheard and discovered her in the cabin on the ship's first day at sea.*

Several schoolboys also took illegally to the mailships. One such occasion involved a lad from a leading Cape Town boarding school. His absence from the Friday supper table was noticed by the headmaster who promptly called for information on the boy's whereabouts. There were no immediate volunteers of information but later that night, in response to deep anxiety, a friend of the boy confided in the headmaster that the absentee was probably on board the Southampton-bound mailship. A radio message to the ship and a quick search led to his early discovery but not before he had made considerable winnings at the games evening. He was transferred to the southbound mailship at Southampton and on arrival in Table Bay was taken off the ship by pilot tug, away from the glare of the press who had tended to treat the boy as a hero.

In most cases, stowaways were prosecuted in the port where they were landed, only to receive either a small fine or a suspended prison sentence. The company found the trials and the sentences frustrating, for the repatriation of a stowaway and the copious correspondence involved in each case cost not only money but valuable time. To solve the increasing stowaway problem in South Africa, but reluctant to close their ships to the public, Union-Castle tried several new schemes, finally settling for that used successfully in Southampton (there was seldom a stowaway on the southbound voyage) whereby a limited number of permits were issued to the passengers themselves for distribution to their friends.

are keeping up well. Accordingly . . . the results for 1973 should show a marked improvement on those of the previous years.

This extract from Sir Nicholas's address implies that while the volume of passenger bookings was declining, the group was expecting greater revenue from sources other than the liners.

The final straw for the mailships was the containerization of the South African-European trade. In response to the demand for container shipping, several joint studies by the State and by the shipping lines through the Southern African-European Conference paved the way for the entire South African-European trade to be containerized by July 1977. Well before that time, members of the Conference had placed orders for fully cellular 50 000-ton containerships for the service between South Africa and north-western Europe, including Britain. The Conference member lines who had undertaken responsibility for the provision of the ships were:

Overseas Container Line (which would take over the Conference trading rights of Union-Castle and Clan Line)	1
Safmarine	4
Ellerman-Harrisons	1
Compagnie Maritime Belge	1
Nedlloyd (formerly Holland-Afrika Lijn)	1
Deutsche Afrika-Linien	1

Besides these, two ro-ro ships would serve the Scandinavian and German trades, and another two the north-western European ports.

Until the completion of these ships, a number of other vessels capable of carrying both containers and break-bulk cargo would be chartered to ensure a smooth transition to 'C-Day' (1 July 1977) when the Southern African-European Container Service was to be born.

Compounded by the other negative economic factors, the decision to containerize the trade meant the unavoidable withdrawal of some of the mailships, none of which could be modified economically to carry significant numbers of containers. The first to go was the twenty-seven-year-old *S.A. Oranje*. In the 1975 annual report of Safmarine, a short paragraph noted the fate of the liner: 'The increased fuel costs have resulted in the operation of the *S.A. Oranje* becoming consistently unprofitable and the ship has been sold to breakers.'

In October 1975, she arrived in Cape Town from Southampton with her usual cargo.

3

Thereafter she called at Port Elizabeth as scheduled, but a gale and heavy seas sweeping the East London roadstead prevented the pilot from boarding and the liner continued her passage to Durban where she was de-stored. With a skeleton crew, she made her first and only passage across the Indian Ocean en route to Kaohsiung, there to be beached for cutting up. It is said that when the old liner was lined up for the beach, she swung away as if reluctant to be scrapped. On the second attempt she crashed on to the beach, thus ignominiously completing a twenty-seven-year career unmarred by breakdown or accident, during which time the vessel completed 187 round voyages totalling nearly three million nautical miles.

In the first class dining saloon on the *S.A. Oranje*, there hung a huge painting of the Union Buildings in Pretoria. The work of the South African artist J. M. Pierneef, it had been commissioned by the Pretoria City Council for the first *Pretoria Castle*, an intermediate vessel built in 1939. When that liner was gutted for war service the painting was put into storage and after the war was transferred to the new *Pretoria Castle* and placed on the bulkhead behind the captain's table. When the ship was destined for the scrapyards, that painting, another by Le Roux Smith Le Roux depicting the City Hall in Pretoria, and two mirrors engraved with the coat-of-arms of Pretoria were presented to the Pretoria Council at a luncheon in April 1976.

The *Edinburgh Castle*, also a heavy consumer of fuel, left the service in May 1976. On her last sailing from Southampton for South Africa en route to Taiwanese breakers, two of her officers with strong Scottish leanings, piped the ship away from the quay. As she sailed down Southampton Water, strains of *The Lament* from the piper stationed on her funnel deck came upriver to those watching from the Town Pier. Of her final departure from Cape Town on 7 May 1976, the *Cape Times* shipping columnist wrote:

> Nostalgic echoes resounded from empty rooms and bare long galleries of the *Edinburgh Castle* which, with only mails and cargo from Southampton, made her swansong in Table Bay yesterday en route to the knackers' yards in Kaohsiung, Taiwan as scrap. She should realise about R1,9 million in terms of current scrap prices.
>
> Members of the crew of less than 50, reclined in formerly luxury suites, the library containing hundreds of books was available to the staff . . .
>
> On the foredeck, lay two spare bronze propellers recovered from a store at Southampton which are going to the scrappers as part of the deal . . .
>
> It is on the decks where the 27 years' service is revealed by the liner. The once smooth wood is now splintering, rough and scarcely waterproof after years of tropical sun and rain.
>
> Furniture is labelled for various addresses and a City hotel is getting chairs from the long gallery. A writing table is destined for the Durban pilots . . .
>
> The steamer will set off from Durban next week on her first and last trip east of Africa, and has required new charts to find her way through the Singapore Straits to Taiwan . . . On arrival in Kaohsiung, the representatives of the scrappers will tell Captain Peter Eckford where to drive the ship up on the mud. They will find a gap between two beached ships in course of demolition and whether the gap is wide enough or not, they will request that he go full astern into the opening and the weight of the ship will push the other two apart.
>
> Damage is of no account . . . The initial landing will buckle the rudder, probably wreck the steering gear, and twist the propeller blades . . .

Captain Eckford had been the fourth officer on the *Edinburgh Castle* during her maiden voyage in 1948.

Because the mail schedule was still in force, substitutes had to fill the gaps left by the withdrawal of the two old mailships. Safmarine's *S.A. Zebediela* and *S.A. Hexrivier* replaced them on the northbound voyages only, returning in ballast from Southampton to Durban to be ready for the next northbound slot in the schedule. Those southbound voyages which would have been allocated to the *S.A. Oranje* and *Edinburgh Castle* were taken by Safmarine chartered or owned vessels, the first being the chartered 20-knot *Benlawers* which sailed from Southampton on 1 November 1975.

Early in 1976 came the announcement that the 'funship' *Pendennis Castle* was to be withdrawn from the mail service in June.

A strong north-wester was blowing and Table Mountain was shrouded in cloud on 2 June 1976, the day the *Pendennis Castle* left on her last voyage after a remarkably short career of only seventeen years. She was sold to Far Eastern interests who intended to operate her as a cruise liner, a forlorn hope when one considers that revenue earned from cargo while on the Cape run scarcely offset the costs of her heavy fuel consumption and high portage bill. As a cruise liner she would carry no cargo to assist in running her at a profit. The nearest her new owners came to achieving their ambition of converting her to a cruise liner was to paint her white and give her a completely red funnel. Thereafter, sporting the successive names of *Ocean Queen*, *Sinbad* and *Sinbad 1*, she spent several

1 *Stowaways being transshipped in mid-ocean from the* Athlone Castle *to the southbound* Pretoria Castle.
2 *A boarding permit for the* Pendennis Castle *on her last call at Cape Town.*
3 *The* S.A. Oranje *sailing from Durban, bound for Taiwanese scrapyards.*

1

years at anchor in Hong Kong before being sold to Taiwanese scrap merchants in 1980. Yet another of the mailships was cut up to feed the furnaces of the steel industry of the Orient.

Immigration to South Africa had once been the lifeblood of Union-Castle on the southbound voyage; now the main immigration point was Jan Smuts Airport, Johannesburg, as increasing numbers of new arrivals chose air travel rather than the twelve-day passage to South Africa. In any case, most of the jobs to which immigrants were coming were located in the industrial heartland of the southern Transvaal, 1 700 kilometres from Cape Town. However, what had been a healthy flow of immigrants to South Africa virtually ceased after the horrific events in Soweto in June 1976 and the ensuing unrest countrywide. No one wanted to settle in a country that appeared to be on the brink of ruin.

With so many factors militating against the continued operation of the mailships, it was not surprising that on the morning of 15 November 1976 a memorandum from the group secretary of Cayzer Irvine was circularized to all staff members, advising them of a statement to be released to the press that afternoon:

> It is with regret that Safmarine/Union-Castle announce that the two remaining passenger mailships operating on the route between the United Kingdom and South Africa are to be withdrawn from service in the latter part of 1977. The ships are Safmarine's *S.A. Vaal* 30,000 tons and Union-Castle's *Windsor Castle* 36,000.
>
> This is a direct result of the forthcoming introduction of a container shipping service on this route which will embrace the shipment of cargo presently carried by the mailships. The container service will be operated by a fleet of specially built cargo-only container ships, the first of which is due to enter service in September 1977.
>
> The *Windsor Castle* and *S.A. Vaal* were built to carry several thousand tons of cargo in addition to 700/800 passengers each, and they are not economically viable as passenger carriers only.
>
> The last sailing of the *Windsor Castle* in the South Africa/United Kingdom mail service will commence at Durban on 31st August 1977, sail from Cape Town on 6th September 1977, to arrive at Southampton on 19th September 1977.
>
> The last sailing of the *S.A. Vaal* in this Service will commence at Durban on 21st September 1977, leave Cape Town on 27th September 1977 to arrive at Southampton on 10th October 1977.
>
> CAPE TOWN
> 12.11.1976.

The statement was as bland as it was inevitable. It neither conveyed any emotion nor bore any reference to the 120-year history of the mail service which would be terminated during the second half of the following year. Some viewed it as insensitive to the close ties that

2

had existed between South Africa and the mailships, and to the fond memories of thousands of people who had travelled on the mailships over the decades. Others simply shrugged it off as an inescapable product of economics.

Under the command of Captain Patrick St Quentin Beadon, the *Windsor Castle* made her last calls at South African ports between August and September 1977. At all the ports on that last downcoast voyage, buffet luncheons were organized to thank those among the shipping fraternity who had played some part in the smooth operation of the mail service. Officials from the port administration, customs, chandlers and agencies enjoyed the lavish Union-Castle hospitality for the last time. In two functions on successive days during the ship's last call at Cape Town, her officers were entertained by the company at the Mount Nelson Hotel, that symbol of elegance and reminder of the halcyon days of Union-Castle when the company had bought the hotel for its more affluent passengers.

Then came the day of the last sailing from Cape Town by a Union-Castle passenger mailship – Tuesday 6 September 1977. Since she was the largest and probably the best known among all the postwar mailships, thousands turned out to see the *Windsor Castle* leave. The four o'clock sailing ritual was exercised as in the past. As the great liner moved away from the quay, the Blue Peter came down, and three deep blasts from her foghorn resounded around the harbour. Arches of water from the fire jets on the tugs saluted the liner as she gathered speed to leave the harbour, while the customary chorus of ships' sirens sent the 'Greatest Liner on the Sunshine Route' into history.

A month later she was renamed the *Margarita L*, de-stored by the small remnant of Union-Castle staff in Southampton, and flying the Panamanian flag but under Greek ownership, she left the Hampshire port for Jeddah to serve as an accommodation ship for contract workers in Saudi Arabia and also for Muslim pilgrims to Mecca – a role she was well suited to. Her accommodation was air-conditioned, she had equipment to desalinate tons of fresh water daily and to generate electricity, while her catering facilities could feed hundreds of people simultaneously. In time, she returned to the Mediterranean, and is currently laid up in Eleusis Bay, Piraeus.

Three weeks after the final departure of the *Windsor Castle* from Cape Town, similar pomp and ceremony were accorded the *S.A. Vaal* for her last northbound voyage. As had

1 *Minus one of her port lifeboats (it had been donated to the local Naval Cadet Unit in Durban) and sailing with a skeleton crew for the delivery voyage to Taiwanese breakers, the* Edinburgh Castle *leaves Durban for the last time.*

2 *Tuesday, 6 September 1977: the* Windsor Castle*, the largest and the last Union-Castle passenger mailship, leaves Table Bay on her final voyage on the mail service.*

1

MAILSHIP PASSENGERS

Although the great majority of passengers returned home with a store of pleasurable memories, there were always a few who found fault with everything and who thrive on being unreasonable, uncooperative or downright antagonistic. Some of the offenders were the aristocrats in first class for whom everything had to be done and whose complaints to the master – or to the chairman of the company – included such trivia as unacceptable hairstyles of certain stewards or the bacon being too crisp.

The excessive exuberance of some tourist class passengers accounted for numerous problems over the years, such as the time when a number of passengers took the Crossing the Line ceremony too far and daubed the purser of the Pendennis Castle *with shoe polish and generally made a nuisance of themselves.*

Each problem brought before the ship's master required handling with the tact and finesse of a seasoned diplomat. Some were amicably resolved and some were not, and there were occasions when irate passengers went so far as to sue the company. One incident concerned a couple travelling first class, who found that the ship had no cot for their child. Nothing could appease them and they stormed off the ship at Las Palmas to await the following week's southbound vessel. The sequel was a successful suit against the company, which was ordered to pay £890 damages and £3 000 legal costs.

Another court hearing in Cape Town concerned a passenger who claimed that he had not been provided with the grade of cabin for which he had paid. While the initial proceedings of the case were conducted swiftly, the judge decided he needed to establish the true nature of the accommodation for himself, and adjourned the hearing until the return of that mailship to Cape Town. After an in loco *inspection, he dismissed the claim.*

Deaths, often followed by burial at sea, dampened the voyage for all, but there were numerous joyous occasions too, none more so than a marriage ceremony or the birth of a baby.

2

Royalty, governors-general, mining magnates, politicians, writers, musicians, film tars – all walked the white scrubbed decks over the years. But although the rich and the famous dominated the news reports on mailship passengers, by far the majority of those on board were ordinary folk – people travelling on an immigration scheme or fulfilling a holiday dream. Many of their memories and memorabilia fill the pages of this book.

3

4

Extracts from the Ship's Official Log of R.M.S. "Windsor Castle."

CAPTAIN P. St. Q. BEADON

Voyage 124 — CAPE TOWN to SOUTHAMPTON via LAS PALMAS

Date	Distance Run	Lat.	Long.	Temp. at Noon Air C	Air F	Sea C	Sea F	ITINERARY
Sept. 6		At Cape Town		14°	58°	—	—	1600: vessel departed Cape Town escorted by S.A.N. 'President Pretorius.' Few clouds, fine and clear. WSW wind, force 2 *Passengers on board: 215 first class. 553 tourist class* Cocktail Music daily by Mike Hill Cinema, 'Silent Movie'
7	408	29°00S	13°00E	17°	63°	16°	61°	Lightly overcast, fine and clear. SE wind, force 3 Clocks retarded one hour during night to B.S.T. Complimentary Dancing Lessons by Peter Glen Captain's Cocktail Party Dancing with the Jimmy Skene Quintet. 'Windsomnia'
8	507	22°25S	07°07E	18°	65°	17°	63°	Lightly overcast, fine and clear. SxE wind, force 3 1200: Vessel crossed Tropic of Capricorn, thus entering Tropics Quiz Time. Cinema. 'The Sweeney'
9	512	15°34S	01°43E	19°	67°	18°	65°	Lightly overcast and clear, fine weather. SExS wind, force 4-5 2000: vessel crossed Greenwich Meridian Children's Deck Sports. Children's Cinema. 'Junior Jukebox' Frog Racing. 'Windsomnia'
10	512	08°36S	03°17W	23°	73°	23°	73°	Partly cloudy, fine and clear. ESE wind, force 4-5 2030: passed 'Safmarine's' Southbound Mailship 'S.A. Vaal' Aquatic Sports. Pantomime - 'Ali the Barber.' 'Windsomnia'
11	483	01°58S	07°47W	26°	79°	24°	75°	Few clouds with fine sunny weather. SExE wind, force 3 1918: vessel crossed the Equator in longitude 09°05W Divine Service conducted by the Captain in the 1st Class Lounge Cricket Practice and Cricket Match— Passengers v. Ship's Officers Classical Concert. 'Tropical Night.' 'Hawaiian Night' in Disco
12	496	04°45N	12°34W	27°	81°	27°	81°	Few clouds, fine and clear. SSW wind, force 3 Crossing the Line Ceremony. Return Cricket Match Cinema, 'Airport '77'
13	489	11 22N	17°19W	29°	84°	29°	84°	Partly cloudy with showers. SE wind, force 2-3 2200: vessel passed Cape Verde and City of Dakar — most Westerly point of Africa Children's Fancy Dress Parade and Tea Party Gala Evening Recalling 120 Years of Cape Mail Service
14	492	19°34N	17°44W	26°	79°	25°	78°	Cloudless, fine with sunny weather. NNW wind, force 3-4 2330: vessel crossed Tropic of Cancer thus leaving the Tropics Children's Fair. Cinema, 'A Star is Born'
15	488	27°26N	15°36W	23°	73°	23°	73°	Partly cloudy and clear, fine weather. NE wind, force 5 1530: vessel arrived at Las Palmas 1930: sailed from Las Palmas Talk on Las Palmas. Tombola. Mike Hill entertains
16	341	32 51N	13°48W	22°	72°	22°	72°	Few clouds, fine and clear. NxE wind, force 2-3 Cinema, 'The Last Tycoon.' 'More Revue.' 'Windsomnia'
17	464	40°17N	11°10W	14°	58°	20°	68°	Lightly overcast with occasional showers. E wind, force 2 2148: rounded Cape Finisterre, entered Bay of Biscay Children's Cinema. 'Junior Jukebox.' Farewell Dance
18	451	47 08N	06 58W	16°	60°	18°	64°	Few clouds, fine and clear. ExN wind, force 6 1745: vessel rounded Ushant thus entering the English Channel Divine Service conducted by the Captain in the Cinema Classical Concert. Tombola. Mike Hill entertains
19	299	At Southampton						E.T.A. Southampton Pilot Station: 0330 B.S.T. E.T.A. Alongside Berth: 0630 B.S.T.

Distance Table Bay to Southampton Pilot Station: 5,942 miles   Average Speed: 20·24 knots

Total distance Cape Town Docks to Southampton Docks: 5,979 miles

1 *The* Sinbad 1 *(formerly the* Pendennis Castle*) at anchor off Singapore. She failed to fulfil the cruise liner ambitions of her new owners and ended her days in Taiwanese scrapyards.*

2 *On 28 August 1970, some sixty miles north of Las Palmas, and twelve hours after he had fallen overboard from the* S.A.Vaal*, William Honeywill was rescued by the ship's seaboat. On hearing that the man was missing, presumably overboard, Captain Alan Freer decided to turn the ship, retrace her course and search for several hours for the missing passenger. Shortly before breaking off the search, Captain Freer ordered a sight on Gran Canaria to confirm the ship's position. He set course towards the island and within minutes Honeywill was sighted in the water and rescued. The need for the alteration of course notwithstanding, the success of the rescue was attributable to the accuracy of Captain Freer's navigation, which had to take into account the sea conditions as well as currents.*

The Windsor Castle *performed a similar rescue in November 1976 when Mrs Margaret Fuller was pulled from the water three hours after she had fallen overboard off the African coast. On that occasion Captain Patrick St Quentin Beadon's supreme navigational skills enabled him to retrace the ship's course for 25 miles and pass within 50 metres of the passenger, at which point Mrs Fuller was spotted.*

3 *Safmarine's* S.A. Hexrivier *in Cape Town, loading for Southampton. She and her sister ship, the* S.A. Zebediela*, were drafted into the northbound mail schedule following the withdrawal of the* S.A. Oranje *and the* Edinburgh Castle.

4 *Extracts from the log book of the* Windsor Castle *on her last northbound voyage for Union-Castle.*

1

2

been the case for the *Windsor Castle*, there were functions at all the ports along the down-coast voyage, but because of her South African connection, and because she was the last passenger mailship on the run, several additional ceremonies marked her farewell at Cape Town. On the day of the final sailing, the boat train, drawn by a steam locomotive, arrived at Cape Town's A Berth from Johannesburg, brimming with passengers and steam enthusiasts and evoking memories of the days when this was a feature of the weekly mailship departure.

That afternoon, bands played on the wharf as the passengers crowded the rails to watch the proceedings. Ashore, the wharf seethed with a throng of humanity, all gazing up at the great white liner, which was dressed overall and flying a long paying-off pennant from the signal halyard at the cross-tree. Meanwhile cars lined the Table Bay coastline, and office workers gathered at vantage points throughout the city to view her departure. Hundreds of those watching must have recalled with deep nostalgia the day they too had sailed in the *S.A. Vaal*, or one of her consorts.

As the gangway was lowered and the tugs took up the slack on their towing hawsers, a thousand helium balloons were released, while pipers from the Cape Town Highlanders played the ship away from the quay. From the wing of the bridge, Commodore Robin McA. Thomson peered down to see the pilot safely off, called for full ahead and ordered a minor course alteration to bring the mailship in line ahead with the frigate SAS *President Pretorius*, the harbour tugs and a host of pleasure craft. With that escort, the great liner moved out into the roadstead and, as so many other fine liners had done on their last

Extracts from the Log of the Final Northbound Voyage of the "S.A. Vaal"

"Voyage Number, One Hundred and Fourteen"

LAUNCHED CLYDEBANK 17-1-61 — COMMODORE R. W. McA. THOMSON

CAPE TOWN TO SOUTHAMPTON

Date	Day's Run	Lat. Long.	Wind Force	Temp. at Noon Air	Temp. at Noon Sea	Itinerary
27-9-77	At Cape Town		Var 3	21.1°	—°	1600 Departed Cape Town 2021 Passed Cape Columbine Cloudless
28-9-77	423	28°19S 13°22E	SE 6	18.0°	15.6°	Ship's Clocks retarded one hour to GMT plus one hour Commodore's Cocktail Party. Welcome Aboard Dance Sunny with few clouds Low S'ly swell
29-9-77	509	21°24S 07°57E	SWxW 2/3	17.1°	16.7°	0506 Crossed Tropic of Capricorn and entered Tropics Cloudy and clear Low S'ly swell Frog Racing
30-9-77	513	14°36S 02°30E	SE 3	18.6°	18.3°	Tropical Night on the Promenade Deck 2230 Crossed Greenwich Meridian and entered Western Hemisphere. Overcast but clearing Low SxE'ly swell
1-10-77	508	08°03S 2°59W	SExS 3/4	22.1°	23.3°	Vaal Revue Sunny with cloudy patches Low SSE'ly swell
2-10-77	508	01°31S 08°24W	SSE 3/4	24.2°	23.3°	1030 Divine Service conducted by the Commodore 1740 Crossed Equator and entered Northern Hemisphere Sunny becoming cloudy Low SE'ly swell
3-10-77	526	05°23N 13°49W	SxW 4	27.5°	26.7°	Vaal Derby Cloudy but clearing Low SE'ly swell
4-10-77	494	12°27N 17°40W	Var. 1/2	27.9°	28.3°	1834 Passed Cape Vert—Most Westerly point of Africa Sunny with light haze No swell The Generation Game S.A. Vaal Flappers
5-10-77	494	20°41N 17°39W	NExE 2/3	21.8°	23.9°	2045 Crossed The Tropic of Cancer and left Tropics Fancy Dress Parade S.A. Vaal Minstrels Sunny with light haze Low N'ly swell
6-10-77	460	27°58N 15°16W	NNW 5/6	22.3°	22.2°	1248 Arrived Las Palmas 1800 Departed Las Palmas 2215 Music From The Shows Sunny with scattered cloud Low N'ly swell
7-10-77	314	32°54N 13°33W	NNW 6	19.5°	22.7°	2115 Olde Tyme Music Hall Sunny with scattered cloud Heavy NNW'ly swell
8-10-77	448	40°02N 10°47W	WSW 5	19.6°	18.9°	2200 Passed Cape Finisterre and entered Bay of Biscay Overcast with scattered cloud Heavy NNW'ly swell Mailship Farewell. Pyjama Party at the Vaal a go-go
9-10-77	482	47°23N 06°27W	NWxW 5	14.1°	14.4°	Divine Service conducted by the Commodore 1621 Rounded Ushant, left Bay of Biscay and entered English Channel. O'cast occl. show's Mod. W'ly swell 2130 Farewell Sing along
10-10-77	294 At Southampton					0330 Expected arrival off Pilot station 0630 Expected arrival alongside berth

TOTAL DISTANCE 5982 MILES - - AVERAGE SPEED 20·33 KNOTS

3

4

5

voyages, continued along the Atlantic seaboard for several miles, before turning to seaward and into the sunset.

Festivale Maritime Inc. bought the *S.A. Vaal*, renamed her *Festivale* and sent her to Japan for a refit, which included the conversion of much of her cargo space to passenger cabins, the upgrading of many of her facilities and several structural changes to her promenade decks – changes that many believed improved her appearance. American tourists fill her now, mainly on cruises out of Miami to the Caribbean.

With some voyages of the official mail contract remaining, Union-Castle chartered several fast vessels to replace – albeit temporarily – the passenger liners. One was the Blue Star ship *Andalucia Star*, a feature of which was her low fuel consumption of 60 tons per day – a substantial saving on the 240 tons of the *Pendennis Castle*.

Although there had been great ceremonial farewells for both the *Windsor Castle* (the last Union-Castle passenger ship to sail from Cape Town) and the *S.A. Vaal* (the last passenger mailship on the run), it was the *Southampton Castle* that made the final voyage under the last Ocean Mail Contract.

Shortly before the vessel sailed at two o' clock on the afternoon of 11 October 1977, a quiet, yet nonetheless poignant, ceremony was held on the wharfside, where the last mailbag was put into the cargo sling by Cape Town's postmaster for hoisting aboard by crane.

At the small luncheon on board, Union-Castle (South Africa)'s managing director, Desmond Lawrence, commented:

The departure today of the *Southampton Castle* has even more significance, though not perhaps the glamour which attaches to the phasing out of our well-known passenger ships. The sailing today marks the end of a contractual arrangement which has existed for 120 years . . . Mail will, of course, continue to be carried by sea – containerisation is the ideal vehicle for this in many ways. Union-Castle's interests in the container era will be invested in Overseas Containers Limited whose first vessel, the *Table Bay*, will be in these waters in November. Union-Castle has for long had very close links with both Southampton and Cape Town, and an affinity has grown between these two cities. This is recognised today by His Worship the Mayor [Mayor of Cape

1 *The* S.A.Vaal *dressed overall on her farewell call at Port Elizabeth.*
2 *Pipers at the departure of the* S.A.Vaal *from Cape Town on 27 September 1977.*
3 *It was customary to provide each passenger with an extract from the ship's log as a souvenir of the voyage. This extract was the last to be printed for a passenger mailship.*
4 *The* S.A.Vaal *leaves Cape Town for the last time. Note the paying-off pennant flying from the signal halyard.*
5 *The* Festivale *(formerly the* S.A.Vaal*) in the Straits of Malacca en route to Japan for conversion to a cruise liner. She is still operating, taking mainly American tourists on Caribbean cruises.*

1

2

Town, Councillor Ted Mauerberger] who is to hand over to Captain Wray-Cook [the master of the *Southampton Castle*] a letter of greeting.

A few hours later, and with very little of the fuss accorded the earlier final departures, the *Southampton Castle* had disappeared over the horizon to close a long and eventful chapter in South Africa's maritime history.

Around the world many ports with large passenger terminals began to experience economic recession as the ocean passenger trade went into a rapid decline. Southampton and the South African ports were equally affected by the ending of the mailships' weekly calls.

In Southampton, thousands of tons of fuel and stores had been taken on each week by the mailships. Maintenance of machinery and equipment had brought work to numerous shoreside personnel, while thousands of pounds had been earned by laundry companies who had cleaned the linen, carpets, curtains and other fittings in the liners. Over the years, hundreds of thousands of people had occupied rooms in the city's hotels, inns and bed and breakfast establishments; indeed, on the night before sailing it was almost impossible to obtain accommodation within a reasonable distance of the harbour without prior booking. Pubs and restaurants enjoyed the benefits of Union-Castle clientele; florists and other shops throughout the city thrived on the dozens of bowls of flowers, fruit and other gifts sent to passengers on sailing day, while hundreds of dockers depended for their livelihood on unloading the 15 000 tons of cargo brought by the weekly liner, and loading a similar tonnage each week for shipment to South Africa. When one considers the volume of passenger traffic passing through Southampton in the heyday of the liners, it is obvious just how great the economic impact of their withdrawal was on the port.

In South Africa, it was estimated that Union-Castle spent more than R200 million per year on repairwork, stores, fuel, port dues and salaries for their local employees, not to mention the thousands of rands spent by the ships' passengers and crews in the country's four major ports. With the ships' withdrawal, all that ceased.

As the liners sailed on their last voyages, hundreds of men looked ahead to retrenchment and little hope of employment elsewhere, particularly as the containerships would carry only a twentieth of the mailships' crews – and mostly foreign nationals.

Among the crew on the *Windsor Castle* on her last voyage were three men whose collective length of service on Union-Castle ships totalled 141 years. Able Seaman Arthur Brown had started his sea-going career in the *Balmoral Castle* in 1929, the same year in which Smoke Room Steward Laurence Byrne went to sea for the first time. His first ship was the *Carnarvon Castle*. Another smoke room steward, Leonard Symes, had notched up forty-five years' service, which had begun on board the intermediate liner *Guildford Castle* in 1932. Messrs Byrne and Symes had been shipmates on the *Capetown Castle* throughout the war, and when the *Windsor Castle* reached Southampton in September 1977, these stalwarts of the company were paid off for the last time.

Such was the lot of most of the mailships' crews, the majority of whom had been with the company for decades; several were second or third generation Union-Castle men.

The link between the Inkson family and Union-Castle, for example, dated back to October 1889, when G.H. Inkson joined the *Norham Castle* as a saloon boy and captain's servant. In all, he sailed in twenty-nine ships, including two spells in the Currie yacht *Iolaire*. He saw the decks of the *Tintagel Castle* crowded with troops on their way to fight in the Anglo-Boer War; as chief steward on the *Dunluce Castle*, he had to cater for troops of the Imperial Guard when they were hurriedly withdrawn from South Africa in 1914 for service in Europe, and he was on board the vessel on her voyage to India during the Gallipoli campaign when she served as a hospital ship, and in many other places within the Mediterranean theatre of war. A footnote in his personal logbook states: 'Patients carried from August 5th '15 [1915] to December 21st '18 [1918] = 48,945.'

He helped to alleviate the suffering of the malaria victims evacuated in the liner from Dar-es-Salaam and he saw Australian ports when the ship repatriated troops to their native land at the close of World War I. For nine years after the war until he came ashore

3

4

5

to the Southampton office, he was chief steward on board a number of the mailships, his last sea-going appointment being the *Walmer Castle*.

Inkson's three sons also joined Union-Castle: the eldest served ashore for forty-four years; another went to sea for eight years before joining the RAF for wartime service; after forty-two years with the company, the youngest son retired from Union-Castle when the Southampton office closed in 1977. A nephew of the old man had also spent some years with Union-Castle.

Then there were the Pyne brothers, and Chief Steward Beckett, whose son followed in his footsteps, as well as numerous other families whose lives had revolved around Union-Castle for as long as they could remember.

Because many of the crewmen lived in the greater Southampton-Portsmouth area, the economy of that area had benefited in a small, yet significant, way when their wages were brought ashore. Shipping companies such as Union-Castle had provided jobs for thousands, ashore and afloat, but the curtailment of the liner services brought massive retrenchment and unemployment, not to mention severely restricting employment opportunities for the younger generation.

The passenger offices in London and Southampton closed, and in time the rest of the Union-Castle operations were swallowed up in the Overseas Container Line service.

Having cleared their desks, Union-Castle employees left for a life on pension or on the dole. Now they reflect on the demise of a company that had been, as many of them have said, 'like a club', and to which so many felt a strong, almost zealous, allegiance. There are still Union-Castle gatherings in various British towns, where tales of better days are told among friends. Among those who travel great distances to meet old colleagues in this way is Bill McEwan who, from junior clerk in the Glasgow office, moved through the ranks to become passenger manager for Southampton and, later, assistant to the area director until the last sailings in 1977. More than thirty-three years with Union-Castle, interrupted only by World War II, are reflected in his enthusiastic recollections of the

1 *A souvenir brochure of the last voyage of the* S.A.Vaal. *According to information inside the brochure, Chief Radio Officer R. Hough served on board for most of her 114 voyages.*

2 *The regional director of posts and telecommunications, Gawie de Kock, places the last mailbag into the cargo sling for it to be hoisted on board the* Southampton Castle *on the final voyage of the mail service. Mr Neil Sempill, left, managing director of Cayzer Irvine (South Africa), and Captain N.F. Wray-Cook, master of the mailship, look on. The container on the foredeck is perhaps symbolic.*

3 *Because they were together for several voyages, each lasting six weeks, a special camaraderie developed between Union-Castle officers. In Southampton, the Red Lion (once the 'court' of the young Prince Harry – later Henry V) was a favourite gathering place.*

4 *Situated on the site of the Gloucester Baths, which had been demolished during excavations for the docks in 1838, the old customs house in Canute Road, Southampton, was a grand building with a porticoed entrance hall and a look-out for the customs officers. In 1892, the building was taken over by the Union Line, and when the Union and Castle lines amalgamated in 1900, the building became the Southampton office of Union-Castle, remaining so until the mid-fifties when, apart from the passenger department, Union-Castle offices moved to the Western Docks.*

5 *Leonard Pyne, MBE (left) and his brother, Sydney, both chief stewards, went to sea at an early age and, after excellent and loyal service spanning more than fifty years each, were honoured by the company on their respective retirements. Leonard Pyne had endured extreme hardship when the* Warwick Castle *was torpedoed in 1942.* *(See page 95.)*

1

POSTCARDS OF THE UNION-CASTLE MAILSHIPS

Once the hobby of small boys and seamen, but now a lucrative trade, the collection of ships' postcards extends back decades. Companies used the postcards to advertise their ships, and on the postcards passengers described to their friends their shipboard experiences, many of which make fascinating reading today as they record shipboard life over the years.

The first Union-Castle postcards were printed shortly after the turn of the century. They were photogravure illustrations, although as early as 1906 the first colour postcards had been issued by the company. Many other styles were used, but the one most familiar was the sepia card, a style initiated possibly in the late twenties. Most ships had several cards during their careers, reflecting modifications as they were made, such as the refits to five vessels in the late thirties.

In the course of its history Union-Castle commissioned several artists to portray a number of its ships, and many of these paintings were used by the company for their official postcards. Some paintings were excellent but most exaggerated the colours, creating an unnatural sea running, or they depicted the ships completely out of proportion. On the whole they did little to enhance the image of the company. Interspersed with colour reproductions of these paintings, the sepia cards continued until the end of the mailship era, though the photogravure style returned with cards of the Pretoria Castle, *some of the cargoships, the* Pendennis Castle *and the last* Windsor Castle.

While several other series of postcards were produced by individual photographers or publishers, those that were issued officially by Union-Castle today change hands for large sums of money.

RECORD PASSAGES SET BY THE MAILSHIPS BETWEEN BRITAIN AND CAPE TOWN

1857 *DANE*	44 DAYS
1863 *SAXON*	31 DAYS
1863 *ROMAN*	30 DAYS 20 HOURS
1865 *SAXON*	28 DAYS 12 HOURS
1871 *SYRIA*	26 DAYS 18 HOURS
1871 *PENGUIN*	24 DAYS 18 HOURS
1873 *WINDSOR CASTLE*	23 DAYS
1876 *DUNROBIN CASTLE*	22 DAYS 12 HOURS
1876 *AMERICAN*	22 DAYS 2 HOURS
1877 *DUNROBIN CASTLE*	21 DAYS 13 HOURS
1877 *BALMORAL CASTLE*	21 DAYS 11 HOURS
1877 *GERMAN*	19 DAYS 9 HOURS
1879 *PRETORIA*	18 DAYS 17 HOURS
1890 *DUNOTTAR CASTLE*	17 DAYS 20 HOURS
1891 *DUNOTTAR CASTLE*	17 DAYS 17 HOURS
1891 *DUNOTTAR CASTLE*	17 DAYS 5 HOURS
1891 *DUNOTTAR CASTLE*	16 DAYS 23 HOURS
1891 *SCOT*	15 DAYS 10 HOURS
1892 *SCOT*	15 DAYS 8 HOURS
1892 *SCOT*	15 DAYS 3 HOURS
1893 *SCOT*	14 DAYS 19 HOURS
1936 *STIRLING CASTLE*	13 DAYS 9 HOURS
1937 *CARNARVON CASTLE*	12 DAYS 13 HOURS
1954 *EDINBURGH CASTLE*	11 DAYS 21 HOURS
1965 *WINDSOR CASTLE*	11 DAYS 12 HOURS
1969 *PENDENNIS CASTLE*	10 DAYS 11 HOURS

2

3

'I'm afraid containerisation can never recapture the magic of the old mail boat departure!'

palmy days of one of the great British lines. And there are dozens of others, both in Britain and South Africa, whose long association with the lavender-hulled ships goes back many decades.

Union-Castle had been a way of life for thousands in Southampton maritime circles, and for 120 years it had been an institution on the South African trade. Captain Strutt, the master of the tiny coal-fired steamship, *Dane*, could never have dreamed of the significance of that pioneering voyage to the Cape in 1857; neither could he ever have imagined the revolutionary changes that were to take place in maritime transport over the next century or so – changes that would raise the embryo mailship company to the pinnacle of influence and prestige, and equally would bring about its sudden demise.

The first fully cellular containership serving southern Europe, Lloyd Triestino's *Africa*, entered Cape Town harbour in July 1977, to be followed by the *City of Pretoria*, a small container vessel which inaugurated the containerization of the north-western European trade. The first of the large containerships on that run, the *Table Bay*, a 53 784-ton vessel capable of carrying 2 436 twenty-foot equivalent unit containers (TEUs) was owned by the Overseas Container Line which took over the Conference trading rights of Union-Castle and Clan Line.

In October 1977, fifteen TEUs – the first containerized shipment of mail from Britain – were landed in Cape Town from Safmarine's *S.A. Nederburg*. The *S.A. Langeberg* took the first northbound containerized mail shipment.

Following a significant downturn in the volume of European cargo – the result of selective trade sanctions imposed on South Africa – the *Table Bay* was withdrawn in 1979, bringing to a close a chapter in the history of the South African trade.

---

1 *A selection of postcards depicting the mailships over the years.*
2 *Bought by the Costa Line in 1978, the* Good Hope Castle *and the* Southampton Castle *were renamed the* Paola C *(above) and the* Franca C *respectively. Both were scrapped in China in 1984.*
3 *From* The Argus, *14 July 1977.*

From The Argus, *14 July 1977.*

'It's an exact replica built by Thor Heyerdahl to prove that the old mailboat run could still be profitable!'

Final reflections

When one considers the enormous influence of Union-Castle in the maritime affairs of southern Africa, and the high esteem in which the company was held by the general public in South Africa, its total demise is not only a matter for nostalgic reflection but also grounds for a study in maritime management.

Some observers believe that had British & Commonwealth/Union-Castle adapted to the inevitable end of the point-to-point passenger trade and become cruise operators, they might still be owning passenger liners. It is argued that if the Greeks could operate the *Amerikanis* (formerly the intermediate liner *Kenya Castle*) for several years, as well as the *Victoria* (ex-*Dunnottar Castle*), and if Festivale Maritime Inc. could run the *Festivale* (ex-*S.A. Vaal*), could not Union-Castle have done so? Two other major British liner companies, heavily involved in point-to-point passenger services in former years, adapted to the changes with considerable success. When the North Atlantic passenger trade ended, Cunard disposed of its liners, opting instead for cruise ships, while P&O employed the 1960-vintage *Canberra* for cruising and today has a relatively large fleet of cruise liners.

In the late fifties and early sixties Union-Castle had tried cruises to the Mediterranean, Azores and Madeira from Britain using some of the intermediates, while the *Reina del Mar* – a cruise liner initially chartered by Union-Castle before their purchase of her in 1973 – had cruised to South America several times, loaded with fun-seeking South Africans. None of these attempts to break into the cruise market was sustained, however, because the ships essentially were not suited to the different function.

Contrary to popular belief and emotive thought, the Union-Castle mailships earned their revenue not from the passenger trade, although that function brought them close to the hearts of thousands; rather, it was the highly tariffed cargo – particularly fruit, liquor, wool and gold – that had brought good profits to the group. Every year the mailships headed the list of freight earners in the Union-Castle fleet. Close behind came the fruit-ships. Containerization changed that.

Some wondered why the company did not opt for more involvement in the international container trade. Both P&O and Cunard did so with enthusiasm, and although the latter company has experienced difficulties in recent years, it enjoyed an initial success on the transatlantic container shuttle. P&O continues with a lucrative container trade to the Far East and Australasia, as well as being an important shareholder in a number of other container operations.

Although several other British and European companies had beaten the high portage bills by engaging in off-shore operations, B&C declined to be involved to any great extent with flags of convenience. The inference is that the downturn in ocean passenger traffic and the advent of the containership were not the only factors responsible for the demise of B&C shipping. Rather, it was a carefully designed strategy to move away from direct maritime involvement, and as surety against the fickleness of shipping, the astute B&C management had for years been steadily diversifying their operations to include interests such as property development, airlines, tourism, oil, insurance and finance.

Indicative of the changes taking place within B&C was the fact that by 1983 no Union-Castle or Clan Line vessels were trading, and the last ship owned by the group, a King Line vessel, was sold in 1986, though through the Overseas Container Line, B&C continued an interest in shipping. In 1987, the Cayzer holding in B&C was bought by a consortium headed by John Gunn, a young tycoon, who proceeded to sell many of the assets of the group to finance the purchase. In the process, many former Union-Castle landmarks disappeared. B&C itself suffered an ignominious end when it was placed under receivership in 1990 following the injudicious purchase of the Atlantic Computer empire, which left the group with deficits of millions of pounds.

A further factor had emerged in South Africa. Since its coming to power in 1948, it was clear that the Nationalist Government would have preferred local vessels to carry the mail, and over the years the subject was debated many times in parliament and elsewhere. The emergence of Safmarine, therefore, had a significant influence on events. Largely independent of the B&C shareholding from 1967, and becoming an increasingly vigorous force in the shipping world, Safmarine was matching and even eclipsing most competitors, including the B&C/Union-Castle operation. This was especially the case once Safmarine had secured dominance in the South African-European Container Service (SAECS) with a majority share in the Europe-South Africa service. In short, when

Safmarine's Astor *(I).*

The St Helena *(II) which came into service in 1990.*

B&C/Union-Castle opted to move away from shipping, Safmarine moved into the vacuum and assumed the leading role in the Conference.

With the withdrawal of the mailships, the Atlantic islands of St Helena and Ascension would have had no regular ocean link for either passengers or supplies. With a subsidy from the British Government, the St Helenian Government and Curnow Shipping Company established the St Helena Shipping Company to operate a service between Avonmouth in Gloucestershire via the islands and Cape Town. In late 1977, it bought the small passenger-freighter *Northland Prince*, which could carry seventy-six passengers, and renamed her *St Helena*. When she was taken over by the British Admiralty for service during the Falkland Islands War in 1982, the tiny *Aragonite* – and later the former Blue Funnel liner *Centaur* – were chartered for the service. The ageing *St Helena* returned after her duties for the Admiralty but, since she was the only regular ocean passengership operating between South Africa and Britain, she was palpably too small to meet the demand for passenger berths. A custom-built vessel of the same name and with a passenger capacity of 140 came into service in 1990.

Safmarine tried to re-introduce the point-to-point passenger service when, in 1984, they bought the German cruise liner *Astor* – a well-appointed vessel with no cargo space but accommodation for some 500 passengers. Commodore Robin McA. Thomson was called upon to command the liner, which made several voyages along the old mailship route. In an attempt to lure back to the sea many who had enjoyed a voyage on board the *S.A. Vaal* or her consorts, an extensive advertising campaign was geared to evoke memories of the days of the mailships. The boat train was revived for some of the sailings from Cape Town and there was an initial rush for berths. However, while she was a remarkable vessel, the *Astor* was probably not suited to the long voyage from the Cape. There was insufficient deckspace, her shallow draught caused her to roll excessively and her high portage bill made her expensive to operate. To tap lucrative German and American tourists in the hope of earning dollars or Deutsch Marks, the *Astor* was put into the cruise market with only occasional voyages between South Africa and Britain during the high season. While undeniably a prestigious addition to the Safmarine fleet, she became too costly and was sold. A second *Astor*, built in 1986 and similar in many ways to her predecessor, never came to South Africa. She was sold in December 1988 after less than two years in service.

In 1990, Safmarine introduced a limited passenger service between South Africa and Southampton on its four large containerships. Treated to excellent cuisine and fine hospitality on board, ten passengers enjoyed very comfortable accommodation and were given the run of the ship. When the British terminal of the SAECS was changed from Southampton to Tilbury in 1992, a call at Zeebrugge prior to Tilbury on the northbound voyage and at Le Havre en route to Cape Town made a pleasant interlude for the passengers.

At the time of publication, the *St Helena* and the four Safmarine vessels provide the only regular ocean passenger link between Britain and South Africa, a very different scenario to that prevailing only a few years previously when the mailships embarked their weekly complement of some 700 passengers.

One of those who enjoyed travelling in the Union-Castle ships was Laurens Van der Post who was a guest of the company for the last voyage of the *Windsor Castle*. In *Yet Being Someone Other*, he wrote:

> Although it is several years now since I made that round voyage in the *Windsor Castle* from Southampton, I have not yet made my peace with the event and doubt if I ever shall . . .
>
> Finally we broke the last of our paper streamers, and passed a lone Scottish piper in a Black Watch tartan standing on the tip of the last breakwater to grace our going with the kind of lament of which only a Highland soul is capable. We were followed out to sea by hundreds of little ships and as they and a snow-storm of gulls escorted us out to the dark blue albatross-haunted roadstead of the South Atlantic, the land spontaneously sent us its own special message of hail and farewell. Wherever we looked from city to Lion's Head, Signal Hill to Sea Point . . . mirrors – of all shapes and sizes reflected the levelling afternoon sunlight back at us . . .
>
> Long after the last of the little ships had given up, the gulls had turned about . . . I remained on deck. I remained there until the Cape itself sank into the sea, because I knew I would never again see it do so in that way . . .

Van Riebeeck's Drommedaris *in Hout Bay.*

The maritime history of South Africa

A CHRONOLOGY OF EVENTS

c.600 BC The Phoenicians become the first to round the Cape of Good Hope. (According to the Greek historian, Herodotus, it seems that they sailed from the Red Sea via the Cape to Gibraltar.)

1487 The Portuguese navigator, Bartholomeu Dias, rounds the Cape from west to east in an attempt to find a sea route from Europe to the East Indies. A mutinous crew forces him to turn back when off the Great Fish River. Nevertheless, his men are the first Europeans to land in southern Africa when they put ashore at Golfo de Santa Maria da Conseicao (Walvis Bay), Angra das Voltas (Lüderitz) and Aguada de São Bras (Mossel Bay).

1497 Vasco da Gama rounds the Cape and is the first European to record sighting the coast of present-day Natal. His arrival near Calicut on 14 May 1498 signals the successful pioneering of the sea route between Europe and the east.

1501 The first recorded 'posting' of a letter in southern Africa. (The letter is said to have been found in a shoe, tied to a tree at Mossel Bay – a watering place well known to Portuguese seamen – in the hope that other seamen would find and deliver it.)

1503 A ship commanded by Antonio de Saldanha, a Spaniard in the service of the Portuguese, makes the first recorded entry into what is today Table Bay, which he names Aguada de Saldanha.

1505 The first recorded shipwreck on the southern African coast occurs near Mossel Bay. (It was a Portuguese vessel carrying pepper and probably other spices.)

1591 The first British ships anchor in Table Bay.

1595 Commanded by Cornelis Houtman, the first Dutch fleet arrives in the East, having sailed via the Cape of Good Hope. (It did not call at the Cape.)

1598 The first Dutch fleet arrives in Table Bay.

1601 Joris van Spilbergen, commander of a Dutch fleet, discovers a large bay which he assumes, erroneously, to be Table Bay – the one discovered by Antonio de Saldanha in 1503. In fact, the bay he had sailed into was unknown to navigators and is present-day Saldanha Bay, which name it acquired from Van Spilbergen.) The fleet continues southwards and sails into a bay which, because it is dominated by a flat-topped mountain, Van Spilbergen names Tafel Baay.

1652 The Dutch establish a refreshment station at the Cape, of which Jan van Riebeeck is the first commander.

1671 The Dutch ship, *Yselstein*, is the first ship to anchor in what becomes known (from 1687) as Simon's Bay.

1689 The Buffalo River mouth – site of present-day East London – is reached by an exploration team sent out by Governor Simon van der Stel.

1700 The first wool is exported from the Cape.
1788 Bound for Batavia, a Dutch ship at Mossel Bay loads the first cargo of export wheat.
1792 Arthur Anderson, founder of the Union Line, is born in Gremista, Shetland Islands, on 19 February.
1795 British forces, under the command of Admiral George Elphinstone, capture the Cape in a minor skirmish called the Battle of Muizenberg. (The British took this step to prevent the Cape from falling into French hands.)
1803 The Cape is returned to the Dutch.
1806 Britain retakes the Cape at the Battle of Blaauwberg.
1813-1814 The British Naval base is moved from Table Bay to Simon's Bay.
1815 The first mail service between Britain and Table Bay is initiated by the British Government.
1816 Port Beaufort at the mouth of the Breede River is established, mainly to serve the Overberg region. (Frequent strandings on the bar at the mouth of the river led to its closure in 1883.)
1820 A large group of British settlers arrives in Algoa Bay. Among other towns, they establish Port Elizabeth.
1823 Lieutenants Farewell and King make the first significant exploration of Durban Bay (Port Natal).
1825 Donald Currie, founder of the Castle Line, is born in Greenock, Scotland, on 17 September.
The *Enterprise*, the first steamship to call at a southern African port, arrives in Table Bay.
The Kowie River mouth is used as a commercial port (Port Alfred) for the first time.
1826 Port Elizabeth is given port status.
1834 The start of the Great Trek by Afrikaner farmers who resent British control. (Over several decades, this 'trek' led to the establishment of the Boer Republics, Transvaal and Orange Free State.)
1838 The *Hope*, the first steamer on the South African coastal trade, begins a service between Table Bay and Algoa Bay.
1842 The *Hindustan* is the first P&O ship to call at Table Bay.
1843 Britain annexes Natal to the Cape Colony.
The tidal dock Southampton is opened. (This became known as the Outer Dock.)
1844 To offload supplies and disembark troops for the Frontier War, the Buffalo River is used as a port for the first time.
1845 The first direct shipping link between Britain and Port Beaufort is forged.
1847 The first commercial use of the Umzimvubu River mouth (Port St Johns).
1848 Aliwal South (later reverting to the Dutch name of Mossel Bay) is founded.
1851 The first regular British mail steamer, the *Bosphorus*, arrives at the Cape.
1852 The *Sir Robert Peel* is the first steamer to cross the bar at Port Natal (Durban).
1853 The Union Steam Collier Company, forerunner of the Union Line, is founded in England.
1854 The first Cape Colonial Parliament is formed.
1857 German settlers arrive at the Buffalo River.
The *Dane*, the first Union Liner on the South African trade, arrives in Table Bay.
1858 The Shaw Savill Line begins operating between Britain and New Zealand.
1859 The Inner Dock at Southampton is completed.
1860 Prince Alfred tips the first load of stone to commence construction work on the Table Bay breakwater.
1861 Harbour work at the Kowie River mouth (Port Alfred) is completed.
1862 Donald Currie establishes Donald Currie & Co. to operate sailing ships to India.
1866 The *Ajax* arrives at Algoa Bay to be the first Blue Funnel ship to visit a South African port.
1867 Diamonds are discovered near Kimberley. However, only after the sale of the Star of South Africa in 1869 is the economic significance of the diamond deposit realized. The subsequent diamond rush brings thousands of immigrants and creates an insatiable demand for supplies from Europe, particularly from Britain.
1869 The Suez Canal is opened, taking most of the ships moving between Europe and the East, including those on the Australasian trade.
Donald Currie establishes the Liverpool and Hamburg Steamship Company to operate a feeder service between Britain and Europe.
Knysna begins to expand as a port.
1870 The Alfred Basin in Table Bay is opened.
The *Western Hope*, the first Cape & Natal Line vessel, arrives in Table Bay.
1872 Donald Currie forms a company to operate steamers to the Cape. (Initially known as the London Line or Colonial Mail Line, this company became The Castle Packets Company Ltd in 1876.)
The first harbour construction work begins at the mouth of the Buffalo River (East London), and the *Bismark* is the first steamer across the bar.
The first Castle steamship, the *Dover Castle*, is launched in Scotland.
The *Westmoreland*, the first of Donald Currie's steamers, arrives in Table Bay.
The *Walmer Castle* arrives in Table Bay. It is the first steamship bearing the suffix 'Castle' to reach southern Africa.
1878 Britain annexes to the Cape Colony the Walvis Bay district and several guano islands off the west coast of present-day Namibia.
The Zulu War brings an influx of shipping to Durban to land troops and stores.
1879 The first Bullard King liner, the *Pongola*, arrives in Durban.
1880 The First South African War brings scores of ships to Table Bay and Durban to land troops and equipment.
Shipping services begin between Durban and Port Shepstone at the mouth of the Umzimkulu River.
1881 The Castle Packets Company Ltd becomes known as The Castle Mail Packets Company Ltd.
Clan Line introduces a service from the west coast of Britain to South Africa.
The first substantial jetty is built at Port Elizabeth.
1882 The *Aberdeen* is the first Aberdeen White Star liner to call at Table Bay.
Rennie's Aberdeen Direct Line's *Dabulamanzi* arrives in Durban. (This was the forerunner of the T.&J. Harrison Line which became a regular trader to South Africa.)
1883 The first South African Steamship Conference is founded by the Union Steamship Company, The Castle Mail Packets Company Ltd, The Clan Line and four other shipping companies.
1885 Simon's Bay comes under the control of the Royal Navy.
1886 The discovery of gold in the Eastern Transvaal has maritime repercussions similar to those caused by the discovery of diamonds. Port Natal takes much of the additional shipping.
1889 The first Portuguese mailship, the *Rei de Portugal*, arrives in Table Bay.
1890 The Empress Dock in Southampton is commissioned.
The Deutsche Ost-Afrika Linien (DOAL) is founded for service to Tanganyika.
1892 The *Drummond Castle* takes the first successful consignment of South African fruit to Britain.
The DOAL liner, *Kaiser*, arrives in Durban to inaugurate a service to South Africa.
Bucknall Line's cargo service to South Africa begins with the arrival in Algoa Bay of the chartered *Viceroy*.
1893 The Union Liner, *Scot*, sets a new record of 14 days 8 hours and 57 minutes for the passage from Southampton to Table Bay.
1895 The *Johannesburg* inaugurates Bucknall's passenger service to South Africa.
1896 The Woermann Line begins services to South Africa.
1899 The outbreak of the Anglo-Boer War leads to a great build-up of shipping in South African harbours, notably Table Bay and Durban.
The *Medic* inaugurates the White Star Line's colonial service.
1900 The Union and Castle lines amalgamate to form the Union-Castle Line.
Shipping services to Port Alfred cease. (The port was officially closed in 1915.)
1901 Port Shepstone is closed as a harbour.
1902 The Dom Pedro Jetty in Algoa Bay is completed.
The first tanker, the *Murex*, arrives in Table Bay.
The British India Steam Navigation Company begins a service between India and South Africa.
1904 The *Armadale Castle* becomes the first mailship to enter Durban Bay.
The *Armadale Castle* takes the first shipment of South African export citrus fruit to Britain.
1905 All major ports are now linked by rail to the Witwatersrand goldfields.
The Victoria Basin in Table Bay is completed.
The Shaw Savill & Albion Line takes financial control of the Aberdeen Line. (Later this service became known as the Aberdeen & Commonwealth Line.)

1906 The Empreza Naçional de Navigaçione, the forerunner of the Companhia Naçional de Navegação, begins operating between Portugal and southern Africa. Their first ship on the run is the *Portugal*.
Andrew Weir and Company, forerunner of the Bank Line service to South Africa, begin trading across the Indian Ocean.
1908 Diamonds are discovered around the mouth of the Orange River.
1909 Donald Currie dies at Sidmouth in Devon on 13 April.
1910 The unification of the Cape Colony, Orange Free State, Transvaal and Natal into the Union of South Africa allows a single economic policy and stimulates economic confidence in the new country. (Shipping services benefited directly from this as a new wave of immigrants arrived and trade increased.)
Simon's Town Harbour is officially opened by the Duke of Connaught.
Union-Castle begins its East African service with the *Guelph* (Britain-Suez-South Africa) and the *Dunluce Castle* (Britain-South Africa-Suez).
1911 Elder Dempster and Royal Mail Line buy out Donald Currie and Company.
The Ocean Dock in Southampton is opened.
T. & J. Harrisons takes control of Rennie's Aberdeen Direct Line.
1912 The South African Government fixes the Ocean Mail Contract with the Union-Castle Line for ten years.
The breakwater and jetty at Mossel Bay are completed.
1913 The Homeward South African Conference is founded.
1914 The Beira Homeward Conference is founded.
The Bucknall Line becomes known as the Ellerman & Bucknall Line.
The outbreak of World War I disrupts shipping activities.
1915 German South West Africa is captured by South African troops.
The *Kangaroo*, owned by the government of Western Australia, becomes the first motorship to call at South African ports.
1918 The end of World War I means a gradual return to normal shipping activities.
The first large-scale iron ore mining in South Africa begins.
1919 The Nederlandsche Zuid-Afrikaansche Stoomvaart Maatschappij commences trading to South Africa. Their first ship on the service was the *Rijndijk*. (This was the forerunner of the Holland-Afrika Lijn, and later the Nedlloyd services to South Africa.)
1921 The Houston Line takes over the local Thesen's Steamship Company which has been operating coastal services since 1869.
1922 The Ocean Mail Contract with Union-Castle is renewed, this time on an annual basis.
The South African training ship *General Botha*, a former Royal Naval cruiser, has its first intake of cadets.
The SS Frontier Steamship Company begins trading between Durban, Port St Johns and East London. (This was the forerunner of African Coasters and later Unicorn Lines.)
The Electricity Supply Commission (ESCOM) is established. (Stimulating industry, and as an importer of capital equipment, ESCOM benefited liner services.)
1924 The first motor vehicle assembly plant is built at Port Elizabeth, stimulating trade to the port.
1925 Navigazione Libera Triestina begins a service from Italy to South Africa via Suez. (This was a forerunner of Lloyd Triestino.)
1926 The *Orca* of Royal Mail Line is the first cruise liner to visit South African ports.
The *Carnarvon Castle* is the first motorship on the mail service.
1927 The first commercial wharf at Walvis Bay is commissioned.
1928 The Iron and Steel Corporation (ISCOR) is founded. (This development had major industrial significance and therefore indirectly benefited shipping services.)
1929 The South African Government, the Perishable Products Exports Control Board and Union-Castle sign an agreement on the shipping of perishable products.
The Great Depression begins. Many ships on the regular South African trade are withdrawn.
1930 The shipping empire of Lord Kylsant collapses.
The Portuguese company, Companhia Coloniale Navigaçione, begins regular sailings between Portugal, Angola, South Africa and Mozambique with the *Mouzinho*.
1932 The Holland-Afrika Lijn is established.
Shaw Savill & Albion absorb the Aberdeen Line on the Australasian service.
Imperial Airways begins an air service between Cape Town and London.
1933 African Coasters is formed to trade along the southern African coast. (Later, African Coasters became part of Unicorn Lines.)
Extensions to Table Bay Harbour (the present Duncan Dock) begin.
1934 To cope with the increasing size of ships, notably the Union-Castle liners, a major tug-building programme is started by the South African Railways & Harbours. The first product of that programme, the *John Dock*, arrives in South Africa.
Iscor produces its first steel.
1935 The Union-Castle Line orders its first refrigerated cargoships, the *Rothesay Castle* and the *Roslin Castle*, to carry South African fruit to Britain.
1936 The Ocean Mail Contract with Union-Castle is renewed for ten years.
The *Stirling Castle* establishes a new record of 13 days and 9 hours for the passage between Southampton and Table Bay.
Thesen's Steamship Company is sold by the Houston Line to Mitchell Cotts of Cape Town.
1937 African Coasters absorbs the SS Frontier Shipping Company.
In response to the increasing size of the mailships, the East London turning basin is enlarged.
1938 The harbour at Port Elizabeth is completed. (In 1933, HMS *Dorsetshire* had been the first vessel alongside.)
The *Capetown Castle*, the largest prewar Union-Castle liner, comes into service. (She was also the largest motor passenger liner in the world.)
1939 The outbreak of World War II.
1940 The Industrial Development Corporation (IDC) is established. (Being in the forefront of industrial development, and with its own involvement in Safmarine from 1961, it played both a direct and indirect role in South African shipping.)
Knysna ceases trading as a port. (It was closed officially in 1954.)
1941 The South African Line (SAL) is founded in Cape Town. (The company only began trading after the war, and later partnered DOAL in a service between north-western Europe and South Africa. It was absorbed by the South African Marine Corporation in 1973.)
1945 The end of World War II. Shipping services gradually return to normal.
Because of wartime exigencies, the completion of the Duncan Dock in Table Bay has been hastened.
The first trunk air service between Johannesburg and London, the Springbok Service, is introduced by South African Airways and BOAC.
1946 The Ocean Mail Contract with Union-Castle is renewed for ten years.
The first sailing of the States Marine Corporation between the United States and South Africa lays the foundation for the establishment of the South African Marine Corporation (Safmarine).
1947 King George VI, the first British monarch to visit South Africa, arrives on board HMS *Vanguard*.
Safmarine's first ship, the *Constantia*, and South African Line's first ship, the *Kaapland*, arrive in South Africa.
Marion and Prince Edward islands are annexed by South Africa.
1949 The Springbok Shipping Company is registered in South Africa by Union-Castle.
Fish canning begins in Walvis Bay, contributing significantly to the volume of cargo shipped through the port.
Union Steamship Company is absorbed by Thesens.
1950 The South African Coal, Oil & Gas Corporation is established. (This stimulated further industrial development in South Africa and contributed directly and indirectly to the amount of cargo shipped.)
1952 The British-based Coast Lines takes over Thesens Steamship Company from Mitchell Cotts.
South African Airways introduces jet aircraft to the Springbok service.
1954 The abolition of the so-called 'sea-competitive railway rates' between South African ports stimulates coastwise cargo movement by sea.
Safmarine's first new ship, the *South African Merchant*, is launched.
1955 Durban Lines is established to operate mainly between Durban and Mozambique.
1956 The British and Commonwealth Shipping Company (B&C) acquires substantial shareholdings in Union-Castle and Clan Line, which are absorbed into B&C.
Union-Castle's Southampton passenger terminal at Berth 102 is inaugurated by the *Edinburgh Castle*.

The Suez Canal is closed owing to hostilities in the area. Hundreds of ships are diverted to the Cape Route, bringing serious congestion problems to all South African harbours.

1957 The Ocean Mail Contract is re-awarded to Union-Castle. (Approved by the South African Parliament in 1956.)
The Suez Canal is re-opened and shipping reverts to normal.
The Royal Navy hands over Simon's Town to the South African Navy, which until then had used Salisbury Island in Durban as its main base. (The Royal Navy continued to use Simon's Town but its South Atlantic headquarters moved to Youngsfield in Cape Town.)

1958 The *Pendennis Castle*, the last mailship ordered by Union-Castle from Harland & Wolff, is launched. (After the B&C takeover of Union-Castle she was modified on the stocks.)
The *Arundel Castle* is the first mailship to be withdrawn and scrapped since World War II.

1959 The IDC takes over a large shareholding in Safmarine from the American company States Marine.
The B&C Group activates the dormant South African subsidiary, Springbok Shipping Company, which takes over the ships and services of Bullard King.

1960 The *Windsor Castle*, the largest mailship on the South African service, arrives in Cape Town on her maiden voyage.
The first Boeing 707 of South African Airways is placed on the Johannesburg-London service.
Bullard King (Natal Line) ceases trading.

1961 South Africa leaves the British Commonwealth and becomes a republic.
The last passenger mailship to be ordered, the *Transvaal Castle*, arrives on her maiden voyage.
Safmarine takes over the Springbok Shipping Company.

1963 Safmarine begins an extensive building programme, which spans more than a decade and encompasses the delivery of refrigerated ships, fast cargo liners and bulk carriers.
Harbour extensions are built at Walvis Bay.

1964 Financial transactions between African Coasters and the mining house, Union Corporation, allow the Safmarine fleet to expand and pave the way for the amalgamation of the major coasting companies in 1966.

1965 Union-Castle introduces the 11½-day schedule between Southampton and Cape Town.
Union-Castle begins to withdraw its passenger-carrying mailships in favour of two cargo mailships, the *Good Hope Castle* and the *Southampton Castle*.
Safmarine's first bulk carrier, the *Sugela*, enters service.
Safmarine buys a controlling interest in Thesen's Steamship Company.
Safmarine buys the *Transvaal Castle* and *Pretoria Castle* and renames them *S.A. Vaal* and *S.A. Oranje* respectively, giving the corporation a significant shareholding in the mail service.
The tanker basin in Table Bay Harbour is completed. (The first tanker arrived in March 1966.)

1966 African Coasters and Smiths Coasters merge to form Unicorn Shipping Holdings. African Coasters remains the main operator and changes its name to Unicorn Lines. Safmarine sells Thesen's Steamship Company to Unicorn Lines in exchange for a large shareholding in Unicorn Lines.
Safmarine and the IDC enter the tanker trade with the purchase of the *Allamanda* and *Lanmar*, followed by other larger tankers.
The British seamen's strike.
The arrival in Cape Town of the *S.A. Van der Stel* inaugurates Safmarine's new dry-cargo liner programme.
The East London grain terminal is commissioned.

1967 The Suez Canal is closed as a result of the Six-Day War, necessitating the diversion of hundreds of ships to the Cape Route. As in 1956-7, harbour congestion becomes a serious problem.
The last Union-Castle intermediate liner, the *Kenya Castle*, is withdrawn from service and sold.

1968 The container terminal at Southampton comes into operation.

1969 The *S.A. Vaal* and the *S.A. Oranje* are changed to the South African registry, and become the first mailships to fly the South African flag.
The first South African vehicle ro-ro ship, the *Greta Delport*, enters service to move vehicles between South African ports.

1970 Unicorn Lines acquires a 32 per cent share in Durban Lines.

1971 The last Ellerman & Bucknall and Holland-Afrika Lijn passenger ships are withdrawn from the South African service.
Safmarine takes delivery of its first Very Large Crude Carrier (VLCC), the *Kulu*.
South African Airways places Boeing 747 aircraft ('jumbos') on the Johannesburg-London service.

1973 Safmarine takes over the South African Line.
Construction begins on the new bulk export terminals at Richards Bay (coal) and Saldanha Bay (iron ore and mineral concentrates).
The Portuguese company, Companhia Coloniale Navigaçione,withdraws its passenger ships from the South African service.

1974 Plans are announced for the containerization of the South African trade.
The Overseas Container Line, in which B&C has an interest, builds the first containership for the north-west Europe-South Africa trade, while Safmarine orders four containerships from French yards. (Another Safmarine vessel, *S.A. Langeberg*, came from Italian yards for the Mediterranean service and was the corporation's first containership.)
Unicorn acquires full control of Durban Lines.
The Portuguese CNN withdraws its last passenger ship on the South African service.

1975 The Suez Canal re-opens and South African shipping activities return to normal.
The last Shaw Savill & Albion passenger liner, the *Northern Star*, is withdrawn from service and scrapped.

1976 The bulk export terminals at Richards Bay and Saldanha Bay are formally opened. (*S.A. Vaal* inaugurates the Richards Bay terminal.)
Lloyd Triestino and British India Lines withdraw their passenger ships on the South African trade.

1977 The containerization of much of the South Africa-Britain trade begins.
Container terminals are commissioned in Cape Town, Durban and Port Elizabeth.
Because of the withdrawal of all except four mailships, the *Andalucia Star* becomes the first non-Union-Castle/Safmarine ship to carry the official mail, although she is on charter to Union-Castle.
The last of the mailships are withdrawn.
The last mailship sailing from Cape Town is taken by the *Southampton Castle* on 24 October.
The first containerized shipment of mail from Britain arrives in Cape Town aboard the *S.A. Nederburg*.
The first fully cellular containership on the South African trade, Lloyd Triestino's *Africa*, docks in Cape Town
Unicorn Lines introduces its first fully cellular containership, the *Voorloper*, for its coastal service.

1978 The *S.A. Helderberg* is the first Safmarine containership on the South Africa-Britain/north-western Europe service.
Berth 206 at Southampton's container terminal is commissioned, as a direct result of the decision by the South Africa-Europe Container Service to use the port as its British terminus.
The *St Helena*, owned by St Helena Lines, inaugurates a new mailship service between Cape Town, St Helena, Ascension and Avonmouth.

1979 The last ship bearing the suffix 'Castle' is renamed.

1984 In an attempt to revive the South Africa-Britain passenger service, Safmarine buys the German cruise liner, *Astor*.

1985 Port Nolloth is officially closed as a commercial port.
The South African Oil Exploration Corporation announces that gas fields offshore from Mossel Bay are to be exploited.
Safmarine sells the *Astor* and a replacement is ordered from German yards.

1990 St Helena Lines replaces its ship with a larger *St Helena*, which continues to operate as a mailship.
Safmarine offers berths for ten passengers on board each of its four large containerships on the SAEC service.

Mailships of the Union, Castle & Union-Castle lines

Only those vessels built or bought specifically for the mailship service are listed below.

It should be noted that the system of tonnage measurement varied over the years, while the tonnage of some ships changed during their period of service. The figures given are those assessed when a ship entered service and can generally be accepted as referring to gross registered tons. Note too that even some official records, such as *Lloyds Register*, contain differences with regard to the tonnage and other details of various ships.

Speed given is designed service speed.

* Denotes a Union liner.

AFRICAN

* *AFRICAN* (1873)
  Steamer. 2 019 tons. Length 96,19 m (315 ft 7 in). Speed 12 knots. Passengers: 1st 100, 2nd 50, 3rd 50. Completed in 1872. In 1881, transferred to the SA coastal service; 1885, sold to F. Stumore & Co., London.
* *AMERICAN* (1873)
  Steamer. 2 126 tons. Length 97,45 m (320 ft). Speed 12 knots. Passengers: 1st 100, 2nd 50, 3rd 100 (dormitories up forward). Ship foundered 23 April 1880 (see page 21).

AMROTH CASTLE SEE *ARUNDEL CASTLE* (1921)

* *ANGLIAN* (1873)
  Steamer. 2 206 tons. Length 95,71 m (314 ft). Speed 11 knots. Passengers: 1st 94, 2nd 50, 3rd 100 in dormitories forward. In 1884, used as a troopship for the conveyance of troops to Egypt with the Gordon Relief Expedition; 1886, placed on the SA coastal service; 1894, sold to Huddart Parker Ltd, Sydney, Australia; 1913, hulked; 1932, scuttled.
* *ARAB* (1879)
  Steamer. 3 192 tons. Length 106,60 m (350 ft). Speed 12 knots. Passengers: 1st 110, 2nd 90, 3rd 50. In 1882, used as a troopship for the Sudanese Campaign; 1883, placed on an experimental voyage Liverpool-Newport News-Baltimore; 1885, HQ ship for naval transport staff in the Sudanese War; 1891, transferred to the intermediate service; 1900, broken up.

ARDTORNISH CASTLE SEE *HAWARDEN CASTLE*

ARMADALE CASTLE

ARUNDEL CASTLE

ARMADALE CASTLE (I) SEE *ROSLIN CASTLE*

ARMADALE CASTLE (1903)
Steamer. 12 973 tons. Length 173,7 m (570 ft). Twin-screw. Speed 14 knots. Passengers: 1st 336, 2nd 174, 3rd 244. Crew: 250. Ordered after the merger of the Union and Castle lines. Was an improved version of Union Line's *Norman* (I) and *Celt* (III) – renamed *Walmer Castle* (I). In 1914, commissioned as auxiliary cruiser in 10th Cruiser Squadron; 1918, resumed the Cape mail service; 1935, withdrawn from service; 1936, scrapped.

ARUNDEL CASTLE (1921)
Steamer. 19 023 tons. Length 192,18 m (630 ft 6 in). Speed 17 knots. Twin-screw. Passengers: 1st 234, 2nd 362, 3rd 274. Four funnels. (The account of her launching gives her passenger capacity as 1 063.) Launched 1919 as *Arundel Castle* having been laid down as *Amroth Castle*. Commenced maiden voyage in April 1921 as the largest vessel yet built for the company. In 1937, withdrawn from service and extensively modernized: four funnels replaced by two, and new bow fitted; 19 216 tons; length 202 m (661 ft); new boilers and bow added 3 knots to speed. In 1939, requisitioned as a troopship; 1947-1950, employed to transport emigrants to South Africa, with accommodation for 846. On her return to the mail service, her passenger accommodation was: 1st 164, tourist 371. 1958, withdrawn from service; 1959, scrapped in Gin Drinkers Bay, Kowloon – the biggest ship to be demolished there.

ATHLONE CASTLE

BRITON

BALMORAL CASTLE

CAPETOWN CASTLE

* *ASIATIC* (1873)

Steamer. 2 066 tons. Length 91,41 m (29 9 ft 11 in). Speed 12 knots. Passengers: 1st 75, 2nd 55. In 1880, transferred to the intermediate service; 1888, sold to H. Martini & Co., Glasgow.

* *ATHENIAN* (1882)

Steamer. 3 877 tons. Length 111,25 m (365 ft). Speed 12 knots. Passengers: 1st 120, 2nd 90, 3rd 50. On 22 October 1882, *Athenian* was the first vessel to use Cape Town's new Robinson dry dock; 1887, re-engined; 1897, sold to the Canadian-Pacific Railway for use in the Klondyke gold rush; 1907, scrapped in Japan.

* *ATHENS* (1856)

Steamer. 739 tons. Length 68,45 m (224 ft 7 in). Speed 11 knots. Built for a Liverpool company and acquired in 1858. On 16 May 1865, lost with all 29 on board while attempting to round Mouille Point in Table Bay during the Great Gale of that year. The seas doused her furnaces and she drifted ashore and broke up (her cylinder head is still visible).

ATHLONE CASTLE (1936)

Motor vessel. 25 564 tons. Length 212,14 m (696 ft). Twin-screw. Speed 20 knots. Passengers: 1st 300, cabin 490. Launched in 1935 by Princess Alice, Countess of Athlone, whose husband, the Earl of Athlone, had been governor-general of South Africa. In 1938, inaugurated the fourteen-day mail schedule. (For her war record, see pages 88-9.) In 1947, after refurbishing, she resumed the mail service; 1965, broken up in Kaohsiung.

BALMORAL CASTLE (1877)

Steamer. 2 948 tons. Length 105,08 m (344 ft 9 in). Speed 10 knots. Passengers: 1st 100, 2nd 50 and 100 emigrants. Sister to *Dublin Castle*. An innovation was the fitting of individual swivel chairs in the dining saloon, replacing the former continuous upholstered benches. In 1882, sold to Spanish interests.

BALMORAL CASTLE (1910)

Steamer. 13 361 tons. Length 173,8 m (570 ft). Twin-screw. Speed 14 knots. Passengers: 1st 320, 2nd 220, 3rd 250. In 1910 became the first of the company's vessels to be fitted with Marconi wireless telegraphy. Carried the Duke of Connaught to South Africa for the opening of the first Union Parliament. In 1914, requisitioned as a troopship; 1915, carried first South African troops to Europe; 1919, resumed the mail service, her accommodation having been modified to take 120 passengers 1st class, 68 2nd and 230 3rd; 1939, withdrawn and scrapped.

* *BRITON* (1861)

Steamer. 1 164 tons. Length 80,47 m (264 ft). Iron. Speed 10 knots. Passengers: 1st 60, fore-cabin 50. The first of many ships claimed by their owners to be 'unsinkable and unburnable'. In 1873, sold to the British Government and became HM Transport *Dromedary*; 1884, scrapped.

* *BRITON* (1897)

Steamer. 10 248 tons. Length 161,65 m (530 ft 4 in). Steel. Twin-screw. Speed 17 knots. Passengers: 1st 260, 2nd 192, 3rd 186, plus 300 in dormitories. Crew: 230. At the time of her maiden voyage on 4 December 1897, she was one of the largest vessels in service to any of the British colonies. In 1900, she was the first Union liner to take a sailing following the company's merger with the Castle Line. On 27 August 1914, sailed from Cape Town in a troopship convoy carrying 4 000 troops. With her in the convoy were *Balmoral Castle*, *Dunluce Castle*, *Goorkha*, *Guildford Castle* and *Kenilworth Castle*. Although occasionally carrying troops, she remained in commercial service until 1915 when she was converted for full-time trooping. In 1920, resumed the mail service; 1925, laid up in Southampton Water as a reserve steamer; 1926, scrapped.

* *CAMBRIAN* (1860)

Steamer. 1 055 tons. Length 74,68 m (245 ft). Speed 10 knots. Passengers: 1st 60, fore-cabin 40. Employed continuously on the mail service until sold to France in 1872.

CAPETOWN CASTLE (1938)

Motor vessel. 27 002 tons. Length 223,72 m (734 ft). Twin-screw. Speed 20 knots. Passengers: 1st 292, cabin 499. Largest Union-Castle motor-driven liner and also longest motorship in the world at the time. In 1939, taken over for trooping duties (see pages 89-91); 1947, first mailship to re-enter service after postwar refurbishment; 1960, engine room explosion off Las Palmas killed seven crew members; 1965, made headlines again when twenty gold ingots were stolen from a temporary strongroom; 1965, re-classified as an 'extra' ship; 1967, scrapped at Spezia.

CARISBROOK CASTLE

CARNARVON CASTLE

CARISBROOK CASTLE (1898)

Steamer. 7 594 tons. Length 147,83 m (485 ft). Speed 15 knots. Passengers carried in three classes and was the first Castle ship to have 1st class sited amidships, 2nd class aft and 3rd class forward. In June 1900, made the last Cape mail sailing from London following a decision to make Southampton the terminal port; 1912, transferred to the East African route; 1914, became a hospital ship; 1922, scrapped.

CARNARVON CASTLE (1926)

Motor vessel. 20 063 tons. Length 192,25 m (630 ft 8 in). Twin-screw. Speed 16 knots. Passengers: 1st 310, 2nd 275, 3rd 266. Crew: 350. First of Union-Castle motorships. Modernized in 1938, when given a single funnel and its relevant statistics changed to 20 133 tons and length 201,5 m (661 ft); accommodation was for 266 passengers 1st class, 245 2nd and 188 tourist. September 1939, converted in Cape Town to an armed merchant cruiser (for full war record, see pages 91-4); 1947-9, used as an emigrant ship to South Africa, with 1 283 berths; 1949-50, refurbished and modernized, her tonnage increasing to 20 141 tons, with accommodation for 216 passengers 1st class and 401 tourist; June 1950, resumed the mail service; 1962, sold to Japanese shipbreakers.

* *CELT* (1855)

Steamer. 514 tons. Speed 8 knots. Employed on Cape run 1857-62. Originally purchased as *Gothenburg* during Crimean War to join *Saxon* on coastal coaling service. In 1862, taken over by Charles Lungley & Co. as part payment for the building of subsequent ships; later renamed *Possedon* (1870) and *Poseidon* (1910); 1932, scrapped.

* *CELT* (1866)

Steamer. 1 439 tons. Length 80,09 m (262 ft 9 in). Speed 9 knots. In 1874, length increased to 89,31 m (293 ft) and tonnage to 2 112 tons. February 1875, wrecked at the mouth of the Ratel River between Cape Agulhas and Danger Point without loss of life. (See pages 19-20.)

DUNOTTAR CASTLE

* *CELT* (1902) SEE *WALMER CASTLE* (1902)

CONWAY CASTLE (1877)

Steamer. 2 966 tons. Length 106,38 m (349 ft). Speed 12 knots. Passengers: 1st 100, 2nd 50, plus 100 emigrants. In 1883, transferred to the intermediate service; 11 May 1893, wrecked at Vatomandry south of Tamatave, Madagascar, while on passage from London to Mauritius.

COURLAND (1872)

Steamer. 1 241 tons. Length 76,33 m (250 ft 5 in). Speed 9 knots. In 1875, transferred to the SA coastal service; 1895, sold to Dada Abdoola, Durban; 1901, sold to a Bombay company; 1925, scrapped at that port still bearing her original name.

* *DANE* (1854)

Steamer. 526 tons. Length 53,9 m (177 ft). Speed 7,5 knots. On completion, chartered to the French Government for the duration of the Crimean War. In 1857, placed on the Southampton-Rio de Janeiro service; 15 September 1857, inaugurated the first Union Line sailing with mails to the Cape Colony, arriving in Cape Town on 29 October. This was the beginning of the mail service, which was to continue for the next 120 years. In 1864, placed on the Mauritius service; 1865, chartered by the British Government to play a part in an expedition to Zanzibar in connection with the suppression of the slave trade; wrecked in Algoa Bay. (See page 15.)

* *DANUBE* (1866)

Paddle steamer. 2 039 tons. Length 101,19 m (332 ft). Iron. Speed 12 knots. Passengers 1st 140, 2nd 68, 3rd 30. Originally built as a two-funnelled paddle steamer for the Royal Mail Steam Packet Company, she was acquired by the Union Steam Collier Company in 1871 and converted to a one-funnel vessel, a single screw replacing the paddles. In 1879, carried the Prince Imperial of France to the Zulu War, in which he was killed; 1888, sold and broken up.

DRUMMOND CASTLE (1881)

Steamer. 3 663 tons. Length 111,25 m (365 ft). Speed 11 knots. Passengers: 1st 120, 2nd 100, 3rd 160. In 1894, transferred to the intermediate service; 28 May 1896, lost off Ushant, sinking so rapidly that no boats could be launched and with only three of her passengers and crew surviving; 1929, Italian salvage teams searching for P&O's *Egypt* in order to recover gold bullion found *Drummond Castle* with a gash from waterline to keel.

DUBLIN CASTLE (1877)

Steamer. Sister to *Balmoral Castle* (1877). 2 805 tons. Length 104,34 m (342 ft 4 in). Speed 10 knots. Passengers: 1st 100, 2nd 50, plus 100 emigrants. In 1882, sold to Compania Transatlantica and renamed *Santo Domingo*; July 1898, wrecked off Isle of Pines near Cienfuegos, Cuba.

DUNOTTAR CASTLE (1890)

Steamer. 5 625 tons. Length 131,98 m (433 ft). Speed 17 knots. Passengers: 1st 160, 2nd 90, 3rd 100. Launched by Lady Currie. First Union-Castle liner to have two funnels. A record maiden voyage from Dartmouth to Cape Town of 17 days 19 hours and 50 minutes, which she bettered twice. In 1904, laid up; 1907, chartered to Panama Railroad Company and used by Sir Henry Lunn Ltd for cruises to Norway and Mediterranean; 1913, sold to Royal Mail Line and renamed *Caribbean*; 1914, requisitioned as an armed merchant cruiser; 26 September 1915, foundered off Cape Wrath with the loss of fifteen lives.

DUNVEGAN CASTLE

EDINBURGH CASTLE (1872)

EDINBURGH CASTLE (1948)

DUNROBIN CASTLE (1876)
Steamer. 2 820 tons. Length 104,34 m (342 ft 4 in). Speed 10 knots. Passengers: 1st 100, 2nd 50, plus 100 emigrants. First true mail steamer designed for Currie's South African service. In 1876, broke existing Cape record; 1877, broke record again. An innovation was that the first class dining saloon extended the full width of the ship with access from the surrounding cabins. On 27 January 1879, sailed from Durban carrying to Britain the first news of the Zulu victory at Isandhlwana; 1883, transferred to the intermediate service; 6 June 1892, became the first ocean-going ship to cross the Durban bar and dock in the inner port; 1893, sold to French buyers; 1914, scrapped in Genoa as *Etoile.*

DUNVEGAN CASTLE (1896)
Steamer. 5 958 tons. Length 137,31 m (450 ft 6 in). Speed 15 knots. Passengers: 1st 200, 3rd 400. (First class passengers were still accommodated in the poop in accordance with sailing ship practice.) In 1904, laid up for a while and then placed on the East African service via the Suez Canal; 10 August 1914, landed the first British Expeditionary Force in France; 1917, carried General Smuts to Britain to join the War Cabinet; 1923, withdrawn from service and broken up in Germany.

* *DURBAN* (1875)
Steamer. 2 875 tons. Length 109,73 m (360 ft). Speed 12 knots. Passengers: 1st 150, 2nd 55. An enlarged version of *Asiatic* and, as in *Dunvegan Castle* (1896), 1st class passengers were accommodated in the poop. In 1888, transferred to the intermediate service; later reduced to carrying cargo only; 11 June 1893, wrecked near Santa Cruz de Tenerife while homeward bound from Natal to Southampton.

EDINBURGH CASTLE (1872)
Steamer. 2 678 tons. Length 102,21 m (335 ft 4 in). Speed 9 knots. Passengers carried in two classes. First steamer in service of Donald Currie & Co. Served as a mail steamer to the Cape and then placed on the inter-colonial service. In 1880, sold to Spanish interests together with *Walmer Castle.*

EDINBURGH CASTLE (1910)
Steamer. 13 330 tons. Length 173,74 m (570 ft). Twin-screw. Speed 14 knots. Passengers: 1st 320, 2nd 220, 3rd 250. September 1914, entered Admiralty service as an armed merchant cruiser, returning to the mail service in 1919; 1938, withdrawn from service but was again taken over by the Admiralty and based at Freetown, Sierra Leone, as a floating accommodation and depot ship; September 1945, due to the high cost of towing her to a European shipbuilding yard, she was taken out to sea and sunk by naval gunfire about 60 nautical miles from Freetown.

EDINBURGH CASTLE (1948)
Steamer. 28 705 tons. Length 227,81 m (747 ft 5 in). Twin-screw. Speed 22 knots. Passengers: 1st 215, tourist 478. Crew: 400. In 1962, refitted with a signal mast on bridge and the foremast cut down to funnel height; 1967, modernized; March 1976 made her final voyage to Durban with passengers, followed by a single cargo-only voyage; June 1976, taken to Taiwan for breaking up.

ELIZABETH MARTIN (1872)
Steamer. 1 246 tons. Length 76,38 m (250 ft 7 in). Iron. Speed 9 knots. Named after Donald Currie's mother and always referred to as the 'Betty Martin'. In 1877, transferred to the SA coastal service; 1879, inaugurated the Cape Town-Natal-Mauritius service; 1882, sold to Greek owners and renamed *Athenai*; 1891, renamed *Samos*; 6 October 1916, sunk by submarine in the Mediterranean.

* *EUROPEAN* (1869)
Steamer. 2 272 tons. Speed 10 knots. Built as the *Europe* for a French company. In 1872, bought by John Ryde and sold to Union Line; 5 December 1877, wrecked off Ushant en route from Cape Town to Britain – no lives lost. (See page 21.)

GARTH CASTLE (1890)
Steamer. 3 705 tons. Length 111,25 m (365 ft). Speed 11 knots. Passengers: 1st 120, 2nd 100, 3rd 160. On 23 July 1881, at a review of the fleet in Leith Roads, leading personalities dined on board; 1890, transferred to the intermediate service; 1901, sold to Elder Dempster & Co.; three months later sold to Khedivial Mail Co. and renamed *Ismailia*; 1923, scrapped as *Brunette.*

* *GERMAN* (1877)
Steamer. 3 028 tons. Length 106,58 m (350 ft). Speed 12 knots. Passengers: 1st 150, 2nd 50. Designed to complete the Cape mail service in 19 days. In 1889, transferred to the intermediate service; 1896, sold to Italian interests to become *Sempione*; October 1902, converted into storage hulk.

GOOD HOPE CASTLE

KENILWORTH CASTLE

KILDONAN CASTLE

GOOD HOPE CASTLE (1965)
Motor vessel. 10 538 tons. Length 180,4 m (592 ft). Speed 22,5 knots. Designed for a mail service of 11½ days, if required. In 1967, refitted to take twelve passengers; June 1973, severely damaged by fire near Ascension Island (see pages 139-141); 1978, sold to Italian interests and renamed *Paola C*; 1984, scrapped in Shanghai as *Paola*.

GOTHLAND (1872)
Steamer. 1 482 tons. Length 76,68 m (251 ft 7 in). Speed 9 knots. Built for Currie's Leith, Hull & Hamburg Steam Packet Co. but chartered to carry Cape & Natal SN Co.'s private mail to the Cape. When this company foundered in 1872 she carried Currie's private mail to the Cape. In 1876, transferred to Currie's Liverpool-Hamburg Line; 1915, sold to the Admiralty as a blockship but never used as such; 1919, sold to a London firm under the same name and again in 1922, this time renamed *Trudy Bremer*; 1924, scrapped in Germany.

GRANTULLY CASTLE (1880)
Steamer. 3 454 tons. Length 109,6 m (359 ft 7 in). Speed 12 knots. Passengers: 1st 120, 2nd 100, 3rd 160. Sister to *Kinfauns Castle* (1880). Designed for easy conversion into an armed merchant cruiser. In 1896, sold to Booth Line and renamed *Augustine* (II); August 1912, sold for £8 250 and scrapped.

HAWARDEN CASTLE (1883)
Steamer. 4 389 tons. Length 116 m (380 ft 7 in). Speed 12 knots. Passengers: 1st 150, 2nd 150, 3rd 100. Sister to *Norham Castle* and *Roslin Castle*. When built she was Castle Line's largest vessel to date. Advertised as *Ardtornish Castle*, she was renamed after W. E. Gladstone's estate in Wales and was launched by Mrs Gladstone. In 1904, sold to Booth Line and renamed *Cyril*; 1905, sank after colliding with the same company's *Anselm* near Para in the Amazon River.

ICELAND (1871)
Steamer. 1 474 tons. Length 76,68 m (251 ft 7 in). Speed 9 knots. Built for Currie's Leith-Hull-Hamburg service. Chartered to carry Cape & Natal SN Co.'s private mail to the Cape in 1872, and also Currie's private mail. In 1873, returned to North Sea trading; 18 December 1876, wrecked on Texel Island.

KENILWORTH CASTLE (1904)
Steamer. 12 975 tons. Length 173,79 m (570 ft 2 in). Twin-screw. Speed 14 knots. Passengers: 1st 350, 2nd 200, 3rd 270. Crew: 250. An improved and enlarged version of *Norman*. In 1914, employed in trooping duties from Cape Town to Southampton; 4 June 1918, in a collision in English Channel (see page 64); 1919, when homeward bound with Australian troops, she was quarantined in Table Bay for three weeks during the great influenza epidemic; 1936, withdrawn from service and broken up.

KILDONAN CASTLE (1899)
Steamer. 9 692 tons. Length 157,07 m (515 ft 4 in). Twin-screw. Speed 16 knots. Passengers: 1st 266, 2nd 171, 3rd 198. Practically identical to *Kinfauns Castle* (1899), she was the last vessel built for Castle Line before the merger in 1900 and was immediately pressed into service as a troopship for the Anglo-Boer War, carrying 3 000 troops on her maiden voyage. In 1900, based at Simon's Town as a prisoner-of-war ship; July 1916, converted into an armed merchant cruiser; 20 January 1917, left Oban for Murmansk with the Allied Mission to Russia in an attempt to prevent a separate peace with Germany; after the war she resumed the mail service; 1931, broken up in Norway.

KINFAUNS CASTLE (1880)
Steamer. 3 507 tons. Length 109,83 m (360 ft 4 in). Speed 12 knots. Passengers: 1st 120, 2nd 100, 3rd 160. Sister ship to *Grantully Castle* (1880). First Castle liner built of steel. In July 1883, carried Thomas Carey with his wife and six children to Cape Town after the Phoenix Park murder trial (see page 27); 1883, sold to Russian Volunteer Fleet.

KINFAUNS CASTLE (1899)
Steamer. 9 664 tons. Other details as for *Kildonan Castle*. When commissioned in 1899 she was Castle Line's largest vessel. In 1914, converted to an armed merchant cruiser; August 1914, captured German sailing ship *Werner Vinner*; September 1914, captured German barque *Heinz* off Port Nolloth, South Africa; November 1914, her seaplane sighted German cruiser *Königsberg* in the Rufidji River in East Africa – the cruiser was destroyed shortly afterwards; after the war, resumed the mail service; 1927, withdrawn and broken up in Holland.

LAPLAND (1872)
Steamer. 1 269 tons. Length 76,3 m (250 ft 4 in). Speed 9 knots. Built for Currie's Leith-Hull-Hamburg service and carried private mail to Cape Town. Employed on South African coastal trade until returning to North Sea in 1882. In 1902, sold to Glen & Co. of Glasgow and renamed *Shuna*; 1906, sold to Greek interests and renamed *Sophia M*; 1908, sold again but retained name; 1911, sold to Turkish owners and renamed *Scutari*, only to revert to her 1908 owners but now named *Varvara*; 9 May 1913, grounded on Island of Mull but was refloated, repaired and purchased from underwriters by yet another Greek firm; 19 July 1917, torpedoed and sunk.

* *MEXICAN* (1883)
Steamer. 4 661 tons. Length 115,27 m (378 ft 2 in). Speed 12 knots. Passengers: 1st 170, 2nd 60, 3rd 50. On entering service, she was the largest mail steamer on the mail run. In April 1885, transported troops to Hong Kong during Russian war scare; April 1900, sank after collision with Tatem's *Winkfield* when homeward bound from Cape Town with 102 passengers, cargo and mail (see pages 47-9).

NORMAN

NORSEMAN

PEMBROKE CASTLE

PENDENNIS CASTLE

* *MOOR* (1882)

Steamer. 3 688 tons. Length 111,25 m (365 ft). Speed 12 knots. Passengers: 1st 120, 2nd 90, 3rd 50. Sister to *Athenian*. In 1894, lengthened by 13,4 m (44 ft), her funnel lengthened and a second funnel added. New tonnage 4 664 tons. In 1901, sold to Royal Mail Line as *La Plata*; 1908, sold to Polytechnic Touring Association for cruising to Scandinavia and renamed *Viking*; 1913, broken up.

NORHAM CASTLE (1883)

Steamer. 4 240 tons. Other particulars as for *Hawarden Castle*. In June 1887, included in Queen Victoria's Jubilee Fleet Review off Spithead; 1903, sold to French interests and renamed *Martinique*; 1932, broken up in Italy. (See also pages 52-3.)

* *NORMAN* (1854)

Steamer. Particulars as for *Dane* (1854). Chartered to British Government for service in Crimean War. In 1856, inaugurated a service from Southampton to Rio de Janeiro; 1857, employed on the mail service to South Africa; 1863, transferred to the SA coastal service; 1864, returned to England to be sold as part payment for new tonnage.

* *NORMAN* (1894)

Steamer. 7 537 tons. Length 149,6 m (490,8 ft). Twin-screw. Speed 17,5 knots. Passengers: 1st 150, 2nd 100, 3rd 100. When commissioned in 1894, she was a great improvement on any vessel on the South African mail service and her design was to be followed, with modifications, for years to come. In 1899, requisitioned as a transport for Anglo-Boer War; 1910, laid up as a reserve vessel at Netley, Southampton Waters; August 1914, with the outbreak of war, she was brought out of reserve for trooping duties and was in the first convoy to carry the British Expeditionary Force to France; 1916, rejoined the mail service; 1917, was again transporting troops to Mediterranean; 1919, returned to the mail run; 1921, with the advent of *Arundel Castle*, transferred to the round-Africa service; 1926, withdrawn from service for breaking up when new *Llandovery Castle* entered the Round Africa service.

* *NORSEMAN* (I) (1866)

Steamer. 1 386 tons. Length 80,09 m (262 ft 9 in). Speed 9 knots. In 1873, sold to J. Hough for conversion into a cable layer and re-sold to Western & Brazilian Telegraph Company, retaining her name; 1892, badly damaged in a gale; 1898, sold for breaking up.

* *NORTHAM* (1858)

Steamer. 1 330 tons. Length 83,52 m (274 ft). Speed 13 knots. Passengers: 1st 97, 2nd 30. Launched for P&O Line and sold back to builders in 1868 as part payment for new tonnage. In 1869, acquired by the Union Line for £16 500 and placed on the mail service; 1875, sold to Sir John Malcolm, converted into a sailing vessel and renamed *Stars and Stripes*, under which name she continued trading to South Africa until destroyed at sea by fire in 1878.

* *NUBIAN* (1876)

Steamer. 3 088 tons. Length 109,42 m (359 ft). Speed 12 knots. Passengers: 1st 150, 2nd 50. In 1891, fitted with triple-expansion engine, two funnels replaced by one and transferred to the intermediate service; 21 December 1892, wrecked in River Tagus while under pilotage.

* *NYANZA* (1864)

Steamer. 2 128 tons. Length 99,75 m (327 ft 3in). Passengers: 1st 143, 2nd 34. Built for P&O Line, which found her to be heavy on coal and sold her to Union Line in 1874 for £26 000. In 1880, converted to screw propulsion; purchased by the Sultan of Zanzibar for use as a private yacht but also used for trading; 1902, broken up.

PEMBROKE CASTLE (1883)

Steamer. 3 946 tons. Length 121,97 m (400 ft 2 in). Speed 12 knots. Purchased on the stocks to become the only Castle liner not built on the Clyde prior to the merger with the Union Line in 1900. Passengers in three classes. Used occasionally as a mail vessel but more frequently employed as an intermediate. In 1906, sold with *Helius* to Turkish Government; August 1914, sunk by Russian warships off Samsoun, Turkey.

PENDENNIS CASTLE (1958)

Steamer. 28 442 tons. Length 232,64 m (763 ft 6 in). Twin-screw. Speed 22,5 knots. Passengers: 1st 197, tourist 473. Launching in 1957 delayed by strike in builder's yard (see page 115); August 1969, set final Union-Castle record for a passage between Britain and Cape Town in 10 days 11 hours; August 1976, sold to Ocean Navigation Co. of Panama and named *Ocean Queen*. Renamed initially *Sinbad*, and then *Sinbad I* in 1978. Although intended for cruising, she made no further commercial voyages and in April 1980 she arrived at Kaohsiung for breaking up.

PRETORIA CASTLE

ROSLIN CASTLE

SCOT

* *PHOEBE* (1851)
Steamer. 613 tons. Length 52,65 m (172 ft 9 in). Speed 9 knots. Acquired by Union Line in 1857 to replace *Union* (1854), and placed on the mail service to Cape Town. In 1861, sold to Union SS Co. of New Zealand; 1865, bought by Intercolonial Royal Mail Steam Navigation Co.

* *PRETORIA* (1878)
Steamer. 3 199 tons. Particulars as for sister ship *German*. In February 1879, while serving as a troopship for the Zulu War, she carried 942 men of the 91st Highlanders on a record passage from Britain to Natal of 24 days 8 hours. In October of the same year, set a new record from Britain to the Cape of 18 days 17 hours. In 1887 was present with *Asiatic* and *Moor* at Queen Victoria's Golden Jubilee Naval Review at Spithead; 1888, transferred to the intermediate service; 1897, sold to Quebec SS Co., retaining her name.

PRETORIA CASTLE (1948)
Steamer. 28 705 tons. Length 227,8 m (74 ft 4 in). Speed 22 knots. Passengers. 1st 215, tourist 478. In 1962, she was fitted with signal mast atop the bridge and her foremast was cut down to funnel height; 1966, transferred to Safmarine (UK) Ltd and renamed *S.A. Oranje*; 1969, her port of registry changed to Cape Town. After having carried over 250 000 passengers without ever having missed a sailing, she arrived in Kaohsiung on 2 November 1972 for scrapping by Chin Tai Steel Enterprises.

* *ROMAN* (1863)
Steamer. 1 282 tons. Length 88,65 m (290 ft 10 in). Speed 10 knots. Started service as mail steamer, later transferred to the intermediate service. In 1872, given new compound engines and boilers and lengthened to 97,96 m (320 ft 9 in); 1888, placed on Southampton-Bremen-Hamburg feeder service; 1889, sold to Turkish owners.

ROSLIN CASTLE (1883)
Steamer. 4 267 tons. Length 115,82 m (380 ft). Speed 12 knots. Passengers: 1st 150, 2nd 150, 3rd 100. Laid down in 1882 as *Armadale Castle* but delivered as *Roslin Castle*. In 1888, refitted and lengthened by 3 metres. New tonnage 4 487 tons. In 1904, sold to German owners and renamed *Regina*; fitted out as a Russian naval store ship for service in the Far East; March 1905, wrecked off coast of Mozambique but refloated, towed to Durban and subsequently sent to Italy for breaking up.

S.A. ORANJE SEE *PRETORIA CASTLE*

S.A. VAAL SEE *TRANSVAAL CASTLE*

* *SAXON* (1863)
Steamer. 1 142 tons. Length 88,65 m (290 ft 10 in). Speed 10 knots. Sold to a Hull-based company in 1876.

* *SAXON* (1900)
Steamer. 12 385 tons. Length 173,74 m (570 ft). Twin-screw. Speed 17,5 knots. Passengers: 1st 310, 2nd 203, 3rd 286. Last vessel to be given a Union Line name. Made maiden voyage with white hull of Union Line and red black-topped funnels of Castle Line. Employed during World War I as a troopship; 1918, re-entered commercial service; June 1931, withdrawn and laid up as a reserve vessel; 1935, scrapped in Britain.

* *SCOT* (1891)
Steamer. 6 844 tons. Length 152,4 m (500 ft). Twin-screw. Speed 18 knots. Passengers: 1st 208, 2nd 100, 3rd 100. Coal capacity 3 000 tons at 170 tons per day. Built at a cost of £254 000, *Scot* was the first twin-screw liner on the Cape route. Her first voyage was in the traditional black livery of Union Line, which later gave way to attractive buff upperworks and cream-yellow funnels. In 1891, set new record of 15 days 10 hours for a passage from Britain to Cape Town; 1892, she broke this record twice; 1893, set a new Britain-Cape Town record of 14 days 19 hours, which stood until bettered by *Stirling Castle* in 1936. In 1896, lengthened by nearly 9 m; 1903, withdrawn from service; 1905, sold to Hamburg-American Line and renamed *Oceana*; 1910, bought by Bermuda-Atlantic Company; 1914, sold to Morse Dry Dock and Repairing Company; 1916, bought by Cia. Transatlantica of Spain and renamed *Alfonso XIII*; 1923, name changed to *Vasco Nunes de Balbao*; 1927, scrapped in Italy. (See also pages 32-3.)

SOUTHAMPTON CASTLE (1965)
Motor vessel. Sister to *Good Hope Castle* (1965) with same specifications. In 1967, accommodation fitted for 12 passengers; October 1977, made last voyage of a Union-Castle mailship between Cape Town and Southampton; 1978, sold to Italian interests and renamed *Franca C*; 1984, scrapped at Dalian as *Franca*.

STIRLING CASTLE

TRANSVAAL CASTLE

WALMER CASTLE

* *SPARTAN* (1881)
Steamer. 3 487 tons. Length 111,1 m (364 ft 6 in). Speed 12 knots. Passengers: 1st 161, 2nd 90, 3rd 50. Together with *Trojan*, Union Line's largest ship to date. Originally mail steamer; 1889, transferred to the intermediate service; 1900, sold to Italian interests; 1902, scrapped.

STETTIN (1864)
Steamer. 759 tons. Length 67,67 m (222 ft). Speed 10 knots. Passengers: 1st 50, emigrants (on Cape route) 50. Built for Leith, Hull & Hamburg SP Co. In 1876, placed on Cape route after wreck of *Windsor Castle* (1872); 1878, reverted to the North Sea trade; 1933, broken up in Scotland at the age of 69 years.

STIRLING CASTLE (1936)
Motor vessel. 25 550 tons. Length 212,14 m (696 ft). Twin-screw. Speed 20 knots. Passengers: 1st 300, cabin 490. In August 1936, beat Britain-Cape Town record set by Union Line's *Scot* in 1893; 1940-45 employed on war service as troopship (see pages 94-5); 1946, refitted and accommodation altered to take 245 1st and 540 tourist class passengers; February 1966, sold to Japanese shipbreakers for £360 000.

* *SYRIA* (1863)
Steamer. 1 932 tons. Length 95,22 m (312 ft 9 in). Iron. Speed 10 knots. Built for P&O Line as a screw steamer and later fitted with paddle propulsion. In 1870, sold by P&O for £30 000 as part payment for *Mirzapore* and resold to Union Line, being reconverted to screw propulsion; October 1871, broke the Britain to Cape record; 1878, taken over by James Laing & Co. of Sunderland as part payment for *Durban*; 1 April 1880, foundered in the Atlantic en route to Liverpool from America .

TANTALLON CASTLE (1894)
Steamer. 5 636 tons. Length 134,21 m (440 ft 4 in). Speed 15 knots. Passengers: 1st 200, 2nd 150, 3rd 140. This was Castle Line's first quadruple expansion engined ship. In 1895, attended opening of Kiel Canal; May 1901, wrecked on Robben Island off Cape Town (see pages 49-53).

* *TARTAR* (1883)
Steamer. 4 425 tons. Length 114,73 m (376 ft 5 in). Iron. Speed 11 knots. Passengers: 1st 170, 2nd 60, 3rd 50. In 1889, fitted with triple expansion engine, increasing her speed by 1 knot; December 1897, sold to Canadian Pacific Railway Co. for transpacific and Gold Rush services; March 1908, laid up following a collision and sold to Japanese for scrapping.

TAYMOUTH CASTLE (1877)
Steamer. 2 069 tons. Length 91,77 m (300 ft 1 in). Speed 11 knots. Passengers: 1st 50. In 1879, proved unsuitable as mail steamer because of small size and transferred to the intermediate service; 1891, sold.

* *TEUTON* (1869)
Steamer. 2 106 tons. Length 100,94 m (331 ft 2 in). Speed 12 knots. Formerly *Glenartney*, one of a group of eight sister ships built originally for Glen Line's China service. In 1873, purchased by Union Line and renamed *Teuton*; 1875, lengthened to 106,68 m (350 ft); 30 August 1881, foundered off Quoin Point, South Africa (see page 22).

TRANSVAAL CASTLE (1961)
Steamer. 30 212 tons. Length 231,7 m (760 ft 2 in). Twin-screw. Speed 22,5 knots. Passengers: 728 in one class. Crew: 425. On 12 January 1966, transferred to Safmarine (UK) and re-named *S.A. Vaal*; 1969, registered in Cape Town; 27 September 1977, made final passenger mailship sailing from Cape Town to Southampton and was withdrawn from service in the October; sold to Festivale Maritime Inc., modified in Japan, and as *Festivale* is based in the Caribbean for cruising.

* *TROJAN* (1880)
Steamer. 3 652 tons. Length 111,1 m (364 ft 6 in). Speed 12 knots. Passengers: 1st 116, 2nd 90, 3rd 50. In 1880, was the largest ship on the mail service; later became an intermediate. In 1899, served as hospital ship for Anglo-Boer War; 1900, scrapped.

WALMER CASTLE (1872)
Steamer. 2 446 tons. Length 99,9 m (327 ft 9 in). Speed 10 knots. Passengers in two classes. Sister to *Dover Castle* (1872), which never went to South Africa, having been destroyed by fire off the Chilean coast while on a charter voyage. *Walmer Castle* was the first Castle ship to arrive in South Africa. In 1880, became an intermediate steamer; sold to Spanish buyers and renamed *Valencia*; 1888, bought by Cuthbertsons and renamed *Gaw-Quan-Sia*; 16 December 1889, collided with *Leerdam* – both vessels sank without loss of life.

WALMER CASTLE (1902)
Steamer. 12 546 tons. Length 173,89 m (570 ft 6 in). Twin-screw. Speed 14 knots. Passengers: 1st 336, 2nd 174, 3rd 244. Crew: 250. Laid down as *Celt* in 1900 for Union Line, she was re-named prior to commissioning. In 1910, carried Lord Gladstone (first governor-general of South Africa) to Cape Town; 1918, engaged in trooping; 1919, rejoined the Cape mail service; 1930, laid up at Netley in Southampton Water as a reserve vessel; February 1932, broken up at Blyth.

WARWICK CASTLE (1877)
Steamer. 2 957 tons. Length 106,35 m (348 ft 11 in). Speed 12 knots. Passengers: 1st 100, 2nd 50, emigrants 100. On 23 January 1889, inaugurated direct service from Flushing to Cape Town; 1891, transferred to the intermediate service; 1897, sold to Booth Line being re-engined and re-named *Jerome* (11); 1911, sold to Turkish buyers; 1921, scrapped as *Kerasounde*.

WARWICK CASTLE

WINDSOR CASTLE (1922)

WINCHESTER CASTLE

WINDSOR CASTLE (1960)

WARWICK CASTLE (1930)

Motor vessel. 20 445 tons. Length 198,58 m (651 ft 6 in). Twin-screw. Speed 17 knots. Passengers: 1st 260, 2nd 243, 3rd 254. Crew: 350. Sister ship to *Winchester Castle* (1930). In 1938, modernized and re-engined for a service speed of 20 knots, and one funnel replaced her former two; tonnage re-assessed at 20 107 tons; 1939, taken over for trooping; November 1942, torpedoed west of Gibraltar (see page 95).

WINCHESTER CASTLE (1930)

Motor vessel. 20 109 tons. Length 192,51 m (631 ft 7 in). Speed 17 knots. Passengers: 1st 260, 2nd 240, 3rd 246. Sister to *Warwick Castle* (1930) and underwent same modifications in 1938. (For her war record, see pages 96-7.) In 1947, employed on emigrant service to South Africa, providing about 1 200 berths; 1948, overhauled prior to resuming the mail service; passenger accommodation modified to take 190 1st and 398 tourist; 5 November 1960, arrived in Japan for scrapping after entry of *Windsor Castle* to the service.

WINDSOR CASTLE (1872)

Steamer. 2 672 tons. Length 102,21 m (335 ft 4 in). Speed 9 knots. Passengers carried in 1st and 3rd classes. In 1872, entered the Indian service as a mail steamer and in the September made a record-breaking voyage from Southampton to Calcutta; 1873, broke Southampton-Cape Town record; October 1876, wrecked on Dassen Island, north-north-west of Cape Town, with no loss of life (see pages 20-21).

WINDSOR CASTLE (1922)

Steamer. 18 967 tons. Length 192,76 m (632 ft 5 in). Other details as for her sister ship, *Arundel Castle* (1921). Launched by Prince of Wales on 9 March 1922. Her name caused problems due to a River Severn excursion steamer bearing the same name. (This latter vessel had to be bought, renamed and then sold to free the name for the new ship.) In 1937, she was re-engined and modified, with passenger facilities altered to accommodate 219 in 1st class, 191 in 2nd and 194 in 3rd. Her new tonnage was 19 141 tons and her length was 206 m (661,3 ft). In September 1939, requisitioned as a troopship; 23 March 1943, sunk by aerial torpedo in the Mediterranean, 110 nautical miles north-west of Algiers (see pages 97-9).

WINDSOR CASTLE (1960)

Steamer. 37 647 tons. Length 238,68 m (783 ft 1 in). Twin-screw. Speed 22,5 knots. Passengers: 1st 191, tourist 591. Crew: 475. Largest ship ever built for the mail service. On 18 August 1960, commenced maiden voyage; 6 September 1977, took final sailing by a Union-Castle passenger vessel from Cape Town to Southampton; 1977, sold to Greek interests, becoming *Margarita L* and converted in Piraeus into a luxury accommodation vessel for service at Jeddah, Saudi Arabia; she later returned for lay-up in Piraeus.

Some statistics

Passenger complements

The statistics given in the tables below reflect each ship's initial passenger capacity. It should be borne in mind, however, that sources give varying numbers and that subsequent minor refits may have changed the totals in some cases.

SHIPS OPERATING BETWEEN WORLD WAR I AND WORLD WAR II

	YEAR BUILT	1ST	2ND/CABIN TOURIST	3RD
NORMAN	1894	150	100	100
BRITON	1897	260	192	186*
KINFAUNS CASTLE	1899	266	171	198
KILDONAN CASTLE	1899	266	171	198
SAXON	1900	310	203	286
WALMER CASTLE	1902	336	174	244
ARMADALE CASTLE	1903	350	200	270
KENILWORTH CASTLE	1904	350	200	270
BALMORAL CASTLE	1910	320	220	250
EDINBURGH CASTLE	1910	320	220	250
ARUNDEL CASTLE	1921	234	362	274
WINDSOR CASTLE	1922	234	360	275
CARNARVON CASTLE	1926	310	275	266
WINCHESTER CASTLE	1930	260	240	246
WARWICK CASTLE	1930	260	243	254
STIRLING CASTLE	1936	300	490	
ATHLONE CASTLE	1936	300	490	
CAPETOWN CASTLE	1938	292	499	

* The *Briton* also had accommodation for 300 passengers in dormitories.

SHIPS OPERATING AFTER WORLD WAR II

IMMIGRANT SHIPS IN THE IMMEDIATE POST WORLD WAR II PERIOD

	TOTAL PASSENGERS (MOSTLY DORMITORY ACCOMMODATION)
ARUNDEL CASTLE	846
WINCHESTER CASTLE	1200
CARNARVON CASTLE	1283

REGULAR MAIL SERVICE

	YEAR BUILT	1ST	CABIN	
ARUNDEL CASTLE	1921	164	371*	
CARNARVON CASTLE	1926	216	401*	
WINCHESTER CASTLE	1930	190	398*	
STIRLING CASTLE	1936	295	540	
ATHLONE CASTLE	1936	245	538	
CAPETOWN CASTLE	1938	243	553**	
PRETORIA CASTLE	1948	215	478	(LATER REDUCED)
EDINBURGH CASTLE	1948	215	478	(LATER REDUCED)
PENDENNIS CASTLE	1958	197	473	
WINDSOR CASTLE	1960	191	591	
TRANSVAAL CASTLE	1962	728		ONE CLASS
SOUTHAMPTON CASTLE	1965	12		
GOOD HOPE CASTLE	1965	12		

* Passenger capacity changed during major refits

** *Capetown Castle* When a one-class 'extra' liner: 787

Comparative lengths, tonnages, power and speed (selected ships)

SHIP	YEAR BUILT	LENGTH METRES	TONNAGE GROSS	BHP	SPEED KNOTS
KILDONAN CASTLE	1899	157,1	9 692		16
ARMADALE CASTLE	1903	173,7	12 973		16
BALMORAL CASTLE	1910	173,8	13 361		14
ARUNDEL CASTLE	1921	192,2	19 023		17
CARNARVON CASTLE	1926	192,2	20 063		16
STIRLING CASTLE	1936	212,1	25 550		20
CAPETOWN CASTLE	1938	223,7	27 002		20
PRETORIA CASTLE	1948	227,8	28 705		22
PENDENNIS CASTLE	1958	232,6	28 442		22,5
WINDSOR CASTLE	1960	238,7	37 647		22,5
TRANSVAAL CASTLE	1961	231,7	30 212		22,5
SOUTHAMPTON CASTLE	1965	180,4	10 538		23

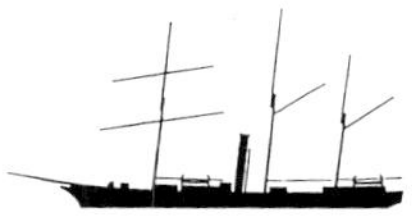

DANE (1857) 53,9m

DUTCH FLUYT (17TH CENTURY)

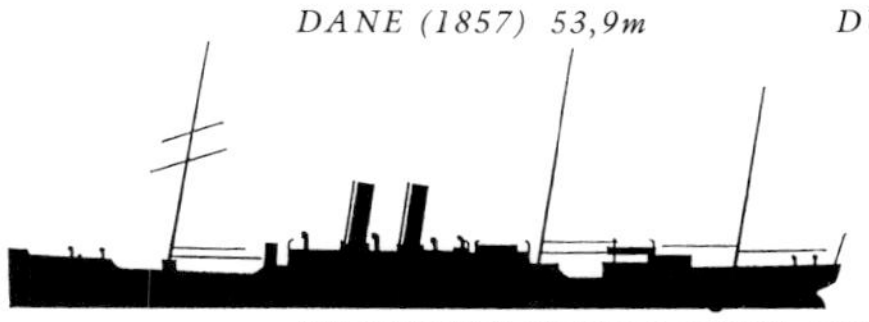

DUNOTTAR CASTLE (1890) 131,98m

BRITON (1897) 161,65m

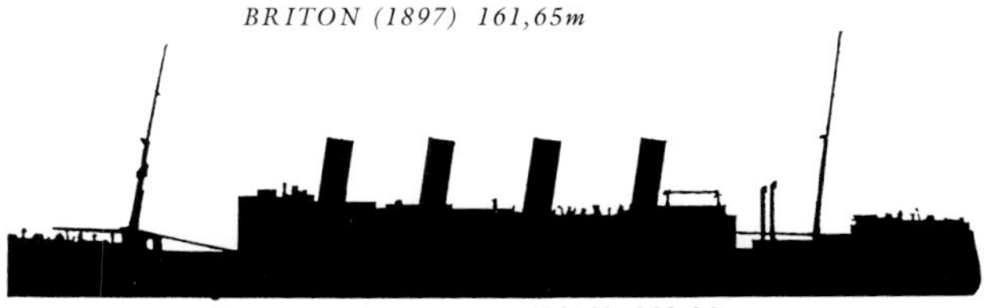

ARUNDEL CASTLE (1921) 192,18m

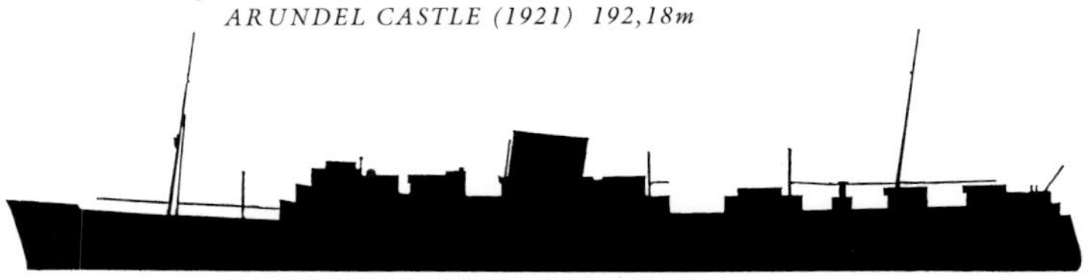

CAPETOWN CASTLE (1938) 223,73m

WINDSOR CASTLE (1960) 238,68m

0 10 20 30 40 50 60 70 80 90 100 METRES

Badges of rank

Accommodation

RMS PENDENNIS CASTLE

LENGTH OVERALL 232,6 METRES
BREADTH OVERALL 25,6 METRES
TONNAGE ABOUT 28 442 TONS GROSS

1 CHARTROOM AND WHEELHOUSE
2 CAPTAIN'S DAYROOM
3 RADIO ROOM
4 OFFICERS' ACCOMMODATION
5 CHILDREN'S PLAYROOM
6 FIRST CLASS LOUNGE
7 FIRST CLASS SMOKEROOM
8 FIRST CLASS CARD AND WRITING ROOM
9 FIRST CLASS LIBRARY
10 FIRST CLASS LIDO
11 FIRST CLASS SWIMMING POOL
12 TOURIST LOUNGE
13 TOURIST LIDO
14 TOURIST SWIMMING POOL
15 TOURIST RECREATION SPACE
16 TOURIST SMOKEROOM
17 FIRST CLASS CABINS
18 SUITE ROOMS
19 DE LUXE CABINS
20 AFT END OF CREW'S ACCOMMODATION
21 FIRST CLASS ENTRANCE FOYER AND SHOP
22 TOURIST CABINS
23 TOURIST ENTRANCE FOYER
24 TOURIST DINING SALOON
25 FIRST CLASS DINING SALOON
26 GALLEYS/FOOD PREPARATION SPACE
27 CARGO HOLD
28 MAIL ROOM
29 ENGINE ROOM
30 BOILER ROOM
31 AUXILIARY MACHINERY
32 STABILISER FIN

Flags and funnels

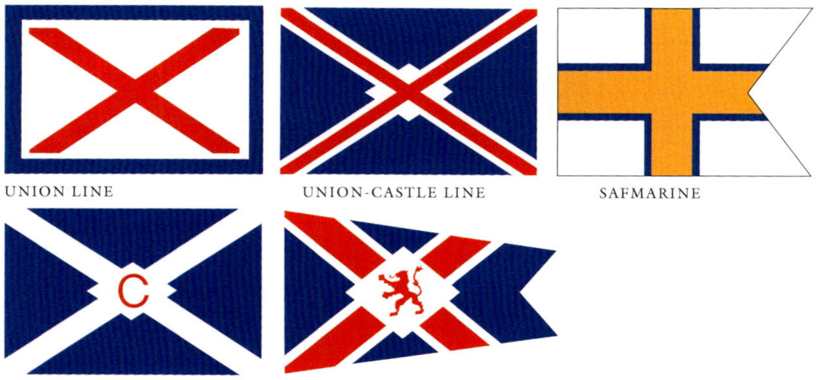

UNION LINE

UNION-CASTLE LINE

SAFMARINE

CASTLE LINE

BRITISH AND COMMONWEALTH SHIPPING GROUP

CASTLE LINE 1862 UNION-CASTLE LINE 1900

UNION LINE 1858-1860

UNION LINE c 1866

UNION LINE 1870

UNION LINE 1891

SAFMARINE 1966

Bibliography

BOOKS CONSULTED

BROWN, A.S. *The Guide to South Africa*. Cape Town: Juta, 1910.
BURMAN, J. *Bay of Storms*. Cape Town: Human & Rousseau, 1976.
CASTLE LINE *The Castle Line Illustrated Handbook*. London: Castle Line, 1898.
CATTELL, P. *The Union-Castle Ocean Post Offices*. Heathfield: P. Cattell, c. 1983.
CHAPMAN, C. *A Voyage from Southampton to Cape Town and back in the Union Company's Mail Steamer "Syria"*. London: Barridge, 1872.
DAMANT, H. *Every Thursday at Four o'Clock*. London: Overseas Visitors' Club, 1977.
DUNN, L. *Ships of the Union-Castle Line*. London: Adlard Coles, 1954.
HAWS, D. *Merchant Fleets in Profile: Union-Castle*. Cambridge: Patrick Stephens, 1979.
HOWARTH, D. & S. *The Story of P&O*. London: Weidenfeld & Nicolson, 1986.
HUGHES, D. & HUMPHRIES, P. *In South African Waters*. Cape Town: Oxford University Press, 1977.
INGPEN, B.D. & PABST, R. *Maritime South Africa*. Cape Town: Struik, 1985.
INGPEN, B.D. *South African Merchant Ships*. Cape Town: Balkema, 1979.
INGRAM, J.F. *The Land of Gold, Diamonds and Ivory*. London: W.B. Whittingham, 1889.
KLUDAS, A. *Great Passenger Ships of the World* (6 vols) Cambridge: Patrick Stephens, 1975-1986.
KNIGHT, E. *Union-Castle and the War 1914-1918*. London: Union-Castle, 1920.
LLOYDS, *Register of Shipping*. London.
MALLETT, A. *The Union-Castle Line: A Celebration in Photographs*. Coltishall: Ship Pictorial Publications, 1990.
Idyll of the Kings. Kendal: World Ship Society, 1980.
MATHERS, E.P. *South Africa and how to reach it by the Castle Line*. London: Simpkin Marshall, 1889.
McCOUGHAN, M. *Steel Ships and Iron Men*. Belfast: Friars Bush Press, 1989.
MIDDLEMISS, N.L. *Gathering of the Clans: History of The Clan Line Steamers Ltd.*
MITCHELL, W.H. & SAWYER, L.A. *The Cape Run*. Lavenham: Terence Dalton, 1984.
MOFFAT, R.W. *John Smith Moffatt*. London: John Murray, 1921.
MOODY, B. *Merchant Ships of the Solent – Past and Present*. Southampton: Kingfisher Railway Productions, 1988.
150 Years of Southampton Docks. Southampton: Kingfisher Railway Productions, 1988.
MOSS, M. & HUME, J.R. *Shipbuilders to the World: 125 Years of Harland and Wolff, Belfast, 1861-1986*. Belfast: 1986.
MURRAY, M. *Ships and South Africa*. London: Oxford University Press, 1933.
Union-Castle Chronicle. London: Longmans, 1953.
NATIONAL MARITIME MUSEUM, Greenwich *The Denny List*. London.
OLIVER, S.P. *On Board a Union Steamer*. London: W.H. Allen, 1881.
PAKENHAM, T. *The Boer War*. London: Futura Publications, 1982.
PORTER, A.N. *Victorian Shipping Business and Imperial Policy: D. Currie, the Castle Line and Southern Africa*. Woodbridge: Boydell Press, 1986.
RITCHIE, L.A. *Modern British Shipbuilding: A Guide to Historical Records*.
ROSKILL, S.W. *The War at Sea*, (3 vols). London: Her Majesty's Stationery Office, 1954.
ROTHERY, H.C. *A Digest of Judgements in the Board of Trade Inquiries into Shipping Casualties 1876-80*.
SOLOMON, V. *The South African Shipping Question*. Cape Town: Historical Publishing Society, 1982.
TURNER, L.C.F. *et al. War in the Southern Oceans*. London: Oxford University Press, 1961.
TURNER, M. *Shipwrecks and Salvage in South Africa – 1505 to the Present*. Cape Town: Struik, 1988.
UNION-CASTLE, *A Union-Castle Album*. London: Union-Castle, 1903.
VAN DER POST, L. *Yet Being Someone Other*. London: Hogarth Press, 1982.
WALKER, E.A.W. *A History of Southern Africa*. London: Longmans, 1968.
YOUNG, G. *Salt in my Blood*. Kommetjie, CP: Midgley, 1975.
Ships that Pass. Kommetjie, CP: Midgley, 1976.
Farewell to the Tramps. Kommetjie, CP: Midgley, 1982.
South Africa on the World Sealanes. Cape Town: Marine Underwriters Association (S.A.), 1991.

NEWSPAPERS AND JOURNALS

Belfast Newsletter, Belfast.
British and Commonwealth Review, British and Commonwealth.
Cape of Good Hope and Port Natal Shipping and Mercantile Gazette.
Cape Times, Cape Town.
Daily Despatch, East London.
Daily News, Durban.
Eastern Province Herald, Port Elizabeth.
Flotsam and Jetsam, Ship Society of South Africa.
Lloyds List.
Lloyds Weekly Shipping Index.
Marine News, World Ship Society.
Natal Mercury, Durban.
Seabreezes.
Seafari, British & Commonwealth.
South African Shipping News and Fishing Industry Review.
The Argus (formerly the *Cape Argus*) Cape Town.
The Southern Evening Echo, Southampton.
The Wheelhouse, S.A. Marine Corporation.
Union Gazette, the Union Line.

Photographic acknowledgements

Where only one photograph appears on a page, only the page number is given below.
Where more than one photograph appears on a page, the page number is given first, followed by the photograph number.

AFRICANA MUSEUM, JOHANNESBURG: 39/3; 39/4; 39/5; 57/4; 75/7; 85/2.
BRIAN INGPEN COLLECTION: 1; 6; 43/4; 48/1; 48/2; 62/2; 66/4; 66/5; 69/3; 69/4; 79/3; 85/3; 90/1; 91/3; 92/1; 92/3; 92/4; 94/1; 96/1; 97/2; 98/1; 98/2; 102/1; 103/4; 104/1; 104/3; 109/3; 109/4; 109/5; 110/3; 124/1; 124/2; 126/2; 130/2; 134/1; 139/3; 144/2; 150/1; 151/3; 151/4; 153/3; 153/4; 154/1; 155/3; 155/4; 156/1; 159/2; 159/3; 166/1; 172/3; 174/1.
CAPE TIMES, CAPE TOWN: 154/2.
C.J. HARRIS COLLECTION: 38/1; 59/3; 67/7; 67/8; 114/2; 123/3; 143/4; 146/1.
DAILY NEWS, DURBAN: 128/5; 128/6.
DESMOND LAWRENCE: 115/4; 134/2
EAST LONDON MUSEUM: 63/4
ERIC EYBERS: 117/4; 118; 128/1; 152/1.
ERIC HOSKINGS: 112/2; 164/2.
ERROL M. CORNISH: 23/2; 23/3; 23/4; 59/2; 61/3; 165/6; 171/7; 172/1.
E. STUART: 79/4
HUGH JAMES: 138/1; 140/1; 169/7.
IAN SHIFFMAN: 135/3; 147/3; 148/1; 153/5; 157/2.
KENNETH TOWERS: 103/3.
LAURENCE DUNN: 174/2.
LOCAL HISTORY MUSEUM, DURBAN: 42/1; 50/1; 71/4; 75/2; 75/5; 84/1; 166/2; 168/2; 168/3; 168/4; 170/1; 171/4.
MOUNT NELSON HOTEL, CAPE TOWN: 4; 5.
NATAL MERCURY, DURBAN: 172/4.
NATIONAL MARITIME MUSEUM, GREENWICH: 8; 9/1; 9/2; 10/1; 10/3; 11/4; 11/5; 14; 26; 32; 11/3; 43/3; 51/3; 51/4; 51/5; 52; 58/1; 60/2; 61/4; 62/1; 63/4;64/1; 72/1; 73/4; 75/3; 75/4; 75/6; 86/2; 87/3; 87/4; 88/1; 89/2; 90/2; 92/2; 95/2; 97/3; 99/3; 99/4; 99/5; 110/1; 110/2; 111/4; 111/5; 118; 123/4; 127/3; 128/3; 128/4; 130/1; 132/2; 133/3; 133/4; 133/5; 136/1; 137/3; 138/2; 142/1; 145/4; 150/2; 155/5; 167/5; 169/5; 172/2.
PENINSULA & ORIENT LINES: 12/2.
RAY RYAN: 124/3.
ROBERT PABST: 83/3; 105/4; 108/1; 119/xx; 128/2; 129/7; 135/4; 146/2; 149/2; 165/4; 165/7; 168/1.
RON FERGUSON COLLECTION: 21; 126/1; 166/3.
SHIP SOCIETY OF SOUTH AFRICA, CAPE TOWN: 28/1; 34/1; 45/3; 49/3; 55; 60/1; 77/5; 132/1; 164/3; 167/4; 167/6; 167/7.
SOUTH AFRICAN LIBRARY, CAPE TOWN: 10/2; 11/6; 23/5; 24/2; 25/4; 51/6; 76/4; 78/1; 102/2; 104/2; 106/1; 112/1; 115/3; 120/1; 120/2; 123/2; 145/3; 164/1.
STATE ARCHIVES, CAPE TOWN: 16 (AG944); 24/1 (AG189); 27 (AG3114); 28/2 (3953); 29/3 (S25); 30 (AG3947); 33 (E8661); 35/3 (S22); 40/1 AG3437); 40/2 (E8575); 42/2 (S898); 47 (AG3889); 67/6 (S408); 80/3 (AG1931); 107/2 (E8595); 165/5 (S84); 170/2 (AG3197).
TERRENCE MCNALLY: 3; 101/3; 107/3; 125/4; 131/3; 141/2.
THE ARGUS, CAPE TOWN: 22/1; 68/2; 137/2; 142/2; 143/3; 152/2; 157/3; 158/1; 171/4.
ULSTER FOLK AND TRANSPORT MUSEUM, BELFAST: 35/2; 36/1; 36/2; 38/2; 38/3; 51/2; 56/1; 56/2; 56/3; 66/1; 66/2; 66/3; 70/1; 71/2; 71/3; 73/5; 73/6; 76/1; 76/2; 76/3; 78/2; 80/1; 80/2; 81/4; 82/1; 108/2; 116/1; 117/2; 117/3; 121/3; 122/1.
UNIVERSITY OF CAPE TOWN, MANUSCRIPTS SECTION, JAGGER LIBRARY: 73/2; 73/3.

The publishers have made every effort to trace the copyright holders of the following illustrative material: 2; 21; 31; 44/2; 65/3; 68/1; 100/2; 125/5; 169/6; 170/3; 171/6, but without any success. They would appreciate receiving any information that will facilitate contact with them.

INDEX

PAGE NUMBERS IN BOLD INDICATE ILLUSTRATIONS

LIST OF SUBSCRIBERS

COLLECTORS' EDITION

Steve Bales
Brenthurst Library
Dave & Di Burger
Christopher A. V. Dadson
Richard & Maureen de Beer
J. P. du Plessis
W. T. F. (Will) du Toit
F. J. Elson
John & Julie Fannin
Fernwood Press
First National Bank, Hillbrow
John E. Franklin
Russel, Bonnie & Gabriella Friedman
Trevor A. Groves
C. J. Harris
David S. Haynes
R. B. O. Hellyer
Laurence Hilton
Rupert & Nadia Horley
A. Ingpen
G. Ingpen
Robert Maingard
Kelly & Carol Manson
M. J. Morley
Gregoire Munro
Carr & Peter Newton
Perishable Products Export Control Board
Chief Executive, Portnet, Johannesburg
M. Raath
Alan Thomas Smith
Gordon R. Stanford
A. E. H. Stead
Pieter Struik
Ann Susman
D. R. Susman
Konrad E. Taeuber
Captain R. J. Taylor
Rudolpho Valente
Rudolph Valente
W. van Rÿswÿck
Nils Erik Warner
Ilse & Stephan Wentzel
Philip A. Wetten

STANDARD EDITION

Den & Jen Adams
Keith A. Adams
Africana Book Collectors
Alexander L. D. Agenbacht
Ian W. Alderton
Keith Allen
Dr D. R. Anderson
George Aubrey

Marilyn & John Bailey
David Baird
Francis Baker
J. T. Baker
G. J. Barker
Professor B. P. Barkhuizen
William Barlow
M. W. Barrow
Captain P. St. Q. Beadon
Alan Crawford Begg
E. Behnisch
Fred Bell
Keith Bentley
Isak & Lieske Bester
Professor Gerhard J. Beukes
Mr & Mrs D. C. Biggs
Paul & Jean Bingle
Henry A. Bird
John E. Bishop
Frederick & Florence Borlase
M. J. M. Bourke-Wright
C. R. Boyd
T. J. Bracher
Frank R. Bradlow
Clifford E. Bragg
P. D. Brandt
Bredasdorp Shipwreck Museum
Ruprecht Brennecke
Dr David N. Brereton
S. A. S. Brown
Stan Brown
Roy & Joan Brunette
Peter N. Buckley
C. R. Bumberry
Dr G. D. Burger
Arie Burggraaf
Clive Bush
Hans Busse
R. Ernest Butland
Chris & Veronika Buys

Mr & Mrs H. A. Calow
Ronald C. M. Caris
Gerald Carson
Gerry & Anne Cartwright
Hon. Charles Cayzer
Rt. Hon. The Lord Cayzer
E. C. Chamberlin
Christopher John Clarke (Harris)
Vivien Clarke
Ted & Estelle Clayson
C. F. Clinning
Peter & Sally Cobbold
M. J. R. Coetzee
Nigel Combes
Arthur Stirk Cook
Mrs D. Cook
B. Cooke
Pietro Corgatelli
R. G. Craseman
C. P. Crompton

Martin E. Damstra
Barrie & Elizabeth Davis
Stoffel de Jager
Ludi de Klerk
K. N. de Kock
Cheryl de Lange
H. R. de Lange
Robert L. de Lange
D. de Milander
G. de Vries
Colin T. Dellar
Diners Club (SA) (Pty) Ltd
W. T. F. (Will) du Toit
E. J. du Plessis
Francois du Randt
Mr M. Duggan

Jack Eastmond
L. Edgecombe
Captain I. S. Edwards
Revd Father M. N. W. Edwards
R. D. Edwards
D. M. Eedes
F. J. Egan
Endangered Wildlife Trust
Felix & Carla Ernst
Greg R. Eva
Charles H. B. Everard

I. G. Farlam
Ferdinand Postma-Biblioteek PU vir CHO
Meeding & Barendien Ferreira
First National Bank, Hillbrow
D. R. Fisher
Gerald V. H. Flack
John Allan Foley
Peter Ford
Dr Brian Fraser
Dr S. Freedberg
Georg & Hannes Fritz
George Richard Fuller
Captain A. H. Fussell

Chris Gaigher & Family
Garlicke & Bousfield Inc
Erika Gerkens
Rupert Gettliffe
Allan Gie
I. F. G. Gillat
Jack Goodwin
W. Gould
T. E. R. Gower
Murray Graham

Elizabeth Jane Greenwood
Grindrod Seafreight
Grindrod Seafreight, Cape Town
Siegfried J. Gross
Iris G. Groves
Gerald A. H. Guy

R. S. Hallatt
Rudolf & Sonia Hanie
Mr G. Hardcastle
M. J. Hargraves
R.H. Harm
Derek Harraway
R. J. N. Harris
Mr & Mrs E. R. Harrison
Jeanie & Jonathan Harrod
J. O. C. Hart
Samantha J. Allen Hartley
Alan McA. Harvey
M. D. Hayhurst
P. J. & M. L. Hendricks
Glynn & Anne Herbert
Robin P. Higgins
C. O. Hill
E. R. Hill
Roy Hirst
Ray E. Hiscock
Hazel Hofmeyr
Graeme N. Hogg
Commodore V. F. Holderness
E. D. Holland
Birgitta Hope
E. G. Hotchkiss
L. J. & S. Howell
N. S. H. Hughes
Graham Neville Hunt
Mr Dudley Hunter
Erika Huntly
Julian Bryan Hutchins

A. Ingpen
G. Ingpen
Mr H. B. Irving

J. S. Gericke Library
P. P. Jacobs
Dr N. H. G. Jacobsen
M. K. Jamieson
Doug & Edna Jardine
A. G. Jeffrey
Ralf Johannsen
Lt.-Cdr. D. Johnson
M. J. Johnson
Reverend David L. Jones
Alarik Jooste
Commodore E. W. Jupp

R. D. Kearney
Jean Keenan-Smith
Captain D. A. Kennedy
D. Kerridge-Walker
Owen Kinahan
Giles King
R. G. King
Anna Kirsten
Ria Kirsten
Michael Klaasen
Bram Klapwijk
F. B. Klinghardt
R. E. Klinghardt

David Garth Knott
Rear-Admiral Martin Kramer S.M. Retd
W. P. Kroon
Chris & Val Kühn
Donald L. Kyle
Edna-May Kyriazis

Lt.-Cdr. J. F. Lamont, LWM MMM
Richard G. & Darryn Lander
D. B. Lawrence
H. D. Lawton
R. Brian Leathem
K. D. Leaver
Stan Lemmer
Letaba Arts & Crafts
Professor & Mrs Owen Lewis
Lifestyle Garden Centre
Mr H. G. Y. Lincoln
Kristian T. Lorentzen
Gaynor Louw
Josua Louw
R. B. Low
D. C. Lowe
Professor Roy A. Lubke

Nina Maclennan
Mr Alistair Macmillan
Jean Macpherson
C. W. Malan
Leon & Pauline Maltz
Michael Marais
Dr Paul Edmond Marchand
Mariner's Wharf (Pty) Ltd
Maritime Brokers & Consultants (Pty) Ltd
John H. Marsh
Amy, Sue & Don Marshall
Eichele Martin
John H. Martin
L. A. Martin & Associates (Pty) Ltd
R. A. McClelland
Ron McDonald
Mrs Patricia Gloria McWalter
Richard Mellor
I. P. D. Merriman
Pierre, Irene & Julie-Mari Meyer
Micor Shipping
W. R. G. Millar
P. D. (Dave) Minnaar
L. H. Mirfin
R. I. Misplon
Mrs S. L. Mitchell
David I. Moor
E. P. Morley
J. L. Morris
Ian Morrison
John Mortimer
Mrs E. E. Moulder
George Müller
Malcolm Murphy
R. D. M. Murray

Valerie Neethling
Louis Owen Nel
Brian Nelson
Michael S. Newman
Eric Nijs

R. S. O'Connor
Peter O'Hare
R. E. Oakley

George L. Oram
W. J. Osborn
Mr A. D. P. Ovenstone
Lindsay & Eileen Owen

David Papmore
W. L. Parfitt
Mr George Lovell Parkes
Charles A. Parsons
B. J. Patchitt
Cynthia Payne
Geoff Peatling
Roydon C. Peden
Jeffry Perlman
Pinelands High School Library Fund
Pastor I. R. Harold Plüddemann
Brendan Pollard
Portnet
Port Manager, Portnet, Cape Town
Laurie Potgieter
Noel Potter
Dr Marius Pretorius
Ken Price

Lorraine & Roger Raab
Jonathan D. Raath
Arthur Rabson
Asok Rajh
W. A. C. Reniers
Rhoades & Stonehouse Families
Alan W. Rich
Harry Riddell
John M. Roberts
D. A. Robertson
Ian M. Robertson
John Robins
Paul Robins
Carol Roehm
Daniel & Margaret Rooks
Dave & Uelah Rosenberg
W. G. M. Ross
J. P. Rourke
Ulrich F. Ruch
Rowland Rumbelow

S.A. Diving Services
Saflink, Durban
Mr & Mrs J.C. Sandeman
H. L. Schaary
Paul Schamberger
Ken Schmulow
N. C. Schofield
P. W. St. L. Searle
Werner K. Seeba
Norman C. Segal
Werner Seidel
Robert William Semple
Philip A. Short
D. J. Sidman
Max David Silverman
Dennis & Ansie Slotow
Dennis Smith
Keith & Dorothy Smith
Ian Spangenthal
W. L. Stanton
Stellenbosch Library
Peter Tuson Still
B. W. Stroeve
Alexi Stylianides
Quentin Sussman

T. K. Swinton ('Stirling Castle' 1957)
David Andrew Sylvester

E. Taeuber
Allan Tait
B. M. Tanner
Captain R. H. Terhordt
Frans Theunissen
Ken Thomas
Andreas Thiemann
Captain M. St. J. Thomson
Commodore R. & Mrs H. Thomson
C. R. Tilney
Pieter Toerien
Rupert G. F. Toms
Craig R. Troeberg
J. Tunstall
Malcolm Turner
Miss P. A. Tyerman
Dr J. C. Tyrrell

UCT Library

Rodolfo Valente
Rudolpho Valente
Douglas van der Horst
M. van der Mark
Rudi van Dÿk
Anne & Errol van Greunen
Danie van Niekerk
Richard Davison van Niekerk
M. & M. A. van Rijswijck
P. W. van Schalkwyk
Paul van Wieringen
Fanie & Julye-Ann Venter
Kirsten, Dirk & Carl Venter
Gerrie Vermaak
Dr J. C. Verwayen
Dr L. Vogelpoel
Lambert Vorster

C. J. S. M. Walden
M. J. Walker
Peter E. Ward
Professor Ian B. Watt
A. V. Weinerlein
Desmond R. Weirich
Olga E. Wells
D. A. Wengrowe
George Bryan & Lorna White
Paul Whitehouse
Keith C. Whitfield
Diana I. A. Whyte
Brian Wicken
R. L. Wicks
Alen Henry Wilkinson
Derrick Willett
C. A. Williams
Roger Williams
D. P. Willson (Shorty)
Jean Wilson
Peter Winckelmann
Mr Peter J. Wordie, CBE
John A. Wyllie

Lionel Young

A. J. Zandbergen
Captain R. J. Zanders
Captain Michael J. Zugg